The State and Social Power in Global Environmental Politics

NEW DIRECTIONS IN WORLD POLITICS,
HELEN MILNER AND JOHN G. RUGGIE,
General Editors

The State and Social Power in Global Environmental Politics

Edited By

RONNIE D. LIPSCHUTZ

and

KEN CONCA

Columbia University Press • New York

Columbia University Press
New York   Chichester, West Sussex

Library of Congress Cataloging-in-Publication Data

Material from Nancy Peluso's article (chapter 3) first appeared in an article
in *Global Environmental Change*, Vol. 3, No. 2, June 1993. This material is
reprinted here with permission of Butterworth-Heinemann, Oxford, UK.

The State and social power in global environmental politics / edited
by Ronnie D. Lipschutz and Ken Conca.
p.   cm.—(New directions in world politics)
Includes bibliographical references and index.
ISBN 0-231-08106-5.
ISBN 0-231-08107-3 (pbk.)
1. Environmental policy—Decision making.
2. Environmental policy—International cooperation.
I. Lipschutz, Ronnie D.
II. Conca, Ken.
III. Series.
HC79.E5S713   1993
363.7—dc20
93-15878
CIP

Printed in the United States of America
c 10 9 8 7 6 5 4 3 2 1

New Directions in World Politics

HELEN MILNER AND JOHN GERARD RUGGIE,
General Editors

For John Holdren

Contents

Foreword

In the flurry of work on human/environment relationships stimulated by the globalization of environmental concerns, this book sets a new standard. It makes three important contributions. The authors whose work is collected here demonstrate, to begin with, that human responses to global environmental change involve sociopolitical dramas; they cannot be understood properly, much less managed effectively, in purely technocratic terms. They then proceed to show that these dramas unfold at many levels—ranging from grassroots social movements to the negotiation of international treaties—which interact with each other in complex ways. To this they add a third element arising from the realization that the world has entered an era of global social change running parallel to global environmental change. The challenge before us is not simply to understand the impact of environmental changes on familiar economic and sociopolitical systems; it is also a matter of comprehending the interactions among two sets of dynamic systems, all of which are complex in their own right and any of which may be subject to nonlinear changes. Small wonder, then, that Ronnie Lipschutz and Ken Conca have chosen to use the imagery of dramas and stages in characterizing the scope of this work.

Global environmental change gives rise to sociopolitical dramas because it has profound consequences for the interests of an array of actors and organized interest groups. Of course, these include countries, like the United States, which now finds itself under growing pressure to reduce its emissions of carbon dioxide—the United States alone currently accounts for about a quarter of worldwide carbon dioxide emissions—despite the painful economic consequences of such measures in recessionary times, or Brazil, which has a domestic political dynamic fostering the destruction of moist tropical forests despite growing pressures from an array of outside forces to protect the forests of Amazonia.

As this book makes clear, however, many other actors have stakes in these dramas, even at the international level. Multinational corporations have developed a considerable capacity to insulate themselves from the regulatory efforts of governments seeking to correct market failures that are damaging to the environment. Yet on occasion, such corporate actors perceive advantages for themselves from the adoption of environmentally responsible policies and become influential players in combatting the impact of global environmental changes, as Du Pont has done in the case of chlorofluorocarbons. Nor can we afford to overlook the increasingly sophisticated activities of intergovernmental organizations, nongovernmental organizations, and even individuals capable of acting as leaders in international environmental dramas. Comparing the run-up to the 1992 United Nations Conference on Environment and Development (UNCED) with the experience of the 1972 United Nations Conference on the Human Environment (UNCHE) makes it clear that we are in the midst of a sea change with respect to the role of nongovernmental organizations. And it would be a serious mistake to ignore the role of capable and persistent individuals like Mostafa Tolba who, as the Executive Director of the United Nations Environment Programme, became a critical player in the drive to establish regimes to combat the pollution of the Mediterranean Sea, to protect the stratospheric ozone layer, and to regulate the transboundary movement of hazardous wastes.

Without denying or diminishing the significance of these international responses to global environmental change, this book drives home the point that human responses to both systemic changes, such as ozone depletion or climate alteration, and cumulative changes, such as the loss of biological diversity, are shaped in large measure by sociopolitical dramas occurring at the national and even at the local level. Partly, this is a matter of limitations on the capacity of national governments to implement within their own jurisdictions rules that they have accepted in international forums. Even more profoundly, however, issues of global environmental change can lead to shifting alliances within societies and to the rise of new social movements capable of affecting public policy through the intensity of their concerns. In the advanced industrial societies, for instance, the prospect of additional environmental regulations has triggered a backlash among property owners who fear drastic losses in the market value of their property. In the developing countries, the same prospect has fanned the flames of resentment against the developed world and, in the process, intensified what may be termed "sovereignty sensitivity." More generally, the rise of global environmental change as a high-profile item on domestic agendas raises hard questions about the delicate and shifting balance between the public sector and the private sector. Yet beneath the surface, there are indications that the general public in many societies is beginning to take seriously the threats that global environmental changes pose for human welfare. The resultant clash between embattled industries and the interest groups associated with them and aroused publics may well provide one of the great political dramas of the next century.

What makes all this particularly interesting to practitioners and scholars alike is that we have embarked on an era of global social change as well as an epoch of global environmental change. The surface manifestations of this development are familiar to all. The socialist economies of the former Soviet bloc have collapsed. Nationalism has reemerged as a force to be reckoned with in parts of Europe and Asia. Countries in a number of the Third World areas are experiencing a turn from military regimes to fledgling democracies. Progress toward economic integration in Europe may finally trigger a functionalist spillover into political integration. AIDS and other pandemics may seriously erode the social fabric, initially in Africa but later in other parts of the Third World as well. Without denying the importance of these developments, there are now reasons to believe, as this book reminds us clearly and thoughtfully, that we may be on the verge of experiencing shifts in the defining characteristics of international society or, in other words, in the "deep structure" of world order. Whether these developments, centering on the nature and roles of sovereignty, nationalism, capitalism, and modernity, bring about a transformation in the character of international society during the near future remains to be seen. But what is crystal clear, even at this point, is that efforts to understand the impacts of global environmental change or human responses to such change which do not take account of the concurrent forces of global social change are doomed to failure.

What lies before us, then, is an extraordinary intellectual challenge. We must find ways to comprehend large-scale and possibly nonlinear changes both in physical and biological systems and in socioeconomic and political systems. And we must learn how to think imaginatively as well as rigorously about the complex interactions between global environmental change and global social change. Meeting this challenge will place a premium on the talents of those able to transcend and, in some cases, break out of the familiar paradigms and methodologies of established scientific disciplines. It is not that the established disciplines have nothing to contribute to our efforts to meet this challenge; far from it. But more and more we need well-trained people who are able with ease to cross disciplinary boundaries and collaborate with colleagues from other fields, even while they hold onto the intellectual capital of their own disciplines.

In this connection, it is surely no accident that most of the contributors to this volume are young scholars associated in one way or another with the Energy and Resources Group of the University of California at Berkeley. Under the able leadership of John Holdren, this program has moved to the forefront in efforts to break down intellectual barriers in order to promote innovative thinking of the sort needed to understand critical interactions among physical, biological, and human systems. To the extent that this book constitutes a measure of its success, the program deserves thoughtful attention on the part of all those interested in understanding global change.

Finally, this volume constitutes a ray of hope for those endeavoring to break out of prevailing customs regarding the specification of subfields and teach courses that compare and contrast human/environment relationships ranging from small-scale traditional societies through national societies to international society. It is not easy to find readings for such courses that are both accessible and imaginative. The growing band of instructors seeking to introduce students to the sociopolitical dimensions of global environmental change across these levels of human organization will welcome this addition to their reading lists.

Oran R. Young, Director
The Institute of Arctic Studies
Dartmouth College
January 1993

Acknowledgments

This volume is the result of more than four years of discussion, writing, and work by many people, some of them associated with the Energy and Resources Group (ERG) at the University of California, Berkeley, and others not. The project was initiated in 1989, under the rubric "Global Resources and Environment: Arenas for Conflict, Opportunities for Cooperation." At that time, one of the editors was a recent ERG graduate, the other still a Ph.D. candidate in ERG. Many of the others were newly minted Ph.D.'s or close to completion, as well. Today, they are almost all in academic positions across the United States. Support came from a number of sources: the MacArthur Interdisciplinary Group in International Security Studies at UC-Berkeley; the University of California's systemwide Institute on Global Conflict and Cooperation; and, through the Pacific Institute for Studies in Development, Environment and Security, from the Rockefeller Brothers Fund, the George Gund Foundation, and the Ploughshares Fund. In March of 1990 a first workshop was held at Berkeley's Clark Kerr campus; a subgroup of those who attended the workshop met twice more over the following year. The result of those meetings you now hold in your hands.

Thus, the number of people who have in one way or another

contributed to, commented on, or critiqued the work of contributors to this volume is enormous; they cannot all be listed here. Among them, however, we single out one individual. For us, John Holdren has been more than just a source of quantifiable data or an expert on more subjects than one could shake a stick at. He has also been an adviser, a mentor, and a friend. Without him, this project could not have been imagined, let alone completed.

Others instrumental in making this book a reality include Kate Wittenberg, Leslie Bialler, and Chad Kia of Columbia University Press; Pat Brenner of the Pacific Institute; Toni Folger-Brown of ERG; Harry Kreisler and his minions at Berkeley's Institute of International Studies; John Ruggie; Oran Young; and two anonymous reviewers of a draft manuscript (you know who you are). To them, and to everyone else who played a part in this particular drama, our heartfelt thanks.

R.D.L. Santa Cruz, CA
K.C. Worcester, MA
January 1993

About the Contributors

RONNIE D. LIPSCHUTZ (general editor), Assistant Professor of Politics, University of California, Santa Cruz; author of *When Nations Clash: Raw Materials, Ideology and Foreign Policy* (New York: Ballinger/ Harper & Row, 1989).

KEN CONCA (general editor), Visiting Professor of Government and Politics, University of Maryland at College Park.

STEVE BREYMAN, Visiting Assistant Professor of Political Science, Marquette University; author of *Spears Into Pruning Hooks: A Political Sociology of the 1980s West German Peace Movement* (Forthcoming).

DANIEL DEUDNEY, Assistant Professor of Political Science, University of Pennsylvania; author of *Pax Atomica: Planetary Geopolitics, Territorial States, and Republican Unions* (Princeton, NJ: Princeton University Press, forthcoming).

LUTHER P. GERLACH, Professor of Anthropology, University of Minnesota; author, with Virginia H. Hine, of *People, Power, Change: Movements of Social Transformation* (Indianapolis: Bobbs-Merrill, 1970).

ANN HAWKINS, Assistant Professor, Program in International Studies, University of Oregon.

BARBARA JANCAR-WEBSTER, Professor of Political Science, State University of New York-Brockport; author of *Environmental Management in the Soviet Union and Yugoslavia* (Durham, N.C.: Duke University Press, 1987); *Women and Revolution in Yugoslavia, 1941–45* (Denver, CO: Arden Press, 1990).

KAREN LITFIN, Assistant Professor of Political Science, University of Washington, Seattle.

JUDITH MAYER, Ph.D. student, City & Regional Planning, University of California, Berkeley. She is the author of a new book to be published by Columbia University Press.

NANCY LEE PELUSO, Assistant Professor, School of Forestry and Environmental Studies, Yale University; author of *Rich Forests, Poor People: Resource Control and Resistance in Java* (Berkeley: University of California Press, 1992).

JESSE C. RIBOT, Lecturer, Dept. of Urban Studies & Planning, MIT; author, with Anne Bergert, of *L'Arbre Nourricier en Pays Sahelien* (Paris: Editions de la Maison des Science de l'Homme, 1990).

JAMES N. ROSENAU, University Professor of International Affairs, The George Washington University; author of *Turbulence in World Politics: A Theory of Change and Continuity* (Princeton, N.J.: Princeton University Press, 1990).

The State and Social Power in Global Environmental Politics

The world's a theater, the earth a stage
Which God and Nature doth with actors fill.
—Thomas Heywood, *Apology for Actors* (1612)

1

A Tale of Two Forests

●

KEN CONCA AND
RONNIE D. LIPSCHUTZ

The arrival of the 1990 burning season brought a new sense of urgency to the various struggles being played out in the rainforests of the Amazon. Local land conflicts among wealthy ranchers, small landholders, landless peasants, and the traditional occupants of the forest showed no sign of abating. The Brazilian government, which had traditionally defined its policies for the region in terms of economic development, national security, and political authority, was proving unable (perhaps unwilling?) to implement effectively its newly expressed concern for the forest and its inhabitants. North American environmentalists and European governments, having temporarily halted their barrage of criticism in the face of some pro-environment symbolism from the newly elected Brazilian government, held their collective breath and watched.

Five thousand miles away, along the northern coast of California, a very different struggle was simultaneously playing itself out. Under the banner of "Redwood Summer," environmental activists sought to celebrate and protect what remained of California's dwindling old-growth redwood stands. Through a series of public events, direct actions, and symbolic gestures, protestors attempted to change the underlying basis of the relationship between trees and people. They sought to define a political space wherein would apply new types of property-rights relationships. In essence, they sought to declare civil rights for trees. At the same time, environmentalists less oriented toward direct action and symbolic politics were also active. They pushed a state referendum to protect what little remained of California's old-growth forests, lobbied Congress and the National Wildlife Service to declare the Northern Spotted Owl an endangered species (a step that would have the effect of preserving old growth stands), negotiated with local lumber companies, and even suggested "debt-for-nature" swaps—a first for the United States.

The immediate results of these efforts were, at best, mixed. In the media, Redwood Summer acquired the tint of the 1960s; given the circus atmosphere and the way the media portrayed the clashes between activists and loggers, it was no surprise that, when the dust had settled, the effort was labeled a failure. There was no grand movement, and no mass conversion of the region's inhabitants. Nothing concrete took place that would have indicated that the forests would, in fact, be protected. The efforts of mainstream environmentalists also yielded mixed results. California voters rejected their ballot initiative (dubbed "Forests Forever") in a climate of fiscal conservatism. But the threat of another expensive initiative battle did provide the impetus for timber companies and environmentalists to begin negotiating a controversial plan for "sustainable forestry" in the region. This in turn led to a decision by two lumber companies to halt the harvesting of their old-growth properties. And, almost one year later, the Northern Spotted Owl was granted endangered status, placing almost 11 million acres of Pacific Northwest forests out of bounds for exploitation.

As in the Amazon, the struggle over California's forests engages a complex cast of characters—in this case, local and national environmental groups, local communities, small timber harvesters, large timber corporations, state and federal bureaucracies, and domestic and foreign timber markets. There are, of course, some important differences. What is at stake in California is not the future of a continental expanse of forest, but rather the remaining scraps of a once-vast resource. The explicitly international dimension is also less readily apparent than it is in the global controversy over the future of Amazonia—even though some 25 percent of northwestern U.S. cutting was destined for Pacific Rim markets by the late 1980s, and with the treatment of temperate-zone forests emerging as an issue in the global debate over tropical rainforests.[1]

Nevertheless, the forest dramas of Amazonia and California share two important features that reflect the central concerns of this book. In the first place, each is being played out through a complex inter-weaving of economic, political, and social cooperation and conflict manifest at a number of different levels: in conflicts pitting local groups against the apparatus of the state and those who control it (agencies, developers, political elites); in cooperation between local movements and environmental organizations from outside the re-gion; in conflicts among competing levels of political jurisdiction (local, national, and multilateral); and in pressures for intergovern-mental cooperation (or perhaps more accurately, regulated competi-tion and conflict) in what might be an emerging international regime to promote so-called "sustainable development." The result is a set of linked dramas whose total interaction will, somehow, determine the "fate of the forests." [2]

In addition, each of these vignettes reflects the multiple meanings of the global environment. When one asks what global environmen-tal change may mean for world politics, as we do, we are confronted with a complication—the "global environment" is several things at once: a complex geobiophysical (and *social*) system; a rapidly emerg-ing issue-area in world politics; an arena in which fundamental con-flicts over power, wealth, and control are played out; and, ultimately, a social construction, through which individuals and groups derive and define competing notions of authority, legitimacy, and sover-eignty. As we see in both California and Amazonia, forests are not merely trees, and if we are to reveal their multiple meanings we must connect them to these arenas of world politics.

This, then, is a book about the politics and meaning of global environmental change. Our concern, however, is only partly with how environmental change—whether it is truly global in scale or merely the cumulative effects of local change—might be affecting the material conditions of individual societies or international politics. Of much more concern to us is how the combination of environmental change and social response seems to be coming to play a growing role in some of the broader processes of change underway in global politics—to occupy more and more, we believe, of the social and political space of the current world order. It may be that environmen-tal problems, conceptions, and constructions are part of larger pro-cesses of systemic transformation that are imminent or already under way. Or, perhaps, the bursts of noise emanating from Amazonia, California, and other places around the planet will die down, and the system will settle back once again into the patterns of the past. In either case, while the fate of the forests and the outcome of other environmental changes cannot be discerned readily from the information now in hand, looking at the dramas themselves may help us sketch one component in the emerging outlines of a new global politics. And in looking for the evidence, we will necessarily expand on the traditional language of international politics, introducing ideas that, while they have emerged in other fields of inquiry, are increasingly central to the study of international conflict, multilateral cooperation, and world order.

Global Environment and World Politics: Emerging Perspectives

As the human impact on the global environment intensifies, and as governments scramble to respond to the resulting stresses, both academics and policymakers are starting to pay closer attention to the links between global environmental change and international politics.[3] This growing analytical interest has unfolded along two principal conceptual axes—one stressing technology and resources, the other political and economic systems. The first axis is populated principally by analysts who emphasize the inherent conflict potential of an increasingly crowded, ecologically-stressed, and resource-scarce planet. The basic thrust of this message—grounded in ecological principles and metaphors and carried primarily by natural scientists with the inclination to study social issues—has not changed significantly since Fairfield Osborn and Harrison Brown turned their attention to these issues in the early 1950s—or, for that matter, since the emergence of a sizable body of work whose origins may be traced back to the nineteenth century. Osborn drew parallels between the mass destruction of World War II and a second, silent war, consisting of "what man has done in recent centuries to the face of the earth and the accumulated velocity with which he is destroying his own life sources." Brown, writing in 1954, suggested that the future prospects for world peace would be directly linked to progress in solving the problems of population growth, resource consumption, agricultural productivity, and economic development.[4]

Since the time of Brown, Osborn, and other "environmentalist pioneers," the list of environmental problems typically cited has lengthened, and the precision of the physical characterization of those problems has grown significantly. But few authors writing in this tradition have given more than cursory consideration to how these trends are grounded in or related to the economic, social, and political structures of current world order.[5] The underlying, planetary level of analysis, though highlighting the need for broadly integrative analysis, tends to ignore the complexity of existing social relations and to draw attention away from the way those relations channel the consequences of environmental change. In particular, much of the growing policy-oriented literature on global environmental change, also laden with ecological metaphors and scarcity paradigms, shares this tendency to discount or ignore the social complexities of international politics. For example, according to James G. Speth, then President of the World Resources Institute:

> To address the environmental challenges of the 1990s, a series of large-scale social and economic transitions is needed. Everywhere, environmental deterioration is integrally related to economic production, technology, the size of human and animal populations, social equity, and a host of other factors. The actions we must take to reverse this deterioration are so many and fundamental that we must think not merely in terms of discrete initiatives but also in broad macro-transitions with multiple benefits.[6]

When such language is unwrapped, it often turns out that the proffered approach to dealing with global environmental change pays little or no attention to the intervening role of social variables. For example, Speth's six steps to "environmental security" begin with technical instruments—population control and renewable technologies—and then leap to the level of significant social-structural change—a new world economy, global equity, sustainable development, and new forms of governance. The call for action—that the nations of the world "come together in recognition of these challenges" and "declare . . . a priority mission of international cooperation and diplomacy in the 1990s"—gives no indication of recognizing the depth, in social terms, of the changes proposed, and does little to suggest where the leverage points for promoting such extraordinary changes might lie.[7]

The second axis in the literature is populated by scholars of international relations, seeking to apply the traditional research agendas of their field to what is seen as a new issue area in world politics. These scholars, though generally paying closer attention to social processes and structures, have effectively re-created the historical divides of international politics as a field of inquiry. Those cast in a "realist" mold, for example, have emphasized resource wars and the high politics of an environment worth fighting over. Those drawing on interdependence perspectives see strong incentives for cooperation, flowing almost automatically from the transnational nature of environmental problems; conflict in this context is seen to be rooted in the inherent fragility of environmental cooperation, and in the various barriers to collective resource management. Still others, steeped in more radical traditions, have interpreted global environmental change as simply the latest venue in the continuing effort of the rich to dominate the poor. And while these competing schools of thought differ notably in their diagnoses of the consequences of global environmental change, they share a tendency to treat such change itself as originating outside the social systems in which its consequences are assessed.[8]

Projecting historical assumptions onto new issues and new contexts frequently yields insights. As we have stressed, the global environment can be thought of, at least in part, as an emerging arena in which preexisting struggles over power, wealth, and control are played out; thus, there will be much to learn from the application of existing frameworks. Nor is the quick abandonment of traditional research programs a recipe for expanding knowledge and understanding; it sometimes seems that theory in the social sciences arises less from the accumulation of knowledge, leading to new and somehow more complete models, than from the fashion of the moment. As Oran Young has pointed out, theory is historically contingent.[9]

In the study of world politics, for example, the most influential theoretical trends of the past three decades—the challenge of dependency theory, the emergence of the concept of interdependence, and the subsequent resurgence of realism—were reactions to the circumstances of the times: the failure of decolonization and development assistance to spur growth and democracy in the Third World; the faltering of postwar regimes for trade and finance with the seeming decline of U.S. hegemony; and the renewal of Cold-War tensions in the Reagan years.[10] Just as in each of these cases new readings of "the facts" stimulated quests for new theory, we argue today that existing theory may be less than perfectly suited to the task of analyzing the political implications of global environmental change.

A particular concern is the relative paucity of cross-fertilization between international relations and other disciplines concerned with issues relevant to global environmental change. This may arise more from historical contingency, and from internal divisions established by practitioners within the discipline, than from the nature of the problems under consideration. The decision to focus principally on power—as opposed to the links among power, authority, rules, and purpose—has meant that the humanities and social sciences (other than economics and, in a limited way, history) have had little to say that fits in with the dominant research agenda in the study of international relations and politics.[11]

Thus constrained, the suggested means of dealing with global environmental change are pretty much limited to the tool kit in hand: intergovernmental agreements and international regimes, debates about partially yielding up national sovereignty, arguments about collective action, and so on. Limited initiatives such as the Montreal Protocol—an agreement to control growth in one narrow class of chemicals, produced in a few places and, by most accounts, amenable to substitution—are taken as precedent-setting models. If the principal challenge is one of designing conventional policy instruments for narrowly conceived problems of market externalities, transboundary pollutants, and common-pool resources, this may be so. But if global environmental change has consequences on a more fundamental level—if it calls into question not just the distribution of power but also the meaning of power, the legitimacy of rules, and the nature of authority—then it may be that the tool kit lacks some important items, and that these are being fashioned elsewhere, beyond the ken of the ordinary round of international activities.[12]

Having thus criticized the literature on global environmental change and interpretations of its political implications, it may be rightfully asked whether we have anything better to offer. How might we better think about the relationship among environmental change, human activity, and international politics? We begin first by assuming that the natural world, the social world, and the world of ideas cannot be treated as purely exogenous to one another. Giving primacy of place to a single one of these "worlds" mischaracterizes the relationship among them, in that a fundamental change in one drives fundamental changes in the others, ultimately feeding back into the original one, as well.[13] This does not suggest that studies focused principally on nature, society, or values are not important. But it does suggest the need to be far more skeptical about the possibility of developing "parsimonious" predictive models. And it suggests that studying the politics of global environmental change becomes an inherently interdisciplinary exercise, requiring the building of language bridges to the other social sciences, the humanities, and the natural sciences.

Environmental Change and Ecological Interdependence

One of the critical elements in the emerging, multifaceted debate on the politics of global change has to do with the relationship between the natural environment and the social world. Stemming the tide of environmental destruction has emerged at or near the top of the list of problems said to define the new international context, and we are often told that the type of international cooperation required to manage global environmental change is fundamentally new as well. This raises some basic questions as to how, exactly, the natural environment and the social world influence one another. Are the goods and services of the natural world so fundamentally woven into the fabric of human society that their depletion, disruption, or diminution alters the basic terms on which societies exist and human beings interact? Does human society exercise such control over nature that environmental problems can also be controlled, and nature itself managed and manipulated to serve human purposes? Or, as we suggest here, is there a complex relationship between the two, in which multiple linkages and feedbacks play themselves out in a hundred different ways, producing a thousand possible outcomes and blurring the very distinction between the natural and the social? [14]

If the relationship between the biosphere and human society were a relatively straightforward one, in which the former only provides the material basis or inputs for various processes that support the latter, then we might expect the economic, political, and social consequences of environmental destruction to be largely instrumental. Shortages of resource "goods" or overabundance of environmental "bads" could be ameliorated by the appropriate substitutions or technological solutions, and conflict emerging from such adjustments minimized by winners compensating losers. Large-scale environmental degradation would challenge governments principally to anticipate such substitution requirements and negotiate such compensations—no small task, but one confined to the traditional terrain of statecraft. But if the relationship is a more complex one, characterized by complex systems of interdependencies and feedbacks, then the types of changes we are seeing might well be much more fundamental (or "structural") in their social consequences, and thus presage basic alterations in human social relationships at a variety of levels. This, in turn, would raise doubts about the possibility of even knowing, much less managing, the consequences of these environmental impacts (which, after all, are the result of *human* actions, activities, and impacts, not simply forces growing out of natural geobiophysical cycles).

This book is premised on the belief that the natural-social link is sufficiently complex that such fundamental changes may in fact be occurring. Our objective is to bite off a relatively small piece of this relatively large cake having to do with the planetary environment and human society. More specifically, we have taken as our task an examination of the implications of global environmental change for patterns of international conflict, cooperation, and politics. We will not present an all-encompassing theory of global change; indeed, our assumption that there are complex interactions among the many "meanings" of the global environment leaves us skeptical of such attempts. We will, however, suggest the emergence of a fundamentally new social dynamic, with which governments, their critics, and their observers may be poorly equipped to deal. We will argue that this new dynamic, which we label *global ecological interdependence*, consists of two seemingly countervailing trends: tighter systemic binding among actors in the prevailing international system, and the simultaneous decay and fragmentation of the traditional authority structure of world politics.[15] We will hypothesize a world in which governments, driven by pressures from without and within, find themselves increasingly bound to common efforts and joint solutions, while at the same time having to grapple with a set of issues to which they are poorly equipped to respond. In such a world, social movements and networks of non-state actors may play an increasingly important role—perhaps in concert with the state, perhaps in competition, and perhaps even as an alternative organizing principle for world politics, based on new constitutive rules and institutional forms.

Global ecological interdependence is thus *global*, in the sense that it takes place in a planet-encompassing space; *ecological*, in the sense that the systems affected encompass not only what we ordinarily think of as "environment" or "resources" but also the relationship of human activities to them; and *interdependent*, in the sense that many different social, political, and cultural "ecosystems" overlap and are intertwined with one another.[16] Working with three such "essentially contested" terms reflects the ambiguity of the phenomena we wish to examine. More important, the contested character of these terms reflects the existence of competing intellectual constructions of the environment, politics, and society. Ultimately, we will argue that global ecological interdependence cannot be understood as simply a physical phenomenon, or even a combination of physical changes and social responses; it also represents an increasingly powerful way in which individuals and groups conceive of their connection to something larger.

Our agenda consists of four central questions. First, *how does global environmental change contribute to global ecological interdependence?*[17] Is environmental change an important cause or component of tighter systemic binding? Of the decay of traditional authority structures? Is environmental change one of the principal causes of global ecological interdependence, or merely a reflection of more fundamental processes at work? Is global ecological interdependence a broadly useful conceptualization of emerging patterns and structures in world politics, or does it merely reflect the environmental slice of a many-layered cake?

Second, *what are the prospects for collectively managing environmental change and ecological interdependence in a constructive fashion?* How manageable is global environmental change? What does "managing" mean in this context, and what would it require? Does global ecological interdependence facilitate environmental "governance," through international arrangements among sovereign parties—or does action require new institutions or forms of governance that might supersede, bypass, or otherwise lessen the role of states? Is collective management possible at all, given the diverse and competing social constructions of the global environment?

Third, *are the processes of world politics being altered by global ecological interdependence?* If so, how? Are traditional patterns of conflict and cooperation changing, or are they likely to change, as a result of environmental change? As a result of growing awareness of, or particular ways of interpreting, such change? Are new types of actors emerging on the world political stage, with the power to undercut or bypass the prerogatives of the nation-state? Are traditional actors developing new ways of participating in world politics? If so, how are such changes altering traditional norms and modes of operation, and how must we change our traditional ways of thinking about world politics as a result?

Fourth, *how are social responses to global ecological interdependence shaping or altering world order?* Is the growing effort to manage the global environment contributing to a transformation in world order, and if so, how would we know? What are the consequences of ecological interdependence and human responses to environmental change for capitalism, sovereignty, nationalism, modernity—in short, for the economic, political, and cultural pillars of the current world order? Is the global environment being redefined? If so, by whom? And is this act of redefinition in turn changing the definition of the international system?

Underlying these questions is a deeper conceptual one: on what level, if any, is globally significant social change taking place? Is it occurring solely or principally at what John Ruggie has called the "physicalist" level, which "sees reality . . . in terms of separate and distinct actors; palpable, discrete, and infinitely divisible properties; and discontinuous events," and in which cause and effect are clearly visible, even if our understanding of the causal relations are obscured by a host of perceptual factors? Or is change happening at the deeper level of process, structures, roles, and relationships, where, as David Dessler puts it, "social forms . . . preexist action?" [18]

In considering these questions, the authors represented in this volume brought a range of disciplinary backgrounds and experiences to a series of three workshops on the broad theme of environmental change and world politics. In spite of the sometimes daunting barriers of language and competing disciplinary conceptualizations, we found that our thinking converged, over the course of the workshops, around several themes: the severe constraints on the capacity of governments, acting alone or in concert, to "manage" the global environment; the emergence of social movements, nongovernmental organizations, and other non-state actors that are somehow linked to the substance or imagery of environmental change; the social and political process by which new institutions emerge, at various levels, in response to the impacts of environmental change; and the struggles over the definition of underlying rules through which the social and political consequences of global ecological interdependence are played out.

In the process of exploring these themes, we found ourselves having taken the first halting steps toward building trans-disciplinary languages to describe social conflict and cooperation at different levels. We also found that our emphasis on the *multiple levels* of environmental cooperation and conflict, and on the *multiple meanings* of the

global environment itself, left us at odds with much of the burgeon-
ing literature on the general theme of resources, environment, security, and international cooperation and conflict. On the one hand,
the social and political complexity involved—the blurring of traditional economic, cultural, and jurisdictional borders, the ability of the
weak to thwart the plans of the strong, and the intertwining of
environmental issues with basic questions of legitimacy, power, and
authority—left us skeptical that global environmental management
could be approached from the rational-technical framework prominent in the literature. On the other hand, we were able to glimpse
the patterns of a certain order in this chaos—of new rules and roles
being established through diverse, interacting processes of social
discourse—that left us not without hope.[19]

Plan for the Rest of the Book

In keeping with our organizing metaphor of drama and stages, the
volume is organized into three separate acts. Act I examines the
capacity of governments, acting alone and collectively, to manage
the consequences of environmental degradation and change. Chapter 2, by Jesse Ribot, and chapter 3, by Nancy Peluso, explore the
severe constraints on the capacity and willingness of Third World
states to act as environmental managers.[20] Ribot examines the interpenetration of market and state in Senegal, and the resulting ineffectiveness of environmental regulations. Peluso, considering cases where
the state has more effective tools at its disposal, shows the inextrica-
bility of environmental management from broader goals of state-
building, control, and coercion. In chapter 4, James Rosenau raises a
more general challenge both to the competence of individual states
and to traditional forms of collective management. Rosenau suggests
that the turbulence resulting from (among other things) growing
skills on the part of individuals and growing dissatisfaction with
government performance, fuel what he has described elsewhere as
the "bifurcation" of world politics—with implications for even the
strongest and most competent of states. Chapter 5, by Karen Litfin,
takes up the question of collective management more explicitly, examining patterns and performance among emerging environmental
regimes. Litfin explores the extent to which institutions, manifested
primarily in international regimes, have developed to compensate for

the growing inability of states to manage individually their ecological interdependence.

Act II examines the role of social movements, institutions, knowledge, and constitutive rules in supporting, challenging, or rendering obsolete the traditional tools of statecraft in global environmental politics. In chapter 6, Steve Breyman looks at the rise of environmental activism and the role of social movements in contesting state legitimacy; he focuses in particular on the various dimensions of knowledge-as-power in a movement context. Chapter 7, by Barbara Jancar, examines a specific example of movement challenges to state integrity; the chapter explores the role of environmental symbolism and movements in the devolution of the Soviet state and the rise of groups centered around nationalist political action. Chapters 8 through 10 then examine the social construction of the environment, and the ways the renegotiation of socially constructed sets of "constitutive rules" may alter the framework for political change. Chapter 8, by Luther Gerlach, focuses on a specific example of the regime "renegotiation" process, the Minnesota drought debates. In chapter 9, Ann Hawkins examines multiple levels of contestation in the renegotiation process, exploring the way the problem of global climatic change has been framed to reflect particular world views and power structures. Chapter 10, by Ronnie Lipschutz and Judith Mayer, then considers the relationship among rules, property rights, and the construction or reconstruction of regimes for natural-resource management.

Act III explores—in an admittedly speculative way—some of the longer-term implications of global ecological interdependence for world politics (and for those who would study it). In chapters 11 and 12, Daniel Deudney and Ken Conca, respectively, develop a set of hypotheses about future configurations for world politics as a logical outgrowth of ecological interdependence. Deudney explores the possibility that effective responses to global environmental problems could lead to an emergent "world domestic politics;" Conca explores the consequences of a global environment "managed" by a set of environmental regimes that remain largely implicit, structured by the broader economic, political, and social pillars of the current world order. Chapter 13, by the editors, then seeks to glean lessons from the case studies, to tie together concepts and cases, and to inquire whether global ecological interdependence does, indeed, represent an indicator of more fundamental systemic change.

NOTES

1. The unwillingness of the United States to merge discussions on temperate and tropical forests contributed to the failure of a proposed forest-management regime at the June 1992 Earth Summit in Rio de Janeiro.

2. The phrase is borrowed from Susanna Hecht and Alexander Cockburn, *The Fate of the Forest* (London: Verso, 1989), which describes the interaction of these multiple processes in the Amazon.

3. "Global change" is a term that has entered policy discourse only very recently, yet its meaning seems already to have been codified in the world's capitals and councils of state to signify "global warming" or, more colloquially, the "greenhouse effect."

4. See, for example, G.P. Marsh, *Man and Nature* (New York: Scribner, 1864; reprinted Cambridge, MA: Harvard University Press, 1965); Fairfield Osborn, *Our Plundered Planet* (Boston: Little, Brown, 1953), pp. viii–ix; Harrison Brown, *The Challenge of Man's Future* (New York: Viking, 1954).

5. For recent variations on the basic themes of Brown and Osborn, see Andrew MacGuire and Janet Welsh Brown eds., *Bordering on Trouble: Resources and Politics in Latin America* (Bethesda, MD: Adler and Adler, 1986); Jessica Tuchman Mathews, "Redefining Security," *Foreign Affairs* 68, no. 2 (Spring 1989): 162–77; Norman Myers, "Environment and Security," *Foreign Policy* 74 (Spring 1989): 23–41; Paul Ehrlich and Anne Ehrlich, *The Population Explosion* (New York: Simon and Schuster, 1990); Barry Commoner, *Making Peace with the Planet* (New York: Pantheon, 1990); Albert Gore, *Earth in the Balance: Ecology and the Human Spirit* (New York: Houghton Mifflin, 1992).

6. James G. Speth, "Environmental Security for the 1990s . . . In Six Not-So-Easy Steps," *WRI Issues and Ideas* (January 1990).

7. Ibid. The most cohesive recent expression of such an agenda can be found in *Our Common Future*, The Report of the World Commission on Environment and Development (Oxford: Oxford University Press, 1987), but similar discussions can also be found in Aldo Leopold, *A Sand County Almanac*, 2d ed. (New York: Ballantine, 1966); Harrison Brown, *Challenge of Man's Future*; and Andrei D. Sakharov, *Progress, Coexistence and Intellectual Freedom* (New York: Norton, 1968).

8. Actually, most students of international relations have treated environmental issues as lower than low politics. Kenneth Waltz regards resource issues as a minor variable in international politics; see *Theory of International Politics* (Reading, MA: Addison-Wesley, 1979). Hans Morgenthau gives resources a more prominent role as an industrial input into the power of nations; see *Politics Among Nations: The Struggle for Power and Peace* (New York: Knopf, 1967). For a survey of the pre-1986 literature on "resources and conflict," see Ronnie D. Lipschutz, *Ore Wars: Access to Strategic Materials, International Conflict, and the Foreign Policies of States*, Berkeley, CA: Ph.D. Dissertation, Energy and Resources Group, University of California, Berke-

ley, 1987, ch. 3. A more recent survey is Thomas F. Homer-Dixon, "On the Threshold: Environmental Changes as Causes of Acute Conflict," *International Security* 16 no. 2 (Fall 1991): 76–116.

Among the realists are Nazli Choucri and Robert North, *Nations in Conflict* (San Francisco: Freeman, 1975); Bruce M Russett, "Security and the Resources Scramble: Will 1984 Be Like 1914?" *International Affairs* 58, no. 1 (Winter 1981/82): 42–58; and Arthur H. Westing, ed., *Global Resources and International Conflict: Environmental Factors in Strategic Policy and Action* (Oxford: Oxford University Press, 1986). Those drawing on independence perspectives include Marvin S. Soroos, *Beyond Sovereignty: The Challenge of Global Policy* (Columbia, SC: University of South Carolina Press, 1986); and Oran R. Young, *International Cooperation: Building Regimes for Natural Resources and the Environment* (Ithaca: Cornell University Press, 1989). Among the radicals are Michael Tanzer, *The Race for Resources: Continuing Struggles over Minerals and Fuels* (New York: Monthly Review Press, 1980). A more recent example of this literature, in which the "radical" element is implicit, is Gilberto C. Gallopin, Pablo Gutman, and Hector Maletta, "Global impoverishment, sustainable development and the environment: a conceptual approach," *International Social Science Journal* 121 (August 1989): 375–98. See also the *IFDA Dossier*, a quarterly publication of the International Foundation for Development Alternatives in Nyon, Switzerland. Some radicals, of course, have stressed that the emerging politics of the global environment could be a force for progressive change as well as for the status quo; see John Ely, "Green Politics and the Revolution in Eastern Europe?" *Capitalism Nature Socialism* no. 4 (June 1990): 77–97.

9. Oran R. Young, *Resource Regimes: Natural Resources and Social Institutions* (Berkeley: University of California Press, 1982).

10. See, e.g., Simon Dalby, *Creating the Second Cold War* (London/New York: Pinter/Guilford, 1990).

11. This statement is not meant to overlook the growing body of work within international relations concerned with exactly these themes. See Nicholas Onuf, *World of Our Making: Rules and Rule in Social Theory and International Relations* (Columbia: University of South Carolina Press, 1989); Alex Wendt, "Anarchy Is What States Make of It: the social construction of power politics," *International Organization* 46 no. 2 (Spring 1992): 391–426; James N. Rosenau and Ernst-Otto Czempiel eds., *Governance Without Government: Order and Change in World Politics* (Cambridge: Cambridge University Press, 1992). Some of the logical consequences of such bridge-burning can be seen in what realism has had to say about natural resources; see, e.g., Daniel Deudney, "Europe as a Natural Republic, ca. 1500–1900," Draft manuscript, June 1990; Geoffrey Parker, *Western Geopolitical Thought in the Twentieth Century* (London: Croom Helm, 1985); Ronnie D. Lipschutz, *When Nations Clash: Raw Materials, Ideology and Foreign Policy* (New York: Ballinger/Harper & Row, 1989).

12. For varying perspectives on the value of the Montreal Protocol as precedent, see Richard E. Benedick, *Ozone Diplomacy* (Cambridge: Harvard University Press, 1991); and Ronnie D. Lipschutz, "Institutionalizing Global Climate Management: Some Lessons from Natural Resource Regimes, Some Thoughts About Implementation," Discussion Paper for a Policy Studies Organization Roundtable Panel on "The Challenges of Potential Global Climate Change for Policy Analysis" APSA Meeting, August 30–September 2, 1990, San Francisco, CA. In complex situations, success may, in fact, blind one to the potential pitfalls of such approaches. As Davis Bobrow and Robert Kudrle have noted, "Nations often get themselves into difficulties through self-disabling errors of commission and omission. They go wrong not so much because of recent failure but rather because success leads them to conclude that their achievements should and can continue without substantial policy reorientation." See "Avoiding the Perils of Success: Japan Looks Ahead," *International Studies Notes* 15 no. 1 (Winter 1990): 16.

On the possible inadequacy of the tool kit see Ronnie D. Lipschutz, "From Here to Eternity: Environmental Time Frames and National Decisionmaking." Paper prepared for a Panel on "De-nationalizing" the State: The Transformation of Political Space, Social Time, and National Sovereignty, Conference of the International Studies Association, Vancouver, BC, 19–23 March, 1991.

13. This system of feedbacks is one manifestation of "interdependence," although it is not one commonly used in the political science literature. In *Theory of International Politics*, Waltz treats "interdependence" as an economic quantity that indicates the degree of trade between two states. John J. Mearsheimer does the same, defining interdependence as a "situation in which two states are mutually vulnerable; each is a hostage of the other in the economic realm" ["Back to the Future: Instability in Europe After the Cold War," *International Security* 15, no. 1 (Summer 1990): 43]. While Keohane and Nye [*Power and Interdependence: World Politics in Transition* (Boston: Little Brown, 1977)] are more sophisticated in their treatment of the concept, they still regard it as a condition arising largely from interstate economic relationships.

14. See for example Dennis Pirages, *Global Technopolitics: The International Politics of Technology and Resources* (Pacific Grove, CA: Brooks/Cole, 1989); H. E. Goeller and A. M. Weinberg. "The Age of Substitutability," in P. H. Abelson and A. L. Hammond eds., *Materials: Renewable and Nonrenewable Resources* (Washington, D.C.: American Association for the Advancement of Science, 1976), pp. 68–73; and H. E. Goeller and A. Zucker in "Infinite Resources: The Ultimate Strategy," *Science* 223 (3 Feb. 1984): 456–62.

15. The term "global ecological interdependence" is not one that originates with us, although we intend to use it here in a specifically *social* sense (rather than the more common, narrowly physical sense). The notion of simultaneous binding and fragmentation is also one whose origins are rather

obscure; for a discussion of these concepts see John G. Ruggie, "Changing Frameworks of International Collective Behavior: On the Complementarity of Contradictory Tendencies," in Nazli Choucri and Thomas W. Robinson eds., *Forecasting in International Relations* (San Francisco: W. H. Freeman, 1978), pp. 384–406; James N. Rosenau, *Turbulence in World Politics* (Princeton: Princeton University Press, 1990).

16. John G. Ruggie writes that "the globe has become a *region* in the international system, albeit a *nonterritorial* one. . . . the concept refers to a subset of social interactions that take place on the globe. This subset constitutes an inclusive level of social interaction that is distinct from the *international* level, in that it comprises a multiplicity of integrated functional systems, operating in real time, which span the globe, and which affect in varying degrees what transpires elsewhere on the globe." "International Structure and International Transformation: Space, Time, and Method," in Ernst-Otto Czempiel and James N. Rosenau eds., *Global Changes and Theoretical Challenges* (Lexington: Lexington Books, 1989), p. 31. Regarding ecological independence, see Amos W. Hawley, *Human Ecology: A Theoretical Essay* (Chicago: University of Chicago Press, 1986).Our use of the term interdependence differs somewhat from the state-centric perspective on interdependence found in much of the international relations and international political economy literature (e.g., Keohane and Nye, *Power and Interdependence*.)

17. We distinguish here between the geobiophysical (environmental) changes taking place around the world and the sociopolitical (ecological) space within which these changes are affecting human civilization. Others have characterized these two realms as the "biosphere" and the "sociosphere." See for example "Reconciling the Sociosphere and the Biosphere," *International Social Science Journal* 121 (August 1989). The extent to which it is meaningful or useful to make such a distinction is the subject of debate, as well.

18. Ruggie's quote is from, "International Structure," p. 29. David Dessler's is from "What's at Stake in the Agent-Structure Debate?" *International Organization* 43 no. 3 (Summer 1989): 452. On page 448 Dessler refers to this as a "positional model, " and goes on to argue (pp. 453–54) that one must distinguish between physical attributes as one instrument of action, and rules that coordinate action: "policy not only relies upon physical capability, but it also requires a framework of meaning through which use of that capability become recognizable as policy. . . ." See also Ruggie, "International Structure," pp. 30–32.

19. We are grateful to Oran Young for pointing out the first of these two themes, as well as for his active participation and consistently insightful commentary throughout the workshops. Luther Gerlach was a consistent champion of the latter, as his chapter reflects.

20. We use the term "capacity" here to denote "specific organizational structures the presence (or absence) of which seems critical to the ability of

state authorities to undertake given tasks"; Peter B. Evans, Dietrich Rüesche-meyer, and Theda Skocpol, "On the Road to a More Adequate Understand-ing of the State," in: P. B. Evans, D. Rueschemeyer, and T. Skocpol eds., *Bringing the State Back In* (Cambridge: Cambridge University Press, 1985), p. 351. See also William Ascher and Robert Healy, *Natural Resource Policymaking in Developing Countries* (Durham, N.C.: Duke University Press, 1990); Joel Migdal, *Strong Societies and Weak States: State-Society Relations and State Capa-bilities in the Real World* (Princeton: Princeton University Press, 1988).

Act I

THE STATE AND GLOBAL
ECOLOGICAL INTERDEPENDENCE

It is widely assumed that environmental problems, however they manifest themselves, should be managed by governments. At the international level, the transborder nature of many such problems requires cooperation and collaboration among governments; at the domestic level, only the state has the tools and the authority to manage resources rationally, internalize costs, and mediate conflicts over competing uses. Most of the strategies put forward for responding to global environmental problems assume that states are willing and able to assume this managerial role.

The chapters in this section cast serious doubt on such assumptions. They challenge the idea that states have the capability to effectively manage resource use in a sustainable fashion, or that the fundamental interests of the state can be subordinated readily to the goals of sustainability. Indeed, it may even be that the state and its administrative organs stand as obstructions to sustainable resource management and environmental protection.[1]

One of the fundamental sources of state power is control over the resources located within the national territory. In most countries, natural-resource goods and environmental services are an important component of this resource base. The power to grant or alter property rights to resources can be an important means of building state alliances with civil society. And the effective use or allocation of those resources can, in principle, serve such other fundamental state purposes as national integration, state-building, preserving (or altering) the prevailing social order, raising revenues, or maintaining the legitimacy of the state itself.

In the industrialized countries of the West this capability on the part of the state is pretty much taken for granted. Historically, the state has in general been well-positioned to influence the flow and exploitation of resources to the benefit of certain users. And it does so within the context of well-developed legal systems that have evolved in parallel to markets (where, in effect, rights to property are bought and sold). The state can also tap into these markets, extracting revenues and resources for its own purposes (indeed, in most Western countries, such extraction accounts for a sizable fraction of total state revenues).

Whether this image of the democratic state as an effective resource manager holds true in a world of ecological interdependence remains to be seen (as indicated below, we have our doubts). But in much of the Third World it is clear that this picture has never applied. Instead, as Jesse Ribot underscores in chapter 2, we see what in many instances are "states" in name only. Rather than having re-created the European dichotomous state, in which laws and markets evolved in parallel, most less-developed countries have had Westernized legal systems imposed on much older patterns of social arrangements. In the struggle for domination, it is no surprise that the older system very often absorbs the newer one. The case Ribot examines here (that of charcoal markets and deforestation in Senegal) illustrates the result: legal efforts to protect the environment are undermined by what Joel Migdal has called the "web of social relations,"[2] becoming as good as no protection at all. Ribot's chapter illustrates that the problem in Senegal has as much to do with the alien nature of the state and its legal system, imposed upon a local system of production, as it does with the relative strength of society vis-à-vis the government. As Ronald Herring has described this problematic in the context of state-society relations in South Asia,

> States in the [South Asian] region mock the theoretical states of academic discourse, dissolving into society with distance from the center, much as blood vessels diminish in size with distance from the heart until they disappear into spaces around cells.[3]

Not all states in the Third World are as weak as Senegal's, of course. In many Latin American countries, for example, the administrative apparatus of the state predates the emergence of what currently constitute the dominant forces in civil society. More generally, many Third World states can lay claim to considerable capacities for intervention in some social spheres. Nancy Peluso (chapter 3) considers the cases of Kenya and Indonesia, where the state attempts to use its substantial military capacities to, in her words, "coerce conservation." In both cases, the military provides a means, when law and markets fail, to pursue state goals—in this case, goals nominally described as environmental conservation and resource development. In Kenya nature reserves have become the conservationist equivalent of war zones, while in Indonesia the deployment of military forces ensures principally that the military are able to determine who takes resources from the forest.

From the outside, observers applaud such actions as necessary to protect reserves and manage forests effectively. Coercive conservation is seen as demonstrating national commitment and capabilities. Yet as Peluso points out, the underlying goals of the state have little to do with conservation per se, and the use of force reflects not the state's strength but rather its very *weakness*—not its autonomy, but rather its inability to apply other means. Coercion may keep out poachers, but in the long run it undermines rather than legitimizes the state's role in resource conservation.

In chapter 4, James Rosenau presents an even broader challenge to the assumption of state competence in environmental management. He argues that even the competence of the strong and clearly differentiated states of the industrialized world is increasingly coming under challenge. While the conventional wisdom posits that environmental problems will drive centralization, Rosenau also sees a countervailing tendency toward decentralization, or "subgroupism." [4] Growing skills among citizens and a new standard of "performance legitimacy" are undermining state capacity and autonomy, as citizens take into their own hands those environmental problems that seem most threatening to their day-to-day lives. Environmental problems exacerbate this more general tendency; the impacts of global ecological interdependence are unevenly distributed *within* societies as well as among them, and national governments will be increasingly hard put to mediate and manage the resulting patchwork of effects.

Taken together, the arguments of Ribot, Peluso, and Rosenau raise doubts about not only the ability of states to manage their ecological interdependence individually, but also the prospects for doing so collectively. The factors they cite—including the fundamental incapacity of governments to control the destructive processes involved, the scarcity of effective policy levers, and the importance of resource extraction (and hence environmental destruction) for state-society alliances—may be far more serious obstacles to collective action than the traditionally cited "barriers" of mistrust, free riding and defection, and transaction costs.

In chapter 5, Karen Litfin examines the experience to date with collective environmental management through the construction of international environmental regimes. Although she sees in this record real possibilities for at least limited collective management, Litfin also underlines some embedded problems often overlooked by students of international regimes. Perhaps most importantly, she points out that most environmental regimes are "embedded in other social, political, and economic institutions" (a theme to which we return repeatedly in subsequent sections). While this could be read as a generalized commitment to environmental quality, Litfin is careful to point out that nonenvironmental considerations and domestic political interests often override such commitments. Even where the commitment to international cooperation is strongest, at the level of international regimes, the relative incapacity of the state system to manage resources and protect the environment is becoming increasingly evident.

None of this is to suggest that states are becoming irrelevant in the face of global ecological interdependence; as these chapters show, governments have fundamental interests in various forms of environmental protection and destruction. And effective responses to environmental problems that do not involve the state are difficult to imagine, at either the international or domestic levels. But it *does* suggest that the focus of analysis must change, casting a more critical eye on the state as a willing and able environmental manager. We pick up this theme in subsequent sections, addressing the issue of how this focus might be altered.

NOTES

1. Although the individual chapters vary in emphasis, they tend to accept the definition of the state put forward by Stepan: "The continuous adminis-

trative, legal, bureaucratic and coercive systems that attempt not only to structure relationships *between* civil society and public authority in a polity but also to structure many crucial relationships within civil society as well." See Alfred Stepan, *The State and Society: Peru in Comparative Perspective* (Princeton: Princeton University Press, 1978), p. xii (emphasis in original).

2. Joel S. Migdal, *Strong Societies and Weak States: State-Society Relations and State Capabilities in the Third World* (Princeton: Princeton University Press, 1988).

3. Ronald J. Herring, "Resurrecting the Commons-Collective Action and Ecology," *Items* (SSRC) 44 (4): 65.

4. These tensions between centralization and subgroupism in international politics are explored on a more general basis in James Rosenau, *Turbulence in World Politics: A Theory of Change and Continuity* (Princeton: Princeton University Press, 1990).

2

Market-State Relations and Environmental Policy: Limits of State Capacity in Senegal

•

JESSE C. RIBOT

Policy analysts working in the international arena often ignore the domestic complexities of developing-country environmental-policy implementation. The generally held assumption is that with an official policy commitment by countries with sufficient finances, infrastructure, technical knowledge, labor and land, policies will be implemented as specified.[1] Putting aside the question of whether such resources exist, a more fundamental question involves the political-economic capacity of the developing state or, more appropriately, its government, to act.

In this chapter, I explore the role of factors beyond the physical and financial means of the state as they affect the state's capacity to manage the use and conservation of natural resources. I examine social and political-economic dynamics that intervene between official environmental management policies and actual management practice. To do this, I focus on the role of market-state relations in the policy process. Drawing on the regulation of rural-urban charcoal markets in Senegal, I argue that policy outcomes are the result of two sets of interdependent factors: first, the political and economic needs of the state and those who occupy its administrative hierarchies—needs which the state policy apparatus is used to pursue; and second, the set of historical social relations linking those in the government to those who participate in the markets that extract, process, transport and distribute natural resources—relations through which policies are applied, transformed, used, and often circumvented or undermined.

After outlining some issues concerning state capacity in the developing world in the following section, I use examples from Senegal's forestry sector to explore these issues. I begin by describing the rural environmental consequences of Senegal's urban charcoal demand and some of the policies that have been implemented to manage charcoal production, transport, distribution and end use. I then focus on a quota system implemented to reduce charcoal production and aid in the management of the charcoal market, and lay out how the quota has been systematically circumvented and undermined. Next, I address the political-economic uses and functions of environmental policy, and some of the environmental consequences of the 'alternative' policy applications. Finally, I look at the articulation of peasant productive relations with the patronage use and functions of these nominally environmental policies.

States and Markets

For the purpose of simplicity, I begin with Alfred Stepan's definition of the "state" as

> the continuous administrative, legal, bureaucratic and coercive systems that attempt not only to structure relationships *between* civil society and public authority in a polity but also to structure many crucial relationships within civil society as well.[2]

While this Weberian definition provides a starting point for examining the state as a structure that attempts to influence society through its policy-making and implementation apparatus, it is limited. In many developing countries, the state is not autonomous from society, as the definition suggests, but is a "captive" of powerful elements within society, as we shall see. Indeed, "states"—and their governing apparatus—are often permeated and restructured by powerful social relations emerging from civil society. I would argue that the state is always at least partially captive of or serving select interests within society. It is a matter of what mechanisms are at work in doing this, not whether or not it is occurring. My interest here is in demonstrating one way that it is occurring within societies where the state's legal-administrative apparatus is interlinked with powerful interests within civil society.

This has important consequences for policy. The capacity of developing states to manage resource use, conservation, and environmentally sound development, or to accomplish most any other end, depends on the financial means of the state (that is, its revenue base), its institutional and physical infrastructure, and the structure of state-civil society relations. This last element is critical, particularly the nature of the state's relation to the markets and institutions it is trying to regulate. It is through this set of relations that control over economic, social, and natural resources is developed and maintained for the myriad purposes of the state and its members. These purposes include economic extraction for investment in industry and infrastructure or for the provision of social services, as well as the cultivation of political and economic alliances—that is, the achievement of the state's development goals and the maintenance of its legitimacy. They include the mix of private and public, social, ideological, and material aims of officials and agents that occupy public office.

The implication, in the words of Theda Skocpol, is that

> Fully specified studies of state capacities not only entail examinations of the resources and instruments that states may have for dealing with particular problems; they also necessarily look at more than states as such. They examine states *in relation to* particular kinds of socioeconomic and political environments populated by actors with given interests and resources.

She goes on to note that a complete analysis of state capacity

> requires examination of the organization and interests of the state, specification of the organization and interests of socioeconomic groups, and inquiries into the complementary as well as conflicting relationships of state and societal actors.[3]

The regulatory problems become evident when we examine the relationship between the state's and society's interests and institutions. The common assumption, that the state can effectively intervene in these institutions and extract resources from them, often does not hold. This can be seen, for example, in the case of markets. The market, as I use the term here, is not merely an arena of supply, demand, and price; rather, it is a social network of exchange and commerce and a conduit for natural resources from their rural origins to their final use.[4] Those who participate in the market are not isolated producers, merchants and consumers interacting solely through competititve exchange; they are producers and consumers related to each other and to members of the state through a network of social ties. By the same token, the state is not a benevolent or objective hand in market regulation, as neoclassical models cast it, and as it is often viewed in the industrialized world. Rather, it includes participants in exchange and accumulation within the market. Consequently, the intervening variables between supply and demand are not merely prices and quantities, but also include the political, economic and social relations between the market and the state and among financiers, merchants, and laborers within the market.

In my exploration of some of these relations and their effects on the policy process I will argue, as does Robert Bates, that on the state side we are faced with a system in which members of the government can use state resources to cultivate clienteles. By channeling benefits to favored individuals or groups they can build political, economic, and social influence and support for themselves, their party, and the state.[5] In short, state-controlled resources are allocated through social relations between the market and state for both political and private ends.

On the market side, access to these state-controlled resources is, I submit, a function of social identity and social relations emerging from dependent agricultural productive relations. This argument is based on Sara Berry's work on the use of social relations as means of gaining access to productive resources.[6] The agricultural productive systems, in which dependent producers must invest in social relations with their patrons in order to maintain access to productive resources, provide the basis for current market-state resource flows.

The implications of market-state relations vis-à-vis state capacity to make and implement environmental policy are far reaching. Where the state and market are intertwined and patrimonial powers preside, policies (environmental policies for this analysis) that limit profits, constrain powerful individuals or groups within society, or are inconsistent with historically accepted rules of market conduct and exchange, are unlikely to succeed. They are more likely to be transformed to serve the purposes of those influential officials and merchants with access to the productive resources of both the state and civil society.

Regulation, Urban Woodfuel, and the Rural Environment

In West Africa, as in most of sub-Saharan Africa, urban as well as rural households depend on woodfuels (charcoal and firewood) for almost all of their energy needs. Many urban centers prefer charcoal over firewood for its hot and even burning characteristics, while rural populations still burn firewood directly. Charcoal-consuming urban centers exert a disproportionately large pressure on the forest resource since charcoal is produced from wood at low conversion efficiencies. Because urban growth is so much greater than rural growth (due largely to rural-urban migration), and because per-capita urban woodfuel consumption is much higher than rural consumption (due to urban use of charcoal), urban centers are consuming a growing portion of the primary woodfuels produced. Because much of the urban growth is due to rural-urban migration and because migrants switch from firewood to charcoal, growth of total woodfuel demand in some countries outpaces population growth. In Senegal, for example, urban preference for charcoal results in the urban twenty-five percent of the population consuming fifty percent of the primary woodfuels produced nationally. Senegal's situation is somewhat extreme. Nevertheless, on the African continent, where urbanization rates are among the highest in the world, urban demand for forest resources—along with its rural social and environmental consequences—is significant and growing.[7]

In the regions from which urban-bound charcoal is extracted, impacts on villages have been extensive. In these regions, urban woodfuel harvesting is degrading the forests on which rural populations depend for food, fuel, fodder, building materials, medicines, dies, and other forest products.[8] In my surveys, for example, villagers consistently blamed charcoal producers for firewood scarcities and for the scarcity of game animals and birds, large posts for home construction, and honey (previously gathered as a cash crop). The concentrated nature of urban demand results in forest clearing around villages that far exceeds local resource use. The result is shortages for village populations whose own consumption alone would probably not degrade the resource. In short, urban woodfuel demand results in village-level economic and subsistence hardships.

The consequences of urban woodfuel demand extend beyond local effects. Several studies have projected exhaustion of Senegal's forest resource if current trends persist.[9] Such deforestation poses a threat to urban energy supply, as well as the availability of other commercial and subsistence forest products, and negative long-term consequences for agricultural and pastoral systems (through, for example, watershed effects and soil erosion). The micro- and macro-climatological effects of these forms of environmental degradation are also of concern.

Senegal's Ministry for the Protection of Nature (MPN—*Ministère de la Protection de la Nature*) and its Forestry Department (*Direction des Eaux, Forêts et Chasses*—housed within the MPN) are well aware of many rural environmental consequences of urban charcoal demand and the potential for woodfuel shortages.[10] In response, the two agencies have implemented measures intended both to reduce demand and increase production, including improved cookstove and charcoal kiln programs, a bottled gas substitution program, woodfuel plantations, and reforestation efforts. Efforts have also been made to manage the natural forests by imposing a quota limiting charcoal production; restricting charcoal production to the most forested regions of the country; drawing up ecologically based allotments of forest tracts for charcoal production; limiting the charcoal production season; prohibiting the cutting of live trees in drought-sensitive areas; and protecting commercially valuable tree species.

In addition, the Forestry Department requires merchants in the charcoal industry to form or join cooperatives and to carry licenses and obtain production, transport, and storage permits. This is part of a larger effort to organize the rural sector for national-development purposes as well as to help tax and regulate the charcoal market. Together, these measures are intended to assure urban woodfuel supply and to protect the resource base, both of which fall under the Forestry Department's jurisdiction.

The achievements of these programs, vis-à-vis managing the forest resource, have been marginal at best. Dissemination of higher-efficiency woodstoves and charcoal kilns has met with little success because of limited efficiency improvements, cost constraints, and social resistance to new cooking and conversion technologies. Similar problems have been faced by programs aimed at substituting bottled gas for charcoal. Attempts to increase woodfuel production through planting have been affected by low survival rates, land and tree tenure complications, and financial constraints. The net result of efficiency, substitution, and planting programs—attempts to increase supply or reduce demand—has been negligible. Urban charcoal demand continues to grow with urban population.[11] Thus, for the

foreseeable future, urban and rural households will continue to depend on natural forests for virtually all of their energy needs.

Natural-forest management programs have been confronted by a
different set of problems. These policies have also had limited effects,
but for political-economic, rather than technical or financial, reasons.
The social and political-economic dynamics of the market, and the
configuration of market-state relations, have undermined the ability
of the state to manage natural-forest extraction. For example, as a
result of market-state links, excess production quotas have been freely
distributed by government agencies to powerful merchants, while
the production season, restrictions on species exploitation, and limits
on the spatial distribution of production have been circumvented—
to the benefit of state officials and agents as well as select merchants.

Policy circumvention and manipulation activities are not, however, mere criminality or fraud, market failures, externalities, or exceptions to the rule of law. Rather, they represent part and parcel of
the tension and cooperation between participants in the market and
agents of the state in an ongoing struggle over control of and access
to productive resources. In this struggle, incomplete jurisdiction of
the state, integration of market and state interests, and the dynamics
of social relations and institutions, render the state unable to manage. Hence, these political-economic dynamics ultimately undermine
the official environmental (or development) functions of state policies.

Contradictory Quotas—the Cornerstone of Market Regulation

A better understanding of these problems can be gained by examining a specific portion of the government's management efforts and
the social dynamics affecting public policies aimed at mitigating the
rural environmental impacts of Senegal's urban charcoal demand. I
focus here on the production-limiting quota in an effort to clarify
why it has not worked as intended. Regulatory policies have had
both positive and negative environmental effects. Rather than protecting forest resources, however, the system of controls deployed to
manage charcoal production has, as we shall see, served mainly to
tax the market, create resource-extraction opportunities, and strengthen
historical social ties and hierarchies within the market and between
the market and state.

The quota is a cornerstone of charcoal production and marketing regulation designed not only to limit charcoal production, but also to serve as part of a system for guiding the spatial distribution of production nationally, the allocation of production permits, the collection of taxes and stumpage fees, and the transport of charcoal within Senegal.

Each year a Forestry Department committee fixes a national quota, which is set well below demand. Prior to the opening of the production season, quotas are allocated to cooperatives by regional committees composed of the regional governor, representatives from the Forestry Department, cooperative presidents, National Union of Forestry Cooperatives, and the regional cooperative association. Allocation is based on the number of members in each cooperative, and the cooperative's production rate for the previous year.

Cooperatives are composed of charcoal merchants, who must be members to obtain a share of a cooperative's quota. With quotas in hand, individual merchants are then able to obtain production permits and to hire the charcoal producers who use them. A production permit specifies a period of validity (usually 30 days) and a production plot. When the production cycle is completed and the charcoal is ready, the merchant is then ready to move the charcoal to market. To do this, he (indeed, they are all men) needs a charcoal transportation permit, which he receives in exchange for a portion of his quota and the payment of stumpage fees and taxes. In this manner, the quota system tracks the temporal and spatial distribution of production, its total quantity, and the taxes and fees derived from charcoal production.

In addition to a national quota set far below demand, the official retail price of charcoal—which is fixed by the government—is set below the market price (or, at least, below the price at which charcoal is actually sold). *Ceteris paribus*, a quota set below demand, combined with a low fixed retail price, should lead to charcoal shortages in the cities. In practice, however, this does not happen, since neither the fixed price nor the quota are respected—evidently, *ceteris* is not *paribus*. Actual production is about 180 percent of the official national quota, while the actual retail price of charcoal is more than 30 percent above the fixed price.[12] How—that is through what channels—does this occur? Why is such a contradictory policy allowed to stand? What are its effects?

Although, in theory, these government regulations should limit production, in practice, the quota is not a fixed quantity. Additional quotas—above and beyond the national annual quota—can be obtained through various social and economic channels. Powerful merchants ask for extra quotas through the intervention of their representatives in the national assembly, government ministers, religious leaders, and friends or relations within the government with the MPN or Forestry Department. Many eventually receive them, and the problem of limited supply is thereby overcome.

In other words, via informal relations with powerful members of government, select merchants are allocated additional quotas. Merchants with fewer connections to the state—that is, merchants of lower status—are not entirely excluded from marketing more charcoal than the official initial allocation specified; they can obtain additional circulation permits (equivalent to having an extra quota) by purchasing confiscated charcoal from regional forestry offices. Rather than gaining access through social status and social relations, they must use whatever economic leverage they may have. Indeed, it is often the case that "confiscated" charcoal is produced by the buyer's workers with the "confiscation" being merely the paperwork needed to purchase access to circulation and marketing in the form of circulation permits. In these ways, access to charcoal marketing is obtained through combinations of social relations and economic leverage. Note that little charcoal enters Dakar without an official circulation permit (obtained through a quota or through the "confiscation" route), since, as some merchants put it, why would anyone take the risk of circulating without a permit when permits are relatively easy to obtain?

Policy for Whom and for What? The Uses and Functions of Environmental Policy

Why the combined quota and fixed-price policy persists can only be surmised. The Forestry Department, the MPN, and the Ministry of Commerce, all of which are jointly involved in the policy-making and implementation process, are certainly aware of the contradictions that exist within the charcoal production system. It is, nevertheless, plausible that the policy arises out of competing and contradictory mandates. On the one hand, the low fixed retail price is a product of political pressures to subsidize urban necessities. Politicians in Senegal are often said to fear the protests that might result if the price of charcoal were raised. In addition, low prices provide indirect support to urban industry through what is, in effect, a wage subsidy. (See note 12).

On the other hand, the Forestry Department is under intense pressure from international and domestic environmental organizations to reduce the impacts of charcoal production on the forests, and it is held responsible, as well, when charcoal shortages do arise. Thus, the Department sets the quota in order to maintain long-term supply by reducing pressures on the forests. It then turns around and allows excess quotas to be allocated to prevent shortages and ease political pressures from industry, merchants, and the urban population. There is also a financial incentive involved here: the Forestry Department and the MPN receive revenues from taxes and stumpage fees, which provides an incentive to keep production up. In short, these agencies are caught between pressures to meet demand and protect the forests: the contradictory policies, and their circumvention (through excess quota allocation and nonenforcement of the fixed price), emerge partly as a product of the struggle between these competing goals.

Another complementary and quite compelling explanation is that powerful members of the government and the market benefit from this set of policies and their circumvention. Clearly, those select members of the market with access to additional quotas benefit from that access. Agents of the state who grant that access also stand to benefit by dint of their power to allocate resources along political, economic, or social lines. These resources can be used to extract economic rents or build political clienteles.[13] This last point may help to explain why, in recent years (1988 and 1989), the Forestry Department and MPN have continued to lower an already unenforced and unenforceable quota. By doing so, the agencies appear to be trying to protect nature. At the same time, the gap between the quota and actual production grows larger, providing state officials and agents with access to a resource for political and economic allocation.[14]

In the case of the quota, in other words, officials create a law *prohibiting* an activity that they can later *allow* for an unofficial fee, or as a "favor," thereby extracting what Robert Bates calls "administratively generated rents." In effect, state officials and agents charge rents on access to what are supposed to be state-restricted resources. Bates goes on to describe a similar situation in Western Nigeria: "The marketing board lowered the prices offered peasant producers for export crops and thereby accumulated surplus revenues. A portion of the proceeds thus generated by the board was transferred to development agencies, which provided capital for loans at subsidized terms to potential investors in the urban industrial sector." Bates explains that "this policy in Nigeria was in fact self-contradictory, and its contradictions became a source of political opportunity."[15]

Elsewhere, Bates argues that in general African governments explicitly use market regulations as "instruments of political organization of the countryside," and see market intervention as "a basis for building political organizations." He observes that: "the prevailing tendency has been to regard these [policy generated] rents as pure social costs—inefficiencies induced by political distortions of market forces. What has not been stressed is that the rents also represent political resources—resources which can be used to organize political support."[16]

Of course, the activities of members of the state and market also serve to enhance officials' and agents' *private* capacities to accumulate both social (with its political element) and economic capital. That is, policies are also manipulated and circumvented so as to allow private acquisition of access to resources for production and survival. Thus, the distribution of state resources serves both individual and state ends, rather than simply being a systematic attempt on the part of the state to maintain its base of political support—a purpose also served by the rationing of state resources.[17]

In Senegal's charcoal market, rents are charged on access to quotas, as well as on permits, licenses, restricted forest access, and other resources allocated by the state—including rents collected by forestry agents from producers for protection from fines. These rents can be in monetary or in social and political forms. They can range from small bribes to agents all the way up to the political support a minister derives from the generous distribution of restricted quotas or permits. Such a system encourages the tightening of restrictions and control over the resource in order to increase rent-extraction opportunities.

In sum, while policies have official functions and uses, they also provide opportunities for unofficial resource use by officials and agents of the state and members of the market. By their nature, pricing and allocative policies shift *legal* authority over resources, and hence influence resource access and control.[18] When the state adds to (in the form of subsidies), takes from (in the form of taxes or fees), or controls resources within the market (as with licenses, permits, quotas, price fixing, health and safety regulations, and the regulation of resource management), these become levers by which individuals in the government can influence resource distribution.[19] Where such levers exist, social ties between the members of the market and state spring into action.

In Senegal, the state is not exogenous to or separate from the market; rather, they are highly intertwined. As elsewhere in Africa, Senegalese charcoal merchants use channels of influence based on relations of patronage, obligation, dependency, and other social and religious ties and institutions (e.g. through Muslim brotherhoods and ethnic relations), along with political and economic channels (such as bribes, payoffs, partnerships, and lobbying), to obtain access to resources under state control. (The social relations linking the market and state can run along numerous lines: ethnic group, class, religious denomination, caste, clan, family, etc.) These social relations integrally link the market and state. This integration is not merely another way of talking about market distortions, but is rooted in a more organic model of the relation between markets and states— a model in which state policy capacity is a function of state-civil society relations.[20]

In the final analysis, charcoal production is still almost twice as high as is the official quota, and it is almost certainly growing along with urban population. The quota places no real limit on charcoal production, with the net result that policies applied to Senegal's charcoal market do not appear to have improved environmental practices: they have not directly reduced charcoal production, nor have they systematically managed forest production toward environmental ends. Rather, these policies have mainly served to further stratify the market and provide social, political, and economic support to select merchants, government officials, and agents.

Productive Ties, State Policy, and the Market-State Relation

Market-state relations are critical to the performance of environmental or any other regulatory policies, since it is through these relations that policies take on both form and function. The market-state relation is cultivated through patronage on the state side as described above. On the market side, it is built through historically rooted social relations of production and exchange. In this section I show how state patronage and peasant-based productive relations integrate to form the basis of market-state relations.

In Senegal's charcoal market, as in much of Sub-Saharan Africa, market relations of production and exchange are intertwined with and embedded in indigenous social relations.[21] Economic historian Sara Berry highlights *social identity* (i.e. one's status in a social-political hierarchy of power and influence), in addition to market exchange, as a key factor in the ability of those participating in commerce to gain access to productive resources.[22] She argues that:

> Since pre-colonial times, Africans have gained access to land, labor, and capital for agricultural production both through exchange and through membership and status in various social units. . . . [U]nder colonial rule specific mechanisms of access changed with changing economic and political circumstances, but the general principle—that access depended on social identity as well as on purchasing power—persisted.[23]

Similarly, in Senegal, historically rooted social relations that depend on social identity—such as noble-captive relations between current Fulbe (a West African ethnic group) charcoal merchants and producers—are integrated with the newer set of market relations. In this new context, these relations continue to serve select individuals or groups (with the appropriate status and/or finances) in their efforts to secure access to productive resources.[24]

In other words, in Senegal, social identity and the selective patterns of resource access it engenders lay the foundation for market stratification. Patterns of stratification, in turn, influence resource flow and distribution within the market and between the market and the state. The quota system, along with other policies applied to Senegal's charcoal market, serves the political function of building a clientele through allocation of state resources along lines of social status—that is, allocation to the powerful members of the market. It simultaneously helps reproduce and reinforce this status-based system of resource access.

In the charcoal market, powerful merchants have gained their influence through their historically privileged position over charcoal producers. The merchants, coming largely from the land-owning nobles, have managed to maintain a system of domination over charcoal producers, who come largely from the first group's stock of former serfs. Throughout the transition from an agriculturally based system of serfdom, rooted in the noble-captive economies of Guinea's Futa Jalon region, to the current set of productive relations found in the charcoal market, many characteristics of nobility, captivity, and mutual dependence have been maintained.

The Fulbe noble-captive system has its roots in the Islamic *jihads* (holy wars) of the mid-1700s, when Islamic Fulbe took Diallonké populations as their serfs. Under this productive system, the captives or serfs depended upon their relations with noble families for access to productive resources. Serfs (women, men, and children) worked five days a week in the homes of their nobles and gave ten to fifty percent of their harvest in return for religious services, medicine, protection, food, and land.[25] Although this system has changed over time, many of its characteristics persist in Guinean agriculture today.[26] Indeed, similar productive systems are currently found throughout West Africa,[27] including Senegal's charcoal market, which is dominated by Fulbe merchants and producers who brought these types of productive arrangements with them from Guinea and have integrated them with similar dependent-productive relations found in Senegalese agriculture.

Before the late 1970s, charcoal producers were dependent on merchants for subsistence advances, tools, religious and medical services, and protection from harassment by foresters. In return, producers were obligated to give half of their charcoal production to the merchant, with subsistence advances and other expenses subtracted from the producer's remaining earnings. As a result, producers often wound up in debt after the production cycle, and were obligated to continue working for the merchant to pay off their debt.

Following some isolated and inconclusive protest by charcoal producers over very poor returns to their labor, one forestry agent catalyzed the abandonment of the sharecropping system in 1979. On his own accord, Forester Amadou Mbaye Ndiaye of the Regional Forestry Service of Tambacounda called a meeting of merchants and producers, demanding that exchange be altered to a negotiated price-per-sack basis, and calling this his "free-market" policy. This unofficial "policy" (or pronouncement) took root and, within two years, producers were being paid by the sack. Under the new system, merchants provided subsistence loans to producers while the charcoal season was underway and purchased the charcoal from them at the end of the production cycle. The loans, of course, were still subtracted from the producer's final income. For a while, the market appeared to be moving toward more competitive exchange, but the merchants lost little time in regaining control over trade.

In particular, the quota system (in which I include quotas, licenses, permits, and cooperatives, since they are so integrally linked) provided merchants with significant advantages in this situation, since it gave them a monopoly over official charcoal marketing channels. The merchants were able to take control of cooperatives because of financial and social entry barriers that producers were unable to overcome. The distribution of production quotas, licenses, and permits through cooperatives gave merchants ultimate control over commerce. The collective organization of merchants into cooperatives, exclusive of producers, provided a forum for collusive fixing of the producer price. And, so, this unique access for merchants strengthened their oligopsonistic position, weakening the bargaining position of producers.[28]

Whereas producers previously had been tied to their merchants through labor-tying debts and extra-economic obligations, and for access to land and credit, they are now obligated to the merchants for access to permits and marketing in addition to protection from foresters and (albeit less important) subsistence loans. Indeed, it may be that the position of the producers is weaker under this new arrangement. Subsistence advances to producers have become smaller and more difficult to obtain with the advent of price fixing, indicating a shift away from debt and interlocking credit-labor markets as a way of maintaining control over price.

In brief, market regulations made the producers *legally* dependent upon merchants, but this new system of production and exchange is not so different from the old. Producers are still dependent on relations of social status for access to merchant-controlled productive resources, although this time around, instead of seed, land, religious services, and protection from other nobles, the relevant resources are marketing and protection from the state. The regulations within the charcoal market have replaced the mechanism by which dependency was maintained, but they have not supplanted the system of dependency.

State interventions in the market thus give the state a handle on the flow of productive resources, making access to the state an essential productive ingredient.[29] The necessity of state access to productive resources, in combination with its selective nature, makes government intervention a mechanism for building political clienteles and for maintaining dependent productive relations. Thus, the relation between the market and state takes on a function for the merchant as well as for the state. While resource control is a means for members of the state to cultivate alliances and to partake in the market, it is also a means for merchants to maintain the dependence of labor. By having exclusive access to marketing, merchants can maintain control over the market. The cost of that maintenance is the investment (as in political loyalty or possibly payments) merchants must make in social relation with members of the state. Members of the state benefit, both politically and economically, from the social investments they receive while merchants benefit from their exclusive access to the state.

Resource access for merchants now requires investment in social relations. Whereas, prior to intervention by the state, the investment ran from the producer to the merchant, now it also runs from the merchant to the state. In effect the system has gone from two tiered—nobles and serfs—to three tiered—state, merchants, and producers. In this latter system it is now the merchants who invest in social relations with the state; they invest resources extracted directly from producers whose dependence these relations help to maintain.

Conclusions

When evaluating the potential for environmentally sound development policies, the nature of the state and its ability to implement resource-management policies must be taken into account. Policies applied to the co-evolved political and economic system of many developing countries ultimately may take on the form of that system. The resources captured by regulatory policies are diffused along social and political-economic lines rather than serving their nominal purposes, and policy-generated resources are used for political-economic ends through these historically-rooted social channels.

The implications for dealing with the effects of global ecological interdependence are not insignificant. The bottom line, which those concerned with environmental protection must recognize, is that even when states express a will and have the finances to implement a given set of policies, there is no guarantee that they will be able to do so. In the "weblike" societies of many developing countries, the ability of the state to execute its will depends on how policies redistribute or limit resources and resource access. These factors are more important than the official intentions or technical ability of the state. In sum, resource management must be viewed through the broader optic of its location in a system of national (and international) markets and under a management largely colored by the difficult relation between the market and the state. Until issues of scarcity, distribution of, and access to resources of the earth and of the state are addressed, sustainable management of the natural-resource base will remain highly problematic.[30]

Understanding the political-economic dynamics between the market and the state may permit the design of policies and measures that address root causes of environmental decline and environmental policy limits. In the final analysis, however, contradictions and conflicts over resource ownership, access, and interests will continuously arise. The state will always have difficulties when it must protect and exploit resources on which it depends both materially and politically. In the face of these contradictions it is the task of the environmental analyst or policymaker to redesign and reimplement policies in what is fundamentally an iterative process. Environmentally sound or "sustainable" development policies will not be implemented once and for all. They will come and go.

NOTES

1. For supporting arguments see Joel S. Migdal, *Strong Societies and Weak States: State-Society Relations and State Capabilities in the Third World* (Princeton: Princeton University Press, 1988), p. 9 and Marilee S. Grindle, *Policy and Policy Implementation in the Third World* (Princeton: Princeton University Press, 1980).

2. Alfred Stepan, *The State and Society: Peru in Comparative Perspective* (Princeton: Princeton University Press, 1978), p. xii; as cited in Theda Skocpol, "Bringing the State Back In: Strategies of Analysis in Current Research," in Peter B. Evans, Dietrich Rueschemeyer, and Theda Skocpol eds., *Bringing the State Back In* (Cambridge: Cambridge University Press, 1985), p. 7. Emphasis in original.

3. Skocpol, "Bringing the State Back In," pp. 19, 20. Emphasis in original.

4. Jesse C. Ribot, "Markets, States and Environmental Policy: The Political Economy of Charcoal in Senegal" (Ph.D. diss., Energy and Resources Group, University of California at Berkeley, 1990).

5. Robert H. Bates, *Markets and States in Tropical Africa: The Political Basis of Agricultural Policies* (Berkeley: University of California Press, 1981).

6. Sara H. Berry, "Social Institutions and Access to Resources," *Africa* 59 no. 1 (1989).

7. Alain Bertrand, "Les Nouvelles Politiques de foresterie en milieu rural au Sahel: Réglementations Foncières et Forestières et gestion des ressources ligneuses naturelles dans les pays de la Zone Soudano-Sahélienne," *Bois et Forêts de Tropiques* No. 207 (First Trimester, 1985): 24; Jean Gorse, "Fuelwood and Domestic Energy: the Fuelwood 'Crisis' in Tropical West Africa," (World Bank, West Africa Agricultural Projects Department, 1985); Gerald Leach and Robin Mearns, *Beyond the Woodfuel Crisis: People, Land and Trees in Africa* (London: Earthscan Publications Ltd., 1988), pp. 178–179; Phil O'Keefe and R. Hosier, "The Kenyan Fuelwood Cycle Study: A Summary," *GeoJournal* 7.1 (1983): 25–28; Asif M. Shaikh and Edward Karch, "Will Wood Work: the Future of Wood Energy in the West African Sahel" (E/DI, Unpublished, 1985); Gérard Madon, "Note sur le contrôle des flux de charbon de bois," (Report ENERDOM/SEN/87, DE-MIDA/World Bank, DEFC-MPN, 1987); Youba Sokona, "Statistiques et bilans énergétiques du Sénégal" (ENDA-MIDA, July 1987); World Bank, *World Development Report 1987* (New York: Oxford University Press, 1987).

8. Anne Bergeret, "Nourritures de Cueillette en Pays Sahélien," *Journal d'Agriculture Traditionnelle et de Botanique Appliquée* 33 (1986); Anne Bergeret and Jesse Ribot, *L'Arbre Nourricier en Pays Sahélien* (Paris: Editions de la Maison des Sciences de l'Homme, 1990).

9. République du Sénégal, "Plan Directeur de Développement Forestier, Phase de Diagnostique: Economie de bois, 1ère et 2éme parties," Ministère du Développement Rural, Secrétariat d'Etat aux Eaux et Forêts (Paris: CTFT/SCET-International, 1981); World Bank, "Senegal: Issues and Options in the Energy Sector" (Report No. 4182–SE, 1983).

10. There has been almost no research on the precise analytic connections between urban woodfuel demand and its social and ecological impacts. Although there have been a few inconclusive studies of the ecological consequences of urban charcoal demand, Senegal's Forestry Department assumes they are significant and widespread. Among the first to recognize the significance of urban demand are: Dennis Anderson and Robert Fishwick, "Firewood Consumption and Deforestation in African Countries" (World Bank Staff Working Papers, Washington D.C., 1984), p. 22; Jean Gorse, "Fuelwood and Domestic Energy: the Fuelwood 'Crisis' in Tropical West Africa" (World Bank, West Africa Agricultural Projects Department, Washington D.C., 1985), p. 1; Kenneth J. Newcombe, "Household Energy Supply: The Energy Crisis That is Here to Stay" (World Bank, East Africa Projects Department, Paper presented at Senior Policy Seminar—Energy, Gaborone, Botswana, 18 through 22 March 1985, p. 3); and Carolyn Barnes, J. Ensminger, and Phil O'Keefe, *Wood, Energy and Households: Perspectives on Rural Kenya, Energy, Environment and Development in Africa*, no. 6 (Stockholm, The Beijer Institute, 1984). Each of these studies is based on work done in Africa. An example of the prevailing focus on rural woodfuel demand is provided by Bina Agarwal, whose experience has been mostly in India; see *Cold*

Hearths and Barren Slopes: The Woodfuel Crisis in the Third World (New Delhi: Allied Publishers Private Limited, 1986); Gerald Leach and Robin Mearns, *Beyond the Woodfuel Crisis: People, Land, and Trees in Africa* (London: Earthscan Publications, 1988), pp. 187–280; Meyers and Leach have recently (1989) written insightfully on these matters. Some of the rural consequences of urban charcoal demand have been addressed by Bergeret, "Nourritures de Cueillette en Pays Sahélien,"; Anne Bergeret, "Rôle Alimentaire des arbres et de quelques plantes herbacées, Communauté Rurale de Sali (Kumbija), Sénégal" (Paper presented at the VII Séminaire d'Economie et Sociologie Rurale, Montpellier, France, 15 through 19 September 1986); Mamadou M. Niang, "La Mise en Place des réformes agrofoncières" in E. Le Bris, et al. eds., *Enjeux Fonciers en Afrique Noire* (Bondy: ORSTOM and Paris: Karthala, 1982); Seydou Niang, "Impact de la production de charbon de bois sur l'écosystème forêt" (Proceedings of Colloque Forêts et Environnement, Institut Sciences de L'Environnement, Dakar, Senegal, May 1989); and M. Arbonnier and B. Faye, "Étude de la forêt classée de Koumpentoum" (Projet d'Aménagement et de Reboisement des Forêts du Centre Est, République du Sénégal, Ministère de la Protection de la Nature, Direction de la Conservation des Sols, December 1988).

11. For discussions of these programs see Chun K. Lai, "Reforestation in the Republic of Senegal: Framework, Description and Analysis" (Report of Consulting Forester, New Haven: USAID, 1984); Chun K. Lai, "Forestry Planning: The Senegalese Experience," *Rural Africana* no. 23–34 (Fall 1985/Winter 1986): 87–94; George F. Taylor II and Edouard G. Bonkoungou, "Introduction," *Rural Africana,* Special Issue on Forestry in the West African Sahel no. 23–24 (Fall 1985/Winter 1986): 1; George F. Taylor II and Moustapha Soumaré, "Strategies for Forestry Development in the West African Sahel," *Rural Africana* no. 23–24 (Fall 1985/Winter 1986): 16; Transenerg, 1985; World Bank, "Republic of Senegal Forestry Project Staff Appraisal Report" (Projects Department, West Africa Regional Office Agriculture III Division, Report No. 3120a-SE, 1981); and World Bank, "Senegal: Household Energy Strategy" (Report No. 096/89, March 1989), pp. 32–35.

12. A World Bank end-use survey determined that consumption in Dakar exceeded the quota by 80 percent. This figure was later revised downward due to protest by members of Senegal's Forestry Department; see Josef Leitmann, "Draft Report on Household Energy Strategies for Senegal (World Bank: Unpublished, 1987); World Bank, "Senegal: Household Energy Strategy," Report No. 096/89 (March 1989). The average weight of a "kilogram" of charcoal sold in Dakar at the official fixed price is 740 to 770 grams; see Smaïl Khennas, "Circuit de distribution, prix du charbon de bois, substitutions: le cas Sénégalais" (Dakar: ENDA-TM, 1987).

13. Bates, *Markets and States* pp. 98–9.

14. For a quantitative discussion of the potential rents created by policies, see Anne O. Krueger, "The Political Economy of the Rent-Seeking Society,"

The American Economic Review 64 no. 3 (June 1974); David Collander ed., *Neoclassical Political Economy: The Analysis of Rent-Seeking and DUP Activities* (Cambridge: Ballinger Publishing Company, 1984); and Jagdish N. Bhagwati, "Directly Unproductive, Profit-Seeking (DUP) Activities," *Journal of Political Economy* 90 no. 5 (1982): 988–1002. Kreuger has coined the term rent seeking to describe the changing or circumvention of laws in order to extract profit. Bhagwati presents an excellent taxonomy of rent seeking and other "Directly Unproductive, Profit-seeking Activities." The rent-seeking literature is loaded with questionable assumptions and implicit values, some of which are enumerated by Warren J. Samuels and Nicholas Mercuro, "A Critique of Rent-Seeking Theory," in Collander ed., *Neoclassical Political Economy.* This literature nevertheless provides a framework for examining what is happening when individuals attempt to profit by circumventing the rules that presumably apply to everyone. The prescriptions that come from the rent-seeking literature (such as a "free market" policy) follow more from the assumptions than from the analysis (see Samuels and Mercuro, ibid.). Rent-seeking analysis and the concept of rent seeking are, nevertheless, still of great value as tools for quantifying the potential for and understanding some immediate economic ramifications of policy circumvention and lobbying.

15. Bates, *Markets and States,* pp. 99, 100.

16. Robert H. Bates, *Essays on the Political Economy of Rural Africa* (Berkeley: University of California Press, 1983), pp. 130, 129. For an excellent example of public resource allocation along class and clientele lines, as well as for the private profit of powerful officials, see Temple and Temple, 1980: 241–248.

17. This situation reflects what Weber calls a "patrimonial office," where the distinction between private and official spheres blur. Weber, 1987: 1028.

18. Krueger, "The Political Economy of the Rent-Seeking Society,"; Bhagwati, "Directly Unproductive Activities"; Collander ed., *Neoclassical Political Economy*; See Catherine Boone, "The Making of a Rentier Class: Wealth Accumulation and Political Control in Senegal," *Journal of Development Studies* 26, no. 3 (April 1990): 425–49. for a precise definition and discussion of such rents and rentier activities.

19. Indeed, the government is always, at least indirectly, such a lever since it defines laws which in turn define resources—laws that define ownership and access. See Samuels and Mercuro, "A Critique of Rent-Seeking Theory," pp. 57–60. Access to the state is paramount to access to leverage over laws (changing or circumventing them) and therefore, over resource use and distribution. Environmental policies, which often restrict quantities of resources used, the zones in which resources can be extracted, or the prices at which resources can be sold, provide ideal opportunities for extracting rents (Krueger, "The Political Economy of the Rent-Seeking Society," pp. 291–293; Bhagwati, "Directly Unproductive Activities," pp. 991–994). Environmental policies are particularly vulnerable to rent seeking since their

formulation and enforcement costs are high, while their constituencies are diffuse and their opponents are fighting for concrete, short-term economic gains; see Douglas North, "Three Approaches to the Study of Institutions," in Collander ed., *Neoclassical Political Economy*, pp. 39–41. Environmental policies are aimed at protecting or managing diffuse resources, making enforcement costly. This is compounded in Africa by lack of sufficient environmental information (research) and trained personnel. In addition, environmental policies are often in direct opposition to concrete economic interests, while their own constituencies are affected only at the margin. Their constituencies are indeed long-term and ideologically driven, rather than being driven by immediate economic gain (or loss). These factors make environmental policies difficult to establish and even more difficult to enforce. Indeed, such environmental policies are particularly susceptible to manipulations at the level of policy formation and implementation, by officials, agents, and those merchants who dominate natural-resource markets.

20. Migdal, *Strong Societies and Weak States.*

21. For a similar thesis based on research in the Sudan see Mohamed A. M. Salih, "Local Markets in Moroland: The Shifting Strategies of the Jellaba Merchants," in Leif O. Manger ed., *Trade and Traders in the Sudan* (Bergen: Department of Social Anthropology, University of Bergen, 1984), pp. 189–212.

22. Also see Max Weber's definition of traditional authority, described by Talcott Parsons, which depends entirely upon the notion of status, or social identity, within a community. Parsons also describes Weber's close linking of property and personal authority: ". . . property rights over things or persons generally carries with it personal authority, usually with at least an element of political jurisdiction, notably over persons and land." He goes on to say, "as the 'means of production' are appropriated within a system of traditional authority there is a strong tendency for it to be accompanied by various forms and degrees of unfree personal status for the persons subject to authority." See Talcott Parsons, *Max Weber: The Theory of Social and Economic Organization* (New York: Oxford University Press, 1947), pp. 61–63. Although it is not clear whether Weber thinks that property is an artifact of status or vice versa, it is clear that property relations are closely linked with status, and to hierarchy vis-à-vis property.

23. Sara Berry, "Social Institutions," pp. 41, 43; and Piers Blaikie, "Environment and Access to Resources in Africa," *Africa* 59 no. 1 (1989): 27 point out that income opportunities are attached to access qualifications. Social identity is one of these qualifications.

24. Social identity as a basis of access to productive resources is distinct from accumulated capital as a basis of access. Although both exist simultaneously in all economic systems, traditional markets are on the social-identity end of the spectrum. It is also important to make clear the distinction between social identity and social relations. Social relations are structures

formed around social identity and which also form social identity. They are the mechanisms, such as friendship, labor tying arrangements or social obligations, through which social identity is exercised and maintained. Similarly, Piers Blaikie "Environment and Access to Resources in Africa," p. 27, argues that income opportunities are linked to access qualifications.

25. William Derman, *Serfs, Peasants and Socialists: A Former Serf Village in the Republic of Guinea* (Berkeley: University of California Press, 1973); Victor Azarya, *Aristocrats Facing Change: The Fulbe in Guinea, Nigeria, and Cameroon* (Chicago: University of Chicago Press, 1978); Philippe David, *Les Navetanes: Histoire des migrants saisonniers de l'Arachide en Sénégambie des origines a nos jours* (Dakar: Les Nouvelles Editions Africaines, 1980).

26. Andrée M. Wynkoop, "Migration and Social Change: The Social Origins of Rural Inequality in the Fouta Djallon," (Paper presented at the Canadian Association of African Studies Annual Meetings, University of Alberta, 7 May 1987).

27. David, *Les Navetanes*; Marguerite Dupire, *Organisation Sociale des Peul: Etude d'Ethnographie Comparée* (Paris: Librairie Plon, 1970).

28. See Ribot, "Markets, States, and Environmental Policy."

29. Sara Berry, "Social Institutions, p. 44 argues that as state control of resources increased in Africa after independence, and social relations between the market and state were cultivated for access to state controlled productive resources, "access to the state became a precondition for doing business successfully."

30. Also see Marianne Schmink and Charles Wood, "The Political Ecology of Amazonia," in Peter Little and Michael Horowitz eds., *Lands at Risk in the Third World* (Boulder: Westview Press, 1987), p. 52.

3

Coercing Conservation: The Politics of State Resource Control

•

NANCY LEE PELUSO

The flurry of ecological awareness and action in the late 1980s has led to a proliferation of international environmental agreements among nation-states. These agreements aim to gain the commitment of official state bodies to conserving tracts of land for wildlife and ecosystem conservation/preservation, reducing air pollution, and supporting allegedly sustainable forms of development. Oftentimes, conservation groups augment the financial and physical capacities of Third World states or state agencies to protect resources with "global" value. Besides international funding, such strategies receive favorable international media support and form part of an ideology of wise global resource management among many Western conservationists.

Such agreements assume that each nation-state, including those which have only recently emerged from colonialism, has the capacity, the internal legitimacy, and the will to manage all resources falling within its territorial boundaries. The implication is that the nation-state should be able to control the behavior of all users of all resources located within the state's (self-) declared jurisdiction, whatever the origin of the state's claim, whatever the nature of competition for those resources, and whatever the nature or origins of resistance to the state's resource control.[1]

These strategies have elicited the formal commitment of many Third World officials and policymakers who, not surprisingly, stand to benefit from their involvement in such initiatives. Some states or state interests, however, appropriate the conservation concerns of international environmental groups as a means of eliciting support for their own control over productive natural resources. Indeed, some tropical developing states use conservation ideology to justify coercion in the name of conservation, often by using violence. The state's mandate to defend threatened resources and its monopolization of legitimate violence combine to facilitate state apparatus-building and social control. "Legitimate" violence in the name of resource control also helps states control people, especially recalcitrant regional groups, marginal groups, or minority groups who challenge the state's authority.

The environmental community, perhaps inadvertently, justifies coercive-protective actions on the basis of moral high grounds which are difficult to dispute, such as the preservation of the world's biological heritage or our common security. Indeed, the recognition of the "urgent need" to defend at any cost endangered species, endangered habitats, or whole ecosystems, is becoming a more frequent part of the discourse of conservation.[2] Those who abhor state violence against its people are in some cases willing to turn a blind eye to the practice of violence or the threat of violence when conservation for (global) common security is being protected.[3] The issue is, thus, more than an acceptance of state violence for national security's sake as a right of sovereign nations.[4] Nevertheless, when a state must resort to violent means of protecting its own or the global community's claims to natural resources, it is an indicator of a failed, incomplete, or nonexistent legitimacy to govern society. Moreover, the states in question may (and often do) apply the tools and equipment they use to establish their resource sovereignty beyond the conservation endpoints envisioned by international facilitators of conservation, and appropriate the moral ideology of global conservation to justify state systems of resource extraction and production.

Two cases have been selected to illustrate the extremes to which coercive resource management can extend: the protection of wildlife, particularly elephants, in Kenya, and the protection of forests in Indonesia. In both cases, the state's "protection" of valuable resources has reached virtually militaristic proportions. In both cases, moreover, coercive conservation has followed or been accompanied by efforts to "develop" the populations against which the state now uses or threatens violence. Development efforts, however, have largely been structured on the state's terms and have failed to consider the political-ecological histories of contemporary resource use patterns. A complete discussion of the interactions between incentives and coercion in resource management is beyond the scope of this paper. Conservation and development strategies for Kenya and Indonesia have been discussed in a number of studies. Documentation or discussion of the militaristic aspects of conservation is more difficult to come by and will remain the key focus of this paper.[5]

My argument relates to states willing to comply with international conservation agreements or Western conservation principles and ideologies that justify its resource management practices. I limit my discussion here to land-based resources because they are geographically bounded, tangible, and visible, and because their management has been centralized under the state in many parts of the world. The state's effectiveness in controlling access to and behavior in forests or wilderness areas represents in many ways a "best case" scenario of its capacity for widespread resource management.

Clashes Between Central States and Local Resource Users

In general, following Skocpol and Migdal, I use the Weberian definition of states as "compulsory associations claiming control over territories and the people within them. Administrative, legal, extractive, and coercive organizations are the core of any state."[6] However, though it is simpler to discuss "the state" as if it were a homogeneous entity with a common purpose under all circumstances, it should be understood that the use of this term does not imply homogeneity.

There are many types of social and political groupings within civil society, with varying capacities to reject or resist the state's will. There are also many factions within a state that vary in their power vis-à-vis each other as well as in their power to impose their will on society. Moreover, many of these factions have goals that fit within the broadly defined goals of the nation as an entity but directly contradict the specific objectives of other state agencies.

Migdal has recently argued that a state's capability to govern is a function of the relations between the state and civil society. The strength of the state to impose its will can be judged through "its capacities to penetrate society, regulate social relationships, extract resources, and appropriate or use resources in determined ways."[7] The state's capacity to govern depends on the degree of its actual authority and, to an extent, on the legitimacy of the ruling components of the state among the various social groups and classes constituting society. Particularly in nation-states formed out of a conglomeration of relatively separate or different cultures and types of social organizations (e.g., those in which a multitude of ethnic groups occupy a portion of the contiguous territory claimed by a nation-state), the ability of state leaders to enforce their policies will range widely. Where resource management and use are concerned, state capacity is reflected in the degree of conformity or conflict between local and national resource managers' intentions and actions. Moreover, a state's successful imposition of its will on its constituents depends on the means of social control and the relative effectiveness of those means in achieving state agendas.[8]

States and state factions can be autonomous from society to the extent that they have goals and interests that do not coincide with those of other parts of society.[9] Particularly in the management of some resources, it is clear that there are many circumstances in which the state or its agents or its leaders are autonomous and interested actors. The extraction of valuable resources such as oil and other minerals, timber, or even some agricultural products, just like the commercial exploitation of rare resources for their touristic and scientific value, is a revenue-generating strategy embraced by most national governments. States generally allocate rights to extract or protect resources in ways that benefit the state itself (in generating revenues to reproduce itself) as well as for the proverbial "greater good of society." Where state interests are translated into parastatal corporate structures, high ranking officers double as government officials and business managers: they are state elites with both personal and professional stakes in the imposition of the state's will. Their decisions about the management of national resources affect both the state's and their individual capital-accumulation capacities and strategies. Internal weakness, in terms of political governance and control of revenue-generating resources, can turn into internal instability and threaten the political-economic positions of the holders of state power. Both as representatives of the state and as individuals, therefore, state actors have an interest in maintaining central control of territories containing valuable resources, and of people with contradictory claims.[10]

It is in developing countries, many of which are still struggling to redress the legacies of colonialism and the difficulties of maintaining multiethnic nation-states, that the most difficult circumstances for conservation are found. The origins of their territorial integration lie in colonialism, and were enforced by colonial armies and arms. Though international colonial pressures may have largely died down in the wake of worldwide independence movements, world market linkages continue to influence the decisions of former colonies by increasing the returns of market activities to the national elites who control the trading links.[11] Despite their contempt for the colonial regimes that preceded them, many contemporary developing states have adopted colonial policies for land and resource control, sometimes making them even more coercive.[12] Moreover, to enforce control where state hegemony is tenuous—because of deep-seated rifts between social groups, regional disparities in resource distribution, or competing concepts of appropriate or rightful use of resources—in many Third World countries, state leaders are increasingly members of, controlled by, or strongly allied with the military.[13]

Power struggles between the state and society are played out constantly in the process of allocation, control, and accessing of resources. Both internal and external pressures on states cause them to manage resources using particular tactics to achieve conservation or (sustainable) production management objectives. A state or a faction of the state may coerce conservation under one or all of three circumstances: when the resources are extremely valuable, when the state's legitimate control of the resource is questioned or challenged by other resource users, and when coercion is considered either the last resort or the easiest means of establishing control over people and territory. State coercion is perhaps most common for resources with high exchange value, such as some tropical hardwoods, or for resources scarce enough to render their greatest value as objects of tourism, as is the case of African wildlife. Resource-funded development strategies are almost always biased toward the enrichment of central actors. In addition, when a state's incomplete hegemony prevents it from sufficiently controlling the people living under its jurisdiction, the state may use both conservation and economic arguments to justify the coercive exclusion of certain groups from valuable resources. Coercion and resource control are intended to increase the state's powers of social control; and these in turn enable the state to extract more revenue from conservation or extractive zones. Finally, development efforts are offered frequently as appeasements to competing resource users. If these fail to establish state control and ensure conservation, coercion may be seen as a final opportunity to preserve the environment and establish social control. When the outcome of state coercive resource management coincides with the goals of outside conservation groups, those factions of the state that produce the results may gain or strengthen the latter's financial and ideological support.

The conservation agenda, which is generally depicted as being in the common interest of the entire global community, is seen by some as a justification for external intervention in what were previously the sole affairs of states.[14] From a local perspective, however, both states and international conservation groups may be seen as illegitimate controllers of local resources.

In general, there are two patterns by which nonlocal actors (whether state or nonstate actors) try to structure controls on local resources. The first involves reorganization of the local status quo: deposing established elites, and replacing them with "environmentally correct" or politically malleable elites, either outsiders or competing insider groups. The second strategy is one of strengthening existing elites; this may involve buying off local leaders and actually changing their allegiance from the local people to the state (or creating a great deal of ambiguity in their expressions of loyalty).[15] Both strategies imply such extensive social changes in the course of imposing a new civil order that they require direct or indirect alliances with the military to enforce control. This generally happens, for example, with the establishment of national parks and wildlife reserves, which require the deployment of military or paramilitary guards to protect the flora and fauna. When international conservation interests have concerns about the implementation of local resource conservation efforts, they may help the state accumulate the tools of power (vehicles, guns, formal legitimacy through legislation), albeit sometimes inadvertently.

International intervention or support does not guarantee the realization of environmental goals or state legitimacy, however. Replacing or strengthening power holders in order to control resources may encourage increasing local resistance or rebellion against state or international controls on local resources. State concerns with the economic value of resources may influence conservation groups to use economic terms to justify their protection and preservation strategies. Whether for intensive production or for preservation, valuation strategies for resource territories frequently disenfranchise local people who had long histories of local resource use and may have played significant, though unrecognized, roles in creating "wild" habitats. Not only does this often have the effect of undermining conservation; it also changes the way resources are perceived, defined, valued, allocated, and used. When these management strategies change who has access to and control over local resources, the use of violence becomes an expedient means of exerting state control, in the name of "conservation" or "legitimate domain."

In sum, externally based resource claimants (including the state itself) frequently redefine resources, the means by which they will be conserved or harvested, and the distribution of benefits from their protection. Such redefinitions often override, ignore, or collide with local or customary forms of resource management. When competition between external and local legitimation mechanisms is played out in the environmental arena, the result is social and political conflict, which causes environmental degradation and ultimately fails to achieve the goals of international conservation interests.

Nevertheless, the state may not "lose." Even if conservation goals are not achieved, the state may succeed in strengthening its capacity to govern via the use of force.[16] No one monitors this type of aggression or this outcome of international conservation strategy. The means of violence and the ideologies of state stewardship of global resources, obtained directly or indirectly from the international conservation community, may facilitate the state's imposition and enforcement of its right to govern.

The Case Studies

Of the two cases chosen to illustrate this trend the clearest and most extreme is that of Kenya and its wildlife conservation areas. I examine the evolution of the alliance between the international conservation community and the Kenyan state agencies that make wildlife protection policies in reserves and parks. The Indonesian case focuses on Java, where a powerful parastatal directly manages luxury woods and hardwoods. In both cases I examine the capacity of the state to control these land-based resources via coercive management mechanisms. I relate the use of coercion to the origins of the state's claims on those resources, the nature of competition for those resources, and the effectiveness of state policies when coercion is used.

I also examine the relationships between coercive state resource management and other aspects of state-society relations. To what extent does the increased militarization of resource control improve or reduce general state capacity to govern? Finally, I explore the role of international environmental groups in explicitly or implicitly supporting coercive state power.

Kenya

The resources discussed in this section are the lands set aside for national parks and wildlife reserves and resources within those lands (wildlife, pasture, and water). The traditional users of these lands, the Maasai, Somalis, and pastoralists of other ethnic groups, have been excluded from access to these lands to various degrees over the past century. State claims to nearly two-thirds of traditional Maasai lands were first made by the British colonial state at the turn of the twentieth century. In 1904 the Maasai, who used to occupy all the land from Mt. Kenya in the north to the border with (and into) what is today Tanzania, were resettled in two reserves. Several years later, those in the northern reserve were resettled again in an extension of the southern reserve. By 1912, they were confined to an area of approximately 38,000 km^2.[17] The British allocated some of the Maasai's traditional lands to European planters whose activities were believed by colonial officials to be "more productive."[18] Early on, however, the British did not subscribe to the theory that the Maasai could not coexist with wildlife. Thus, in 1906 they created the Southern Game Reserve—a wildlife reserve *within* the Maasai reserve because the Maasai were not believed to threaten wildlife, having coexisted with the region's wild game for thousands of years.[19]

It was not until the 1940s and 1950s that the colonial government gave in to pressures from game hunters and some conservation groups to set aside rangeland exclusively for wild game. At that same time, the state wanted to settle the Maasai in fixed places, which meant changing their traditional migratory cattle-raising practices. The Amboseli Basin, occupying some 3,200 km of both the Maasai Reserve and the Southern Game Reserve, was an important source of water during dry season for the region's wildlife as well as the Maasai and their cattle. Dams and boreholes to provide water outside the Amboseli basin were constructed to benefit the Maasai. As the number of Maasai cattle increased, as they continued to migrate to areas where wild game also sought drinking water, and as hunters threatened wildlife in a different manner, conservationist interests grew more concerned that the wildlife dependent on the Basin waters were being threatened. Along with big game hunters, they pressured the colonial government to create reserves where human use would be more restricted. The Southern Game Reserve was abolished in 1952 and four smaller reserves were created, including a new one outside the area of the old Southern Game Reserve, called Maasai Mara. In the 1950s, hunting was first outlawed within these reserves, although the government issued permits for hunting outside the reserves. In the early 1960s livestock grazing was also forbidden in an 80 km^2 area of the Amboseli reserve, which was a direct threat to Maasai lifestyles and livelihoods.[20]

The Maasai did not so easily give up their traditional patterns of migration to seasonal water supplies; nor were water development efforts sufficient to permit them to do so. When their principal means of livelihood was restricted by reserve authorities, the Maasai responded by killing rhinoceroses and elephants. A decade later, some allegedly began collaborating with ivory poachers. They also resisted further appropriation of their access rights by increasing their use of the area surrounding the livestock-free zone, and later demanded tenure rights to all these lands.[21]

Meanwhile, another development increased the state's direct interest in the protection of wild game and the reservation of parklands: the increase in wildlife-oriented tourism beginning in the 1960s. Some tourism revenues, including hunting fees, were given to various Maasai district councils as an incentive to win their acceptance of the reserves.[22] Fees and revenues grew through the 1960s and early 1970s, after Kenyan independence. Not all district councils, however, truly represented the interests of the people in the immediate vicinity of the reserves and parks. In Amboseli, for example, the Kajiado Council receiving park revenues was 150 km from the park boundaries. Thus some Maasai were benefitting from the Park's existence, but not necessarily those who had the most to lose from the Park's creation.

The value of wildlife tourism soon became clear to the central government. In 1974, the government designated 488 km^2 of the Amboseli basin as a national park, while still negotiating with the Maasai. In 1977 this area was reduced to 390 km^2, which was gazetted as a park and would remain free of livestock. A de facto buffer zone was to be established around the core area of the park, and group ranches—a brand-new form of social organization for these

Maasai—were established to further the government's intentions of sedentarizing the Maasai. In addition, the Maasai were expected to allow wildlife to graze on these ranches in exchange for a "wildlife utilization fee," which was supposed to compensate them for losses of water and grazing area to their own livestock.[23]

By 1989, tourism in Kenya was contributing about 20 percent of the nation's total foreign exchange.[24] By 1991, tourists were spending some 50 million dollars a year to view elephants and other wildlife.[25] In this way, as Knowles and Collett have pointed out, the creation of national parks to protect wildlife has not only separated the Maasai from their livestock production base and created a mythical nature devoid of humans for tourist consumption but also provided the government with the financial means to "develop" and "modernize" them.[26] Moreover, "National Parks and Game Reserves are never justified solely in terms of the economics of tourism: both the conservationists and national governments support the creation and maintenance of these areas with *moral arguments* based on the need to conserve wildlife and the intangible benefits that conservation confers on humanity."[27]

The plans for development of the Maasai in Amboseli have not worked as well as they have in Mara. Some blame the failure on the basic conflict in the lifestyles of the Maasai and their unwillingness to allow outsiders to make decisions about their lives and their uses of resources. Collett, for example, claims that the main reason the provision of water supplies outside the park has not achieved the government's development goals is the preference of the Maasai for a migratory, pastoralist lifestyle.[28] However, a recent report by the World Bank indicates that there were also significant technical problems:

> [The conflicts] may be attributed . . . to failure to implement the agreements, to the lack of an official written agreement outlining the management responsibilities of the different parties and policy changes. The water pumping system, financed by the New York Zoological Society and the World Bank, worked well for a few years and then began to fail due to technical and administrative problems which were not corrected by the central Government which had built it. An inadequate water supply left the Maasai little option but to return to find water inside the Park. The problems were aggravated by a drought in 1984, in which the Maasai lost a substantial part of their livestock and received no assistance from the park authorities. The wildlife utilization fees were paid regularly until about 1981, then the payments became sporadic without explanation to the Maasai. The agreement for

group ranches to retain a portion of Park entry fees fell through, perhaps due to administrative changes. . . . Anticipated income from tourism did not increase as quickly as expected. . . . Construction of new lodges and viewpoint circuits on group ranch lands did not materialize as expected. Finally, the 1977 hunting ban eliminated anticipated income from safari hunting license fees.[29]

In the past few years, the basic conflicts over land and resource rights in Kenyan national parks and reserves have been reconstructed in terms of a government mandate to stop the poaching of wildlife, especially of elephants and rhinoceroses. Major international environmental organizations, including the Worldwide Fund for Nature, the African Wildlife Foundation, World Conservation International (WCI), the International Union for the Conservation of Nature (IUCN), Conservation International, and the National Geographic Society have publicized the poaching issue and its threat to global and African biodiversity. The efforts of these and other environmental groups led in 1985 to the creation of the Convention on International Trade in Endangered Species (CITES). By 1991, 105 world nations had signed the CITES declaration to ban the raw ivory trade in their effort to protect elephants in Asia and Africa.[30]

A great deal, however, has been left out of the international discussion of the poaching issue, and neither the origins nor the implications of the proposed solutions to the poaching problem have received the critical analysis they merit. Two gaps in the conservation community's discussion are particularly glaring. The first is the lack of historical perspective on the political and ecological contexts within which parks were created to protect wildlife, and the resulting dismissal of local people in creating particular environments. The other is the failure to consider the political-economic implications of the provision of arms and other equipment intended (at least ostensibly) to protect wildlife.

In April 1989, Richard Leakey became the director of Kenya's Wildlife Service. Since then Leakey has made his mark by firing administrative and field staff believed to be involved in the illegal ivory or rhino horn trade, by giving raises to underpaid and overworked park rangers, and by arming these rangers with automatic rifles and helicopter gunships in order to wage war more effectively on the poachers invading Kenya's national parks. Wage war they have: within two years of his taking over, more than a hundred poachers had been killed, many of them with no chance for discussion or trial; the rangers are licensed, like military in a state of emergency, to shoot-to-kill.[31] The Wildlife Service has also reclaimed direct control over the Maasai Mara Reserve, where the combination of wildlife management with local participation and benefits had reportedly been more successful. The government claimed that the reserve had been inadequately maintained and was deteriorating, denying earlier reports that elephants and rhinoceros populations within this park had been increasing while antipoaching costs were virtually negligible.[32]

The questions here are obvious. Who are the poachers and from where do they derive their claims and their support? Why were they able through the 1970s and much of the 1980s to eliminate, according to the Worldwide Fund for Nature, some four-fifths of Kenya's elephant population?[33]

In their campaigns to save animals, international conservation groups never specify who the poachers are, although some fingers are pointed and accusations made. A letter to members from the WWF, for example, says "Some poachers, tribesmen displaced from traditional occupations by drought or civil war, use primitive methods to kill elephants and transport tusks. But most use high-powered weapons and even airplanes and various sorts of poisons." [34]

What tribe these "tribesmen" are from is not clarified, whether they are Maasai, or Kikuyu, or one of the smaller ethnic minorities within the country. Later in the letter, however, "Somali tribesmen" are directly implicated, as well as people from an apparently different social group, i.e., "Somali officials." In reference to ivory tusks sold or stockpiled within Somalia, the letter says, "These tusks were not legally confiscated. Instead, they probably were poached from Kenya's nearby Tsavo National Park by well-equipped Somali tribesmen, then smuggled out of Kenya with the complicity of Somali officials." [35] The Somali president himself also apparently wrote a letter guaranteeing his government's purchase of ivory tusks from neighboring countries.[36]

The WWF does not specifically accuse the Maasai of killing wildlife for ivory, but implies that their increasing populations are a major threat to the survival of the elephants and other wildlife. Nowhere in the letter to WWF members is it mentioned that the Maasai and other pastoral and hunter-gatherer groups coexisted with elephants and other savannah wildlife over thousands of years; or that people—as well as the elephants—play an important role in creating and maintaining the contemporary savannah habitat that supports them both. Rather, they imply that the presence of the Maasai is a new phenomenon to which elephants must adapt: "One broad cause of the decrease in elephant numbers is surely the advance of human populations into *their* habitat. . . . To some extent, elephants are able to adapt to the growing presence of pastoralists such as Kenya's Maasai." [37]

Chadwick, writing for National Geographic, reflects a more explicit "people versus wildlife" view, with only conservation researchers and supporters exempt:

> Tusks became a sort of underground currency, like drugs, spreading webs of corruption from remote villages to urban centers throughout the world. . . . The seventies saw the price of ivory skyrocket. Suddenly, to a herder or subsistence farmer, this was no longer an animal, but a walking fortune, worth more than a dozen years of honest toil. . . . Ivory was running above a hundred dollars a pound, and officials from poorly paid park rangers to high ranking wildlife ministers had joined the poaching network. . . . [In addition]. . . . Poaching gangs, including bush-wise bandits called *shifta* from Somalia, armed with AK 47 assault rifles, were increasingly turning their guns on tourists. This has all but shut down Meru National Park in the north. [38]

What is wrong with this description is its "snapshot" of a contemporary situation, with the camera angled in such a way as to keep the background out of focus. Everyone in the picture is considered equally guilty, regardless of the roots of their involvement, their power to prevent its happening, their public stance, or the historical basis of their claims to being where they are in relation to the wildlife and the lands. Both the average reader and the writer of the article are unfamiliar with the social history of these "wildlife habitats" and this gap in understanding is neither missed nor deemed necessary. The story, after all, is about people against nature. The people *for* nature, the heroes, are not the local people who lived alongside wildlife for thousands of years before their lands were appropriated by colonial and contemporary state agencies and carved into parks. The implicit heroes are Western wildlife scientists, environmental activists, and the conservation armies who rout the poachers. The indigenous people are implicated because of their proximity to the parks and the logistics of outside poachers gaining access, although it is unlikely that any "peasant farmer" sees one hundred dollars for any pound of ivory he has had a hand in obtaining. Peasants in this view are also guilty of "encroachment" on the elephants' habitat—the areas from which they were excluded not many decades ago: "Ultimately, though, people, not poachers, and growth, not guns, pose the most serious long-term threat to the elephant's survival." [39]

Ironically, Chadwick hints at another motive underlying the involvement of certain state and would-be state actors in this conservation drama: "To currency-strapped governments and revolutionaries alike [ivory poaching] was a way to pay for more firearms and supplies. In the eighties Africa had nearly ten times the weapons present a decade earlier, which encouraged more poaching than ever." [40]

Hence the "need" for increasing the power of the "good" government officials, particularly those working in the parks. As the WWF letter explained, "Anti-poaching forces have been traditionally paid poorly, had insufficient training and equipment, and were understaffed. Moreover, they rarely enlisted the aid of nearby villagers by offering them economic incentives." [41]

As a result, WWF and its partners (IUCN, TRAFFIC, and WCI) began providing "emergency assistance to key African wildlife departments," improving ranger incentives and providing antipoaching equipment and training. They claim that "the only long-term security for elephants in Africa lies in strengthening national capabilities in wildlife conservation and management." Moreover, to its credit, WWF and other groups are "working to ensure that protected areas benefit from the income generated through access fees." [42] Leakey also asked the African Wildlife Federation for assistance, which AWF has provided, including airplanes and vehicles for antipoaching patrols in Tsavo National Park. Though it is a relatively small operation, AWF occasionally takes a more direct role in coercive wildlife protection by "mounting extra patrols when an emergency arises." [43]

That these aircraft, radios, vehicles, night-goggles, and other antipoaching equipment might serve another purpose besides conservation has been a secondary consideration in view of the emergency status of the quest to protect these wildlife. And yet, in an article appearing in January 1989, three months before Leakey's takeover and the subsequent high-powered, highly publicized crackdown on poaching, reports from Kenya showed how the government was already using its mandate to protect and manage resources to assert its authority where local people had resisted state controls on their activities since the colonial period. [44]

Ostensibly to settle a dispute over grazing rights between Somali and Borana groups residing in the north, the government sent in police, army helicopters, military aircraft and the paramilitary General Service Unit. Over 600 people were detained and "large numbers" were killed in the course of the current incident. The conflict is not a new one: a 1984 clash left 2,169 people dead, and in 1987 some 200–300 Home Guards, none of them Somali, were armed "to assist in policing grazing rights and local disputes." [45]

Many of these disputes date from the time that the Kora National Reserve was created, when Somali pastoralists were excluded from access to parklands for grazing. Whole communities of Somalis were resettled onto arid lands in Borana districts. In the course of their resettlement, they were deprived of pasture and water for their livestock. Seeking these resources in the vicinity of the reserve, they are harassed by the Kenyan security forces in the same manner as illegal Somalis engaged in the smuggling trade. The present government's harassment of both the settled and nomadic Somali in the region is couched in conservation rhetoric, but dates back to the region's efforts to secede from independent Kenya in 1967. The colonial government also had difficulty establishing its authority previously. In the course of the recent clash near the Kora reserve, it was reported that, "Under the state of emergency, security forces have powers to act without warrant and detain without specific reason . . . clean-up operations are commonplace." [46] Moreover, the officials involved in the political security operations now form an integral part of the antipoaching operations.

The political implications of this trend in conserving Kenyan wildlife are clear. Though equipment and funds may be allocated to protect nature, they can directly or indirectly be used by the state to serve its own political ends. In this way, the commitment to preservation of wildlife for tourism and research serves both the economic and political interests of the Kenyan government, while its actual effectiveness in doing so is questionable.

Indonesia

The resources discussed in this section are the lands officially classified as state forest lands and the forest species claimed by the state on Java, including teak, rosewood, and mahogany.

The Indonesian state maintains control over the management of production forests through two different forms of what it calls sustained yield management. On Java, production forests are largely organized into state-managed forest plantations, some of which are more than 100 years old. Particularly near production forests, but also near forest reserves, peasants have been formally excluded from all but the most limited forms of access to the forest lands since Java was first governed by the Dutch colonial state at the turn of the nineteenth century. Outside of Java, forest management and people's access to the forest differs. (The diversity of "Outer Island" forest circumstances makes a discussion of these forest management systems beyond the scope of this paper.) As in the Kenya case, the peasants of Java "threaten" the forest (and the state's intentions) largely because of their subsistence activities. The state-supported timber management policies threaten the peasants' access to agricultural land and agroforestry production systems.

Most forest lands in Indonesia were declared the property of the colonial state in 1870, as a result of the *Domeinverklaring,* a decree defining and separating private and state property. Included within the state lands were any formerly cultivated lands that had been in fallow for more than three years. The declaration remained intact after independence, however; it was translated in 1960 into the Basic Agrarian Law. The Forestry Law of 1967 also confirmed the status of certain lands as state forest lands.

The policing of these forests, and the militaristic style of forest security, are critical elements of the Indonesian sustained yield management system in Java. The reason for increasing military and police involvement in forest protection is the increasing discontent with the exclusive management system, despite the foresters' alleged commitment to social forestry in some parts of the Javanese forest.[47] Part of the reason for this is that social forestry is applied only on the most degraded of the forest lands.[48]

Most forestry consists of the plantation production of timber—mainly teak, mahogany, and rosewood—and tree resins, such as rosin and copal. The current management system was originally established by the Dutch colonial government in the late nineteenth century, after some two centuries of increasingly centralized controls on the natural forest and fallowed agricultural lands of the island. As under the Dutch, Indonesian state foresters directly manage the forests; production forests are under the jurisdiction of a parastatal forest enterprise, the State Forestry Corporation (hereafter SFC). Employees of this parastatal make and implement detailed management plans to establish, maintain, and harvest forest products. They also retain a monopoly on the exchange and transport of all primary production of teak, which contributes 92 percent of the SFC's annual income.

Though Java's forests cover nearly a quarter of the island, they tend to be scattered rather than large contiguous areas and are surrounded by densely populated, predominantly agrarian settlements. More than 20 million people in over 6,000 villages—a fifth of the island's population—inhabit villages adjacent to or enclosed by state forest lands, making them subject to the SFC's jurisdiction. The only legal access villagers have to the forest and its forest products is for the collection of deadwood for fuel, and the collection or use of non-timber forest products, limited in number or variety because of the dominance of forest species in the plantations.

During reforestation of clearcut tracts, selected villagers also gain access to land for the first two or three years of the 40–80 year life cycle of the primary forest species, using the land between newly planted rows of trees to plant agricultural crops. At the end of one of these cycles, all the trees in a tract, representing a sustainable proportion of the district's total forest base (1/40, 1/60, or 1/80 of the district's total forest area), are clearcut. Even fewer people are hired seasonally to participate in logging, thinning, clearing brush, or tapping resin as day laborers for the SFC. Longer-term involvement of villagers comes in social forestry areas, nearly 250,000 hectares of SFC land. Many of these lands are extremely degraded, however, and the majority of the benefits of land rehabilitation still accrue to the SFC. Moreover, villagers' access to reforestation land and to other forestry employment is controlled entirely by local staff of the SFC.

Forest police began patrolling the forests of Java in the late nineteenth century under the Dutch. In 1962, President Sukarno authorized arming the forest police with pistols, putting them on a par with the military and the police; no other institution, state or private, and no civilians, are allowed to own firearms under Indonesian law. While lack of funds in the early years precluded the arming of all forest police, today nearly all the foresters in the teak forest districts carry guns.[49]

The police functions of these foresters are written into forest policy, and justified because they are meant to protect strategic resources claimed by the state: "Police security activities in the forest . . . according to Government Regulation No. 28, 1985, are designed to secure and guard the rights of the state to the forest lands and forest products."[50]

Policy clearly states that foresters are to use both "preventive" and "repressive" means of securing the territorial borders and the standing trees. Preventive measures include the usual patrolling of forest lands, getting to know forest villagers, checking the permits of students, scouts, tourists, researchers, and officials from other administrative branches, checking forest-product transport permits, and supervising "people who have a traditional relationship with the forest." [51]

Repressive measures become necessary when preventive measures fail to check theft or forest damage. The infrastructure of forest repression has become impressive indeed within the past fifteen years. Forest security is implemented at several levels of intensity, from the forest police who operate at the same level as labor foremen (*mandor*); to the Special Forest Police (*Polisi Chusus Kehutanan*, or PCK) who are a level higher, equivalent to forest guards (*mantri*); and the Long Distance Patrols (*Patroli Jarak Jauh* or PJJ), also called BRIMOB, like the mobile brigades of police and military that they imitate. The latter institution operates as a sort of forest SWAT team. The first of these forest policing mechanisms originated under the Dutch, the second under Sukarno, and the third is the creation of the SFC. The evolution of the forest police to include paramilitary operations to retrieve teak and teak "thieves," represents the most critical change in the nature of territorial forest control since the colonial period. [52]

Their training and operations provide some indication of their importance to the structure and implementation of forest management. Both forest guards and PCK receive at least three months of training in police methods and basic criminology; both carry guns. In many teak forest districts, *mantris* spend as much of their time engaged in high-powered security activities—stakeouts and the like—as in planning reforestation, logging, thinning, or forest labor organization. The PJJ's operation units consist of three to five PCK, several representatives from the local military post and/or the nearest police station, a representative from the forest district office, a driver and a vehicle. The team is driven into a forest area close to an area of suspected teak theft; the unit members synchronize watches and scatter to seek illicit wood and suspects. These security functions are not only part of the daily routine of forest protection but also part and parcel of the state's strategy for social control throughout the island. According to the head of forest security and agrarian affairs for the SFC:

>Conscious of the burden of implementing [forest management] tasks
>and the strategic position of the State Forestry Corporation in serving
>the country and in the development of our people, particularly within
>the scope of [our] participation in directing socio-political security and
>safety in Java, an island which has traditionally [and] historically acted
>as a barometer of political hegemony and power in the archipelago, all
>SFC troops are expected to play fundamental roles as Security Agents
>capable of detecting political, economic, social, cultural, and military
>troubles among the people. . . . Unlike other businesses . . . the SFC
>has a special mission related to the conditions of the territory it man-
>ages. These conditions have resulted in the SFC's being an enterprise
>with two functions.[53]

The politico-military functions of these state foresters has led many
of them to perceive themselves as modern-day heroes of the state,
protectors of state resources. This attitude is clearly intended by both
forestry and political security policymakers.

One contradiction that influences this security system is that foresters have jurisdiction over trees and forest territory, while jurisdiction over the people lies with the civil administration: subdistrict
officers, village heads, and others. While part of a common state
structure, the loyalties and interests of civil administrators do not
always coincide with those of the foresters. The foresters' primary
response to this has been to forge alliances with civil administrators,
a program which is beyond the scope of this discussion.[54] However,
the social-control intentions of these alliances is represented by the
provision that all special BRIMOB operations cannot proceed into a
village without the explicit, on-site approval of the village head.

Although the government has developed social forestry programs
for some disenfranchised forest users in Java, these concessions pale
in comparison to the gross profits earned by the timber industry.
Moreover, as in Kenya, these development efforts benefit the state
more than the local people in many ways. As mentioned above,
social forestry opportunities in Java are limited to the most degraded
forest lands, which the state has otherwise given up for lost. Any
increased production benefits the state, and the SFC never gives up
its rights to control those lands.

Organs of the state in Java interact differently with international
conservation interests than was the case in Kenya. While conservation groups do not arm the Indonesian government in an effort to
help protect tropical forest habitats, they do play a role in legitimating the state's use of violence to protect its claims to the nation's

natural resources. By lobbying for sustainable forestry, for example, and defining sustainable forestry in the terms traditionally used by Western foresters or ecologists (which generally neither acknowledge nor consider the role of people in creating so-called natural environments), they emphasize the formal, scientific, planning aspects of forest management. Most recently, the Rainforest Alliance's certification of Java teak as part of its "smart wood" program has provided the SFC with international legitimation for its management programs.[55] As a direct result of this certification, the so-called green market, including many "environmentally correct" gardening catalogues, has begun endorsing Java teak. Consider the following trademark explanation from a recent Smith and Hawkin gardening catalogue:

> The Plantation Teak ™ from which we make our teak benches, chairs, and tables does not come from rainforests. It is carefully grown on tree farms in Java, and its harvesting is certified as being beneficial to the economy and the ecology of the region.[56]

They note elsewhere, however, that the Java teak is supplied to them through Thailand—a highly unlikely situation. Their message is that teak is acceptable if it is not extracted from rainforests (as is teak from parts of Thailand and Burma, for example), and that the conditions of production—in plantations where some forest laborers have become more marginalized than they were under the Dutch colonial state—do not matter. Moreover, the state's alleged compliance with a loose set of "social sustainability criteria" developed by the rainforest group is backed up by forest SWAT teams and a management philosophy that explicitly (and unabashedly) includes "repressive and preventive" components. The conservation group, therefore, in concert with the green market, has legitimized the SFC's coercive management tactics.

The Java case also differs from Kenya in that the structures of control and the means of violence are not spreading from the natural resources sector to the rest of society. Rather, they are spreading from the institutions of social control already dominating civil society, and being applied to the control of natural resources by and for the state. Finally, in both Kenya and Indonesia, outside conservation groups help legitimate the state by negotiating an ideology of acceptable state resource management on their terms, not those of local people.

Conclusion

The environmental community's tacit or explicit support of coercive conservation tactics has far-reaching consequences. First, local resistance to what are perceived as illegitimate state claims and controls over local resources is likely to heighten, and may lead to violent response, sabotage of resources, and degradation.[57] Second, and most important, the outside environmental community may be weakening local resource claimants who possess less firepower than the state. While some conservationists are also "arming" local non-government organizations with symbolic and financial support, their ultimate goal is as much or more to influence state policy as to empower local resource users. The ethics underlying the spread of Western conservation ideologies, without considering their inevitable transformation when accepted or appropriated by developing states, require close reexamination.

In a recent publication entitled *Conserving the World's Biodiversity*, a consortium of the wealthiest mainstream environmental organizations and the World Bank detailed an extensive analysis and a set of strategies to protect the world's biological resources from their most ubiquitous predator: humankind.[58] The authors, all scholars or environmental policy analysts, based their concerns on solid science, documenting the demise of certain components of the environment. On the other hand, many of the policy prescriptions are uncomfortably imperialistic. Most disturbing is a short but pointed section toward the end of the document on "The Special Case of the Military." The section lists a number of indicators to support its contention that conservationists worldwide would do well to "systematically" approach national "defense services" "to provide their support for positive action in the conservation of biological resources."[59] Though every one of the nine indicators listed raises questions about their validity and about the ethics of justifying military involvement in conservation, two have particularly disturbing implications related to the arguments presented above.

> The military is concerned primarily with national security, and it is increasingly apparent that many threats to national security have their roots in inappropriate ways and means of managing natural resources; the military might therefore reasonably be expected to have a serious interest in resource management issues.

> As conflicts between people and resources increase in the coming years, the military will require detailed understanding of the biological,

ecological, social, and economic issues involved *if they are to deal effectively with these conflicts.*[60]

These assertions are disturbing; they imply the state and its security forces are neutral mediators in conflicts over natural resources. The examples given here are part of a growing body of evidence showing that, wherever the state directly claims, controls, or manages land-based resources, state organizations and individual state actors have strong vested interests in the commercial exploitation of resources. Their control over the territories within which the resources occur, and over the people living within them, is a major aspect of their strategic territorial control. Militaries, paramilitary organizations, and state agencies often create or exacerbate resource-based conflicts by their participation in protective activities, their involvement as actors, or their coercive tactics. It is far from clear, therefore, that "the various national military establishments operate for the benefit of their respective nations," as the authors of *Conserving the World's Biodiversity* claim.[61] Just as some military leaders can be co-opted to work for the sake of conservation agendas, conservation groups' resources and ideologies can be co-opted for separate military agendas. Once coercive conservation tactics are accepted, such co-optation is nearly impossible to prevent.

Failing to venture beyond the *concept* of thinking globally and acting locally, the writers of international conservation initiatives often brush aside or simply ignore the political implications of empowering states to coercively control access to natural resources. The militarization of resource control—whether for protection or production—leads to damaging relations with the environment, not benign ones. Whatever their approach on the ground, these conservation groups seek ultimately to change state policy and practice. Unfortunately, coercive conservation also strengthens or extends the state's military capacity—not only with the weapons of enforcement but also with new "moral" justifications to legitimate coercion in enforcing a narrowly defined "global community's" environmental will.

NOTES

1. Piers Blaikie, *The Political-Economy of Soil Erosion in Developing Countries* (London: Longman, 1985); Nancy Lee Peluso, *Rich Forests, Poor People: Resource Control and Resistance in Java* (Berkeley, CA: University of California Press, 1992).

2. Daniel Deudney, "Case Against Linking Environmental Degradation and National Security," *Millennium: Journal of International Studies* 19 no. 3 (1990): 461–476.; Jeffrey A. McNeeley, Kenton R. Miller, Walter V. Reid, Russell A. Mittermeier, and Timothy B. Werner, *Conserving the World's Biodiversity* (Washington, D.C.: Worldwide Fund For Nature, 1988).

3. Deudney, "Case Against Linking."

4. Charles Tilly, "War-making and State Making as Organized Crime, " in Peter B. Evans, Dietrich Rueschemeyer, and Theda Skocpol, eds., *Bringing the State Back In* (Cambridge: Cambridge University Press, 1985). [Hereafter Evans et al.]

5. See, for example, Nicholas K. Menzies and Nancy Lee Peluso, Rights of Access to Upland Forest Resources in Southwest China," *Journal of World Forest Resources* 6 no. 1 (p. 82, 1991): 1–20; David Western, "Conservation-based Rural Development," in F. R. Thibodeau and H. H. Field eds., *Sustaining Tomorrow's World: A Strategy for Conservation and Development* (London: University Press of New England, 1984); Agnes Kiss, *Wildlife Conservation in Kenya* (Washington: The World Bank, 1990); David Anderson and Richard Grove eds., *Conservation in Africa: People, Policies, and Practice* (Cambridge: Cambridge University Press, 1987); Peluso, *Rich Forests, Poor People*; Nancy Lee Peluso and Mark Poffenberger, "Social Forestry in Java: Reorienting Management Systems," *Human Organization* 48 n.4 (1989): 333–44; Charles Barber, *State, People, and the Environment: The Case of Forests in Java* (Ph. D. dissertation, University of California, Berkeley, 1989); Michael Dove, "Swidden Agriculture and the Political Economy of Ignorance," *Agroforestry Systems* 1 no. 1 (1983): 85–99; Michael Dove, "Peasant versus Government Perception and Use of the Environment: A Case Study of Banjarese Ecology and River Basin Development in South Kalimantan," *Journal of Southeast Asian Studies* 17 no. 3 (1986): 113–36.

6. Theda Skocpol, "Bringing the State Back In: Strategies of Analysis in Current Research," in Evans et. al., p. 7.

7. Joel Migdal, *Strong Societies and Weak States: State-Society Relations and State Capabilities in the Third World* (Princeton, NJ: Princeton University Press, 1988), p 4.

8. Ibid., p. 22.

9. Skocpol, "Bringing the State Back In," p. 9.

10. Stephen Bunker, *Underdeveloping the Amazon: The Failure of the Modern State* (Chicago: University of Illinois Press, 1985); Richard Robison, *Indonesia: The Rise of Capital* (Canberra, Australia: Asian Studies Association of Australia, 1986).

11. Eric Wolf, *Europe and the People Without a History* (Berkeley, CA: University of California Press, 1982).

12. Michael Watts, *Silent Violence: Food, Famine, and Peasantry in Northern Algeria* (Berkeley, CA: University of California Press, 1983); Ramachandra Guha, *The Unquiet Woods: Ecological History and Peasant Resistance in the Indian*

Himalaya (Berkeley, CA: University of California Press, 1990); Peluso, *Rich Forests, Poor People.*

13. Tilly, "War Making and State Making."

14. World Commission on Environment and Development, *Our Common Future* (New York: Oxford University Press, 1987); Lester Brown et. al., *State of the World 1990* (New York: W.W. Norton, 1990).

15. See Gillian Hart, *Power, Labor, and Livelihood* (Berkeley, CA: University of California Press, 1986); Robison, *Indonesia.*

16. Tilly, "War Making and State Making"; Migdal, *Strong Societies.*

17. W. K. Lindsay, "Integrating Parks and Pastoralists: Some Lessons from Amboseli," in Anderson and Grove, *Conservation in Africa*, pp. 152–55.

18. David Collett, "Pastoralists and Wildlife: Image and Reality in Kenya Maasailand," in Anderson and Grove, *Conservation in Africa*, p. 138.

19. Ibid.

20. Lindsay, "Integrating Parks," pp. 153–5.

21. David Western, "Amboseli National Park: Enlisting Landowners to Conserve," *Ambio* 11 no. 5: 302–308, p. 304; Lindsay, "Integrating Parks,", p. 155.

22. Western, "Amboseli National Park," p. 305; Lindsay, "Integrating Parks,", p. 154.

23. Lindsay, "Integrating Parks,", pp. 156–7; Kiss, *Wildlife Conservation*, p. 72.

24. Joan N. Knowles and D.P. Collett, "Nature as Myth, Symbol, and Action: Notes Towards an Historical Understanding of Development and Conservation in Kenyan Maasailand," *Africa* 59 n.4 (1989): 433–60, p. 452.

25. Douglas H. Chadwick, "Elephants—Out of Time, Out of Space," *National Geographic* 179 n.5 (1991): 2–49, p. 11, 17.

26. Knowles and Collet, "Nature as Myth," p. 452.

27. Collett, "Pastoralists and Wildlife," p. 129; emphasis added.

28. Ibid., p. 144.

29. Kiss, *Wildlife Conservation*, p. 72.

30. Chadwick, "Elephants," p. 14.

31. Ibid., pp. 26–31.

32. Kiss, *Wildlife Conservation*, pp. 71, 74.

33. McNeeley et. al., *Conserving the World's Biodiversity*, p. 1.

34. World Wildlife Fund, "A Program to Save the African Elephant," World Wildlife Fund Letter no. 2, 1989, p. 6.

35. Ibid., pp. 8–9.

36. Ibid., p. 9.

37. Ibid., pp. 4—5; emphasis added.

38. Chadwick, "Elephants," p. 24.

39. Ibid., p. 14.

40. Ibid., p. 24.

41. World Wildlife Fund Letter, p. 7.

42. Ibid., p. 10.

43. African Wildlife Foundation, "1989 was a Very Good Year: Annual Report," *Wildlife News* 25 no.2: 3–5.33.

44. "Kenya: Crackdown on Somalis," *Africa Confidential* 30 no. 1 (1989): 6–7.

45. Ibid.

46. Ibid.

47. Social forestry is essentially a movement in international forestry to involve forest villagers and other local forest users in making forest management decisions. Most forms of social forestry involve some kind of joint management between professional foresters and forest villagers on state or private lands.

48. Nancy Lee Peluso, " 'Traditions' of Forest Control in Java: Implications for Social Forestry and Sustainability, *Natural Resources Journal* 32 no. 4 (1992): 1–35.

49. Forest guards carry guns only in the teak forests because of the high value of the teak trees. Guns are not carried by guards in pine or other types of non-teak forest in Java.

50. Djokonomo Darmosoehardjo, Penguasaan Teritorial Oleh Jajaran Perum Perhutani (Jakarta: Perum Perhutani, 1986), p. 5. [Hereafter Djokonomo].

51. Ibid., p. 9.

52. Peluso, " 'Traditions' of Forest Control in Java."

53. Djokonomo, p. 1.

54. On the formation of these intrastate alliances between the center and peripheries of power, see Barber, *State, People, and the Environment*; Peluso, *Rich Forests, Poor People*; Hart, *Power, Labor, and Livelihood*.

55. Rainforest Alliance, "The 'Smart Wood' Certification Program." Manuscript, 1991.

56. *A Catalog for Gardeners (Summer)* (Mill Valley, CA: Smith and Hawkin, Ltd, 1991), p. 38.

57. Blaikie, *The Political-Economy of Soil Erosion*; Susanna Hecht and Alexander Cockburn, *The Fate of the Forest: Developers, Destroyers, and Defenders of the Rainforest* (New York: Verso, 1989); Guha, *Unquiet Woods*; Peluso, *Rich Forests, Poor People*.

58. McNeeley, *Conserving the World's Biodiversity*.

59. Ibid., p. 131.

60. Ibid., emphasis added.

61. Ibid.

4

Environmental Challenges in a Turbulent World

•

JAMES N. ROSENAU

In a recent book I offer a "bifurcationist" paradigm that may have some utility for the study of environmental and resources problems in world politics.[1] Or at least the ensuing analysis undertakes to trace how some of the core premises of the paradigm might be used to explore the multiplicity of environmental issues that are clamoring for attention.

Two prime sets of tensions are presumed by the model to be unfolding on an unprecedented scale during the present era. One set consists of the tensions between change and continuity; the other involves the tensions that flow from the clash of centralizing and decentralizing dynamics that shape the changes and sustain the continuities. Such tensions, of course, are as old as organized societies, but they can nevertheless be regarded as essentially new dimensions of world politics because for the first time they have become global in scope. Change anywhere in the world today can have consequences everywhere else, just as any centralizing or decentralizing

I am indebted to Ken Conca for a number of helpful reactions to an earlier version of this chapter.

tendencies in one locale can have repercussions for comparable locales everywhere.

The bifurcationist paradigm posits the unfolding of these tensions in world politics as bounded by three prime parameters that normally serve as limits constraining the day-to-day fluctuations of its variables. One of these parameters operates at the micro level of individuals, one functions at the macro level of collectivities, and the third involves a mix of the two levels. The micro parameter embraces the orientations and skills by which citizens of states and members of nonstate organizations link themselves to the macro world of global politics. I refer to this set of boundary constraints as the orientational or skill parameter. The macro parameter is designated the structural parameter, and it refers to the constraints embedded in the distribution of power among and within the collectivities of the global system. The mixed parameter is called the relational one; it focuses on the nature of the authority relations that prevail between individuals at the micro level and their macro collectivities. Each of these parameters is conceived to be presently under such stress that, together, they have cumulatively fostered a profound transformation of the global system, what I regard as the first genuine turbulence in 300 years.[2]

Five prime systemic tendencies are viewed as interactively having brought on the turbulent transformation. One involves the shift from an industrial to a postindustrial order and focuses on the dynamics of technology, particularly on those technologies associated with the microelectronic revolution that have made social, economic, and political distances so much shorter, the movement of ideas, pictures, currencies, and information so much faster, and thus the interdependence of people and events so much greater. A second is the emergence of issues—such as atmospheric pollution, terrorism, the drug trade, currency crises, and AIDS—that are the direct products of new technologies or the world's greater interdependence, and are distinguished from traditional political issues by virtue of being transnational rather than national or local in scope. A third dynamic is the authority crises that stem from the reduced capacity of states and governments to provide satisfactory solutions to the major issues on their political agendas, partly because the new issues are not wholly within their jurisdiction, partly because the old issues are also increasingly intertwined with significant international components (e.g., agricultural markets and labor productivity), and partly because the compliance of their citizenries can no longer be taken for granted.

Fourth, with the weakening of whole systems such as states, subsystems have acquired a correspondingly greater coherence and effectiveness, thereby reinforcing tendencies toward decentralization (what I call "subgroupism") at all organizational levels that are in stark contrast to the centralizing tendencies (such as nationalism) of earlier decades and that are in deep tension with the centralizing tendencies (transnationalism) of the present fostered by the new interdependence issues and the globalization of national economies.

Finally, there is the feedback of the consequences of all the foregoing for the skills and orientations of the world's adults who constitute the groups, states, and other collectivities that have had to cope with the new issues of interdependence and adjust to the new technologies of the postindustrial order: with their analytic skills enlarged and their orientations toward authority more self-conscious, today's persons-in-the-street are no longer as uninvolved, ignorant, and manipulable with respect to world affairs as were their forebears. Most important for present purposes, the refined skills of citizens have diminished their habitual patterns of compliance and heightened their sensitivities to the diverse aggregative processes whereby micro actions get converted into macro outcomes. As indicated by the numerous street rallies that toppled regimes in Eastern Europe, people are now more confident that what they do matters, that the large macro processes of communities, societies, and international systems are not so remote as to be impervious to their inputs.[3] Since environmental problems are to a large degree shaped by myriad actions at the micro level, since the noxious consequences of such problems are intimately linked into the daily routines of all citizens, and since the alleviation of these problems can only be accomplished through the cumulation of actions taken by individuals, the micro transformations that are presently underway on a global scale are bound to be crucially relevant to the success of any program designed to meet resource and environmental challenges.

The interactive impact of these five dynamics as sources of the bifurcation of the state system is summarized diagrammatically in figure 4.1. Here it is implied that none of the dynamics is in itself sufficient to have brought about a global transformation, but that their convergence in recent years has had a substantial impact on the overall structures of the system and the way that issues on the global agenda get processed. This impact is not necessarily salutary or consistent. The five dynamics interactively reinforce each other, but the result can promote animosity and conflict as much as reconcilia-

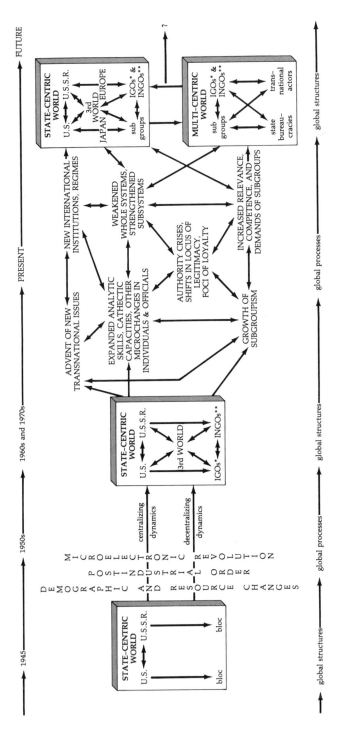

STATE-CENTRIC WORLD

U.S. ←→ U.S.S.R.

bloc

bloc

DEMOGRAPHIC, APPROACHING DISTRIBUTION OF RESOURCES OVER TECHNICAL CAPACITIES CHANGES

centralizing dynamics

decentralizing dynamics

STATE-CENTRIC WORLD

U.S. ←→ U.S.S.R.

3rd WORLD

IGOs* ←→ INGOs**

ADVENT OF NEW TRANSNATIONAL ISSUES

NEW INTERNATIONAL INSTITUTIONS, REGIMES

EXPANDED ANALYTIC SKILLS, CATHECTIC CAPACITIES, OTHER MICROCHANGES IN INDIVIDUALS & OFFICIALS

WEAKENED WHOLE SYSTEMS, STRENGTHENED SUBSYSTEMS

AUTHORITY CRISES, SHIFTS IN LOCUS OF LEGITIMACY, FOCI OF LOYALTY

GROWTH OF SUBGROUPISM

INCREASED RELEVANCE, COMPETENCE, AND DEMANDS OF SUBGROUPS

STATE-CENTRIC WORLD

U.S. ←→ U.S.S.R.

3rd WORLD

JAPAN EUROPE

IGOs* & INGOs**

sub groups

MULTI-CENTRIC WORLD

sub groups

IGOs* & INGOs**

state bureau-cracies

trans-national actors

?

1945   1950s   1960s and 1970s   PRESENT   FUTURE

global structures ← global processes ← global structures ← global processes ← global structures ← global processes ← global structures

*IGOs–International Governmental Organizations
**INGOs–International Non-governmental Organizations

tion and cooperation. Indeed, the turbulence of world politics is in good part sustained by a relentless tension between the centralizing tendencies fostered by interdependence issues on the one hand and the decentralizing tendencies induced by authority crises, subgroupism, and more analytically skillful citizens on the other.

Interdependence Issues

As the foregoing implies, the diplomatic and military issues that have long occupied a central place in world politics have been supplemented with a series of "interdependence" issues, conflicts that have their roots less in the needs and demands of independent national states and more in the needs and wants of people that span the borders of countries. Diplomatic and military policies are generated by aspirations within societies, but interdependence issues derive their strength from the increasingly broad range of ways that the aspirations of societies overlap and cannot be satisfied exclusively through the actions of their governments. Interdependence issues are quintessentially transnational in the sense that confronting them, much less resolving them, can occur only if states pool their resources and cooperatively address their shared dilemmas. Thus it is, for example, that currency crises have been met by the convergence of finance ministers, the threat of AIDS by health ministers, and the challenge of the drug trade by attorneys general. No single government can handle these crises through its own actions. Governments cannot appeal to the loyalties of their citizens, or call on them to sacrifice short-term gains for long-term benefits, with any hope of ameliorating the problem. They cannot denounce a foreign enemy, divert attention from the problem, or otherwise avoid or postpone facing up to the need for action. Rather, it is the very nature of interdependence issues that top governmental leaders have to reach out to counterparts abroad for help and coordination if sharp fluctuations in exchange rates, the spread of disease, or the movement of cocaine are to be offset, domestic restlessness quelled, and a modicum of internal stability and national security maintained.

Clearly, many of the environmental problems that have accompanied the explosion of technologies and the expansion of economies in recent decades fall in the domain of interdependence rather than domestic or international issues. The pollutants that take root in the atmosphere, water, and soil of the earth cannot be confined within national boundaries. They are carried downwind, under water, and through the produce of the soil well beyond their place of origin. They pose threats for which national cultures and historic policies offer little guidance. They embrace a variety of expertises and at the same time they are profoundly political in the sense that they manifestly affect the wellbeing of people in every social class and in all walks of life.

No less important, there are innumerable environmental problems, virtually all of which can be separated out for political action by single-issue groups capable of mobilizing support in and across the two worlds of world politics, thus adding to the complexity and density of global structures. A telling example of the mobilization potential of environmental issues is provided by the Soviet Association for Ecology and Peace, a private group in the Soviet Union that brought pressure to bear on the U.S. Federal Energy Regulatory Commission to take steps to protect the crane during relicensing proceedings involving the Kingsley Dam on the Platte River in Nebraska. Such pressure was exerted because the Platte River habitat is a prime staging ground for cranes, ten percent of which nest in Siberia following their spring migration from the United States.[4]

Put differently, the fit between the structure of the interstate system on the one hand and the global distribution of resources and the dispersion of the pollutants fostered by their utilization on the other is not even close. Many of both the resources and pollutants are ubiquitous and fluid in geographic space. As a result, they encompass whole regions and continents through processes of nature over which nation-states have not traditionally exercised control. They move like (and sometimes with) the winds across and around national boundaries, endlessly defying the conventional mechanisms on which the interstate system has long relied to resolve disputes.

It follows that one useful way to frame the conceptual challenge posed by environmental problems is to approach them from a bifurcationist perspective and probe how the dynamics enumerated above may affect and sustain them as interdependence issues. Put in question form, how are environmental issues likely to unfold as the bifurcated two worlds of world politics become increasingly competitive? How are such issues likely to be processed within and among polities? Under what circumstances will they confound domestic political processes by intruding the demands of environmentally concerned actors abroad? Conversely, how might cooperative endeavors undertaken by transnational actors be undermined, dominated, skewed, or otherwise affected by the internal politics of particular states? How are resource and environmental issues likely to contribute to the authority crises confronting states and governments? To what extent, and in what ways, might they intensify the processes of subgroupism, and what is their potential for refocusing subgroups' tendencies in transnational directions? How might the world's more analytically skillful citizens respond to the worsening of environmental conditions? Will they be increasingly capable of coping with the technical arguments and the diverse proofs on which the arguments rest? Are they susceptible to being mobilized on behalf of the incremental steps required to prevent incipient movement toward eventual disaster? What, in short, are the fundamental characteristics of global resource and environmental problems as transnational political issues?

Ripple Effects of Environmental Change

While this is not the place to undertake a full response to such questions, some of the prime ways in which environmental changes may further the processes of bifurcation and turbulence can usefully be identified. Perhaps the most self-evident consequence of environmental problems is the aforementioned likelihood that they will operate as a relentless pressure for assessments and solutions undertaken either through the cooperation of national governments or the creation or reinforcement of supranational agencies. Since it is in the very nature of environmental challenges that they ignore and span the boundaries of countries, national and subnational governments are bound to be wanting in their efforts to reduce the noxious effects of the challenges. Any success they enjoy in getting those within their jurisdictions to alter their routines in favor of the environment are bound to be insufficient inasmuch as part of the problem originates outside their jurisdictions. So all concerned are likely to reach out to counterparts in other jurisdictions, thereby sustaining and intensifying the centralizing dynamics that weaken states and strengthen transnational endeavors.

But it is important to stress that the consequences of environmental issues are not confined to impelling national and sub-national governments toward ever greater transnational cooperation. Such issues may also be conducive to strengthening the decentralizing tendencies fostered by authority crises, subgroupism, and the expanded competencies of citizens. Environmental change contributes to the elevation of citizens' skills by virtue of the large degree to which its recognition and assessment turns on the nature of science, facts, evidence, and proof.[5] When individuals anywhere become increasingly involved in environmental questions they unavoidably become increasingly preoccupied with questions about the state of knowledge relevant to such matters. Consider the example of global warming: once the issue enters a person's political consciousness, all kinds of unfamiliar puzzles arise. What is known about the warming process? Is that why there is a drought in my part of the world? How adequate are the measurements and trend lines of mean temperatures depicted in the local newspaper? Is the recent rise just a blip in a long-term stable pattern, or does it signify warming? Is it really possible that any of the routines that I and my family follow contribute to a global trend? People may well differ in their answers to such puzzles, but their involvement in them is bound to enhance their sensitivities to the epistemological and methodological premises around which environmental issues revolve. In turn, this more refined sensitivity induced by the scientific roots of environmental problems is likely to expand the skills of citizens with respect to other types of issues and, thus, to intensify further the dynamism of global turbulence.

Given more data- and proof-oriented citizenries, the highly scientific nature of environmental changes may also reinforce turbulent processes through their impact on the relational parameter whereby authority relations between macro- and micro-level actors are established and maintained. A major dimension of the worldwide changes that have occurred in authority structures involves a shift in the nature of legitimacy. For reasons too numerous to elaborate, the longstanding practice whereby citizens accord legitimacy to macro authorities on the basis of the traditional premise that one unquestioningly complies with the directives of those constitutionally entitled to issue them has begun to shift toward what might be called "performance legitimacy"—that is, toward a practice of complying with directives on the basis of the performance record of those who issue them.[6] Thus, for instance, did Marcos experience the erosion of his legitimacy in the Philippines and, perhaps even more manifest, thus did the shift to performance legitimacy result in the progressive deterioration of Gorbachev's capacity to evoke compliance in the Soviet Union. At the core of this transformation in authority structures is a capacity and inclination to recognize discrepancies between the proposed and the actual, between the claim and the outcome, between the alleged and the evidence—capacities and inclinations which are surely enriched and sharpened by the growing relevance of issues that turn on the adequacy of scientific proof.

It follows that the more environmental and technological issues come to dominate the global agenda, and until such time when the evidence relative to them becomes so unmistakable as to be regarded as solid proof by most observers, the greater is the likelihood that authority structures will move from being in place to being in crisis. Indeed, once the evidence does become clear-cut, it can be argued, the scientific bases of environmental problems has the potential of enhancing the legitimacy of supranational actors as the data on global warming, the ozone gap, etc., highlight the limits beyond which national governments can address such problems on their own.

The decentralizing dynamics fostered by subgroupism can also be accelerated by environmental challenges. As indicated by the recent history of the environmental movement—by as disparate developments as the pressures that gave rise to the United Nations Conference on the Human Environment in June 1972, or the widespread local efforts to encourage the recycling of glass, metal, and paper—problems posed by environmental degradation or resource scarcities may readily serve as foci around which subgroups can coalesce. Since such problems are no more respectful of socioeconomic lines than they are of political and geographic boundaries, they can evoke convergence on the part of a wide array of diverse people who may be endangered by a local or more encompassing environmental threat. Moreover, since such threats tend to be of long duration, there is plenty of time for the sentiments and involvement on which subgroupism flourishes to evolve and mature. And the more convincing the evidence of a threat becomes, the more tightly are the ties that bind environmentally minded subgroups likely to be drawn. Environmental problems, in other words, seem ideally suited to create their own constituencies and to never lack for want of support.

In short, to inquire into the dynamics of global environmental change is also to probe those that sustain global social change. The two types of change occur simultaneously. They are inextricably linked to each other. And they are so profoundly and pervasively interactive that it is only for reasons of analytic convenience that they are examined separately.

Variability Among Issues

In order to explore further the challenges posed by environmental problems, some important distinctions must be drawn. To focus on global resources and environments is not to address a single set of issues. Rather, as the aforenoted migration of cranes so clearly indicates, such a focus encompasses a multitude of diverse issues that can be categorized in a variety of ways. Here the multiplicity of issues are conceived to involve two broad arenas, one for nature's products (resources) and another for its degradation (environment), and each of these in turn subsume important distinctions that can be drawn in terms of the newness of the resources and the form and scope of the degradations.

Consider, for example, those resources that are of recent origin elsewhere than on or under land: in ocean beds, outer space, climate and the geosynchronous orbit.[7] Their recent origins (either because only lately have they been identified in non-land realms or because only lately have new technologies made their utilization possible), and their location outside national jurisdictions, endows such resources with several characteristics that set them apart from other types of interdependence issues. First and foremost perhaps, the new nonland resources give rise mainly to distributive rather than redistributive issues, a distinction to which we shall return shortly. Second, the new resource issues are much less infused with symbolic content than other interdependence issues. Their focus is on the allocation, utilization, and management of very concrete phenomena. Being tangible and observable products of nature, they are less subject to considerations of status, hierarchy, and many other intangible symbols that attach to the products of human relationships.[8]

Third, none of the new resource issues embrace large constituencies. Unlike most interdependence issues—such as energy crunches, currency crises, food shortages, and population explosions, which respectively involve masses of motorists, investors, farmers, and parents—the seabed, outer space, radio frequencies, and other new natural resources do not presently have any direct and immediate bearing on the daily lives of millions of people. Potentially, to be sure, their relevance to humankind is considerable, but for the time being this relevance is largely circuitous and indirect. Consequently, those whose welfare might be threatened by proposed solutions to the issues are unlikely to be aware of the threats because the causal chains that lead from the utilization of the resources to their door-steps are so lengthy and complex; or, if they somehow become conscious of the chains and the threats lying behind them, they are likely to feel that there is not much they can do about breaking into and affecting such remote and intricate causal processes. In short, the politics of new resource issues is unlikely to be sustained by the hue and cry of mass publics or burdened or facilitated by their mobilization and intervention.

Fourth, partly because the interests of mass publics in the issues are not recognized, but mostly because of the slow pace at which nature's processes unfold, the issues associated with new natural resources are not likely to be marked by dramatic climaxes. Where terrorism, territorial clashes, currency crises, and other types of issues erupt suddenly and compel attention as "hot" issues, those involving the nonland realm evolve in small increments and almost never command the headlines of the world's media. The specialist can discern droughts leading to famines or environmental pollution leading to disease, but forecasts of doomsday ahead if such patterns are allowed to continue carry little weight in the face of the current, more dramatic crises around which other types of issues revolve. Stated differently, the onset of problems derived from new natural resources is likely to be detected only by specialists whose salience and clout in the political arena is quite limited.

Finally, and by no means least important, the issues associated with new natural resources are highly technical and not readily assimilated by simple and overarching value systems. They involve levels of information and comprehension attained only by specialists and thus they are issues that tend to be waged in the moderate discourse of science rather than the more inflammatory rhetoric of politics. As previously noted, in other words, perhaps no issue area on the global agenda relies more heavily on scientific proof as the means through which persuasion and influence is exercised than does the one embracing controversies over environmental degradation and new natural resources.

An example in this regard is provided by the issue of how much sewage the ocean can absorb without damage to undersea life and to humans who consume its resources. This is not a question around which politicians can mobilize followers and debate on the basis of symbolic values or appeals to unqualified loyalties. Rather, to achieve agreement, compliance, and/or active support the facts must be offered, their derivation legitimated, and their application delineated.

Changes in the amounts of silver, chromium, DDT, and other harmful compounds in ocean waters off metropolitan shores have to be clearly demonstrated and the ways in which the changes were measured have to be persuasive if those who contest such issues are to progress toward their goals. To be sure, facts never speak for themselves. They can be developed only in the context of some kind of value system and, obviously, different value systems can lead to different conclusions as to what the scientifically derived facts mean. It matters, for instance, whether one believes research on sewage systems should be oriented toward uncovering how humans can least disturb ocean habitats or toward how much disruption the ocean can accommodate. Notwithstanding the centrality of such important value dimensions in any new resource issue, however, it is still the case that issues involving nature's structures and processes are bound to be differentiated from all other types of issues by the large degree to which the procedures of science underlie their argumentation and resolution.

If we now factor in land-resource and environmental issues, the need for differentiation becomes even more acute. Like the nonland realm of resources, those issues which originate as opportunities or problems in agriculture, forests, industry, and human and animal populations are highly variable insofar as the politics they evoke is concerned. It would be a grievous analytic error to proceed as if the shared attributes of these problems are such as to allow for lumping them together as a common set of issues. On the other hand, developing a typology that meaningfully differentiates among the various issues can also lead to grievous distortions. Many resources and environmental challenges, for example, can be managed in a multiplicity of contradictory ways. Trees can be used for timber or to hold the soil in place. The atmosphere can serve as a dumping ground or as a regulator of a hospitable climate. Accordingly, depending on their goals and circumstances, people are likely to respond differently to an environmental challenge, some viewing it as loaded with opportunity and others seeing it as threatening their wellbeing. Environmental and resource problems, in short, do not consist only of technical/physical attributes; they are also marked by profound social and political dimensions and any typology which ignores them runs the risk of fostering misleading and erroneous interpretations.

Indeed, the dilemmas inherent in typologizing resource and environmental issues are so acute that it is easy to argue against proceeding from a formulation that posits hard and fast boundaries between types and to opt instead for an analysis that focuses on central

TABLE 4.1
Four Types of Environmental Issues

	Distributive	Redistributive
Goods	I. newly discovered resources (e.g., in outer space, the oceans)	II. technological breakthroughs (e.g., in genetics, agriculture)
Bads	III. newly identified environmental problems (e.g., global warming, ozone gap, toxic wastes)	IV. worsening of longstanding pollutants (e.g., in atmosphere, waterways)

tendencies that cut across all types of problems. Since the distinctions among issues cannot readily be dismissed, however, the ensuing discussion offers both a broad typology and an assessment of central tendencies. More precisely, the typology developed below is supplemented with caution as to its limitations and, subsequently, with an attempt to tease out overall trends that may attach to all resource and environmental issues despite the differences among them. This is accomplished, first, by presuming that the analysis of any type of issue can proceed on the basis of *ceteris paribus* and, then, by relaxing this presumption as it becomes ever more clear that other things are almost never equal.

The typology derives from an assumption that if a modicum of clarity is to be achieved in tracing the impact of citizens, publics, subgroups, governments, and a bifurcated global structure on the arenas of politics wherein resource and environmental problems are processed, it is important to locate these problems along at least two basic dimensions, one that distinguishes among such issues in terms of the quality of their consequences ("goods" versus "bads") and another that differentiates among them in terms of their allocative foundations ("distributive" versus "redistributive" issues).[9] As can be seen in table 4.1, this formulation yields four basic types of resource and environmental issues.

That these four types of issues give rise to very different politics can be readily demonstrated. Their profiles vary noticeably if assessed in terms of the time frames, horizons of observability, forms of proof, levels of information, concerns of elites, and predispositions of citizens that underlie their political dynamics. Table 4.2 outlines these differences; here it can be seen that Type IV issues (the redistribution of bads) are much more highly politicized than any of the other three. Involving as they do threats in the near term that are clearly discernible and part of personal experience, and being rooted in questions of equity as to how onerous burdens should be redistributed, Type IV issues seem bound to evoke intense involvement on the part of publics and activity on the part of a broad spectrum of elites. With smoggy skies and smarting eyes providing immediate experience in support of the scientific evidence that pollutants are a threat to health, Type IV issues lend themselves well to expression through high degrees of organization and mobilization. The domestic and international consequences of the nuclear accident at Chernobyl are a classic example of the deep and pervasive dynamics of Type IV issues.

Other things being equal, however, many (and perhaps most) environmental opportunities and problems fall in the other three categories, all of which involve long-term stretches of time and vague horizons of observability before they reach fruition as aspects of daily life. The time lag between the transformation of newly identified goods—whether they be newly discovered resources or newly developed technologies—into immediately available opportunities that people are willing to seize has been fifty years or more.[10] And the data on when (and whether) newly identified bads—such as the greenhouse effect—will materialize as tangible threats to life and property seem insufficiently clear at present for Type III issues to undergo a transformation into the politics of Type IV issues.[11]

Specialists and concerned elites may see dark clouds on the horizon, broad gaps in the ozone layer, and signs of a global warming, but the likelihood of most people—again assuming other things are equal—taking warnings of such long-run trends seriously would seem to be very small indeed. If near-term success in reversing or halting these trends is to be recorded, it would appear that concerned elites will have to develop convincing proofs if decisive actions by governments are to occur. Otherwise most environmental issues are fated to be locked into that stalemated form of politics whereby the urgings of experts and a few organizations of attentive citizens is no match for the reluctance of politicians to make financial commitments in the face of ambiguous evidence and circuitous horizons of observability. Leaders and attentive citizens may be uneasy that circumstances are so dire as to warrant treating them as Type IV issues, but not until the consequences of the long-term threats are immediately experienced is the politics of crisis likely to become pervasive.

TABLE 4.2
Salient Attributes of Four Types of Environmental Issues

	I.	II.	III.	IV.
Type of issue	Distributive goods	Redistributive goods	Distributive bads	Redistributive bads
Time frame[a]	Long-term	Long-term	Long-term	Short-term
Horizon of observability[b]	Obscure	Vague	Direct	Direct
Form of proof[c]	Tenuous	Technical controversial	Technical controversial	Reinforced by experience
Elite concerns	A few specialists	Relevant specialists & bureaucrats	Relevant specialists & politicians	Widespread among elites
Predispositions of citizens' involvement	Unconcerned	Limited interest	Uneasiness	Intense
Mobilizability of subgroups	Extremely difficult	Difficult	Somewhat difficult	Easy
Organizational activity	Low	Low	Moderate	High

NOTES
[a]For the appreciation of goods and bads
[b]Clarity of the stages through which the opportunities or problems will loom as relevant to daily routines
[c]Nature of the evidence available to demonstrate the viability of the opportunities or problems

The Impact of Global Turbulence

But other things are rarely equal. The conclusion that relatively few resources and environmental issues evoke the characteristics of Type IV issues derives from a politics-as-usual perspective. It does not allow for the aforenoted five dynamics that underlie the present turbulence. If full allowance is made for the interactive impact of these dynamics, the politics of all resource and environmental issues may increasingly come to resemble Type IV issues. Assuming, for example, that authority crises have become more pervasive, states less effective, subgroups more coherent, and citizens more analytically skillful than was the case in earlier eras of world politics, then much of the foregoing assessment needs to be revised. From a bifurcationist perspective, resource and environmental issues have the potential for reducing the time frame, clarifying the horizons of observability, highlighting the adequacy of proofs, proliferating elite activities, evoking widespread citizen involvement, and heightening the mobilizability of groups that normally characterize the passage of issues through the processes of world politics. In effect, under conditions of global turbulence resource and environmental issues seem especially susceptible to the Type IV politics of crisis that attach to the redistribution of bads. The susceptibility will vary depending on whether the issues involve bads or goods and distributive or redistributive dynamics, but in all cases tendencies in a Type IV direction are likely to be readily discernible.

It follows that, with the Cold War and American-Soviet rivalry no longer the predominant issue on the world's agenda, the way is open for other global preoccupations to surface as the central focus of concern. Environmental and resource issues may well be especially suitable for elevation to the top of the global agenda. The advent of a multicentric world as a consequence of the bifurcation of the global system opens up a host of new organizational channels through which environmental bads are likely to be recognized, pondered, and addressed. The mushrooming of subgroupism has added to the incentives and social support that encourage people to jump aboard the environmental bandwagon. The expansion of analytic skills has enlarged, among other things, the capacity of people to employ scenarios that trace causal dynamics across longer stretches of time, thereby better enabling them to experience earlier and more fully the fears that attach to long-term threats. The skill revolution has also been accompanied by a shift from traditional to performance criteria of legitimacy, which further heightens their inclination to assess rather than merely accept the arguments for or against environmental policies. The crises of authority that have weakened governments may have also supplemented the readiness of citizens to listen to the experts who forecast long-term threats to their health and welfare. There are, in short, a number of ways in which the dynamics underlying structural bifurcation may hasten the transformation of resource and environmental politics into a Type IV format.

The specific instance of transformations from Type III to Type IV issues, moreover, involves exactly the set of challenges on which social movements flourish. People who join such movements tend to be attentive to public affairs and thus especially inclined to trace back from distant threats the requirements for action in the immediate present. And once a social movement forms or focuses around a newly identified environmental (Type III) problem, it is likely to initiate the kind of momentum that quickly narrows the perception of time between current luxuries and future upsets.[12]

It might be countered that these hints that the turbulence perspective can usefully be applied to resource and environmental problems suffer from a fatal flaw, that they rest too heavily on analogies to Eastern Europe, that mobilizing more analytically skillful citizens to topple oppressive governments embraces quite a different set of considerations than those which obtain in the case of Type I, II, and III issues. In the latter cases the proofs are too technical and the dangers too remote to activate the widespread support needed to move reluctant politicians into considering and adopting pro-environmental policies. Only in response to immediate opportunities or threats, such an argument concludes, do people exert the pressures and make the sacrifices that Type IV issues induce.

But such reasoning does not precede from an appreciation of the extent to which world politics has been engulfed by turbulence. The premise that people throughout the world have become analytically skillful and cathectically competent cannot be easily exaggerated. The supporting evidence is too extensive, varied, and impressive to be dismissed as mere idealism.[13] To be sure, it is not conclusive proof; and there is surely great variability in the degree to which expansion has occurred in different parts of the world, but the evidence suggests that no part of the world has been immune to these micro changes.

In the interest of exercising caution against misleading interpretations of the fourfold typology, several possible weaknesses, if not fatal flaws, inherent in it can usefully be noted. First, there is the aforementioned difficulty of environmental challenges having multiple dimensions and thus being subject to classification in more than one of the types derived in table 4.1. The Amazon, for example, can be treated as any one of the four types, depending on who defines the challenge: it is an issue of distributive goods from the point of view of the Brazilian government (tapping previously unexploited resource riches), of redistributive goods to cattle ranchers (who seek to alter the traditional pattern of land use, gaining control for a nontraditional economic activity), of distributive bads to the forest peoples (whose lives are being disrupted by the negative consequences associated with the new activities), and of redistributive bads to much of the international environmental community (worsening the already serious problems of tropical-forest disappearance, climate change, and species extinctions). While it is thus clear that issue type is highly dependent on who gets to define the problem— and that much of the controversy surrounding the problem is a function of different conceptions of where it falls on the good-bad and distributive-redistributive continua—this typological difficulty may not be as misleading as it seems at first glance. Not only is it offset by the overall trend induced by the dynamics of turbulence (summarized below); but it may even facilitate clarification in the sense that by tracing how various groups differently classify the same issue, the analyst gets a deeper insight into the conflict it engenders.

A second note of caution concerns the classification of problems in terms of the dimensions that comprise the rows of table 4.2. It can well be argued that while all these dimensions are important, it is not the goods-vs-bads and distributive-vs-redistributive distinctions that are driving the differences among the issues. Why, it might be asked, does table 4.2 treat the horizon of observability as "obscure" for new goods but "direct" for new bads? Or why are elite concerns narrower and forms of proof more tenuous for Type I than Type IV issues? Consider, the argument might continue, how the Third World has stirred up much more of a fuss on being shut out of seabed nodules and satellite orbitals (new goods) than on being stuck on the receiving end of some complex and indirect chains of environmental destruction (new bads). Similarly, it is reasonable to presume, contrary to the entries in table 4.2, that "new bads" (Type III) are often more alarming and contentious than "old bads" (Type IV) to which people have become habituated.

In short, while a general case can be made for each of the entries in the cells of table 4.2, the point of these contrary examples is that none of the entries are likely to hold under all circumstances and that caution must thus be maintained in applying the typology. Still, whatever qualifications may have to be made in ascribing characteristics to different environmental challenges, the analytic scheme suggested by table 4.2 serves to highlight the dimensions along which variability occurs in the politics of environmental issues.

Conclusion

If the talents of people everywhere are changing in the direction of greater competence, the politics of Type IV issues may be closer at hand than seems to be the case at first glance. Type I, II, and III issues are not inherently distant from the political arena. What keeps them far away is the difficulty people have in discerning their immediate relevance. But that difficulty may well be easing as the turbulence of our time gathers momentum.

The implications of this application of the bifurcationist perspective to resource and environmental opportunities and problems seem clear. In a period when the institutions and habitual patterns of world politics are undergoing profound transformation, the political foundations of issues involving environmental degradation are no less volatile. These are issues that can reach deep into the micro level of individual experience. They are issues that can lend themselves readily to aggregation and mobilization, and thus to quick movement up through and across ever more encompassing systems, from the local community to the geographic region to the national society to the international system. And they are issues that derive their dynamism from circumstances that can supersede differences of culture, status, and hierarchy. Poisoned air, contaminated water, and toxic wastes are no less noxious for the rich than the poor, no less fearful for traditional cultures than modern ones.[14]

Increasingly, in short, environmental issues are politically explosive. They show numerous signs of evoking an overall tendency toward the characteristics of Type IV issues—toward being contested in a context that is immediate, intense, short-term, and broadly conflictful among a range of well-organized groups. And, no less important, environmental issues have all the ingredients that conduce to cooperation on a global scale even as their foundations can also serve as incentives to intense conflict at all levels of social organization.[15] In a world where uncertainty is rife as long-standing patterns break down and as the complexity of social systems make the fixing of blame increasingly difficult, global politics may be only one environmental catastrophe away from a volatile turning point in which a concern with the nature of nature becomes a worldwide obsession that leads either to new forms of global order or to new cascades of pervasive disorder.

The very possibility of this turning point highlights the significant question of whether and how environmental politics are likely to feed back on the systemic dynamics that have given rise to the bifurcation of global affairs. If it is the case that the forces sustaining present-day turbulence are fostering a transformation of environmental politics in the direction of Type IV issues, what impact will these transformations in turn have on the very forces that precipitated them? Are Type IV issues likely to reinforce positively the centralizing tendencies in both worlds of world politics? Or are they likely to dampen negatively these tendencies and reinforce the decentralizing tendencies toward weakened states, subgroupism, and expanded analytic skills? Or is their impact likely to be negligible because environmental issues will never supersede traditional forms of conflict—such as trade disputes and boundary wars—on the global agenda? Or, to cite yet another possibility, will their repercussions be of both a centralizing and a decentralizing nature? Are environmental issues, in short, likely to become the driving force of world politics in the future?

Answers to such questions are not easily developed. Much depends on the pace at which elites and publics in different parts of the world converge around Type IV definitions of environmental issues.[16] The quicker and the more pervasively such a convergence develops, the greater is the likelihood that environmental changes will serve as the driving force of world politics. That is, since presumably a convergence around Type IV definitions will occur in local as well as national and international contexts, it has the potential of operating as a powerful stimulus to the evolution of supranational norms and institutions. No other set of interdependence issues seems as capable of initiating and sustaining a centralizing momentum on such a scale. On the other hand, if the convergence around Type IV definitions is slow, halting, and uneven, the greater will be the likelihood that environmental problems will not hinder tendencies toward authority crises and subgroupism. If, that is, most people proceed from Type I, II or III definitions, they will be free to devote their energies to other, business-and-politics-as-usual concerns and tilt the balance in decentralizing directions.

To anticipate the long-term systemic impact of environmental politics, in short, is to estimate how long it will take before the proofs of nature's noxious responses to humankind's exploitation of its resources becomes irrefutable and ominous. Environmental catastrophes may hasten redefinitions toward Type IV issues; but if it is assumed that the continual exploitation of nature can lead only to an ever more precarious existence for people everywhere, the key variable is the adequacy of the proof of immediate, life-threatening dangers lurking in the environment. Once such proofs become commonplace, world politics seems likely to move onto a new global order in which intense and creative cooperation marks the interaction between the state-centric and multicentric worlds, with actors in both domains moving to establish transnational mechanisms for coping with, if not reversing, nature's deadly course.

NOTES

1. James N. Rosenau, *Turbulence in World Politics: A Theory of Change and Continuity* (Princeton: Princeton University Press, 1990).

2. One of these parameters operates at the micro level of individuals, one functions at the macro level of collectivities- and the third involves a mix of the two levels. The micro parameter embraces the orientations and skills by which citizens of states and members of non-state organizations link themselves to the macro world of global politics. I refer to this set of boundary constraints as the orientational or skill parameter. The macro parameter is designated the structural parameter, and it refers to the constraints embedded in the distribution of power among and within the collectivities of the global system. The mixed parameter is called the relational one; it focuses on the nature of the authority relations that prevail between individuals at the micro level and their macro collectivities. An analysis and history of all three parameters is presented in Rosenau, *Turbulence in World Politics*, pp. 87–112; turbulence, defined as the onset of high degrees of complexity and dynamism with respect to all three paramenters, is elaborated upon in chapter 3.

3. For a discussion of the close link between the toppling of regimes in Eastern Europe and greater analytic skills and confidence on the part of individuals and publics, see James N. Rosenau, "The Relocation of Authority in a Shrinking World," *Comparative Politics* 24 (April 1992): 253–272.

4. Larry B. Stammer, "Soviet Group Backs Cranes in U.S. Dam Case," *Los Angeles Times*, February 17, 1990, p. A24.

5. Nor is the increasing relevance of scientific modes of thought confined to environmental problems. For an extensive discussion of how a wide range of technologies seem bound to expand the role played by evidence and proof in international affairs, see Rosenau, *Turbulence in World Politics*, chs. 8 and 15.

6. For a discussion of the sources and complexities of the shift to performance legitimacy, see Rosenau, *Turbulence in World Politics*, pp. 381–83 and 429–30.

7. The discussion in this and the next four paragraphs is amplified in James N. Rosenau, "New Natural Resources as Global Issues," in Rene-Jean Dupuy ed., *The Settlement of Disputes on the New Natural Resources* (The Hague: Martinus Nijhoff, 1983), pp. 25–34.

8. For a conceptual elaboration of the consequences that flow from the distinction between issue-areas that encompass tangible or intangible phenomena, see James N. Rosenau, *The Scientific Study of Foreign Policy* (New York: Nichols Publishing Company, 1980), pp. 160–68.

9. Stated most succinctly, a distributive issue is one in which resolutions can be reached through disaggregation without regard to limited resources, whereas a redistributive issue involves finite resources and is thus not susceptible to unlimited degrees of disaggregation. For an extensive discussion of this distinction, see Theordore J. Lowi, "American Business, Public Policy, Case-Studies, and Political Theory," *World Politics* 16 (July 1964): 677–715.

10. Cf. Ortwin Renn, "High Technology and Social Change," *High Tech Newsletter*, Vol. 1 (1983): 15.

11. For an example of the intensity of the scientific debates that can attach to the question of whether newly identified bads may actually come to pass, see David L. Wheeler, "Scientists Studying 'Greenhouse Effect' Challenge Fears of Global Warming," *The Chronicle of Higher Education*, January 31, 1990, pp. A5, A6, A9.

12. For a succinct and cogent discussion of the role social movements can play in international affairs, see R. B. J. Walker, *One World, Many Worlds: Struggles for a Just World Peace* (Boulder: Lynne Rienner Publishers, 1988).

13. See Rosenau, *Turbulence in World Politics*, chap. 13.

14. Some qualification of this self-evident proposition needs to be introduced. Noxiousness is not entirely an objective condition. It is experienced in the context of culture and priorities. Thus Third World governments contend that their First World counterparts can afford to be sensitive to environmental bads because they already have the luxury of an industrial order, but that they are prepared to risk some noxious consequences if that is necessary to increase the productivity of their economies.

15. For a good discussion of how the world's "collective fate" is susceptible to both cooperative and conflictful outcomes, see Oran R. Young, *International Cooperation: Building Regimes for Natural Resources and the Environment* (Ithaca: Cornell University Press, 1989), chaps. 4, 8, and 9.

16. Poll data gathered by the Louis Harris Organization for the United Nations Environmental Programme indicate that such a convergence may well be underway. Although the samples were not large, Harris found that concern with environmental problems has become global in scope. A majority—and, in some cases, a large majority—of people in thirteen countries perceived a worsening of their environments over the previous ten years. Only in Saudi Arabia did a majority report it had gotten better, and one suspects this finding might be quite different if the Saudis had been polled after the environmental degradations unleashed by the Iraqis over Kuwait and in the Gulf. More important, most respondents anticipated that the processes of environmental degradations would worsen and thus looked to their governments to attach higher priority to the need for environmental protection. Indeed, huge majorities of 75 to 100 percent in each surveyed country agreed that more should be done by national and international organizations to address environmental problems. And perhaps most notable of all, as Louis Harris put it, "alarm about the deterioration of the environment and support for much tougher environmental programs are not confined to Western countries, but are found in the East and West, in the South and North, and in the rich and poor countries of the world." A globally shared Type IV definition, it would seem on the basis of poll data, is very much in the offing. For discussions of these data and alternative interpretations of the openness of publics to learning about environmental challenges, see Lester W. Milbrath, "The World Learns About the Environment," International Studies Notes 16 (Winter 1991): 13–17, and *Symposium, Environmental Problems a Global Threat* (Muscatine, Iowa: The Stanley Foundation, 1989), pp. 6–7 (the Harris quote is reproduced in the latter item, p. 6).

5

Ecoregimes: Playing Tug of War with the Nation-State

•

KAREN LITFIN

The State of the State

The status of the nation-state in an increasingly interdependent world has been a matter of debate since the end of World War II. The unleashing of the nuclear genie prompted some to envision a world government that would replace the nation-state system.[1] By the 1970s, the complex web of global economic relations caused others to speculate that national sovereignty would soon be rendered obsolete by the growth of multinational corporations.[2] Others hoped that ecological independence would inspire a new world order to replace the nation-state system.[3] Yet nation-states have persisted and have managed their growing interdependencies, however inadequately, through various forms of cooperation. In one way or another, this phenomenon of "cooperation under anarchy" has dominated the international relations literature for the past decade.[4]

The recent surge of interest in international environmental problems, along with the recognition that many of them are truly global in nature, raises the question of the state anew. Whether out of prudence or cowardice, I balk at making my own predictions. Observation of recent events in light of two distinct arguments, however, suggests an emergent trend along the lines of what James Rosenau has labelled "the bifurcation of world politics."[5] Rosenau argues that the traditional state-centered structure of the international system now "coexists with an equally powerful, though more decentralized, multi-centric system," dominated by nongovernmental organizations (NGOs) and other transnational actors.

On the one hand, global ecological interdependence could usher in a new era of governmental activism around a new set of welfare concerns, thereby reversing the recent trend in many places toward reducing the role of government in people's lives. Since major environmental problems will not be resolved by the invisible hand of the market, it can be argued, the state will find itself engaged in "an unprecedented degree of domestic intervention and international cooperation."[6] Only the state has the human and financial resources to mount the large-scale scientific and technical projects for detecting, monitoring, and preserving the global environment. Only the state, standing at the intersection of domestic and international politics, has sufficient authority, political legitimacy, and territorial control to influence the myriad causal agents of environmental deterioration. Thus, global ecological problems can be expected to bolster the power and legitimacy of the state in new ways.

On the other hand, this argument suggests that states and markets are the only institutional mechanisms available when in fact a whole array of non-state actors has taken the lead in efforts to preserve the global environment. In particular, scientists and social movements have instigated virtually all existing international environmental agreements, and in many cases were key actors in their negotiation, implementation, and monitoring. Moreover, these non-state actors are infusing new rules, processes, and norms into both new and existing social structures. Ultimately, these developments may signify a shift in fundamental social values and worldviews away from the dominant industrial paradigm toward a more holistic, long-term, and global ecological paradigm.[7] This paradigm shift would arise from the structural contradiction between Earth as an integrated system and the nation-state system based upon the principles of sovereignty and territorial exclusivity. The implications of such a shift for international relations would be dramatic, generating new identities, roles, and interests to challenge the nation-state system.

These two visions of the future are not necessarily contradictory. As Rosenau argues, the multicentric world of non-state actors can coexist with the state-centric world, an argument supported by emerging practices in global environmental politics. An examination of recent institution-building bears out Rosenau's claim that the state has become "both indispensable and inadequate." [8] Although mainstream theorists argue that new international institutions merely confirm the adaptability of the nation-state system, and Rosenau seems to accept their view,[9] I will argue that some important new dynamics are at work. It would be imprudent, however, to predict the withering away of the state; nation-states remain key actors, even if their interests, identities, and power are rendered problematic by the growing importance of non-state actors.

The past two decades have witnessed an unprecedented level of international activity with respect to environmental concerns. As the negative side-effects of economic processes increasingly cross national boundaries, a range of actors has called into question the ability of existing political institutions to cope. In many instances, they have successfully induced national governments to enter into international agreements. One observer puts the number of multilateral environmental conventions at more than 150, and the number of bilateral agreements in excess of 500.[10] Though these instruments constrain national prerogatives, and to that extent encroach on sovereignty, their benefits are seen as outweighing their drawbacks simply for the measure of protection they promise.

Description alone, to say nothing of analysis, of these agreements could fill volumes. Nonetheless, it is possible to document some recent trends with respect to the actors involved in initiating, negotiating, and implementing environmental regimes. One can also trace some trends regarding the kinds of principles and structuring mechanisms expressed in these regimes. Finally, without going into great detail on individual agreements, one can draw some general conclusions about the effectiveness of existing institutions in fulfilling their purpose of environmental protection. These are the aims of this chapter.

The Concept of Regimes

First, a few definitions are in order, to clarify the high degree of ambiguity surrounding my main analytical terms. Institutions should not be confused with organizations, although they often have organizational entities associated with them. Rather, institutions, which are intangible, give a sense of "solidity" to social life by expressing the structural properties of social systems.[11] Oran Young's definition captures the essence of the concept: "Institutions are social practices consisting of easily recognized roles coupled with rules or conventions governing relations among the occupants of these roles."[12] Whether normalized or simply routinized, institutions exist at all levels of social life and include practices as diverse as marriage, warfare, and markets. Regimes, a closely related notion, have been defined by Stephen Krasner as "sets of implicit or explicit principles, norms, rules, and decision-making procedures around which actors' expectations converge."[13] Like institutions, regimes can be tacit or implicit, de jure or de facto. While the terms regime and institution are often used synonymously, they are distinct. Institutions, which consist of actual social practices, are manifestations of regimes, and regimes are the guiding principles behind those practices. In practice, however, the two are coupled, so that a change in one entails a change in the other; if routinized practices change, then so too will the principles governing actors' expectations, and vice versa.

The literature on international regimes has tended to focus on negotiated regimes within the economic issue area.[14] Military and security issues have been viewed as less amenable to regime analysis because regimes are thought to be less relevant in zero-sum situations.[15] Since international environmental problems, by definition, negatively affect more than one country's perceived interests (even if to differing degrees), they may present opportunities for cooperation on the basis of mutually inclusive interests. They may also provide new terrain for preexisting struggles over power and wealth. While regimes and institutions can be understood broadly in terms of routinized practices and general principles, my focus is on formally negotiated environmental regimes among nation-states. Even with such a narrow scope, I argue that new actors, normative principles, and forms of state power are emerging that provide strong evidence for the bifurcation of world politics.

Regime Formation

Two classes of explanation dominate the literature on international regime construction; neither does a good job of accounting for environmental regimes. The first sees regimes as either provided or imposed by a hegemonic power, depending upon whether the hegemon is seen as altruistically providing a public good or simply imposing its own narrowly defined interests on weaker actors.[16] The second category explains regimes as expressions of egoistic self-interest on the part of the parties.[17]

In the first place, both sorts of accounts look to states as the impetus for regime creation. Yet the impetus for recent environmental regime formation frequently, if not typically, emanates from a variety of non-state actors, including regional integration organizations, scientific organizations, environmental pressure groups, and the United Nations' specialized agencies.

Several agreements have been spearheaded by the World Wildlife Fund (WWF) and the International Union for Conservation of Nature and Natural Resources (IUCN), including the Convention on the International Trade in Endangered Species (CITES) and the World Conservation Strategy.[18] The Economic Commission for Europe (ECE) played a pivotal role in bringing about the 1979 East-West agreement on acid rain, the Convention on Long Range Transboundary Air Pollution.[19] While the International Whaling Commission has been in existence since 1948, that regime, and even the very rationale for its existence, has been fundamentally transformed through the work of environmental NGO's like Greenpeace.[20] The United Nations Environment Programme (UNEP) has probably been the single greatest catalyst for environmental agreements since 1975, with its accomplishments ranging from its Regional Seas Programme with eleven action plans around the globe to the 1987 Montreal Protocol to protect the ozone layer. Though UNEP is, strictly speaking, a membership organization for states, it has developed an independent identity and has served as an important forum for nongovernmental organizations and other non-state actors. Finally, without the work of scientists, either as individuals or collectives, none of these agreements would have come about.[21]

If state-centric theories of regime initiation are off course for environmental issues, then those emphasizing the role of a hegemonic state are doubly misguided. What international-relations scholars refer to as the "theory of hegemonic stability" emerged in the late 1970s as an effort to explain the erosion of regimes in the world political economy as a function of the decline of American power.[22] Hegemonic decline allegedly leads to less international cooperation and fewer regimes. Without debating the validity of this theory with respect to political economy,[23] it clearly tells us very little about environmental regime formation. The recent period of intensive environmental regime-building, beginning in the mid-1970s, coincides with what most observers regard as a period of dwindling U.S.

hegemony.[24] Proponents of hegemonic stability theory have not claimed that the existence of a great power automatically produces extensive international cooperation—they claim merely that it is a necessary condition. But the timing of the recent increase in environmental regime formation casts doubt on this assertion.

There is no hegemonic power in international environmental politics. While U.S. leadership was important at the 1972 United Nations Conference on the Human Environment in Stockholm, which stimulated UNEP's formation and two generations of institution-building, the U.S. role has been more equivocal on many issues.[25] Consider the resistance of the U.S. to an acid rain agreement either bilaterally with Canada, or multilaterally as part of the European-based "30-percent Club" for reducing sulfur dioxide emissions.[26] More recently, the U.S. has blocked international agreement on targets for reducing greenhouse gas emissions.[27] These experiences suggest that major states may exercise veto power, even if they are not hegemonic. This is not to deny that large countries sometimes play important entrepreneurial leadership roles.[28] The efforts of France, particularly through its environmental ministry, were important in bringing about and implementing pollution controls under the Mediterranean Action Plan.[29] Similarly, the U.S., through its Environmental Protection Agency, was a catalyst in the 1987 Montreal Protocol.[30]

Furthermore, in those limited instances when regimes are initiated by nation-states, those states are far more likely to be "victim states" than "hegemonic powers." For instance, small island states like the Maldives have been among the most vocal advocates of a global warming agreement to forestall a rise in the world's sea levels.[31] Sweden and Canada come to mind in the case of acid rain.[32] Environmental destruction is particularly apt to galvanize national concern when the resources at stake have important cultural or symbolic value, like the Muskoka Lakes-Haliburton Highlands Region of Ontario, Canada and the Black Forest of Germany, both of which were casualties of acid rain.[33] Obviously, countries are most likely to speak out when they believe that their vital interests are at risk, lending support to interest-based explanations of regime formation.

The Social Construction of Knowledge and Interests

Approaches based upon rational-choice assumptions, however, mistakenly accept interests as straightforward.[34] This is especially misleading for environmental issues, where the very existence of a problem may be doubted and its true magnitude may not emerge for years to come. As such problems expand across space and time, experts are increasingly called upon to help states define their interests. For some environmental problems, such as marine pollution and management of international fisheries, the primary interactions are among technical experts. For others, like ozone depletion in the 1970s and global warming more recently, substantial disagreement may exist among scientists regarding predictions of environmental degradation and the probable impact on human society.[35]

Large-scale environmental problems are science-driven, but this does not mean that they necessarily lend themselves to political consensus. In fact, knowledge itself is a potential source of conflict, particularly when major interests are at stake in the face of unresolved scientific uncertainties. And knowledge production is a contentious process, especially when associated with "trans-scientific" problems straddling the border between science and policy.[36] Even with a relatively narrow range of scientific uncertainty, nations can easily interpret the available knowledge according to their perceived interests. During the Montreal Protocol negotiations, for instance, the principal adversaries based their positions on the same scientific assessment, a report which concluded that few uncertainties remained with respect to the science of ozone depletion.[37] Nonetheless, the European Communities (E.C.) argued for only a freeze on CFC production, while the U.S. proposed a 95-percent phaseout. Even when scientists are outspoken and unified in their policy recommendations, as they have been on the global warming issue, political action may be blocked. The demand for knowledge empowers new actors on the scene, and may even generate new regimes, but the problems remain inescapably political.

One key factor in determining how interests are conceived is the time frame employed. Most environmental problems will outlast the policymakers charged with addressing them. Getting politicians, whose temporal horizons rarely extend beyond the next election, to adopt an intergenerational perspective can be no easy trick. Convincing bureaucrats may not be much easier. In the short run, environmental protection inevitably affects some interests negatively. Even within governments with relatively robust environmental programs, some players will object; likely opponents include budget offices, the military, and commerce departments; industries targeted for regulation will complain most loudly. Thus, the interest in environmental protection is not an obvious one, and it frequently depends upon the adoption of a long-term perspective.

Because national interests are unclear, conflict arises at the intra-governmental level over whose definition will prevail. The state no longer appears as a unitary actor making rational decisions, but is splintered into competing bureaucratic and economic interests, particularly for the most far-reaching environmental problems. The interagency "minuet" over the U.S. strategy in the ozone negotiations, for instance, pales in comparison to the virtual warfare that has characterized the climate change problem.[38] Because scientific and technical knowledge are crucial factors in determining how interests are defined, there is also competition among agencies for who will frame and interpret that knowledge. Domestic and international policies become inextricably linked, so that traditionally domestic agencies, such as energy and environment ministries, emerge as important international actors. The levels of analysis, from subnational to national and international, blur as the state and its interests are increasingly problematized.

To characterize interests as engendered purely within the state, however, would be a gross oversimplification. Rarely has a nation taken the lead in preserving the global environment without substantial pressure from social movements and other non-state actors, whether from within or without. Consider the role of Greenpeace and other groups in stopping the slaughter of whales and, more recently, dolphins; or the work of the Canadian Acid Rain Coalition in both the U.S. and Canada; or the role of the West German Green Party in reversing West German Federal Republic, and even European Community, environmental policies during the 1980s. The pivitol role of knowledge in defining interests also works to the advantage of non-state actors. Once information becomes public, it resembles a collective good in that it is available to whoever would use it. Knowledge can help social movements become key international players, as did the National Resources Defense Council in its bid to monitor superpower compliance with a nuclear test ban.[39] Movements do not need their own costly research programs to be influential; with sufficient technical expertise to interpret existing studies in light of their own values, they can gain access to the media and other sources of political influence.

The ability of scientific knowledge to foster environmental action can be greatly enhanced by the emergence of an apparent crisis. The more sudden, visible, and dramatic the shock, the more likely it is to precipitate international action. The 1986 Chernobyl disaster and the ensuing negotiations to update the nuclear accident regime under the auspices of the International Atomic Energy Agency (IAEA) are a case in point.[40] Visibility may be crucial in order for an environmental disaster to inspire international regime-building. For instance, two giant oil spills in the late 1960s, one from the grounded *Torrey Canyon* off the British coast and the other from an oil well run amok near Santa Barbara, California, led to a complete revision of the regimes governing marine pollution—even though almost all oil pollution at sea comes from routine operations, with less than 5 percent of it generated from accidents.[41]

Moreover, an event not identified by scientists as an environmental disaster may nonetheless produce an atmosphere of crisis. The Antarctic ozone hole, discovered just before the Montreal Protocol negotiations, was not predicted by any of the atmospheric models and had not been conclusively linked to CFCs, so negotiators explicitly agreed to ignore it during their deliberations.[42] Yet there is little doubt that it was a major factor in determining the context and the eventual outcome of the negotiations. Similarly, the discovery of massive forest death in Central Europe during the early 1980s led to the signing in 1985 of the sulfur dioxide protocol by twenty-one countries, even though the dieback had not been conclusively linked to acid rain—and the less visible damage to Scandinavian lakes had been so linked years before.[43] Thus, a dramatic event may even circumvent the received knowledge in stimulating political action.

The apparent importance of crises for catalyzing environmental regime change bodes poorly for those problems of a more gradual and cumulative nature. This observation is particularly alarming because the damage associated with these problems is often irreversible. Consider the loss of global biodiversity. During the last quarter of this century, as many as one million species may become extinct—an average of one hundred extinctions daily.[44] Yet this profound ecological degradation could go virtually unnoticed by an urbanized humanity. Likewise, the steady disappearance of the tropical rainforests, home to the bulk of Earth's species, is nearly invisible to most people. Global warming is another creeping problem, one that is unlikely to produce a dramatic crisis until it is too late. A few hot summers and other climate disturbances may temporarily sound the alarms, but the return of apparently normal weather may put the brakes on any movement toward international regime construction.[45]

Trends in Regime Structure and Content

Not only have the past two decades witnessed a dramatic increase in the number of negotiated environmental regimes, but there have also been significant changes in the actors involved, the issues covered, and the norms and principles expressed in them. Existing institutions may still be inadequate to forestall future ecological crises. But recent environmental regime-building does express an acutely needed broadening of spatial and temporal horizons. These changes reflect a growing recognition of the globalization of ecological interdependencies.

While the involvement of new kinds of non-state actors in environmental regimes represents an important development, the number of nations party to such treaties has increased greatly, a trend reflecting the geographical globalization of environmental politics. International environmental agreements date back to the commissions set up in the mid-nineteenth century to govern such bodies of water as the Rhine and the Danube Rivers.[46] Around the turn of the century, conservation efforts resulted in a wave of treaties protecting migratory wildlife.[47] Until recently, though, most agreements have been bilateral or have covered only small regions. Those agreements with a larger geographical scope, such as the 1911 Fur Seal Convention and the 1946 Whaling Convention, were generally limited to controlling over-exploitation of particular species. Since the 1970s, however, agreements have tended to be multilateral, covering increasingly extensive geographical regions. Most countries, for instance, participate in at least one of UNEP's Regional Seas Programmes. Countries of the European Community are standardizing their environmental regulations, so that in the near future they will be governed by the same regimes in all activities affecting the environment.[48] Despite a rough start in the 1970s, CITES has evolved into a global treaty, with eighty-seven parties as of 1985.[49] The Montreal Protocol, the first global agreement to regulate specific chemicals, was ratified by sixty-five countries as of 1990.[50]

In addition to an expanded spatial perspective, recent environmental institution-building exhibits a temporal reorientation from a compensatory approach toward a preventive approach. Under the 1941 Trail Smelter Arbitration, still the most prominent case in international environmental law,[51] a state is entitled to compensation for actual damages caused by foreign activities, but cannot prevent those activities in advance. Yet many regimes negotiated since the 1970s have institutionalized preventive measures, particularly as concerns have shifted from overexploitation to pollution. Examples of treaties devoted to preventing marine pollution include the 1972 London and Oslo Dumping Conventions, the 1973 Convention for the Prevention of Pollution from Ships, and various components of UNEP's Regional Seas Programme.[52] Since the causes of the Antarctic ozone hole were not known during the negotiations, the Montreal Protocol may also be considered a preventive agreement. According to Richard Benedick, chief negotiator for the United States, that treaty was "based at the time not on measurable evidence of ozone depletion or increased radiation but rather on scientific hypotheses, [and] required an unprecedented amount of foresight."[53]

The shift to a more future-oriented outlook is also evident in the plethora of monitoring and informational regimes launched over the past two decades. In some cases, as in the World Weather Watch,[54] this has simply involved strengthening existing informational regimes, which may also entail a shift in their purposes and activities. In other cases, particularly those associated with UNEP, important new networks have been established. UNEP's INFOTERRA network, considered the world's "most advanced operational international information referral system," provides policymakers from all parts of the globe with sources of environmental information.[55] The Global Environmental Monitoring System (GEMS), affiliated with the World Meteorological Organization (WMO) and UNEP, is "the most comprehensive non-military monitoring system in existence."[56] Strong international ties within the scientific community have laid the foundation for ICSU's mammoth International Geosphere-Biosphere Program (IGBP), modeled after the highly successful International Geophysical Year in 1957.[57] Research generated by the IGBP will lay the basis for future global ecological regimes.

In some cases, what has begun as an informational regime under an umbrella convention leads to a more stringent control regime. This was the case with the 1985 Vienna Convention, which led to the Montreal Protocol, as well as with most agreements negotiated under UNEP's Regional Seas Programme. A few informational regimes, however, are not even successful in accomplishing their limited objectives; the 1978 Amazon Pact, for instance, contained provisions for the exchange of scientific and technical data which were not implemented in the pact's first ten years.[58]

Some environmental regimes are flexible instruments, designed to incorporate new scientific knowledge as it becomes available. Because of the causal uncertainties about the Antarctic ozone hole in 1987, the Open-Ended Working Group for the Montreal Protocol was established to recommend treaty revisions in light of new knowledge.[59] Likewise, parties to CITES convene biannually to revise the list of endangered species. Thus, in their institutional structure, these agreements resemble the General Agreement on Tariffs and Trade (GATT), the international trade regime in which an enduring agreement on certain basic principles can be periodically adapted to new circumstances.

Perhaps the most important institutional development is a philosophical shift in the constitutive principles of recent environmental regimes. With the dramatic post-World War II increase in population and technological pressures, resources formerly perceived as vast or even unlimited are now seen as scarce and endangered. Consequently, the principles of open access and free use that formerly governed the global commons, i.e., the oceans, the atmosphere, and outer space, have proven themselves inadequate to the point that "tragedy of the commons" has become virtually a household term.

Two very different solutions present themselves, both of which have been adopted in recent regimes: national and international management. The Third U.N. Conference on the Law of the Seas (UNCLOS), for instance, embodies both approaches. The extension of territorial waters from the traditional three miles to a two hundred mile Exclusive Economic Zone (EEZ) rests on the supposition that nations will manage their coastal waters with more foresight than prevailed under the "freedom of the seas" regime. Although a nation's activities within its EEZ are restricted, so that the regime "involves states in their own self-government,"[60] in essence the EEZ represents simply a geographical expansion of the nation-state system.

The second approach to governance of the nonterrestrial commons, international management, is more innovative, but it remains to be seen both how effective and how enduring that strategy will be. The proposed International Seabed Authority (ISA), also established at the 1982 UNCLOS, is perhaps the most ambitious attempt at international management of a global commons. The ISA, intended to oversee the mining of manganese nodules in the deep sea, attempts to institutionalize the principle that certain resources are "the common heritage of mankind." The common heritage doctrine, first applied to the world's oceans by the Maltese U.N. Ambassador

Arvid Pardo in 1967, has its roots in the 1959 Antarctic Treaty and the 1967 Outer Space Treaty, both of which refer to their respective domains as "the province of mankind." [61] Although this principle was never fully applied to the world's oceans, it did inform the 1972 Seabed Treaty prohibiting nuclear weapons on the seabed, as well as the later ISA proposal. [62] In its most radical form, the common heritage doctrine suggests that national sovereignty is obsolete as a way of managing the global environment, particularly in light of its disregard for future generations, and that it should be superseded by a new norm of planetary stewardship. At present, the common heritage doctrine remains a rather abstract and lofty ideal. [63]

Because they are evolving, the underlying norms and principles embedded in international environmental institutions are not always clear. Even when there is agreement on a principle, there can be considerable disagreement over how to apply it. Consider the ozone fund, established in 1990 to help developing countries switch to nondepleting chemicals. Developing countries point out that the industrialized world is the source of the problem in making their case that the fund simply institutionalizes the well-recognized polluter-pays principle. Yet some critics in industrialized countries view the fund as a reversal of that principle, for it compels nations that are potential victims of developing countries' pollution to absorb the costs. For these countries, the fund is "a bribe to discourage free-riding." [64] The same opposing perceptions apply to the proposed World Atmosphere Fund, which would assist in the transfer of technology to developing countries to limit greenhouse gases and would be many times larger.

An important question is raised by this discussion: how do new norms in international society come to be institutionalized? One likely possibility is through something like the process by which "soft law" becomes "hard law" on the international scene. UNEP has become rather adept at guiding nations through the process of first establishing a framework (or "umbrella") convention that recognizes the existence of an environmental problem and facilitates information-sharing, subsequently adding actual control measures. UNEP used this format in its Regional Seas Programme and in the ozone negotiations. Soft law is more acceptable than hard law for countries that are jealously guarding their ability to make sovereign decisions. [65]

The danger, however, is that regime formation may go no farther than a declaration of intent or an agreement to share information, in which case there is no new regime since actors' behavior remains unchanged. The World Conservation Strategy, an agreement adopted by more than seventy countries to preserve genetic diversity, may well go that route. The 1979 European Convention on the Long Range Transportation of Air Pollution, heralded at the time as a landmark agreement, only established a consensus that acid rain could pose an environmental hazard. We will not know whether the treaty has any teeth until the year 1993, when the convention's protocol reducing sulfur dioxide emissions by 30 percent is due to take effect.

It would be a mistake, however, not to look beyond the interactions of nation-states and international organizations to document the institutionalization of new environmental norms and practices. In the absence of pressure from social movements, nations might never move beyond vague declarations of intent. Moreover, organizations based in one country can use the actions of other nations to pressure their own governments into adopting stronger environmental measures. The moral authority that comes from setting a good example often leaves less responsible nations politically isolated. When combined with pressure from social movements, this sense of isolation can prompt countries to act. Consider, for instance, Japan's whaling practices; or policy shifts by the U.K., and later the U.S., on acid rain controls; or, more recently, Brazil's efforts to slow deforestation. In each case, a nation that was slow to enact certain policies was persuaded, at least in part, by pressures from abroad to modify its practices.

In the most general terms, the primary reason that so many principles and declarations of intent go unfulfilled is that environmental regimes are embedded in other social, political, and economic institutions. Although treated as such, the environment is not really a separate domain, but a cross-cutting aspect of every sector. All institutions partake of environmental regimes, albeit typically of the tacit sort, in that they have environmental consequences. Most obviously, environmental damage is a side-effect of economic activity or, as economists call it, an "externality." [66] Certain activities that are intrinsic to contemporary life, particularly in the industrialized countries, are inherently destructive. As mentioned earlier, for instance, almost all oil pollution from tankers comes from routine practices.

Furthermore, contemporary economic institutions are virtually guaranteed to contribute to the destruction of the environment. Consider the postwar trade regime under GATT. The priority given to creating a liberal trade order means that national pollution controls can be restricted on the grounds that they present non-tariff barriers to trade, both in industry and agriculture.[67] Likewise, a strong argument can be made that environmental abuse has been institutionalized in the major international development organs. Although the primary sources of development funding, including the World Bank, signed an agreement in 1981 to integrate environmental factors into their lending practices, many projects have failed to do so.[68] Without important changes in the dominant economic institutions, the prognosis for the future may not be much better. The Brundtland Report, which will figure prominently in the 1992 U.N. Conference on Environment and Development, has popularized the term "sustainable development."[69] Yet that report proposes a five-fold increase in the gross world product through major influxes of capital, with no major revisions in the world's economic institutions.[70]

Another set of tensions exists between environmental and political institutions, particularly pertaining to the central institution of national sovereignty. This tension is starkly evident in Principle 21 of the Stockholm Declaration of the 1972 U.N. Conference of the Human Environment, which reflects an attempt to insert a new norm of environmental responsibility into international relations. According to Principle 21, states have "the sovereign right to exploit their own resources pursuant to their own environmental policies and the responsibility to ensure that activities within their jurisdiction or control do not cause damage to the environment of other States or of areas beyond the limits of national jurisdiction."[71]

The first part of the principle reflects a conventional understanding of national sovereignty, whereas the second half is broad enough to encompass the common-heritage doctrine. Given existing institutions, only sovereign states can solve international environmental problems, yet in order to do so they must sacrifice some of their sovereignty. Perhaps the conception of national sovereignty could be broadened to include not just rights, but responsibilities.[72] Indeed, this appears to be one of the primary, if unstated, goals of the environmental movement.

Rather than attempting to restructure fundamental political and economic institutions, recent environmental regimes represent a piecemeal approach to global ecological interdependence. The idea that an expanding network of regimes, each oriented to a relatively narrow task, might collectively lay the basis for a more comprehensive approach, is not new to the study of world politics. So-called 'functionalist' theories saw similar potential in the growth of economic interconnections after World War II.[73] Yet there is good reason to believe that current environmental regimes offer too little, too late.

Effectiveness of International Environmental Institutions

The ability of negotiated regimes to effectively deal with the problems that give rise to them is constrained by the degree of compliance they enjoy, but even with full compliance a regime may not go far enough. Although substantial research has been done on compliance with international agreements concerning arms control, trade, and human rights, there is almost no work on compliance with international environmental accords.[74] However, some general observations can be made. Environmental treaties share some compliance problems with treaties in general: they tend to lack formal enforcement mechanisms; they may never be ratified; and they may be implemented by a different national administration than that of the negotiators. There are also some distinctive problems with environmental agreements, including the decentralized nature of the activities involved, and the inability of small states, whose environmental regulatory programs are often meager, to monitor and enforce them. Consider the difficulties involved in implementing the revised Montreal Protocol, which calls for a ban on CFC's by 1996; bear in mind that this is a relatively centralized industrial activity.

Despite the many opportunities for noncompliance, there are also some important factors that may promote compliance. To some extent, agreements are self-enforcing. The fear of retaliatory linkage, for example, can be a strong incentive for cooperation and compliance.[75] Moreover, national governments face inward toward their domestic constituencies, not just outward to the international arena, so that countries with influential environmental movements may have an additional incentive for compliance. In the long run, a powerful source of compliance may be concern for reputation, which also motivates some nations to act in the first place. Of course, until stronger environmental norms become more universally adopted, concern for reputation is unlikely to be the most important factor in guaranteeing compliance.

The mere existence of an agreement, even with full compliance, says nothing about its ability to tackle a problem. The Montreal Protocol, for instance, is considered a far-reaching agreement. Yet even with full compliance under the new revisions, another ten billion tons of CFC's will be emitted into the atmosphere—an amount equal to half of all production historically.[76] The strongest indictment of existing institutions comes from the recognition that, despite the flurry of institution-building over the past two decades, the quality of the global environment has degenerated over the same period.[77] If we are to be honest with ourselves, environmental quality must be the principal measure of effectiveness.

Despite the apparent ineffectiveness of international environmental institutions, they may be important in other ways. First, current regimes have at least increased both the quantity and the dispersion of information. Thanks to these cooperative arrangements for information sharing, more people can hope to learn about environmental degradation sooner than they would have otherwise. The social empowerment that could evolve from this proliferation and diffusion of knowledge may eventually lead to more effective environmental institutions. Second, the transgovernmental networks that have been formed since the 1970s may prove useful for establishing more far-reaching agreements in the future. Finally, given the magnitude of the environmental problems we are likely to confront in the future, existing regimes have an important symbolic value in that they help counteract the sense of helplessness we might otherwise feel.

Conclusion

One question that inevitably arises is whether conventional political institutions are being transformed to address humanity's recent emergence as "a large-scale geologic force."[78] A possible source of change might be found in the growing prevalence of non-state actors in transnational environmental regime-building. Yet nation-states remain the only parties to agreements; NGO's can at best prod their governments into agreements and monitor their compliance later. Another possibility is that certain principles, like the common heritage doctrine, could represent the emergence of new global environmental norms. But, as mentioned above, such principles are largely limited to the realm of soft law. There may be good reason, then, to conclude that global environmental institutions will function in a way that is analogous to national intervention in market economies, tending to reform yet bolster existing institutions.[79] Nothing is surprising about this; social structures seem to have an inherent tendency to reproduce themselves.[80]

Such an interpretation would, however, miss much of what is new and interesting in global environmental institution-building. While the nation-state system may remain at center stage, it is clearly being pulled simultaneously in many directions. To speak of a world of unitary national actors with precisely defined interests coming together to negotiate environmental regimes on the basis of their mutual interests is simplistic to the point of distortion. Social movements and scientists have emerged as core participants in all phases of the process, from placing issues on the agenda to monitoring compliance with agreements. The knowledge-based nature of environmental problems has opened up the playing field to a profusion of unconventional players. New time frames and spatial horizons are being introduced in international politics, even if they are not always adhered to. New norms and principles are being suggested in a global arena, even if they are rarely institutionalized.

What is remarkable about the emergence of this multicentric world of non-state actors is that it has occurred within the realm of ordinary international practices—alongside the state-centric system. There are convincing reasons, then, to believe that the two worlds may coexist and continue to interact in complex ways.

Nonetheless, experience in environmental regime-building warrants a healthy skepticism about whether the nation-state system can smoothly adapt to ecological interdependence via traditional forms of multilateral, state-centric institutions. Non-state actors, particularly scientists and social movements, are key in all phases, from regime construction to implementation. And with them come new norms, which challenge the principles of sovereignty and territorial exclusivity that define the nation-state system. Whether these challenges are great enough to undermine the existing system is a question that only time can answer.

NOTES

1. For a history of proposals to transcend the nation-state system, ranging from the postwar world government movement to the functionalist supranationalism of the 1970s, see Wesley T. Wooley, *Alternatives to Anarchy: American Supranationalism since World War II* (Bloomington: Indiana University Press, 1988).

2. Raymond Vernon, *Sovereignty at Bay: The Multinational Spread of U.S. Enterprises* (New York: Basic Books, 1971).

3. See Richard Falk, *This Endangered Planet: Prospects and Proposals for Human Survival* (New York: Random House, 1971).

4. Kenneth Oye ed., *Cooperation Under Anarchy* (Princeton: Princeton University Press, 1986).

5. James N. Rosenau, *Turbulence in World Politics: A Theory of Change and Continuity* (Princeton: Princeton University Press, 1990), chap. 10.

6. Charles William Maynes, "To Save the Earth From Human Ruin, Enact New World Laws of Geo-Ecology," *Los Angeles Times*, September 4, 1988, p. V-6.

7. See Dennis Pirages, "Environmental Security and Social Evolution," *International Studies Notes* 16 no. 1 (Winter 1991): 8–12.

8. Rosenau, *Turbulence in World Politics*, p. 249.

9. Rosenau, op.cit, pp. 245–46; see also Robert O. Keohane, *After Hegemony: Cooperation and Discord in the World Political Economy* (Princeton: Princeton University Press, 1984).

10. Konrad von Moltke, "International Commissions and Implementation of International Environmental Law," in John E. Carroll ed., *International Environmental Diplomacy: The Management and Resolution of Transfrontier Environmental Problems* (Cambridge: Cambridge University Press, 1988).

11. For a meta-theoretical analysis of institutions and social structure, see Anthony Giddens, *The Constitution of Society: Outline of the Theory of Structuration* (Berkeley: University of California Press, 1984), 16–37.

12. Oran R. Young, *International Cooperation: Building Regimes for Natural Resources and the Environment* (Ithaca: Cornell University Press, 1989), p. 32. For a similar definition, see Robert O. Keohane *After Hegemony*, p. 246.

13. Stephen D. Krasner ed., *International Regimes* (Ithaca, NY: Cornell University Press, 1983), p. 2.

14. See Krasner, *International Regimes*; Keohane *After Hegemony*; Peter Cowhey, "The International Telecommunications Regime," *International Organization* 44 no. 2 (Spring 1990): 169–200; Charles Lipson, "International Cooperation in Economic and Security Affairs," *World Politics* 37 no. 1 (Winter 1984): 1–23.

15. Krasner, *International Regimes*, p. 8. Friedrich Kratochwil argues persuasively that security institutions, from deterrence to warfare, are indeed norm-governed practices which rely upon a shared universe of signification for their proper functioning; see his *Rules, Norms, and Decisions: On the Conditions of Practical and Legal Reasoning in International Relations and Domestic Affairs* (Cambridge: Cambridge University Press, 1989).

16. The most widely cited proponent of the first viewpoint is Charles Kindleberger. See his *The World in Depression, 1929–1939* (Berkeley: University of California Press, 1973). For an illustration of the second perspective, see Robert O. Keohane, "The Theory of Hegemonic Stability and Changes in International Economic Regimes, 1976–77," in Ole Holsti *et. al., Changes in the International System* (Boulder, CO: Westview, 1980).

17. For examples of the latter see Charles Lipson, "The Transformation of Trade: The sources and Effects of Regime Change" and Arthur A. Stein, "Coordination and Collaboration: Regimes in an Anarchic World," both in Krasner, *International Regimes*.

18. See Simon Lyster, *International Wildlife Law* (Cambridge: Grotius Publications Limited, 1985).

19. Gregory S. Wetstone, "A History of the Acid Rain Issue," in H. Brooks and C. Cooper eds., *Science for Public Policy* (Oxford: Pergamon Press, 1987), pp. 163–196.

20. See Lyster, *International Wildlife Law*; also, J. Scarff, "The International Management of Whales, Dolphins, and Porpoises: An Interdisciplinary Assessment," *Ecology Law Quarterly* 6 no. 2 (1977): 343–52.

21. David Edwards, "Review of the Status of Implementation and Development of Regional Arrangements on Cooperation in Combating Marine Pollution," in Carroll, *International Environmental Diplomacy*; U.N.Environment Programme, *Action on Ozone* (Nairobi: UNEP, 1989).

22. Robert Gilpin, *U.S. Power and the Multinational Corporation: The Political Economy of Direct Foreign Investment* (New York: Basic Books, 1975); W. P. Avery and D. P. Rankin eds., *America in a Changing World Political Economy* (New York: Longman, 1982).

23. For some critiques of hegemonic stability theory, see Keohane, *After Hegemony*; Peter Cowhey and Edward Long, "Testing Theories of Regime Change: Hegemonic Decline or Surplus Capacity?" *International Organization* 37 no. 2 (Spring 1984): 5–22; and Duncan Snidal, "The Limits of Hegemonic Stability Theory," *International Organization* 39 no. 4 (Autumn 1985): 581–614.

24. For an opposing perspective, see Bruce Russett, "The Mysterious Case of Vanishing Hegemony; or, Is Mark Twain Really Dead?" *International Organization* 39 no. 2 (Spring 1985): 207–231.

25. Allen L. Springer, "United States Environmental Policy and International Law: Stockholm Principle 21 Revisited," in Carroll, *International Environmental Diplomacy*, pp. 45–66.

26. James L. Regens and Robert W. Rycroft, *The Acid Rain Controversy* (Pittsburgh: University of Pittsburgh Press, 1988).

27. "U.S. View Prevails at Climate Parley," *New York Times*, November 8, 1990, p. A9; "Bush Assailed Over Global Warming," *Los Angeles Times*, February 6, 1991, p. I-5.

28. See Oran Young, "The Politics of International Regime Formation: Managing Natural Resources and the Environment" *International Organization* 43 no. 3 (Summer 1989): 373–74.

29. Peter Haas, "Do Regimes Matter? Epistemic Communities and Mediterranean Pollution Control" *International Organization* 43 no. 3 (Summer 1989): 395–97.

30. The prominence of national environmental agencies in constructing certain regimes suggests that the state should not be viewed as a monolithic

entity, but rather should be decomposed into its constituent parts, as a bureaucratic politics perspective would maintain.

31. Maumoon Abdul Gayoom, President of the Maldives, speech before the U.N. General Assembly, New York, October 19, 1987.

32. See Wetstone, "History of the Acid Rain Issue," and Amin Rosencranz, "The Acid Rain Controversy in Europe and North America: A Political Analysis," in Carroll, *International Environmental Diplomacy*

33. John E. Carroll, "The Acid Rain Issue in Canadian-American Relations: A commentary," in Carroll, *International Environmental Diplomacy*, p. 145.

34. Stephen Krasner distinguishes between the dominant utilitarian, choice-theoretic approaches in the social sciences, and institutionalism, which looks at how social structures define the identities of individuals and their patterns of interaction. See his "Sovereignty: An Institutional Perspective," in James Caporaso ed., *The Elusive State: International and Comparative Perspectives* (Newbury Park, CA: Sage Publications, 1989). My own analysis proceeds from the second approach.

35. R. Michael M'Gonigle and Mark W. Zacher, *Pollution, Politics, and International Law: Tankers at Sea* (Berkeley: University of California Press, 1979); Douglas M. Johnston, "Marine Pollution Agreements: Successes and Problems," in Carroll, *International Environmental Diplomacy*, pp. 199–206; Barbara Johnson, "Technocrats and the Management of International Fisheries," *International Organization* 29 (Summer 1975): 745–770; see also Lydia Dotto and Harold Schiff, *The Ozone War* (New York: Doubleday, 1978), and Intergovernmental Panel on Climate Change, *IPCC First Assessment Report* (Geneva: World Meteorological Organization, 1990).

36. Alvin Weinberg, "Science and Trans-science," *Minerva* 10 no. 2 (April 1972).

37. WMO/NASA, *Atmospheric Ozone 1985* (Washington, D.C.: NASA, 1986).

38. See Richard E. Benedick, *Ozone Diplomacy: New Directions in Safeguarding the Planet* (Cambridge: Harvard University Press, 1991), chap. 5. For some insight into U.S. interagency debates on global warming, see the GAO Report, "Global Warming: Administration Approach Cautious Pending Validation of Threat," January 1990.

39. "U.S. Group Can Study Soviet A-Test," *New York Times*, December 20, 1986, p. A8.

40. See Young, *International Cooperation*, chap. 6.

41. M'Gonigle and Zacher, *Pollution, Politics*, pp. 5, 17.

42. U.N. Environment Programme, *Ad Hoc Working Group of Legal and Technical Experts for the Elaboration of a Global Framework Convention for the Protection of the Ozone Layer* (UNEP/WG.148/3, p. 15).

43. For an accessible review of the science of acid rain, see Volker A. Mohnen, "The Challenge of Acid Rain," *Scientific American* 259 no. 2 (August 1988): 30–38.

44. Norman Myers, *The Sinking Ark: A New Look at the Problem of Disappearing Species* (Elmsford, NY: Pergamon Press, 1979), p. 31.

45. The First World Climate Conference in Toronto occurred fortuitously during the very hot summer of 1988. The extreme temperatures and drought in Europe and North America suddenly made global warming seem credible to many. According to one prominent climatologist, "The irony is that a solid case of good physics had been given too little credibility for 15 years, whereas one, essentially random, hot event in 1988 has perhaps given us too much credibility." Stephen Schneider, "Doing Something About the Weather," *World Monitor*, December 1988, p. 35.

46. H. Bourne, "International Law and Pollution of International Rivers and Lakes," *University of British Columbia Law Review* 6 (1971), p. 115.

47. See Lyster, *International Wildlife Law*, pp. 62–66.

48. "The Environment in Europe," *Bulletin of the Institute for European Environmental Policy* 37 (November 1986).

49. Lyster, op cit., pp. 240–41.

50. Friends of the Earth, *Atmosphere* 3 (October 1990), p. 7.

51. Springer, "U.S. Environmental Policy," pp. 47–48.

52. Robert J. McManus, "Ocean Dumping: Standards in Action," in David Kay and Harold Jacobson eds., *Environmental Protection: The International Dimension* (Totowa, NJ: Allanheld, Osmun & Company, 1983), pp. 119–139; and Alan B. Sielen and Robert J. McManus, "IMCO and the Politics of Ship Pollution," in Kay and Jacobson, pp. 140–183.

53. Richard E. Benedick, "Ozone Diplomacy," *Issues in Science and Technology* 6 no. 1 (Fall 1989): 43–50. The extent to which the Montreal Protocol was truly a preventive agreement is debatable. A few observations showed some total global ozone loss since 1980. (See Testimony of James Hansen and Sherwood Rowland, Hearings before the Senate Subcommittee on Environmental Pollution, Committee on Environment and Public Works, June 10 and 11, 1986.) Benedick himself used these uncertain measurements to sway his fellow negotiators. In one speech, he declared that "both satellite and land-based measurements suggest that the process of ozone destruction may already be underway." (See *Current Policy*, No. 931, Department of State, February 23, 1987).

54. See Seymour Brown et. al., *Regimes for the Ocean, Outer Space, and Weather* (Washington, D.C.: The Brookings Institution, 1977), pp. 235–36. WWW has moved from simply observing and forecasting short-term local weather conditions to monitoring for global climate change.

55. Anthony J. Dolman, *Resources, Regimes, World Order* (New York: Pergamon Press, 1981), p. 17.

56. ibid., p. 17.

57. National Research Council, *Toward an Understanding of Global Change: Initial Priorities for U.S. Contributions to the International Geosphere-Biosphere Program* (Washington, D.C.: National Academy Press, 1988).

58. Erwan Fourere, "Emerging Trend in International Environmental Agreements," in Carroll *International Environmental Diplomacy*, pp. 29–44.

59. For a description of the revision process, see Benedick, *Ozone Diplomacy*, chap. 11.

60. John Gerard Ruggie, "International Structure and International Transformation: Space, Time, and Method," in Ernst-Otto Czempiel and James N. Rosenau, *Global Changes and Theoretical Challenges: Approaches to World Politics for the 1990s* (Lexington, MA: Lexington Books, 1989), p. 23.

61. Brown et. al., *Regimes*, p. 129.

62. With the U.S. rejection of the ISA, the Law of the Sea Treaty (and with it the common heritage doctrine) have yet to be fully implemented. Although the common heritage doctrine received much attention at the 1992 U.N. conference on environment and development, it was not institutionalized in any of the agreements adopted there.

63. For a discussion of the difficulties involved in institutionalizing the common heritage doctrine in international law, Patricia Birnie, "The Role of International Law in Solving Certain Environmental Conflicts," in Carroll *International Environmental Diplomacy*, pp. 95–122.

64. *The Economist*, June 16, 1990, p. 20.

65. Peter H. Sand, "The Vienna Convention is Adopted," *Environment* 27 no. 5 (June 1985): 19–45. While soft law does not entail any material obligations on the part of the signatories, it can still be very important in establishing certain expectations.

66. The term itself suggests that environmental considerations take a back seat to immediate economic objectives. On the economic theory of externalities, see E.J. Mishan, "The Postwar Literature on Externalities," *Journal of Economic Literature* 9 (1967): 21–24.

67. For a critique of the most recent Uruguay Round of trade negotiations, see the special GATT issue, *The Ecologist* 20 no. 6 (November-December 1990).

68. Henning and Mangun, pp. 297–98.

69. World Commission on Environment and Development, *Our Common Future* (Cambridge: Oxford University Press, 1987).

70. For critical review of *Our Common Future*, see Larry Lohmann, "Whose Common Future?" *The Ecologist* 20 no. 3 (May–June 1990): 82–84.

71. *Report of the United Nations Stockholm Conference on the Human Environment*, UN Doc.A/Conf.48/14 (1972).

72. Michael Manley, ex-premier of Jamaica, quoted in Dolman, *Resources, Regimes, World Order*, p. 197.

73. Functionalism has generally been applied to transnational economic cooperation, but environmental problems may fit the theory as well or better. See David Mitrany, *The Functional Theory of Politics* (London: Martin Robertson, 1975).

74. Harold K. Jacobson and Edith Brown Weiss plan to fill this gap. See

their paper, "Implementing and Complying with International Environmental Accords: A Framework for Research," presented at the 1990 Annual Meeting of the American Political Science Association, San Francisco.

75. This point has been demonstrated by Robert Axelrod through use of game-theoretic models, notably his model of an iterated Prisoner's Dilemma. Robert Axelrod, *The Evolution of Cooperation* (New York: Basic Books, 1984).

76. Friends of the Earth, *Atmosphere* 3 no. (October 1990), p. 6.

77. Norman Myers, "What Happened to Utopia?" *International Wildlife* 17 no. 4 (1987): 36–37; cited in Henning and Mangun, p. 290.

78. W. Vernadsky, "The Biosphere and the Noonsphere," *American Scientist* 33 (January 1945): 1–12, quoted in Lynton K. Caldwell, *Between Two Worlds: Science, the Environmental Movement, and Policy Choice* (New York: Cambridge University Press, 1990), p. 51.

79. This argument extends Ruggie's analysis of global informational regimes for the environment to environmental regimes in general. See John G. Ruggie, "On the Problem of 'The Global Problematique': What Roles for International Organizations" *Alternatives* 5 (1979–80): 517–550.

80. See Giddens, *The Constitution of Society.*

Act II

(RE) CONSTRUCTING THE GLOBAL ENVIRONMENT: GLOBAL ECOLOGICAL INTERDEPENDENCE AND POLITICAL CONTESTATION

Social facts, such as conflict, cannot be explained by natural
facts, such as the environment, but only by other social facts.
—Reidulf K. Molvær, "Environmentally Induced Conflicts?
A Discussion Based on Studies from the Horn of Africa,"
Bulletin of Peace Proposals 22 (1991):175–188.

If global environmental change is a physical reality, global ecological interdependence is a social construction. On one level it is a construction of the authors represented in this volume—a metaphor that helps us think about emerging global patterns of social relations. It is also, we would argue, a construction whose basic features can be seen on a far broader scale. The chapters in this section reflect, on a variety of social scales, actors who perceive the tensions between binding and fragmentation that we set out in chapter 1, and who respond accordingly.

These processes of social construction occur in response to the physical manifestations of environmental degradation, to be sure. But they also occur in response to a broad range of political, social, and economic institutions that link the local and the global. Such institutions include the political ordering of states and the social ordering of cultures; the activities of international organizations and transnational movements; and the ordinary and mundane practices of people, as they go about their daily lives. In our view, failure to recognize these two fundamental points—that different people and groups construct their understanding of the global environment in different ways, and that these competing processes of construction are mediated by a host of complex social institutions—lies at the heart of the "limits to growth" that we perceive in both the global-change literature and the emerging attempts to craft responses to global environmental problems.

To be sure, the terrain facing both academics and activists is new and uncertain: many environmental issues differ, fundamentally and dramatically, from the military and economic issues that have made up the traditional fare of international politics. The social and physical characteristics that form the core of many environmental problems—uncertainty, irreversibility, technical complexity, extended time horizons, thresholds, and path-dependence[1]—force us, at the very least, to re-examine the validity of traditional assumptions about actors, perceptions, interests, and relationships. And the poor fit among the borders of the world's ecological, political, cultural, and socioeconomic systems makes it difficult to trace cause-and-effect across social, spatial, and temporal levels. Scientists are increasingly recognizing land, oceans, atmosphere, and biota as part of a single system, coupled with human social systems in complex fashion. Many processes of environmental change are thus part of a complex interweaving of local, regional, and global cause-and-effect.[2]

Thus local environmental change can have global causes and consequences, in that local ecosystems are tied to socioeconomic systems of transnational extent through complex networks of exploitation, production, and exchange. While soil erosion is essentially a local phenomenon occurring simultaneously in many places across the planet, its causes (e.g., global-market pressures) and consequences (e.g., the impact on global food production and distribution) may be socially linked on a far broader scale.[3] Conversely, global environmental change can have local causes and consequences. Globally linked biogeophysical systems can aggregate local causes—such as the carbon-dioxide emissions of a multitude of factories, automobiles, and burning forests—and redistribute the consequences in completely new patterns that will vary dramatically with locale.

The complexity of these connections has produced competing uses of the term "global." Often, such competing uses simply reflect confusion or oversimplification of underlying physical mechanisms; the concept of "global" warming, for example, is really an aggregation and averaging of what will inevitably be highly variable local consequences, resulting from the sum of geographically and politically dispersed activities. In this case what is "global" is neither cause nor consequence, but the mechanism linking the two.

The chapters in this section, however, stress that competing uses and conceptions of the term "global" reflect not simply terminological confusion, but also competing processes of social construction. As the "tale of two forests" in chapter 1 illustrated, different actors (and analysts) take very different meanings from the idea of "global." Some find a material, technical meaning, in the sense of a global ecosystem; others stress the social sense of the term, and emphasize the role of international economic and political structures; and still others emphasize a cultural, value-oriented sense of planetary ethics and global society.

When manifest among the actors in the dramas themselves, these multiple conceptions of "global" help to produce what Ann Hawkins (chapter 9) describes as "contested ground." As the definition of the problem is globalized, such contestation is likely to intensify, if for no other reason than the broad distribution of causes and consequences over a large number of nation-states, geographic regions, societies, and cultures. How are these meanings constructed? Clearly, they are shaped by the ongoing competition for power among competing social groups. But they also arise from the struggle to define the foundation of knowledge and concepts that form the basis for such competition. Karen Litfin has argued elsewhere that "Environmental crises . . . are not just physical phenomena, they are informational phenomena." The very way in which a crisis is defined, or constructed, on the basis of knowledge and stories, comes to empower some actors over others.[4] Thus it is important to see the environmental "contests" among actors also as definitional struggles that in some sense prefigure the traditional politics of interest.

The chapters in this section thus address not only the material effects of global ecological interdependence but also the construction of political and social spheres of action within which response to those effects occurs. In chapter 6, Steve Breyman argues that the success of ecology movements depends on the effective mobilization of resources; he examines the role of one particularly crucial resource, namely knowledge, in both its technical and practical forms. Knowledge, according to Breyman, is not only of the instrumental type, necessary for devising technical solutions to environmental problems. Because they also tend to be repositories of a practical, operational, local knowledge, social movements have also been able to gain influence and control over resource management. To the extent that this latter point is acknowledged by policymakers, and put into practice, so-called global environmental problems become localized.

Barbara Jancar, in her chapter on the relationship among environmental politics, nationalism, and decentralization movements in the disintegration of the Soviet Union, shows how particular official definitions of permitted and prohibited political activity can lead to very unexpected outcomes. The roots of the Soviet environmental "movement" can be traced to the Khrushchev era, but it was only with the onset of glasnost and perestroika in 1985, and the nuclear disaster at Chernobyl, that the concept of environment became explicitly linked with nationalism and decentralization, providing an apparently "nonpolitical" basis for organizing against the Union. By offering a competing definition of political space—centered on environment, democracy, and nationalism—opposition movements were able to create conditions of "chaos," thus setting the stage for the new political entities that are just beginning to emerge.

Luther Gerlach, writing on drought in Minnesota, offers a very different picture of the social and political effects of global ecological interdependence. There we see how lack of rain placed stress on the delivery of resources, which led to official efforts to reallocate rights to water. The result was a messy, statewide social drama, acted out not only over which Minnesotans needed how much water and why, but also over the very meaning of "water" and "Minnesota." In effect, the drama *is* the politics; it is the key to working out the situation. Only by generating a shared understanding of roles within the political society that is Minnesota—something that legislative action or command-and-control agencies could never do—is it possible to get to the next step of defining entitlements.

In chapter 9, Ann Hawkins examines this process of "working out" on a larger social scale; she explores competing social constructions of the global environment, through an analysis of the politics surrounding the conceptualization of global climate change. Hawkins points out that while the politics of climate change reflect the traditional cleavages of North-versus-South, state-versus-citizen, and urban-versus-rural/indigenous, it also mirrors competing efforts to control the definition of global climate change. She cites three competing paradigms for global environmental "management," each of which empowers some actors and disempowers others. Given the degree of contestation facing the now-dominant "global" paradigm, Hawkins raises serious doubts about the prospects of that paradigm succeeding in practice.

Ronnie Lipschutz and Judith Mayer look more closely at the process of working out roles, stakes, and rules where resources are concerned. Their focus is more general than in the chapters by Ger-lach or Hawkins; they present a framework for understanding how political and social contestation for entitlements is an ongoing, and sometimes highly theatrical and orchestrated, process. They argue that struggles over resources are not merely distributive ones; they are also challenges to the state's authority to define property rights. By acting within a larger cultural and social sphere, activist move-ments as diverse as Redwood Summer and the Brazilian Rubber Tappers' Union are attempting to legitimate the redefinition of who constitutes a stakeholder in a resource system, a prerequisite to the discussion of entitlements or distribution.

Like the chapters in the preceding section, these chapters suggest that the management of global ecological interdependence will be anything but simple. To be sure, the physical parameters of the problem are inherently complex, encompassing as they do an enor-mous range of locations and activities. But it is the social and political complexities that are likely to confound management as it is now generally conceived. Under these circumstances, the process of re-defining the task—by redefining the boundaries of the problems and roles of various stakeholders—must be seen not as an obstruction to effective management, but rather as an essential component.

NOTES

1. See, for example, William C. Clark, "The human ecology of global change," *International Social Science Journal* 121 (August 1989): 315–46.

2. This has been the theme of a number of the recent scientific confer-ences on global change. See for example *One Earth One Future* (Washington: National Academy of Sciences Press, 1990), which summarizes the proceed-ings of the 1989 Forum on Global Change and Our Common Future.

3. Piers N. Blaikie, *The Political Economy of Soil Erosion* (London: Long-mans, 1985).

4. Karen Litfin, "Transnational Scientific Networks and the Environment: The Limits of Epistemic Cooperation," Paper presented to the 1991 Western Regional Conference of the International Studies Association, Nov. 1–2, Los Angeles, p. 24.

6

Knowledge as Power:
Ecology Movements and Global
Environmental Problems

•

STEVE BREYMAN

Upon this gilted age, in this dark hour
Rains from the sky a meteoric shower
Of facts—they lie unquestioned, uncombined,
Wisdom enough to leech us of our ill
Is daily spun, but there exists no loom
To weave it into fabric.
—Edna St. Vincent Millay,
Sonnet No. CXL

"Grandpa, what is power?"

"Power is to be able to act well in life with what one knows and has in hand." [1]

Power is German Greens demonstrating against nuclear power. It is Brazilian rubber tappers struggling to preserve the forests upon which their livelihoods depend. Power is Indian peasants resisting hydroelectric projects that will flood their land. It is North American environmentalists confronting governments and corporations in federal courts. Around the world, ecology movements are demanding and creating the power to shape their own environments. [2]

Some of this citizen action is resistance to the depredations of developers both public and private, and some takes the form of broader campaigns for progressive change. The term "ecology movements" can mask very real differences among reform environmental-

I gratefully acknowledge the research assistance of Guo Sujian, and the helpful advice and criticism of Ken Conca, my Working Group colleagues, and an anonymous reviewer, in the writing and revision of this chapter.

ists, ecofeminists, deep ecologists, and social ecologists. And ecology movements frequently intersect and overlap with movements labeled peace, feminism, and human rights, among others.[3] Whether the essence of a local power struggle is preserving the environment, a people's right to survival, or some other purpose is problematic; ecology claims may or may not also be claims for structural justice. There is no ontologically correct vantage point: it is the perspective of the antagonists or observers that determines, for them, what the fight is "really" about. Regardless of the vectors of citizen action, however, its success depends on "act[ing] well in life with what one knows and what one has in hand." In other words, success depends on gaining power through the effective mobilization of resources.[4]

Ecology movements, despite their imperfections, inspire hope for an uncertain future. They are both causes and consequences of global ecological interdependence. Movement activists, simple and sophisticated, are working, locally and globally, to "save the planet" and its residents. Environmental thinkers have offered a new social paradigm to replace the outdated but still dominant ideology of endless growth, boundless faith in neopositivist science and technology, patriarchy, elitist decision-making, and unbridled materialism. Around the world, the movements that have grown up around these new ideas are schools of participatory democracy and vehicles for citizen empowerment. They are social laboratories for the responsible and sustainable management of ecological interdependence—a task for which states appear inadequate. Whether in countries overdeveloped or underdeveloped, environmentalists battle much of what is wrong with our world and its societies: pollution and environmental degradation, human rights abuses, poverty, exploitation, greed, government arrogance, and corruption.

To fight this good fight requires power. The concept of power is, of course, "essentially contested:" basic value differences among theorists have given rise to a plethora of images.[5] Nevertheless, it is possible to briefly trace the rough outlines of the relationship of ecology movement power to knowledge. My intention is not to offer a well-developed conception, but to prepare a path for an analysis of knowledge as a resource for environmentalists, the primary aim of this chapter.

Power for ecology movements includes especially the power to shape human interaction with the biosphere and the power to decide on the fate of natural resources and the commons, to determine the rate, nature, and direction of economic development. To obtain and wield this power, movements must possess knowledge of the workings of the biophysical world, of the characteristics of natural resources, and of the nexus between resources, environment, and humanity. When individual activists and movement organizations act upon such knowledge as they attempt to control their environments and their own lives as well, we can then speak of knowledge-as-power. This simple formulation helps guard against reductionism, of the historical materialist variety or any other. For as Russell wrote: "The fundamental concept in social science is Power in the sense in which Energy is the fundamental concept in physics. Like energy, power has many forms, such as wealth, armaments, influence on opinion. No one of these can be regarded as subordinate to any other, and there is no form from which the others are derivable."[6]

And this conception of knowledge-as-power is highly flexible: it can fit, more or less comfortably, into some leading theories of power. These theories, following Lukes, can be divided into the one-, two-, and three-dimensional faces of power.[7]

The one-dimensional or Weberian view of power is closely linked to the leading postwar model of political power in the United States: pluralism. Power is seen by pluralists as a function of the use of resources to influence decisions in desired directions (pluralist power is decisional power); policy outcomes are consequences of choices made by organized individuals. Following Weber, these behavioralists view power as an attribute of readily observable conflictual relationships between individuals where the preference of one party dominated those of another.[8] Individuals are conscious of their interests, which take the form of articulated policy preferences, and pursue them more or less vigorously depending on the intensity with which they are felt and the effectiveness of their organization. Individual or group inaction stems from satisfaction with the status quo or inadequate organization. Knowledge-as-power neatly fits the pluralist scheme. Knowledge becomes power for and when movements use it to affect policy decisions and when it aids movements in the organization and mobilization of their interests.

The two-dimensional conception of power considers the focus on decisions a central weakness of the pluralist model. Critics emphasize the importance of issues not on the agenda, not subject to public discussion; through non-decisions, elites delimit both the issues open to and the participants in public debate.[9] To equate interests with preferred policy options ignores individuals and groups that lack the skills and social esteem necessary to press their claims in the political sphere.[10] Other two-dimensional approaches suggest power may flow from individual or group position in the social structure (as in the case of corporations), rather than necessarily and directly from political action. For Mills, those who control public and private institutions—the "power elite"—are those who hold power in society.[11]

Knowledge-as-power helps challengers emerge from the obscurity described by the two-dimensional view: it allows them to force decisions by the more powerful. Routinized non-decision-making becomes more difficult. The luxury of the powerful to employ social values and institutional processes to truncate political debate, a consequence both of their reputational power and of their penetration of decision-making circles, may be taxed by challengers who are able, thanks to knowledge, to form and make their preferences public and have these preferences taken seriously by decisionmakers and opinion leaders.[12]

Radical analysts are dissatisfied with the two-dimensional image. In their view, it ignores the power of ideology, the capacity of elites and their intellectual servants to structure public beliefs, values, and desires to secure compliance with the norms and behavior that serve their needs.[13] A three dimensional conception of power eschews the centrality of conflict to power; "political power," writes Friedland, "may be silent, voiceless."[14] The focus is on, instead, the power to shape, without conflict, individual perceptions and preferences. Wants and desires, institutions and arrangements successfully molded by ideology, by this third face of power, actually work to forestall conflict. The powerless are unable to divine their real, objective interests, interests not served by the ideologically constructed institutions, attitudes and practices, and thus do not contradict the interests of the powerful.[15]

Knowledge-as-power also fits with the third face of power. It is at its most dramatic when it can cast critical light on power relations hidden by the heavy drapery of ideology. Knowledge-as-power serves the needs and interests—subjective and objective—of movement organizations when it challenges dominant ideological formulations and practices that support environmental degradation, and when it offers constructive alternatives for ordering human relationships with the earth.

To repeat, the success of ecology movements depends on the effective mobilization of resources. What resources are available to ecology movements? How are resources mobilized? What are the barriers to mobilization? What comes of movement challenges? Why do movements succeed and why do they fail? These are questions central to an analysis of resources as determinants of movement outcomes.[16] This is not to say that the outcomes of challenges by ecology movements are solely determined by movement resources. Rather, I am arguing only that, whatever the various and dynamic patterns of social control and political opportunity that condition a movement's sociopolitical context, an analysis focused on resources can serve as a starting point for the explanation of the outcomes of movement action.[17]

I will concentrate here on a single crucial but under-studied resource, knowledge, which of all the potential resources available to ecology movements best reflects both the promise and the problems of the globalization of environmental issues and the groups that champion them. My analysis explores how and why knowledge is a resource for ecology movements, and some of the roles knowledge plays in mobilizing those movements. Several suggestions for locating knowledge-focused studies in the context of research on (and by) social movements follow the analysis of knowledge as movement resource.

Knowledge and Ecology Movements

The resources available to ecology movements are manifold: organization, money, activists, leadership, tactics, strategy, to name several. Among the most important is knowledge, which can be a political lever, a powerful tool for recruiting and fundraising, a stimulus for new actions, and a validation for actions already chosen.

Knowledge can be used in the pursuit of movement aims to define interests and to monopolize or share claims to meaning. The power this endows on those who control it makes the politics of knowledge conflictual. Authoritative claims to knowledge can provide leverage to influence policymakers and realize other goals. Behold the *Exxon Valdez* spill.[18] Environmental organizations in the United States naturally hoped to capitalize on the accident. Indeed, donations to environmental groups surged in the wake of the disaster. Assessing the damage to Prince William Sound became a highly contentious undertaking as damages translate into dollars. To this day, the public is still unable to learn the full truth as specific data about the effects of the spill remain "litigation-sensitive." Scientists are subject to gag orders, and scientific cooperation and candor is nonexistent. This is no mere legal question, for the greater the devastation, the greater the political clout for the ecology movement. Sufficient information has been leaked, manipulated, and otherwise made public by various parties to yield some victories for the movement, including continued protection for the Arctic National Wildlife Refuge from oil exploration.

Knowledge as education may also be an indispensable recruiting and organizing tool for popular movements in both developed and developing worlds. While widespread illiteracy and innumeracy are not insurmountable obstacles to mobilization, better educated activists improve a movement's chances for success.[19] This was certainly the case for the Civil Rights movement in the United States where, for example, Martin Luther King, Jr. attended the famed Highlander Center in Tennessee and literacy campaigns were conducted by grassroots movement workers. Saul Alinsky, organizer and educator of activists, gleaned practical, reproducible knowledge, his "rules for radicals," from decades of trial and error. This collected wisdom passed on from one generation of activists to another and from one movement to another, and the necessity for elementary education of some movement constituencies illustrates the importance of education, without which mobilization would prove considerably more difficult.

Environmental education in the West complements leadership training and literacy crusades. Movement educational campaigns build upon recruitment efforts in order to organize the energies of new recruits and veteran activists by stressing the basic scientific competence of movement adherents regarding environmental problems, by alerting members to both long-term and immediate threats to the environment in order to stimulate action, by examining controversies over concepts and issues germane to the movement (such as environmental ethics and environmental economics), and, in general, by enhancing the proficiency, motivation, and morale of movement constituents. In Brazil, Projeto Seringueiro, organized by the National Council of Rubber Tappers, "aims to encourage the rubber tappers to identify more closely with the forest, to understand it, to learn more about it and defend it."[20] Other programs have been arranged by students of Paulo Freire and by the Ecumenical Documentation and Information Center; for rubber tapper, activist, and martyr Chico Mendes, "The strengthening of our movement has coincided with the development of the education programme. . . . all our advances, the fight against the destruction of the forest, the organizing of the cooperative and the strengthening of the union, were all possible thanks to the education program."[21]

The political power and mobilizing potential of knowledge not-withstanding, the connection between knowledge and political action is, to say the least, complex. For certain movement groups, knowledge may be no more than a validation of previously chosen courses of action to save the environment and its inhabitants. Many organizations are predisposed toward action regardless of "the science" of a particular problem. Their ecological values and holistic world views mandate humanitarian and ecological rescue efforts on the basis of the intrinsic worth of human beings and the ecosystems to which they belong. Never an end in itself, knowledge acquires an ex post facto instrumentality; it becomes even less than a means to an end. For other groups, the opposite is true: scientific confirmation and assessment of a problem is a prerequisite for action. The differing approaches are explained, I think, by the varying positions reserved for science in these groups' ideologies, by the extent to which they have shed the dominant social paradigm of positivist scientific rationality.

Governments, like those movement groups still wed to notions of scientific rationality, also seek knowledge-based justifications for their actions. For states under pressure from ecology groups, knowledge can be an impetus to international action provided such action does not question the legitimacy of prevailing political, social, and economic systems. The failure of diplomatic fruits such as the Montreal Protocol and the Convention on International Trade in Endangered Species to challenge the precepts of modern, industrial capitalism helps explain their successful negotiation.[22] Any scientific uncertainties about the roots, extent, or ramifications of environmental threats—and such uncertainties about global ecological problems are considered legion by many in power—allows states to delay, postpone, and otherwise resist action.

These uncertainties can also mask the essence of the struggles among ecology movements, states, and corporations; struggles which are not about science or knowledge per se. For Cotgrove, "the protagonists face each other in a spirit of exasperation, talking past each other with mutual incomprehension. It is a dialogue of the blind talking to the deaf. . . . the debate [cannot] be settled by appeals to the facts. We need to grasp the implicit cultural meanings which underlie the dialogue."[23]

Bush Administration budget director Richard Darman is one of these uncomprehending protagonists. According to Darman, "Americans did not fight and win the wars of the twentieth century to make the world safe for green vegetables."[24] And yet, despite appearances, there may be no misunderstanding at all. Adversaries may very well know their respective positions and stakes. Environmentalists in Southern California know why the few remaining undeveloped parcels of coastal land are slated for resort hotels. Malaysian activists know why trees fall in Sarawak. European industrialists know why there is opposition to toxic waste dumping in the North Sea. Canadian utilities know why native peoples resist the James Bay hydroelectric projects. While competing knowledge claims are the language in which such conflicts are frequently expressed, these are at root struggles over power in its varied manifestations—political, economic, social, and cultural—and wearing its three faces.

Understanding the varied ways in which knowledge can be mobilized requires a closer look at how movements generate and acquire knowledge. Such knowledge originates in the realms of both organized science and everyday experience. Grassroots networks accumulate knowledge about local conditions by breathing air, drinking water, tilling soil, harvesting forest produce, or fishing rivers, lakes, and oceans. Practical knowledge is also generated by scientists and shared with or appropriated by environmental groups. Some of the larger ecological organizations have their own scientific staffs; smaller groups rely on the assistance of volunteer scientists or, as in the case of the vast majority of grassroots networks, go without the benefits of direct scientific research and advice. Whereas scientific knowledge is generalizable, the domain of the specialist, local knowledge is unique and specific, the wisdom of the grassroots. It is a site-specific relative of what Lindblom and Cohen call "ordinary knowledge": knowledge that "does not owe its origin, testing, degree of verification, truth status, or currency to distinctive . . . professional techniques but rather to common sense, casual empiricism or thoughtful speculation and analysis."[25]

The relative and varying weight assigned to these distinctly different, noninterchangeable components of knowledge by movements may be seen as a dimension of the clash between world views with widely varying conceptions of the role of knowledge in structuring the economic and technological sphere of people's lives. Milbrath suggests the conflict is between the "dominant social paradigm," with its emphasis on economic growth, progress, and the central role of science and technology in the modern world, and the "new environmental paradigm," which stresses quality of life, holism, social justice, and grassroots democracy in the postmodern world.[26] The binary division between lore and science is eroded over time at the hands of alliances between scientists and grassroots activists, ranging from those linking environmental scientists and mainstream environmental lobbying organizations to those between anthropologists who have "gone native" and indigenous peoples in conflict with outsiders.[27] Coalitions between scientists and environmentalists are now recognized as central to the initiation, negotiation, implementation, and evaluation of international environmental agreements.[28] And attempts to combine local lore and universal science into new forms of knowledge-as-power is a central thrust of the globalization of the environmental movement. Before turning to a discussion of the possibilities and pitfalls associated with such efforts, a brief discussion of these two types of knowledge, and the mobilizing potential of each, is in order.

Science and Environmental Policy-making

The "progressivist-positivist" planning model arose at the turn of the century in the United States.[29] The model depicts neutral scientists providing value-free information (unsullied by politics, an arena dominated by special interests and the ignorant) to government administrators. Scientific legitimacy rests on the nonideological nature of science and scientists. Government officials, armed with this scientific advice, then democratically determine solutions to public problems. Though under attack by deep ecologists, postmodern social critics, philosophers of science, and others, the model still enjoys widespread currency.[30]

This aging model of the relationship between science and politics in industrial democracies is more normative than descriptive, for several reasons. Society's goals and the solutions to collective problems were not then and are not now arrived at via popular participation but rather through "iron triangles" and neocorporatist decision-making. Second, the incorporation of science into the policy-making process was never as smooth or uncontested as the model avers—recall the public health battles over sewer construction, arguments about horses as means of transportation, and the politics of the formation of the American Medical Association, all raging during the Progressive era in the United States. Third, public administration was and is in many cases and in many places corrupt, lax, or idiosyncratic, rendering scientific advice superfluous.[31] Further damage is done to the model when the veil concealing the internal dynamics of scientific enterprise is lifted to reveal operations similar to other large institutions: competition for funding and honors, bureaucratic strife and turf battles, fraud and egoism. Science and its practitioners fall prey to the same shortcomings endemic to business, religion, and government, as illustrated by cases as diverse as the space program, nuclear-weapons design, nuclear power, cold fusion, and AIDS research.[32]

The concerted broadside against science, technology, and the positivist planning model (or prescription) is of recent origin. Science became vulnerable at least partly through the efforts of social movements and allied individuals: the "mothers' movement" against atmospheric nuclear testing, Rachel Carson's alert about DDT in *Silent Spring*, the consumer movement sparked by Ralph Nader, citizen reactions to the Santa Barbara oil spill, the appropriate technology response to the Green Revolution in the Third World, Barry Commoner's *Science and Survival* and *The Closing Circle*, the first Earth Day, and the general counter-culture of the mid-1960s to early-1970s. And this vulnerability in turn provided an opening for greater ecology-movement participation in the environmental policy process.

Environmental policy-making in the West is marked both by popular participation and technical expertise.[33] Problems arise when the imperatives of expertise clash with citizen input. Environmentalists are the stimulus for the increasing frequency of these clashes. People tire of losing battles against ecologically harmful "progress" and learn to distrust the science that informs decisions on development projects. And they tire of hearing government lawyers, seeking to dismiss citizen-initiated lawsuits, say "Plaintiffs refuse to accept the verdict of those best qualified to resolve such matters . . . Congress has wisely left these technical matters to the technicians."[34]

In many Western countries, ecology-movement action has been effective in raising the costs to government and business elites of ignoring public concerns—concerns fostered by these same citizen organizations. In the United States, public participation in the planning process is now mandated by law, while in Canada, special agencies have been created to encourage public input. Ecology movement participation in the policy process became routine with the requirement that administrative agencies seek public input and with the growth and professionalization of the movements.[35] While the transition to an "open planning" process has been anything but smooth and uncontested, challenging groups are now legitimate actors, more than just bit-part players, on the decision-making stage.

Public hearings are one node of interaction and communication among governments, corporations, and environmental movements, one front on which the ecological battle proceeds. Such hearings, along with other developments deriving from the growing vulnerability of science and the evolution of the new ecological paradigm, have given rise to charges that science has been corrupted by association with contentious policy processes. The problem is, according to the critics, that ends (supposedly chosen politically) and means (supposedly chosen scientifically) are often blurred to the extent that politics comes to shape science and science becomes politicized.[36]

But just what is politicized science? Apparently it is science that has been tarnished in the rough and tumble of the policy process, compromised by the machinations of nonscientists. It is not exactly corrupted science, that sort bent to the will of political or corporate overlords, but it has been delegitimized to some extent nonetheless. Politicized science characterizes those instances when technocracy breaks down or is challenged, those instances when movement intervention in policy-making transcends mundane public hearings. It is what Alvin Weinberg calls "trans-science," what Emery and Trist refer to as "turbulence." [37]

Trans-science and turbulence signify expansions of democracy, whose march once-insulated elites bemoan. Instances of trans-science are more likely when the "system uncertainties" and "decision stakes" are high and include people's livelihoods, ways of life, or health.[38] Nuclear power is the classic example. And yet it is unclear whether science itself is any more "politicized" now than it was prior to the expansion of civilian nuclear power in the 1950s. What is clear is that more and more people, including a swelling number of scientists, demand socially responsible science, technology, and decision-making processes. To describe the change as politicization is to demean it, to smear those who dissent from policy-making–as–usual. A better formulation may be to say that as the stakes rise, so does the turbulence.

But is "turbulence" a good word to describe the sociopolitical changes accompanying higher stakes? Turbulence connotes a process in which the jetliner of modern science encounters some rough air; after a few small adjustments by government, university, and corporate pilots, Air Science continues on course. According to some accounts this is indeed what has happened: greater citizen participation has not been able to curtail many of the "externalities" of technology spawned by science; local opposition may be overwhelmed by the resources available to business and officialdom.[39] Increased citizen input has been a ruse, a sop thrown to noisy activists who have a voice in the process, but one drowned out by those of developers and state agencies.[40]

But discounting the effectiveness of citizen and movement participation in policy-making is too easy. Granted that such popular roles may not address the roots of the ecological crisis, the need for brakes on runaway development remains real. Environmental policy-making in advanced industrial states is in the very early stages of a transition from the neopositivistic applied-science model to the holistic systems perspective of a Green world view. The choice for movements is not between building alternative grassroots networks for living and working, as suggested by some, or taking part in the policy and electoral processes, as recommended by others. Varied movement organizations can and must do both. The challenge for movements is the unremitting cultivation and mobilization of both local lore and scientific data, a task that can further the self-actualization of individuals and the collective mandates of groups.

Local Lore

Grassroots activists can be the "keepers of the residual [national] cultural and economic heritage" in the face of intense pressure to develop and modernize along the lines of the dominant paradigm.[41] As Shiva explains, "The illiterate women of the hill villages did not need professional forest hydrologists to tell them of the role of the forests in protecting land and water stability of mountain watersheds, they had drunk this knowledge with their mothers' milk, and had it reinforced as they grew with religious myths and folklore."[42]

This legacy is part of local networks' mythology and may be a powerful resource that poor people's movements can draw upon for moral sustenance and strategic direction.[43] Religious references work to muster people because they use an age-old and spontaneous mode of mobilizing village communities. And possession of this heritage allows movements to act as condensers of symbols, as "signifying agents" actively engaged in the interpretation of knowledge and the production of meaning. Organizations are empowered to frame events and conditions in order to mobilize potential adherents, garner bystander support, and demobilize antagonists.[44]

Local lore is not the exclusive property of movements in the South, of course, any more than universal science is that of the North. There are Western traditions of use to environmentalists, such as the New England town meeting, the Bill of Rights, the Diggers, Native American spirituality, and the place of the forest in German literature and culture. And yet, while First-World movement groups in the North must contend with a cultural inheritance of the squandering of resources and a Christian tradition that justified and apologized for the ensuing destruction, Third World groups can often find strength in the society's dominant cultural legacy.[45]

The pervasive changes in natural resource management brought on by colonialism, and continued by newly independent developmentalist regimes, overwhelmed the local knowledge and methods of peasants, fishermen, and forest dwellers. But these changes also gave rise to sporadic protests and more sustained turmoil, sometimes allied with national liberation movements. The resurrection of the concept of "the commons" by environmentalists and researchers may eventually vindicate the local if not universal wisdom of ancient modes of production and relationships to the earth, still in practice in spite of Adam Smith, Karl Marx, the Green Revolution, and over two centuries of industrialism.[46]

Ecology movements like the Chipko in India and the Greens in industrialized countries call for a reconstitution of science, rationality, technological and social choice, and economic growth.[47] In practice, this means that Chipko activists work to reassert the lost hegemony of their folk knowledge against the dominance of scientific forestry. Modern silviculture commodifies the former commons into "resources" of purely commercial value. Biomass of high use value for residents of the woods but low exchange value for landowners and the state is destroyed. The result in India has been desertification, uncontrollable floods, and the loss of people's means of survival. Grassroots ecologists' critique of reductionist science, based on their self-interest, customs, and culture, contains the germ of an alternative knowledge system, similar to Feyerabend's notion of science in a free society:

> In a free society intellectuals are just one tradition. They have no special rights and their views are of no special interest (except, of

course, to themselves). Problems are not solved by specialists (though their advice will not be disregarded) but by the people concerned, in accordance with the ideas they value and by procedures *they* regard as most appropriate. [People] . . . combining flexibility and respect for all traditions will gradually erode the borrowed and self-serving "rationalism" of those who are now using tax money to destroy the traditions of the taxpayers, to ruin their minds, rape their environment and quite generally to turn living human beings into well trained slaves of their own barren vision of life.[48]

An ecological perspective, founded on local wisdom, on a recognition of the interrelationships of ecosystems and of the holism of nature, provides citizens' movements with the epistemological tools for the reconstruction of neopositivist science and for an alternative approach to the management of global ecological interdependence.

Global Environmental Policy-making, Knowledge, and Mobilization

The process of international environmental policy-making typically begins when a "problem" is identified, usually by scientists, and often based on partial data and incomplete understanding.[49] Specialists within or allied with movements are among the first to learn of the nature and magnitude of the problem, and movements play a crucial role in getting the word out. Demands quickly follow that something—usually by governments—be done about the problem. Public awareness of the problem is critical to getting it on the government's agenda; delay at this point may later narrow the range of available policy responses.

Once it is on the agenda, the problem becomes an "issue"; problems are issues waiting to happen. Issues are social-psychological constructions that tend to redefine problems so as to make them amenable to policy options, and thus become subjects of more or less public debate. These constructions are especially complex if the issue as defined is both international and environmental. Such issues may be fundamentally ecological or biophysical in the way they are framed, yet inevitably have political, cultural, and socioeconomic dimensions as well.

Traditionally, issues must first be of national concern before states are willing to consider their international or global ramifications. For example, the venerable problem of collective security is still viewed by most decisionmakers through the lens of national security (although this is changing).[50] Successful arms control—the Limited Test Ban Treaty, the Nonproliferation Treaty, SALT—results from public pressure on, and the private initiative of, domestic elites. The gaze is inside looking out. This has been the case too for certain international environmental agreements such as those protecting migratory birds; the impetus for state action emanates from scientific and citizen observations of declining bird counts. The problem is first recognized and then becomes an issue domestically, whether it be radioactive fallout from the Nevada Test Site or fewer ducks during open season in the Dakotas. Movements help shape national environmental issues and elevate them to the international arena.

Has the globalization of environmental issues, for which ecology movements are in part responsible, altered this process? There are signs that what movements know, how they know it, and what they do with what they know are increasingly giving new form to both the style and substance of global environmental policy. And the globalization not simply of the issues involved, but of the movements themselves, may be exacerbating both these tendencies and the sometimes stark choices facing movements in choosing how knowledge is wielded, and for what purpose.

In the traditional process of international environmental policy-making as sketched above, movements play a critical role in minimizing the time from recognizing the problem to setting the agenda by alerting their constituencies and by stimulating the broader public through the mass media.[51] And yet, while international environmental organizations are thus actively and directly engaged in the formulation and implementation of global policy, their role to date has been more that of a public interest lobby than a means by which to give power to citizens. They give people a voice, but merely an indirect one. The extent to which that voice truly reflects the opinion of their constituencies on particular approaches to specific issues is problematic. And the question of more meaningful popular participation beyond representation by a small circle of movement professionals goes unasked. In staking a claim to a place at the policy table, movements have been either unable or unwilling to mobilize masses of people around global problems like biodiversity and climate change on a scale comparable to opposition to nuclear power.

The gathering of indigenous peoples and movement organizations from around the world at the Earth Summit in Rio de Janeiro may signal both a new willingness and a new capacity to move along the continuum from elite representation to mass mobilization. There may be no sustained mass mobilizations, however, until the effects of global environmental problems encroach on people's lives in the way of a new missile or power plant in their communities. (This begs the question as to whether mass mobilizations ought to be a means for the realization of ecology movement ends, a point to which I return below.)

Anti-nuclear-power movements and anti-nuclear-weapons movements have shown the paramount importance of a tangible evil; there is no substitute for something hard and shiny like a missile or a nuclear generating plant to rally people. (The Nuclear Freeze movement provides an obvious exception to this generalization; in this case, the budgetary impact of the arms race and growing awareness of the very real dangers substituted for more tangible symbols.) Knowledge under such circumstances becomes concrete, perception existential. Perhaps desertification will have to greatly accelerate in the North. Perhaps the climate will have to change dramatically before mobilization escalates considerably. There may have to be a "shocker" akin to the 1969 Santa Barbara oil spill before mobilization becomes highly agitated and perhaps it needs to happen in a place like Santa Barbara.[52] The location has a dual significance: idyllic Santa Barbara's pristine beaches were despoiled by sticky petroleum, resulting in large losses of marine life and tourist revenues; and Santa Barbara is in California, with its wide array of well-developed and resource-rich ecology groups.

In the absence of such tangible events or symbols, movements face at least two knowledge-related dilemmas: how to use knowledge to foster a remote but effectively mobilizing symbolism, and whether to do so on an elite or mass level. To wait for a shock may allow time needed for crucial immediate action to pass. By the time a crisis gives rise to a sufficient collective response it could be too late to reverse the damage. Extinct species are gone forever. It is this sense of urgency, based on sometimes sketchy scientific knowledge, that movements try to foster. In the absence of a catalytic event, organizers trying to rally adherents in the West must rely on a more remote symbolism.[53] Outside of the United States and Western Europe, this is less of a problem. Unbreathable air and undrinkable water are everyday concerns of Eastern Europeans. Desertification or deforestation have immediate ramifications for survival in the South. Pleas for heightened sensitivity or empathy, redefinitions of security, or a view to the long-term are unnecessary. Lethal threats have become real.

In the absence of such tangibility, to reiterate, knowledge is dispersed through a discourse of remote symbolism. How this knowledge of remote threats is interpreted and acted upon depends largely on individual values. For "postmaterialists" and others operating within the new ecological paradigm, the holistic view of "human beings as one" provides fertile soil for action predicated on awareness of seemingly distant dangers. For those with egocentric values, the risks must be closer, more immediate, and must threaten material well-being.[54]

In this context of remote symbolism, what constitutes knowledge is itself multifaceted. It is first of all awareness of the existence of a problem via the mass media or movement communications. These news sources are sometimes linked: many movement groups work diligently to enlist the support of the mass media in alerting the larger public to the presence and scope of the problem. Second, knowledge consists of some facility with the science of the problem. Mobilizing for an as-strict-as-possible covenant on the phase-out of chlorofluorocarbons (CFCs) requires understanding how these compounds react with atmospheric gases. Third, knowledge is cognizance of the connections between the problem and the larger world. Take the example of climate change: many First World interests would prefer to focus attention on the destruction of forests in the Third World and ignore that the bulk of greenhouse gases is the result of activities in the industrialized countries. Fourth, knowledge is recognition of how grassroots activists are battling local consequences of global problems. Such information can give rise to concerns about how to help them. The dilemma of remote symbolic discourse is one of producing these separate components of knowledge and weaving them into an effective mobilizing blend.

A second dilemma is whether to pursue elite or mass strategies of knowledge-based mobilization. On one hand, the sort of multidimensional knowledge sketched above can precipitate the complex changes in world view, technique, and time frame that might (assuming a causal connection) lead to the macro shifts in the control of the political economy necessary for truly effective global environmental policy-making. On the other hand, what of the possibility that global-scale problems are not amenable to mass mobilizations? A perspective that cared not at all for the liberating potential of involving wider publics in global problem-solving might consider mass participation unnecessary, frivolous, even counter-productive. Instrumentally focused elite groups might question the investment of resources required to "explain the science" to the general public.

Murray Bookchin, for one, thinks mass mobilization should not be the preferred means toward movement ends. Huge demonstrations and short-term mobilizations like Earth Day and Redwood Summer tacitly accept, according to Bookchin, the current environmentally rapacious social order. Movement actions designed to influence liberal corporate capitalism or bureaucratic state "socialism" are doomed to lesser-of-evils trade-offs which can only delay, not prevent, the ultimate destruction of the biosphere.

> To "play by the rules" of the environmental game means that the natural world, including oppressed people, always loses something piece by piece until everything is lost in the end. As long as liberal environmentalism is structured around the social status quo, property rights always prevails over public rights, and power always prevails over powerlessness. Be it a forest, wetlands, or good agricultural soil, a "developer" who owns any of these "resources" usually sets the terms on which every negotiation occurs and ultimately succeeds in achieving the triumph of wealth over ecological consideration.[55]

Barry Commoner sounds a similar klaxon when he scores the corporate environmentalism of large organizations like the National Wildlife Federation and World Wildlife Fund, and committees like the Acid Rain Roundtable. The latter, a small Klatsch of corporate executives and leaders of Washington-based environmental groups, excluded mine workers in its deliberations over reduced emissions of sulfur dioxide and nitrogen oxide.[56]

Assuming, with some justification, that scientist-activist networks consider popular education both means and end, the question emerges: is it necessary to educate the public to rouse them? My own sense is that some basic ideas about the nature and dimensions of a problem, and some more-or-less-specific notions about cures, are essential for effective and sustained citizen incitement. Maybe it is enough for scientists to alert movement leaders, who then rally the masses through emotional or fear-based campaigns. Returning again to a lesson from the peace movement: European citizen expertise on defense issues during the early 1980s typically came after these citizens had already been mobilized by the threat of an impending hardware deployment. These tens of thousands of citizens knew enough initially to oppose the Euromissiles; what they later learned about decapitation strikes, throw weight, and hard target kill capability only confirmed and "rationalized" their fears and made many of them extraordinarily articulate, informed, and thus more effective challengers of elite decisions. They also became educators themselves and were responsible for the recruitment of enormous numbers of their formerly apathetic or uninvolved fellow citizens. One moral of this story is that issue-areas previously the province of a handful of insulated elites—the nuclear priesthood—were found, despite their arcane, abstract, sanitized jargons, to be accessible to the average educated citizen. My sense is that a similar process of education, acculturation, and activation is under way in the case of global environmental threats.

Linking Local Knowledge and Universal Science

As suggested above, ecology movements are both a response to and a reflection of global ecological interdependence. A critical component of the globalization of environmental issues has been a series of efforts to build North–South movement coalitions. The choices facing movements, and the general challenge of integrating universal science and local lore into an effective mobilizing discourse, will play a significant role in defining the character, scope, and durability of these alliances.

In the industrialized nations, opponents of environmentally hazardous development are attacked as selfish not-in-my-back-yard (NIMBY) pests; in the South, they are castigated as ignorant ingrates stooping in the way of "progress." One First World movement response to this criticism has been to raise the stakes, to decry destructive projects as unfit not only for local communities but as generally unacceptable, giving rise to a new acronym, NOPE: not-on-planet-Earth.[57] This conscious stakes-raising tactic of globalization—a symbolic upping of the ante—has converged with the attempts of many Third World activists to question the universal prescription of economic growth toward a post-industrial standard of living as a desirable and attainable goal. Contends Indian organizer Anupam Mishra,

> If bringing Western development was so necessary, our governments could have encouraged a healthy debate on the question, convincing the people of its importance for their own well-being. But they chose the other way—of ridiculing us, by labelling our culture as backward, by branding our simple knowledge as ignorance and superstition and then forcing us to join their elitist race for scientific development to make us "civilized."[58]

Surmounting these problems, a common concern for students of global change, entails new levels of cooperation between movements all over the world.[59] Bridges are under construction between movements in Western Europe and their neighbors to the East, including former Soviet republics. Links are being forged among environmentalists in the Americas. Asian activists are making alliances among themselves and with global ecology organizations. Regional bodies of tribal peoples are making common cause and overcoming ancient antagonisms. The ties between varied movements may be seen as the construction of new institutions that both respond to, and deepen, global ecological interdependence.

Movements North and South have begun to converge on efforts to propagate Green alternatives to standard growth schemes. Plans for the expansion of city-suburb mass transit links serve as alternatives to building more freeways. Conservation is pitched as a substitute for the construction of new electricity-generating power plants. Brazilian rural workers' unions propose "extractive reserves" to buttress their case for defending the forest. Such proposals, often innovative blends of native wisdom and science, are a means for ecology movements to transcend "business as usual," and counter mean-spirited criticism. Notions such as steady-state economics, bioregionalism, small-is-beautiful, human scale, limits to growth, and the like now contend, although hardly on an equal footing, with the dominant development paradigm.[60]

Alternative ideas evolve in the symbolic realm, in contests of discourse between vested interests and insurgents. The trends of these contests have, of course, real consequences for movements. Much may depend on hard-won experiments and pilot projects, the short-term spoils of modest victories in the struggle for cultural hegemony. Experiments with challenging conceptions are in part a product of alliances among scientists, local activists, and remote movement groups.

Scientists can be supportive allies in the struggles of Southern movements, and Northern environmentalists can reinforce these coalitions by bringing together grassroots wisdom and scientific insight. According to Chico Mendes, "In this fight, our only defense is the pressure put on the authorities by Brazilian society and the international scientific community." [61] The rubber tappers' union relies on a small network of academics and the Institute of Amazon Studies, which Mendes called a "strategic center of the movement," for communication and information assistance. While the indigenous peoples of the Indian state of Bastar do not need specialists to warn them about the dangers of replacing diverse hardwood forests with pine plantations, scientists and Northern environmental organizations have been of use in lobbying against bilateral aid and commercial or World Bank loans necessary for huge development projects.[62] Third World ecologists can also help themselves by helping their Northern neighbors (and vice versa) as the successful visits to Washington of Chico Mendes and Yanomami Indians attest. These visits helped U.S. organizations more effectively work the halls of power on behalf of Amazonian ecosystems and peoples.

Activists North and South echo the sentiment that "developing true partnerships between environmental groups and indigenous peoples is one of the most important things we should be engaging in. It is both moral and practical."[63] But what are "true partnerships"? And on what alternative paradigms are they to be based? One alternative to the conventional development model is the concept of sustainable development. The roots of the idea are complex and still developing, and myriad sustainable development schemes have appeared. Sustainable development is attractive to many ecologists in that it confronts both poverty and environmental degradation. But it has also been criticized as elitist, technocratic, and too quick to compromise on core issues such as the need for growth.[64]

Similarly, debt-for-nature swaps are heralded by many environmentalists as innovations that provide a dual set of benefits: they lessen, however slightly, the cruel burden of debt weighing upon the Third World (and, of course, the suffocating pressure of indebtedness is most painfully felt by those classes least able to resist it), thus addressing a root cause of ecological destruction; and they protect green expanses, however limited, from greedy developers and needy colonists, thus providing immediate relief from deforestation and species extinction. Yet, such swaps do not challenge the prevailing growth paradigm, and are hardly unmitigated successes from the perspective of local peoples. And debt-for-nature agreements tend to decide rainforest land issues over the heads of local peoples, though this appears to be changing.[65]

Forest dwellers were also excluded from the formulation of the Tropical Forestry Action Plan (TFAP), a framework for the funneling of money to developing countries to promote "sustainable" silviculture. Negotiated in 1985 by the World Bank, the United Nations'

Food and Agriculture Organization and the World Resources Institute, the Plan has not prevented an increase in the rate of global deforestation. In 1990 a coalition of ecology groups called for a moratorium on funding for TFAP because, among other failings, it destroys local economies and ecosystems by encouraging capital-intensive, externally controlled logging. The Coordinating Body for the Indigenous Peoples' Organizations of the Amazon Basin (COICA), representing more than a million tribal people of South America, declared in 1989 that while appreciative of ecology movement efforts, "It should be made clear that we never delegated . . . power to the environmentalist community nor to any individual or organization in that community." [66]

A number of models for a more meaningful integration of local and universal knowledge have begun to emerge. One example is provided by Participatory Action Research (PAR), a conscious merger of science and local knowledge designed to empower local communities.[67] A central question for PAR is how to link the pursuit and accumulation of knowledge aimed at effecting social change with popular movements. One objective is the production of rigorous analytical works, stemming from the local knowledge of ordinary people and activists, that enrich the general fund of science as well as popular wisdom. Although not specifically aimed at boosting the prospects of ecology groups, PAR shows promise as a method to connect grassroots struggles and the resources of remote constituencies of conscience.

Another potential aid in linking local knowledge and universal science is the research-action strategy of Alain Touraine.[68] His methods of *l'intervention sociologie* and its process of autoanalysis are designed to stimulate discussions within social movements and to enable activists to situate their efforts within the larger patterns of social domination. Italian sociologists too have been busy devising new approaches to understand and assist local endeavors.[69] Participatory methods frame research questions jointly and collaborate with activists, rather than treat them like objects or data. These methods can be seen as "phenomenological holism"—researchers attempt to grasp the logic of local conflicts while grounding them in fundamental structures of social power. Local knowledge is the starting point for participatory researchers who consider their task the melding of ordinary knowledge with science in a symbiotic problem-oriented dialogue.[70]

Conclusion and Future Research

The environment has moved from an item rather low on the world agenda to the forefront of public concern. At a recent Commonwealth summit, the environment was at the top of the agenda. The environment was a major issue in recent Indian and Brazilian elections, and the Organization of African Unity designated 1991 the Year of the Environment. "If the world is serious about tackling the environmental crisis . . . ," argues Mostafa Tolba, "there is no alternative to global cooperation and the generation of additional resources that goes far beyond anything we see today."[71] Ecology movements are an important progenitor of this refurbished global agenda and are crucial in arousing the global cooperation necessary to genuinely confront the crisis. Engendering innovative and improved knowledge for movements increases the likelihood that states, especially the rich, will devote the additional resources required for renewed efforts to face the coming challenges—a still promising strategy despite its inadequacy at the Earth Summit.

Cooperation is essential to making headway on the plethora of environmental problems facing the world. As the example of knowledge has shown, it is possible for movements North and South to be resources for each other, to be of mutual benefit. Thus, perhaps the most important area for future inquiry involves the kinds of coalitions that are possible between Northern and Southern organizations, between indigenous and colonial peoples. What are the conditions for the creation of environmental alliances? Are the interests and issues of groups in diverse regions converging? Or is the tentative and tenuous unity merely tactical? Must differences of ideology and goals be surmounted for groups to work together? How have movement antagonists attempted to stymie coalition-building? How can such attempts be overcome? Research to improve the prospects for transnational complementarity, to develop the theory and practice of associations within and between environmental movements, would surely prove fruitful.

Another area of interest to students of global change concerns the relations and interactions between movements and states, some dimensions of which were addressed above. This is partly a question about social control: the processes, both coercive and persuasive, whereby authorities secure conformity to societal norms. How and why do states facilitate or hinder movement activities? How can movements counter these efforts? It is also a question of evolution in the state system, that is, of the extent to which the state system can be said to have been transformed by large political-economic forces—the nuclear revolution, growing international economic interdependence, shifts in polarity—and the implications of these changes for nongovernmental actors. These changes are in the essential compass of the state; at the same time that capitalist states' bureaucratic tentacles reach further into the remaining recesses of civil society, individual states, no matter how large and powerful, appear less and less capable of performing what liberals take to be their fundamental function: the provision of national security and citizen welfare. Ecology and other movements moved to fill this political space, a void left not by the retreat or defeat of the state—for states have yet to fully surrender to multinational corporations, international organizations, or some still to be defined heirs—but by its "failure." [72]

The continuing, if diminished, vitality of the state confronts movements at every turn. States remain important determinants of movements' political opportunities.[73] Ecology movement groups, however, have choices, limited though they may be; among their scant options is the mode by which they engage the state. Possible modes include bypassing, challenging, pressuring, and supporting the state.[74] The first involves the construction of alternative networks for the delivery of collective goods. Challenging the state could include fundamental attacks on the legitimacy of a regime and calls for revolutionary transformation, or reformist challenges to state action involving litigation or electoral activity. Pressuring the state entails traditional lobbying or unconventional protest. Supporting the state occurs when the goals of movements and states intersect.

These modes of operation are partly functions of the knowledge available to movements and partly products of other factors internal to movement organizations—though, again, states prefigure much movement action. The modes are overlapping and interdependent; some groups may be better equipped to act in one or two modes but it is also possible for an environmental group to engage in all four either simultaneously, during different campaigns, or during separate phases of the group's career. Studies of how and why movement organizations make the choices they do are interesting; research on the conditions under which choices can be said to be good or bad, right or wrong, is most valuable.[75]

A third focal point for future research returns to the question of mobilization: what explains the absence of great masses of people mobilized for redress of global ecological grievances? Are these issues just too big, too remote? Can distinctions be drawn among efforts on different environmental problems? Has greater mobilization occurred around deforestation than around the problems of species extinction? There was a Redwood Summer, but as of yet no Greenhouse Summer. Are diffuse events such as Earth Day—which serve as multiring circus tents for issues—appropriate localizing responses to global problems? Efforts—scientific and activist—to specify the local ramifications of global ills appear promising. Again, the tangibility of a threat may help account for the level of mobilization. Some modicum of knowledge about a problem or set of problems is necessary before mobilizations can be massive and sustained. What are the conditions for sustainable mobilization? What are the barriers or limits to usable knowledge? When is knowledge not enough?

I claimed in this chapter that knowledge is a resource for ecology movements and tried to show how and why this is so. Much of the discussion thus centered on the core theoretical argument that movements gather and employ resources, in this case knowledge, to realize ends great and small. Globalization of the issues, and of movements themselves, has complicated the role of knowledge and the task of mobilizing it adequately, but has not eclipsed the centrality of effective mobilization of knowledge to attain movement goals. If the analysis here is correct, then environmental movements will increasingly be recognized as critical to the social processes of global ecological interdependence. Authorities will take heed, scholars will take note, and citizens will take part.

NOTES

1. Conversation between Colombian peasant organizers quoted in Orlando Fals Borda, *Knowledge and People's Power: Lessons with Peasants in Nicaragua, Mexico and Colombia* (New Delhi: Indian Social Institute, 1988), p. 1.

2. By "movement" I mean people mobilizing themselves and other resources to change other people (values, attitudes, lifestyles), structures (institutions, cultures), and relations (links between people and structures) using means which tend toward the unconventional for ends which may include the radical. Activists typically come together in organizations which vary as to their formality, structure, leadership, ideology, tactics, and goals, but usually constitute the action networks of a movement.

3. This overlap is partly explained by the socially constructed nature of the labels themselves, and by the set of values common to activists in diverse

movements. For one Indian activist and researcher, "Ecological disruption and economic exploitation [and ecofeminists would add the oppression of women] are intrinsically linked; and this linkage stares everyone in the face when resources are scarce, people are many, and new modes of production are resource intensive and resource wasteful and consume resources needed for survival." See Vandana Shiva, "People's Ecology: The Chipko Movement," in Saul H. Mendlovitz and R. B. J. Walker eds., *Towards a Just World Peace: Perspectives from Social Movements* (London: Butterworth, 1987), p. 253.

4. "Resources" are broadly defined to include all persons, entities, and relationships which can aid a movement or movement organization in negotiating dilemmas, solving problems and attaining goals. There are three sources of mobilizable resources: the movement's beneficiary constituency, any conscience constituencies, and nonconstituency institutions. The first term refers to those beneficiaries of movement activities who also supply resources, and the second to those sympathizers who provide resources but are not directly or materially benefitted by the work of the movement. Institutional resources are those provided by legal codes, police protection, foundation grants and so on. On constituencies, see Jo Freeman, "Resource Mobilization and Strategy: A Model for Analyzing Social Movement Organization Actions," in John D. McCarthy and Mayer N. Zald eds., *The Dynamics of Social Movements* (Cambridge: Winthrop, 1979), pp. 172–177. "Mobilization" refers to the processes by which movement organizations gather and invest resources for the pursuit of goals.

5. For more about the strife over conceptualizations of power, see Steven Lukes, *Power: A Radical View* (London: MacMillan, 1974). I also draw on the discussion of power in Roger King, *The State in Modern Society: New Directions in Political Sociology* (Chatham, NJ: Chatham House, 1986).

6. Bertrand Russell, *Power: A New Social Analysis* (London: George Allen & Unwin, 1988), pp. 10–11. This is not to say that knowledge is identical to other forms or sources of power. It has its own particular characteristics—origins, manifestations, exercise—which, as relevant to ecology movements, are explored throughout this chapter.

7. Lukes, *Power*.

8. See Robert Dahl, *Who Governs?* (New Haven: Yale University Press, 1961) and Nelson Polsby, *Community Power and Political Theory* (New Haven: Yale University Press, 2nd ed., 1980). Weber understood power as ". . . the chance of a man or a number of men to realize their own will in a social action even against the resistance of others who are participating in the action." Quoted in Dennis Wrong, *Power: Its Forms, Bases, and Uses* (New York: Harper & Row, 1979), p. 21. Not all behavioralists follow Weber so closely; Talcott Parsons thought power a resource that transcended conflict situations. See his *Sociological Theory and Modern Society* (New York: Free Press, 1967). For a critique of behavioralist conceptions of power, see King,

The State in Modern Society. A Marxist critique of pluralism can be found in Charles H. Anderson, *The Political Economy of Social Class* (Englewood Cliffs, NJ: Prentice Hall, 1974).

9. See, especially, P. Bachrach and M. Baratz, "Two Faces of Power," *American Political Science Review* 56 (1962) and their *Power and Poverty* (New York: Oxford University Press, 1970). For a critique of their work, see G. Parry and P. Moriss, "When is a Decision Not a Decision?" in Ivor Crewe ed., *British Political Sociology Yearbook* (London: Croom Helm, 1974).

10. Frances Fox Piven and Richard Cloward, *Poor People's Movements: Why They Succeed, How They Fail* (New York: Vintage, 1977).

11. C. Wright Mills, *The Power Elite* (New York: Oxford University Press, 1956). Mills was criticized by Marxists who objected to his failure to develop a class analysis of capitalist society, to his reluctance to consider the power elite a ruling class, and to his characterization of non-elites as masses rather than classes.

12. On dispositional or reputational power, that stemming from the assessments of fellow influentials in the community, see Floyd Hunter, *Community Power Structure* (Chapel Hill, NC: Chapel Hill Books, 1953). It was Hunter's elitist (nonpluralist) findings about the operation of community power in the United States that moved Dahl and Polsby (see note 8) to conduct their studies. On situational power, that stemming from the structural overlap between the networks of economic and social elites and those of political decision-makers, see G. William Domhoff, *Who Rules America Now? A View for the '80s* (Englewood Cliffs, NJ: Prentice Hall, 1983).

13. This conception of ideology is close to that of Gramsci, Althusser, and the later Marx. Ideology in this regard is more than a system of ideas, more than the political consciousness of a class. It links Gramsci's concept of hegemony with Althusser's notions of ideology in general, which functions to secure cohesion in society, and particular ideologies, designed to secure the domination of particular classes. See Louis Althusser, *Lenin and Philosophy and Other Essays* (London: New Left, 1971); Antonio Gramsci, *Selections From the Prison Notebooks* (New York: International, 1971); Jorge Larrain, *Marxism and Ideology* (London: MacMillan, 1983).

14. Roger Friedland, *Power and Crisis in the City* (London: MacMillan, 1982), p. 2. Totally voiceless power is, of course, rarely achieved. This is why even the most powerful capitalists in the United States come together in interest associations such as the Business Roundtable and the National Association of Manufacturers.

15. Such conceptions of "false consciousness" reject the behavioralist equation of interests and wants. It is possible, of course, for people to want things contrary to their interests, to mistake their interests, or to be unaware of the motives for their actions. Critical theorists assign responsibility for the creation and reproduction of false consciousness to the functioning of capitalist ideology industries: popular culture, advertising, etc. See Herbert Mar-

cuse, *One-Dimensional Man* (London: Routledge and Kegan Paul, 1964); Jürgen Habermas, *Legitimation Crisis* (Boston: Beacon, 1975).

16. These questions are the parameters of a theoretical framework which links movement origins, resources, and resource mobilization through social control and political opportunity to the aftermaths of movement challenges. Such a framework should aid case studies and other empirical work necessary to build and test a theory for the explanation and prediction of environmental movement success and failure. I consider this chapter an initial foray toward construction of the framework.

17. The focus on movement resources has been the preserve of resource mobilization/management theories, which stress the microeconomic rationality of collective action, the importance of organization and movement entrepreneurs, and the contingency of political opportunities. At the risk of overgeneralization and at the price of some ethnographic detail, an analytic concept like resources can cut across time, space and culture. See John D. McCarthy and Mayer N. Zald, "Resource Mobilization and Social Movements: A Partial Theory," *American Journal of Sociology* 82 (1977); Anthony Oberschall, *Social Conflict and Social Movements* (Englewood Cliffs, NJ: Prentice-Hall, 1973); and Charles Tilly, *From Mobilization to Revolution* (Reading MA: Addison-Wesley, 1978). Alternately, New Social Movement theory arises from the macro-structural Marxian and Weberian traditions and explains movement origins and behavior in terms of changing social structures. See Alberto Melucci, "The New Social Movements: A Theoretical Approach," *Social Science Information* 19 (1980); and Claus Offe, "New Social Movements: Challenging the Boundaries of Institutional Politics," *Social Research* 52 (1985). Work has commenced to find complementarities between the two approaches. See Herbert Kitschelt, "Resource Mobilization Theory: A Critique," in Dieter Rucht ed., *Research on Social Movements: The State of the Art* (New York: Campus, 1986); and Bert Klandermans, Hanspeter Kriesi, and Sidney Tarrow eds., *From Structure to Action: Comparing Social Movement Research Across Cultures* (Greenwich, CT: JAI, 1988). My approach, while focused on resources, is sensitive to the concerns of new social movement theory, and I proceed in the spirit of synthesis.

18. This passage taps Jeff Wheelwright's *Weathering the Spill* (New York: Simon & Schuster, forthcoming).

19. For numerous examples of illiterate activists making headway against pervasive oppression, see Arthur Bonner, *Averting the Apocalypse: Social Movements in India Today* (Durham: Duke University Press, 1990).

20. Chico Mendes, *Fight for the Forest: Chico Mendes in His Own Words* (London: Latin America Bureau, 1989), p. 32.

21. Ibid., pp. 32, 35.

22. This is not to say that treaties that fail to confront the power of capital are bound for success—many treaties found unobjectionable in boardrooms founder.

23. Stephen Cotgrove, *Catastrophe or Cornucopia: The Environment, Politics and the Future* (New York: Wiley, 1982), p. 33.

24. This is a passage from a speech Darman gave at Harvard University excerpted in "The Talk of the Town" column of *The New Yorker*, June 18, 1990, p. 25.

25. Charles E. Lindblom and David K. Cohen, *Usable Knowledge: Social Science and Social Problem Solving* (New Haven: Yale University Press, 1979), p. 12. For an account of the importance of knowledge in organizational adaptation, see Ernst B. Haas, *When Knowledge is Power: Three Models of Change in International Organizations* (Berkeley: University of California Press, 1990).

26. See Lester Milbrath, *Environmentalists: Vanguard for a New Society* (Albany: State University of New York Press, 1984).

27. Such transnational networks, when they are organized around both a shared causal understanding and shared political goals, have been referred to as "epistemic communities." The term is generally used to refer to elite scientist-activist networks. See John Gerard Ruggie, "International Responses to Technology: Concepts and Trends," *International Organization* 29 (1975): 557–584; Peter Haas, "Do Regimes Matter? Epistemic Communities and Mediterranean Pollution Control," *International Organization* 43 (1989): 377–404. For an interview with activist anthropologist Darrell Posey, see Susanna Hecht and Alexander Cockburn, *The Fate of the Forest: Developers, Destroyers and Defenders of the Amazon* (London: Verso, 1989).

28. See Karen Litfin's contribution to this volume; Richard Elliot Benedick, *Ozone Diplomacy: New Directions in Safeguarding the Planet* (Cambridge: Harvard University Press, 1991); John E. Carroll ed., *International Environmental Diplomacy: The Management and Resolution of Transfrontier Environmental Problems* (Cambridge: Cambridge University Press, 1988); and Peter M. Haas, *Saving the Mediterranean: The Politics of International Environmental Cooperation* (New York: Columbia University Press, 1990).

29. This paragraph draws on a paper by Luther P. Gerlach, "The Problems and Prospects of Institutionalizing Ecological Interdependence in a World of Local Independence," presented to the Ecological Economics Conference, U.S. Forest Service, St. Paul, Minnesota, April 1990, and the sources he cites.

30. It finds support, for example, in Sheila Jasanoff, *The Fifth Branch: Science Advisors as Policy Makers* (Cambridge: Harvard University Press, 1990).

31. On the neglect shown the advice of bureaucratic analysts, see Martha S. Feldman, *Order without Design: Information Production and Policymaking* (Stanford: Stanford University Press, 1989). For a top-down view of the politics of advice, see Arnold J. Meltsner, *Rules for Rulers: The Politics of Advice* (Philadelphia: Temple University Press, 1990).

32. Space constraints prevent me from extending this critique to examine controversies such as those over the fact-value distinction, the ontological

implications of quantum mechanics, technocracy as ideology, and postpositivism in the social sciences. For a discussion of some of these issues, see Frank Fischer, *Technocracy and the Politics of Expertise* (Newbury Park: Sage, 1990).

33. For an overview and synthesis of two decades of political science research on the topic, see James P. Lester ed., *Environmental Politics and Policy: Theories and Evidence* (Durham: Duke University Press, 1989).

34. Joseph L. Sax, *Defending the Environment: A Strategy for Citizen Action* (New York: Knopf, 1971), p. i.

35. On public participation in environmental policymaking, see Albert E. Utton, W.R. Derrick Sewell and Timothy O'Riordan eds., *Natural Resources for a Democratic Society: Public Participation in Decision-Making* (Boulder: Westview, 1976). On the professionalization of movements, see John D. McCarthy and Mayer N. Zald, *The Trend of Social Movements in America: Professionalization and Resource Mobilization* (Morristown, N.J.: General Learning Press, 1973).

36. This examination of the "politicization of science" charge borrows from Gerlach, "The Problems and Prospects."

37. See Fred Emery and Eric L. Trist, *Toward a Social Ecology* (New York: Plenum, 1973); cited in Gerlach, "The Problems and Prospects."

38. On uncertainty and decision stakes, see Gerlach, this volume. Transscience is also more likely in North America and Western Europe where high levels of citizen skills, vigorous social movements, and the growing prevalence of ecological values combine to undermine the cultural hegemony of science and centralized technology. See Ronald Inglehart, *Culture Shift in Advanced Industrial Society* (Princeton: Princeton University Press, 1990).

39. See Murray Bookchin's critique of the tendency of reform environmentalists to weigh risks and benefits and to opt for the lesser of evils in *Toward an Ecological Society* (Montreal: Black Rose, 1980).

40. While popular resistance may lose specific encounters, it may also raise the costs of mega-projects high enough to rule out the proliferation of similar fiascoes. See Henry F. Bedford, *Seabrook Station: Citizen Politics and Nuclear Power* (Amherst: University of Massachusetts Press, 1990); and David E. Apter and Nagayo Sawa, *Against the State: Politics and Social Protest in Japan* (Cambridge: Harvard University Press, 1984). The record is less clear in Western Europe. See Dorothy Nelkin and Michael Pollack, *The Atom Besieged: Extraparliamentary Dissent in France and Germany* (Cambridge: MIT Press, 1981). On the other hand, there is the catch phrase common among slow-and-no-growth activists in Southern California: "Every victory is temporary, every defeat permanent."

41. Shiva, "People's Ecology," pp. 253–54.

42. Ibid., p. 257. Among these myths is that of the goddess Shiva's hair, a symbol for the hydrological role of the Himalayan forests in mediating the descent of the sacred Ganges.

43. My point here is not to ignore instances of ecological abuse in pre-colonial India, but rather to provide an example of the social construction of local knowledge as movement resource.

44. See David A. Snow, E. Burke Rochford, Jr., Steven K. Worden, and Robert D. Benford, "Frame Alignment Processes, Micromobilization, and Movement Participation," *American Sociological Review* 51 (1986).

45. The concept of "stewardship" has recently arisen in certain Christian theological circles as an alternative to the traditional notion of humanity's "dominion" over the environment.

46. On the temporary merger of ecology and independence movements in a different context, see Jancar, this volume; David R. Marples, *Ukraine Under Perestroika: Ecology, Economics and the Workers' Revolt* (New York: St. Martin's, 1991); and Jan Arveds Trapans ed., *Toward Independence: the Baltic Popular Movements* (Boulder: Westview, 1991). Three very different works for which the notion of the commons acts as focus are Harlan Cleveland, *The Global Commons: Policy for the Planet* (Lanham, MD: University Press of America, 1990); Luther P. Gerlach, "Cultural Construction of the Global Commons," in Robert H. Winthrop ed., *Culture and the Anthropological Tradition: Essays in Honor of Robert F. Spencer* (Lanham, MD: University Press of America, 1990); and Bonnie J. McCay and James M. Anderson eds., *The Question of the Commons: The Culture and Ecology of Communal Resources* (Tuscon: University of Arizona Press, 1987).

47. One such redefinition of "rationality" is a subject of John Dryzek's *Rational Ecology: The Political Economy of Environmental Choice* (Oxford: Basil Blackwell, 1987). See also the "comprehensive rationality" of Jürgen Habermas in *Theory and Practice* (Boston: Beacon, 1973) and *Knowledge and Human Interests* (Boston: Beacon, 1972).

48. Paul K. Feyerabend, *Science in a Free Society* (London: Verso, 1978), p. 10; cited in Shiva, "People's Ecology," p. 260.

49. This discussion of the policy process draws on Lynton Keith Caldwell's *International Environmental Policy: Emergence and Dimensions* (Durham, NC: Duke University Press, 1984). Also see Marvin S. Soroos, *Beyond Sovereignty: The Challenge of Global Policy* (Columbia, SC: University of South Carolina Press, 1986).

50. See Steven Kull, *Minds at War: Nuclear Reality and the Inner Conflicts of Defense Policymakers* (New York: Basic, 1988).

51. Movement organizations can also dispute the science or analysis used by state agencies during agenda-setting. See Jeremy Leggett ed., *Global Warming: The Greenpeace Report* (Oxford: Oxford University Press, 1990); see also the vast intellectual production of the critical peace research network, peace movement groups, and individuals in Western Europe and North America in the 1970s and 1980s, which challenged deterrence—the foundation of NATO security policy—and the weapons deemed necessary to shore up deterrence.

52. Roderick Frazier Nash brought the term "shocker" to my attention.

53. On the praxis of symbolism, see Murray Edelman, *The Symbolic Uses of Politics*, rev. ed. (Urbana: University of Illinois Press, 1985).

54. On postmaterialism, see Ronald Inglehart, *The Silent Revolution* (Princeton, NJ: Princeton University Press, 1977).

55. Murray Bookchin, *Remaking Society: Pathways to a Green Future* (Boston: South End, 1990), p. 15.

56. See Barry Commoner, *Making Peace with the Planet* (New York: Pantheon, 1990).

57. Luther Gerlach brought this new phrase to my attention.

58. Quoted in Thijs de la Court, *Beyond Brundtland: Green Development in the 1990s* (London: Zed, 1990), p. 15. In his critique of linear economic growth Mishra cites Gandhi's response to the question of whether, after independence, India might approximate Britain's standard of living: "It took Britain half the resources of the planet to achieve this prosperity; how many planets will a country like India require?"

59. For some ideas about how movement organizations can develop new competencies and better work together, see David C. Korten, *Getting to the 21st Century: Voluntary Action and the Global Agenda* (West Hartford, CT: Kumarian, 1990).

60. See, for example, William Ophuls, *Ecology and the Politics of Scarcity* (San Francisco: Freeman, 1977); Herman Daly ed., *Toward a Steady-State Economy* (San Francisco: Freeman, 1973); Kirkpatrick Sale, *Dwellers in the Land: The Bioregional Vision* (San Francisco: Sierra Club, 1985); E. F. Schumacher, *Small is Beautiful* (London: Abacus, 1974); Hazel Henderson, *The Politics of the Solar Age* (New York: Anchor, 1981); Kirkpatrick Sale, *Human Scale* (London: Secker & Warburg, 1980); Donella H. Meadows et al., *The Limits to Growth* (New York: New American Library, 1972); and Jonathan Porritt, *Seeing Green* (Oxford: Blackwell, 1984).

61. Mendes, *Fight for the Forest*, p. 60.

62. On the halting "greening" of the multilateral lenders, see Bruce Rich, "The Emperor's New Clothes: The World Bank and Environmental Reform," *World Policy Journal* 7 (Spring 1990): 305–329; and The Bank Information Center ed., *Funding Ecological and Social Destruction: The World Bank and International Monetary Fund* (Washington: Bank Information Center, 1989). For a specific study of the World Bank's role in financing ecological mayhem, see Robert S. Anderson and Walter Huber, *The Hour of the Fox: Tropical Forests, the World Bank, and Indigenous People in Central India* (Seattle: University of Washington Press, 1988). United Nations Environment Program Executive Director Tolba is concerned, however, that well-meaning First World ecologists might gain too much leverage with the World Bank: "The worst mistake that could be made is for the rich to apply conditionality to new aid and loans. And to turn environmental protection into a non-tariff barrier." See

Mostafa Tolba, Foreword to Peter Brackley ed., *World Guide to Environmental Issues and Organizations* (London: Longman, 1990), xi.

63. Jim Barnes of the Environmental Policy Institute, cited in Andre Carothers, "Defenders of the Forest," *Greenpeace* (July-August 1990), p. 12.

64. On sustainable development see Robert Goodland ed., *Race to Save the Tropics: Ecology and Economics for a Sustainable Future* (Washington: Island, 1990); David Pearce, Edward Barbier, and Anil Markandya, *Sustainable Development: Economics and Environment in the Third World* (Hants, UK: Elgar, 1990). On the genesis of the concept see William Ascher and Robert Healy, *Natural Resource Policymaking in Developing Countries: Environment, Economic Growth, and Income Distribution* (Durham: Duke University Press, 1990). Among the critics are Lori-Ann Thrupp, "Politics of the Sustainable Development Crusade: From Elite Protectionism to Social Justice in Third World Resource Issues," unpublished manuscript, June 1989; and de la Court, *Beyond Brundtland*.

65. The collective action of the Siriono people of Bolivia forced a "complete restructuring" of the 1987 swap negotiated by Conservation International (CI) with the Bolivian government. CI official María Teresa Ortiz now says "CI will only continue with the plan if the Indians participate." James Painter, "Indians Seek Revision of Debt-for-Nature Swap," *Christian Science Monitor*, September 18, 1990, p. 4.

66. Cited in Carothers, "Defenders of the Forest," p. 12.

67. My discussion of PAR taps Fals Borda's *Knowledge and People's Power*. PAR's ideological wellsprings are the theories of dependencia, the countertheory of subversion, the theology of liberation, dialogical pedagogy, and a reinterpretation of the work of Marx and Gramsci on the commitment and neutrality of scientists. Pilot projects were launched in Latin America in the 1970s, wider-ranging and refined endeavors in the 1980s. Other sources include Peter Reason and John Rowan eds., *Human Inquiry: A Sourcebook of New Paradigm Research* (New York: Wiley, 1981); and Juliet Merrifield, *Putting the Scientists in Their Place: Participatory Research in Environmental and Occupational Health* (New Market, TN: Highlander Center, 1989).

68. See Alain Touraine, *Sociologie de l'action* (Paris: Editions du Seuil, 1965), *The Voice and the Eye* (Cambridge: Cambridge University Press, 1981), and *Solidarity* (Cambridge: Cambridge University Press, 1983).

69. See Alberto Melucci, *Nomads of the Present: Social Movements and Individual Needs in Contemporary Society* (Philadelphia: Temple University Press, 1989) and the sources he cites.

70. Also see the discussion of participatory research in Fischer, *Technocracy*.

71. Foreword to Brackley ed., *World Guide*, p. xi.

72. On the diminished capacity of the state, see Habermas, *Legitimation Crisis*; and Martin Jänicke, *State Failure: The Impotence of Politics in Industrial Society* (University Park, PA: Pennsylvania State University Press, 1990). On

the relevance of the large, and small, changes in world politics to environmental problems, see James Rosenau's contribution to this volume and his *Turbulence in World Politics: A Theory of Change and Continuity* (Princeton: Princeton University Press, 1990).

73. Charles Tilly assigns little or no choice to what he calls "national social movements" independent of choices structured by state action. See his "States and Social Movements," in Charles Bright and Susan Harding eds., *Statemaking and Social Movements: Essays in History and Theory* (Ann Arbor: University of Michigan Press, 1984). An assessment of political opportunities allowing for more movement maneuvering room can be found in Jo Freeman, "Resource Mobilization and Strategy."

74. Ken Conca suggested this four-fold typology. For another mode, somewhat analogous to my description of bypassing the state, see Evelyn Pinkerton, "Intercepting the State: Dramatic Processes in the Assertion of Local Comanagement Rights," in McCay and Anderson, *Question of the Commons*. Other modes or their hybrids can no doubt be formulated. The point is that a typology of this sort might be useful in assessing change in the state system by delineating the modalities of movement-state interaction.

75. Worthy historical and analytical work on the effectiveness of movement strategies, the wisdom of movement choices and the outcome of movement challenges has been done by William A. Gamson, *The Strategy of Social Protest* (Homewood, IL: Dorsey, 1975); and Piven and Cloward, *Poor People's Movements*.

7

The Environmental Attractor in the Former USSR: Ecology and Regional Change

●

BARBARA JANCAR

The fall of communism in Eastern Europe and the Soviet Union has been attributed almost universally to the failure of the so-called so-cialist economic experiment. It is significant, however, that it was not economic failure that brought hundreds of thousands of people into the streets. Nor was it economic failure that spawned the multitude of grassroots movements and organizations that led, ultimately, to the abdication of the Communist Parties of Eastern Europe and the slow, tortuous breakup of the Soviet colossus. What first brought people into the streets was the state of the environment, the recognition that something was terribly wrong with their living conditions.

Between 1985 and 1989, under the impetus of glasnost and the disaster of Chernobyl, the Soviet media were providing ever more grisly information on environmental tragedies occurring throughout the country. In the cities, people organized against what was happening. Environmental protest was in full swing. Yet, only two years later, environmental activism saw a precipitous decline, its place taken by a resurgent nationalism that has since broken up the fragile federal consensus in Yugoslavia, opened the festering wounds of the Czech-Slovak relationship, and brought about the end of the USSR as a single state.

In this chapter, I investigate the dramatic shift from "warrior for ecology" to "champion of nationality" that took place among the most outspoken members of the Soviet population between 1989 and 1991. I first describe my conceptual and analytical frameworks for understanding this change, and then apply them to the Soviet situation.

"Strange Attractors"

My investigation is premised on three conceptual frameworks. The first is the notion of "attractors," a concept borrowed from chaos theory, which has been developed by the natural sciences. The second is "metastability," and the third is "Gaia." I use these concepts by way of metaphor and not as tools for rigorous analysis. Nonetheless, they can help us to understand what is happening in the former USSR.

Chaos

Chaos theory holds that dynamic, nonlinear systems that appear orderly may become completely disorganized over time, as the "initial conditions" in the system constantly change. One classic example of this process is the boiling of water: if you apply heat (initial condition) to water, eventually it boils and makes a phase transition to steam. Chaos theory applies to that transition point between the two phases, finding a pattern in seemingly chaotic, random turbulence. Some systems in chaos may shift to a new, stabilized state; others may never stabilize into an identifiable form. Nonetheless, in chaotic systems there can be found repetitive patterns of interaction that, although never identical, are similar to one another. These patterns tend to form around what theorists call "strange attractors," points in a system that appear to attract other points to them. In addition to the tendency of systems to become chaotic under the impact of ever-changing initial conditions, computer models used recently in biological research also suggest that complex systems tend toward what is termed "anti-chaos," or self-organization.[1] Chaos, in other words, can trigger movement toward antichaos.

Metastability

A second analytical frame of reference rests on a model of ecosystem dynamics, hypothesized from research in the biological sciences. This model of metastability presumes that ecosystems are not static, with any single point of stability but, rather, are constantly evolving. Moreover, at any given time there can be more than one "stability region," depending on the relationship between an ecosystem's resilience and its stability.[2] The system's behavior is said to be "discontinuous" when its elements move from one region of stability to another—during which time the behavior of the system becomes chaotic—because they "become attracted to a different equilibrium condition." The new order may be chronologically related to the old, but the break between the two is complete and irrevocable, and there is no turning back.[3]

Gaia and Surprise

Our perception of and ability to manage human society, and the natural ecosystems within which it exists, are related to a third set of concepts, namely gaia and surprise. The gaia hypothesis posits a global biochemical tendency toward system equilibrium (or metastability around specific equilibrium conditions) that is, to an as yet undetermined degree, controlled by natural systems on earth.[4] Gaia may be considered the first organizing principle of the global environment. Surprise relates to the impact of local human activity on the global environment. Surprise is the unexpected event that occurs when a perceived reality differs sharply from that which was anticipated,[5] and when the unexpected imposes itself upon our consciousness and our selective attention is no longer able to screen out the event by reference to old explanations and rationalizations. According to Harvey Brooks, surprise may occur as an unexpected, discrete event of a technological, natural, political, or economic nature, or as some combination of the four. An example of this would be Chernobyl, which was not only a technological surprise but a political one as well. Surprise may also be the result of a sudden discontinuity in a long-term trend, as happened in the Soviet Union in the 1980s, with the advent of perestroika and glasnost. Or, surprise may arise from the sudden emergence into political consciousness of new information, such as the relationship between chlorofluorocarbons (CFCs) and the Antarctic ozone hole.[6]

We can integrate the gaia and surprise hypotheses with the concepts derived from chaos theory and ecosystem dynamics to illuminate the consequences of global ecological interdependence as follows: the unexpected discovery that human action on the local level can influence global environmental equilibrium and trigger global environmental change has thrown the world and its constituent state political systems into disequilibrium. Out of this emerges two competing sets of tensions, change versus continuity and centralization versus decentralization. These tensions have led to an erosion of authority around the world and the search for new modes of governance to replace those which increasing numbers of people believe have abjectly failed to secure the survivability of life on this planet as we know it.[7]

As those pursuing decentralization disassociate themselves from existing modes of authority at the state level, they push toward greater autonomy at the substate level. In their insistence that the human community at the international level recognize their legitimacy and right to freedom of action, these substate actors operate under the pull of two sets of "strange attractors" in the turbulent international arena: the attraction of democracy and the attraction of substate identity, be it ethnicity, race, or nationalism. But the old state order is unwilling to relinquish its power and thus serves as the attractor for those political and economic forces preferring continuity to the uncertainties and disequilibrium of change.

Global Environment

The global environment constitutes the fourth attractor in the framework I am developing here. The gaia hypothesis renders the environmental movement incapable of permanent attraction to either substate autonomy or the old state institutions, but urges it to seek to form new institutions that can directly relate local human activity to global environmental change, thus securing the ecological integrity of the planet. The world has entered chaos, a nonlinear discontinuous period of change, where surprise provides the changing initial condition, which at some moment in time will trigger the antichaos or spontaneous self-organization principle. A new order, I claim, is being born.

Strange Attractors at Work

The former Soviet Union provides an excellent laboratory within which to apply this analytical framework. The policies of perestroika and glasnost were offered as the Soviet political elite's response to the first "surprise" of irreversible discontinuities in the economy. At that point, the old order saw change as a modification of, not a radical change in, the system and acted accordingly. Consequently, the split between the centrifugal forces of change and the centrists seeking continuity was inevitable. Chernobyl was the second surprise, and with it came a recognition that local technological failure could trigger wide-ranging political and social consequences. It was at this point that the fourth attractor, the global environment, entered the scene, so to speak. Not only was the old order blamed worldwide for environmental failure, it was also put in the unhappy position of having to seek assistance from the global community to deal with the consequences of the disaster. As political authority eroded, grassroots movements increased both in numbers and in intensity.

Based on the source of their attraction, these movements fell into three general categories: (1) democracy and civil rights; (2) national or ethnic autonomy; and (3) the environment. The first two traced their modern beginnings to the dissident movements, formed following the thaw of 1956, that were subsequently repressed and forced underground.[8] The environmental movement began in the corridors of the biology department of Moscow University, which was the first to reassert its links with the tsarist environmental tradition and the heady environmentalism of the 1920s.[9]

With the advent of glasnost, the three movements converged in their singleminded desire to get rid of the old regime. By the end of the eighties, however, the movements had divided, subdivided, and divided again, in a typical chaotic pattern. The nineties began with growing fragmentation and attempts to form larger movements from the fragmented units. After five years of tumultuous change, the Communist Party remained the one established political force, although it, too, was breaking up over the issues of continuity and change, and centralization versus decentralization. The opposition was completely fragmented, unable to impose its will. Environmental issues were more critical than ever, but neither the eroded center nor the emerging periphery had sufficient power to do anything about them. The evolving turbulence eventually brought on the disintegration of the Soviet with all its attendant consequences.

The transition from one "metastable" state to another is not in and of itself a negative phenomenon. If the assumptions of chaos theory are valid, there is a pattern in the turbulence which, at some point, will trigger the tendency toward self-organization, as the old system disintegrates into a new one. Thus, I regard conditions before and after August 1991 as a "process" of transition, and not as a discontinuous interregnum between one "phase" state and another. The political forces which move to the fore in this process are those that may be expected to "crystallize" spontaneously into a new, stable order at some future time.

The question thus becomes: can we discern a pattern in the disorder leading up to 1991 and thereafter? To answer the question, I propose to apply three aspects of my model to current post-Soviet reality: the role of "surprise" and the change in initial conditions in shaping politics in the former Soviet Union, the impact of gaia on the behavior of the informal groups, and the role of democracy, nationalism, and the environment as "strange attractors" during the turbulent period.

"Surprise" as a Change in Initial Conditions

Over the past thirty years, three kinds of surprise operated on the Soviet stage: political, economic, and environmental. The first two are difficult to separate one from another, since both grew out of events in the 1950s. Khrushchev's speech to the 20th Congress of the Communist Party of the Soviet Union (CPSU) in 1956 was the first political surprise, and constituted the initial condition for the undermining of the Party's authority. From there, the way led to the signing of the Helsinki Agreements in 1975, which put human rights at the top of the dissident agenda. Thence to perestroika and, finally, to the CPSU's, and the country's, dissolution.

Khrushchev's speech ushered in a brief period of liberalization. Soviet science was freed from its chains of dogmatism exemplified by Lysenko, and was able to renew its contacts with the outside world. Literature and art began to test the limits of socialist realism and to write more realistically about Soviet conditions. And perhaps of greatest importance, Khrushchev opened up a possibility for the rebirth of civil society with his doctrine of the "all-people's state," and his call for the transfer of state functions to volunteer popular groups, or *druzhiny*.[10] Some of these groups represented a further state intrusion into private life, while others managed to retain their autonomy and freedom of action until the Gorbachev era. Among these were the student environmental *druzhiny*, discussed below.

Space does not permit a detailed recounting of the chain of surprises and change; suffice it to say, however, that glasnost (openness) was a direct outgrowth of the political changes wrought by the 1956 speech and the 1975 Helsinki human rights provisions. The idea of glasnost, developed by a narrow circle of individuals, including Gorbachev, Shevardnadze, and Yakovlev, argued that as Soviet science and technology could not be modernized without the end of ideological supervision, so Soviet society could not be mobilized to take a responsible role in the Soviet economy without the freedom to criticize and express alternative courses of action. Gorbachev saw glasnost as only the right to make constructive criticism, but events overtook him. Glasnost ultimately provided the ideological legitimation for the proliferation of all kinds of grassroots movements in every republic of the Soviet Union, some of them carryovers from the earlier period.

Economic surprise also came in discontinuous stages. By the mid-1980s, global developments in technology and the conduct of business had put the Soviet Union so far behind that the leadership could no longer close its eyes to economic stagnation and deterioration. Perestroika ("restructuring") was the center's admission that a one-party, centrally planned economy was no longer capable of generating efficient economic growth. This admission went to the heart of the communist ideology, which held that only under socialism could the economy attain its maximum efficiency and productivity. The command economy had become an anachronism.

But perestroika was not only a response to economic surprise; it also became a surprise in itself. It required a whole new orientation toward work and production—the kindling of initiative, and the spirit of entrepreneurship among peoples who had no experience of them; it demanded responsibility and commitment. All of these were virtues that the command system had, in the past, found politically dangerous. When coupled with glasnost, moreover, perestroika led to two unanticipated outcomes. On the one hand, it provided the economic legitimation for the growth of grassroots activism, as it tore away the economic underpinnings of suppression. On the other, it confirmed the inability of the leadership to maintain further control over the economic, political, and cultural life of the Soviet Union and its East European satellites.

Within the USSR, the various nationalities very quickly understood the implications of these changes. First the Armenians, then the Balts, Georgians, and Moldavians demanded the right to choose their own independent path. In 1989, Eastern Europe broke away; in 1990, the Russian Republic passed legislation to move toward a market economy; by the end of 1991, the Union was gone, too. Increasingly, the central government in Moscow was seen as a brake on, rather than a catalyst for, change. Constant changes in initial economic and political conditions had shifted the initiative from the center to the republican periphery. Further development now depended on the changes in conditions at the subfederal level.

Environmental surprise followed the others. Here, too, the effects were cumulative. In the late 1960s, the domestic controversy over the future of Lake Baikal revealed the tip of the environmental iceberg.[11] As students were organizing environmental initiatives at the university, their elders began cautiously to do environmental battle in the prestigious halls of the institutes of the USSR and republican Academies of Sciences. In 1972, the Soviet Union took part in the first world conference on the environment held under UN auspices in Stockholm. The Helsinki Agreements further committed the Soviet leadership to an environmental posture. One result was that protection of the environment rapidly moved to the forefront of the Soviet agenda. While most environmental data were still treated as a matter of national security, increasing numbers of articles and editorials were published in the mass media, reporting on pollution caused by the industrial ministries, the inadequacy of measures to attack the problem, and the damage caused by pollution.

During the 1970s, environmental management was institutionalized.[12] Environmental inspectorates were set up in all the industrial ministries, and lead organizations were identified to coordinate environmental management in each environmental area (water, air, forests, land). But largely because of the center's monopoly of planning, these developments did virtually nothing to arrest pollution. Republican, regional, and local governmental authorities were powerless to stop the environmentally destructive behavior of enterprises within their jurisdictions, because these were answerable only to their superiors in the appropriate ministry in Moscow.

In an effort to forestall further adverse developments, scientists within the republics began to take risks by making public their cases to the international community. They also tried to stop destructive environmental practices by networking across institutes and regions. By the end of the Brezhnev era, pro-environmental specialists had become so visible that groupings of them were associated with specific institutions, such as the USSR Academy of Sciences Institute of Geography, Institute of State and Law, the Far Eastern Division of the Academy, Siberian branch, and the Estonian Academy of Sciences.[13] But it took a much greater environmental surprise to cause real mobilization.

Chernobyl was the second, and greatest, environmental surprise, and it had three decisive consequences. First, it led to a complete breakdown of public confidence in the ability of the leadership to handle the accident's effects and, by inference, to deal with anything else. It also contributed to the rapid strengthening of independence movements in the Ukraine and Belorussia. Second, Chernobyl turned the public against virtually all large-scale energy projects undertaken by the central authorities, whether they were hydroelectric dams, nuclear power, or oil. And, third, Chernobyl turned the policy of glasnost from rhetoric to reality. After a week of silence, the Soviet government began to release information about the accident.

With this, the dam broke; there poured forth a torrent of information in the mass media on subjects about which the average Soviet citizen was ignorant: events in Soviet history, the Second World War, drug addiction, crime, and the environment. As the reports came in, the full extent of environmental degradation in the USSR came home to all who cared to read the periodicals: the health of young and old ruined by pesticides and erosion in the cotton growing areas of Central Asia, the drying up of the Aral Sea, pollution in the coal producing region of the Don Bas, the Kola Peninsula turned into a wasteland. The procession of horror stories led to increased criticism of the Communist regime. It was no longer a question of what kind of change, but *how* to move toward a more democratic system. Environmental surprise thus proved to be the last, and perhaps critical, shift in initial conditions, moving most of Soviet society away from any interest in restructuring the one-party command toward a policy of complete change.

The Impact of Gaia

Gaia was a factor in Soviet politics from the time when, with the movement to protect Lake Baikal, the environment first arrived on the federal agenda. Included in the reasons for Baikal's preservation were the presence of life forms that had survived from earlier eras only because of its immense depth and unique ecosystem, and its status as the largest freshwater lake in the world. Both reasons made it an important global resource, and when Soviet scientists argued their case, they stressed that decisions made about Baikal had global implications.[14] Nationalism was, indisputably, another factor at work in the Lake Baikal issue. A leader in the fight to preserve the lake was the rural writer Valentin Rasputin who, more recently, has made no secret of his association of environmental values with the preservation of Russian culture and history.[15]

Gaia played an even more important role in the arguments surrounding the hotly debated projects of the Brezhnev years, the gigantic Siberian and Volga river diversions. Here too, the Siberian environmental lobby, led by Rasputin, played the Great Russian card. But the argument that captured the attention of the international scientific community had to do with possible changes to the Siberian climate and, by extension, to global climate.[16]

Again, however, it was the two major disasters during the Gorbachev era—Chernobyl and the dessication of the Aral Sea—that brought to the fore the global implications of poor Soviet management of the domestic environment. In the Soviet Union, environmental groups mobilized to prevent the further spread of nuclear power in virtually every republic and, after Chernobyl, these groups mushroomed. By 1989, there were over 300 such groups in Leningrad alone. In the Ukraine, Yurii Shcherbak brought together most of the Ukrainian groups into the umbrella organization, *Zelenyi svit* (Green World), later using it to organize the Green Party of Ukraine along the lines of the European Green Parties.[17] After 1986, the major Western environmental organizations, Friends of the Earth and Greenpeace, went to Moscow to connect with Soviet groups. Contact between Soviet environmentalists and their Western counterparts became almost routine. Nuclear disaster and environmental degradation were too important a matter to leave to one country to handle alone.

The drying up of the Aral Sea was a less publicized disaster, and it showed the limits to environmental mobilization. While essentially a regional problem, the fate of the Aral exemplified the prevailing human tendency to embark upon giant projects with insufficient study of their possible consequences.[18] In this case, the disaster was the product of modern day hubris, the deliberate Soviet policy during the Brezhnev years to provide the final solution for the irrigation of

Central Asian cotton. The Aral Sea problem thus makes a global statement about the relationship between sound development policy and environmental integrity. But the level of environmental organization—especially, local—around this problem has been much lower than that over Chernobyl. Thus this disaster makes a different statement about the relationship between environmental activism and international efforts to remedy a situation, to wit: among politically marginal populations, where there is no highly visible gaia effect, there is little international effort, and weak local effort.[19]

The impact of gaia on Soviet politics may be described as reciprocal. On the one hand, poorly conceived development policies in Siberia, Estonia, and Central Asia forced Soviet environmentalists to spread the story internationally in order to forestall, or halt, the worst aspects of the policies' consequences. On the other, the environmental surprise caused by the policies was so large that it could not be kept a Soviet secret and thus attracted immediate international attention. The gaia theory holds that all human activity on the local level affects the global environment, and gaia's pull forced the Soviet Union into an international context. The procession of environmental tragedies of global proportions that has struck the Soviet Union has internationalized the problem of the management of Soviet environmental degradation and made global cooperation essential.

Democracy, Nationalism, and the Environment as "Strange Attractors"

If we look at pre-transition politics in the former Soviet Union we see turbulence, but turbulence characterized by a distinctive pattern of evolution. First, the general pull of all the attractors has been toward decentralization and change. Second, the center attractor became increasingly isolated as groups split off. Third, the formations and reformations of groups have tended to occur where democratic and environmental fields of attraction intersect, or where these two intersect with nationalism. The direction of the splits and reformations was toward inclusivity in the democratic and environmental sectors. Fourth, the nationalist attractor exercised a much more clearly defined pull and there was less divisive activity within its field. The nationalist attractor may or may not have operated within the field of the democratic attractor. By contrast, the environmental attractor and democratic attractors operated increasingly along parallel lines.

The pattern was directed toward change and decentralization and suggested several possible outcomes. One would have been for the center to prevail. But vitality and action lay in the fields of the democratic and environmental attractors. A purely nationalist outcome forecast continued turbulence, especially if all the nationalities were to insist on autonomy. If nationalism were to stabilize at the republican level, the pattern predicted a decentralized but not necessarily democratic or pro-environmental outcome.

By 1992, the national attractor was clearly in the ascendancy, particularly in the periphery of the former USSR. Ethnic wars raged in the Caucasus, Moldava, Azerbaidjan, and Armenia, while a savage civil war in Tadzhikistan threatened to draw in the adjacent Uzbek population. The Baltic republics threw down a tough citizenship challenge to their resident ethnic Russians. Everywhere turbulence continued. However, nationalism seemed to exert less attraction in Ukraine, Belarus, and Russia, where democratic and environmental values continued to exercise a strong attraction. Even though the democratic and environmental movements in these latter republics became fragmented and unstable, these defects could be turned into assets as the movements searched for new modes of cooperation to bring about their return to center-stage. A brief look at the history, geography, and function of the three movements may help to clarify emerging strategies and options.

History

We can trace the role of the environmental groups, and their relationship to the civil rights and nationalist movements, in the onset and progress of turbulence in what was the Soviet Union. As I noted above, the democratic, nationality and civil rights movements of the 1980s grew out of the dissident movement that started during Khrushchev's rule. Dissidents sought not the overturning of the regime but its modification, by making the authorities adhere to the letter of the laws that they themselves had signed into force. National demands, often infused with religious elements, generally came from those nationalities which had had some previous experience with nationhood, or from those which had been forcibly uprooted by Stalin. These groups were notable in the Muslim republics, in Catholic Lithuania, and in Ukraine. Great Russian nationalism and orthodox Slavophile ideology returned to the Russian intellectual scene as well.[20]

Generally speaking, the intellectual foundations of the civil rights movement may be found in two different ideological groups, divided by Rudolf Tokes into the moral-absolutist and instrumental-pragmatists. The first was committed to reshaping Soviet political culture along what was considered to be more ethical lines; the second was composed of liberal members of the scientific, technical, educational, and academic elites, primarily from the scientific community.[21] These groups first emerged during the political thaw of the Khrushchev period. By 1970, the two groups were converging in their demands for more civil and nationality rights, in part because of a change in perception of leading Soviet scientists away from a very elitist ideology to a more pragmatic one. The literary and artistic community also experienced liberation during the thaw. Although the thaw did not mean that one could write and paint at will, dissidence for the creative community came to mean testing the waters and pushing Party guidelines to their limits.[22] The result of this process was the Moscow Civil Rights group.

The environmental movement developed separately from the other two, beginning in the elite setting of the biology department of Moscow University (MGU), where the science faculty had had historically close ties with the All-Russian Society for the Protection of Nature. The movement itself grew out of one of Khrushchev's rough attempts toward democratic reform: the encouragement of informal volunteer organizations, or druzhiny. In 1960, a student druzhina for nature conservation at MGU received the right to organize; by 1979, there were 29 student environmental groups with a total membership of around 3,000 operating from the major university centers of the USSR. By 1990 the Association of Druzhiny for Nature Conservation (DOP) included 134 groups from all over the Soviet Union.[23]

The movement was very proud of its relative independence and the large network of participating groups. It also was extremely careful to preserve its unique legal status as a registered organization not under the patronage of any mass organization, ministry, or institute. It was highly elitist and thus made no effort to be a mass organization. But its concern to maintain this unique status made the movement reluctant to undertake any actions that might in any way be considered "political." The movement thus shied away from all discussions on how to reverse the deteriorating environmental situation. There was, however, increased frustration as the activities of these groups changed nothing. By the mid-eighties, many druzhiniki found themselves sitting on the sidelines with empty hands as perestroika swept the country.[24] The students' mentors, the environmental lobby of scientific experts and literati, were also careful not to engage in "politics." As privileged employees of privileged institutions, environmental scientists preferred to keep their apolitical status, and not risk their research facilities, contacts abroad, and preferential living conditions. Since environmentalism at this time had no popular basis, job security meant keeping in step with the administrative hierarchy.

During the seventies and eighties, one generation of students replaced the other. As the older students left, the environmental movement gradually lost its glamour. Following Chernobyl, the student movement was in a weak position to capitalize on the proliferation of grassroots environmental organizations or provide the necessary leadership.

By 1988, the chief characteristic of the Soviet environmental movement was fragmentation. In December of that year, however, scientists and students, many of whom were former members of the student movement, came together to organize the Socio-Ecological Union. The Union was constituted as an umbrella organization uniting local grassroots environmental groups from all over the USSR. The political acumen and activism of the Union resulted ultimately in its being named the official Soviet agent in the USA/USSR Cooperation in Nature Conservation under the Environmental Agreement.[25]

This brief history of the three movements—civil rights, nationalist, environmental—highlights several factors that ensured their survival during the Brezhnev era and defined their relative "starting positions" in 1985. One factor almost equally common to all of them is "networking." Each movement developed networks of contacts within the Soviet Union as well as abroad, and every network included a means of communication and disseminating information by courier, underground publishing, and word of mouth. Networking was essential for the survival of informal groups under the former communist system.

A second factor was the saliency of the movement. In this category, public awareness of, and access to, the issue were critical. Here, nationalism clearly came first, followed by civil rights, especially when coupled with nationality rights, with environmentalism last. Seventy years of communism did not succeed in replacing the primary allegiance of Soviet citizens to their ethnic groups. Nationalism, however, has to be put in context. During the Khrushchev and Brezhnev years, while there were no dissident movements in Central Asia, the Soviet constitution permitted an official national language and press in each of the Central Asian republics. Hence, whenever the republican leaderships felt any displeasure with or resentment of the center, these attitudes could be put into print. As the seventies and eighties progressed, more and more anti-Russian sentiment found its way into the national republican press. In this respect, the quiet revolt that was brewing in Central Asia may be appropriately compared to the independence movements in the former British colonies of Africa and Asia against domination by a totally different culture and race.[26]

A third factor was complexity. National identity was basic, coming after town and family identify, whereas the rights of freedom of speech and assembly were not intuitively obvious. Behind the latter lay a whole moral and political philosophy regarding the human condition and the ends of humanity that required an education to understand. Environmental issues were the most complex and comprehensive of the three. The students were unable to exert leadership of the movement after 1986 because they had had little prior experience either with solving environmental problems or developing and implementing an environmental program.

Chernobyl awoke the Soviet public to the seriousness of environmental deterioration, and the immediate reaction was a desire to do away with any and all development that risked the environment. The rejection of development was accompanied by a rejection of the political system that could let such disasters happen. Again, the response was simplistic, with people thinking that free elections and a democratic government would immediately solve all environmental problems.

Finally, there was the factor of political sensitivity. With its monopoly of the mass media and state security, the regime was able to control both the growth of dissidence and the access of the dissidents to decision-making.[27] This control, in effect, insulated the political decisions regarding elite maintenance from policy and administrative decisions on economic and social affairs, with two very important consequences for the environmental movement.

From first to last, the Soviet leadership viewed environmental issues as, essentially, a matter for *administrative* and not *political* decisionmaking. In retrospect, this was a major error on the part of the authorities. At the end of the sixties, there had emerged a gray area of semi-legitimacy within which those seeking pragmatic reform of the regime could urge more attention to socialist legality and human rights within the socialist framework. Environmental issues became part of this gray area, while political democracy and nationality rights remained among the impermissible demands. Environmental criticism steadily increased. After 1972, discussion of environmental issues became sufficiently acceptable that they could be used as a foil to conceal national and civil rights agendas.[28]

By contrast, efforts to expand the semi-legitimate areas of scientific and artistic expression continuously came up against the censorship barrier, and national autonomy and political pluralism remained nonissues until well into the Gorbachev era. Thus, during the seventies, environmental issues acquired a symbolic function, especially in the area of nationality rights, that in the first years of glasnost brought huge numbers into the streets of the republican capitals to demonstrate against pollution and, by inference, for national autonomy. But because few people had any idea of the complexity of environmental problems, or of the sacrifices that might be demanded of them to implement environmental programs, the issues never acquired the status of issues in their own right among the general public. As in Eastern Europe, once it became possible openly to take action in the more obviously political areas of national autonomy and democracy, the rationale for popular interest in environmental issues collapsed. The movements lost their political force.

Second, because environmental issues were less politically sensitive, environmental experts and student activists were not automatically thrust into dissidence, but could work openly with less fear of government reprisals than could civil and nationality rights advocates. In many East European countries, environmental experts argued over whether it was necessary to change the regime to save the environment; for example, Janos Varga, the biologist founder of the Hungarian Danube Circle, insisted that "the environment knows no regime." Thus, while lower political sensitivity enabled student and scientist environmentalists to work on environmental problems, it produced a less politicized pool of activists. In Eastern Europe, after the scientist leaders of the informal pre-transition environmental movements were co-opted into the new democratic governments as experts in 1989–1990, there was no one to take their place. The huge mass of followers disappeared.

The history of the informal movements thus contains the seminal weaknesses of current transition politics. The strongest attractor remains nationality. Democracy was an attractor of and for the elite. The environmental attractor never achieved real autonomy, because the complexity of the issues obscured the political component inherent in them. Instead, environmental issues were increasingly used as foils to cover up what were perceived to be the more basic issues of nationality and human rights. As a result, environmental issues today are low on the lists of republican priorities.

Geography

Contrary to what might be anticipated after the accident at Chernobyl, the seriousness of an environmental event was not a good predictor of the formation of grassroots environmental groups in the Soviet Union. A 1990–1991 Institute of Geography study of the environmental movement in the former Soviet Union (FSU),[29] found that among the three basic cultural regions, Europe, Eurasia (Russia), and Asia, environmental groups were concentrated mostly in the major cities in Europe and Eurasia. The largest numbers of groups were located in the European region, in the Ukraine, primarily Kieve and Lvov, the two "capitals" of Ukrainian nationalism, in the capitals of the three Baltic republics, and in what was then Moldavia. In Russia, Moscow, and Leningrad (now St. Petersburg) had by far the largest number of environmental organizations. The few groups in the Caucasus were based in the capitals. A very few groups could be found in the capital cities of the Central Asian Republics, also in the capital cities. The study showed no organization in the area affected by the Aral Sea disaster until Moscow activists went down to organize.

Soviet scholars liked to explain their political scene by the presence or absence of a politically active social strata. Geographer Evgenii Schwartz criticized the student environmental movement precisely for its failure to take a more critical political stance.[30] In his view, environmental groups gained a mass following only when the issues at stake were seen as critical by a large enough stratum of the population with national aspirations. His analysis seems to be borne out by the facts.

Of the FSU's three cultural areas, that with the strongest political traditions and links to political and national developments in Europe was the European section—the Baltics, the Ukraine, Moldavia, Armenia, and Georgia. Much of this area had access to the European mass media so that people were able to keep abreast of events in East Central Europe. The environmental groups were among the first grassroots groups to organize. Everywhere they were met with hostility by the authorities. Under these circumstances, it was preferable to take refuge in numbers, and so the environmental organizations formed in 1986–1987 quickly gave up their autonomy and joined the popular fronts pioneered in the Baltic Republics. Subsequently, Green Parties throughout the region pulled out of the fronts and formed independent organizations.

If nationalism lay behind the formation of environmental groups in the western republics, the environmental concerns which prompted the proliferation of groups in Russia were more personal and much more apolitical. Fear of harm to themselves and their families' health most certainly was the impetus behind the protest of local environmental groups over local conditions. Although nationalism was doubtless behind the desire of groups like Leningrad's *Spasenie* (Salvation) to preserve cultural monuments, environmentalism with a Great Russian "face" was little evident in the activities of most local groups, the DOP, or the Moscow-based Socio-Ecological Union. While Valentin Rasputin, Pamyat, and the Russian Patriotic Bloc advocated the preservation of Russian nature in terms of the preservation of Russian values,[31] the mainstream of Russian environmentalism paid little attention to these issues.

As a consequence, the environmental movement in the Russian Republic initially pushed out in all directions, with hundreds of local and issue-specific groups each protesting a particular environmental wrong. Only in 1987 were umbrella groups formed. Once again, however, these addressed specific environmental issues. *Spasenie*, for example, sponsored the organization of a Council on Ecology, which united 300-odd groups under a single association for the purpose of promoting pro-environmental candidates in the 1989 elections in the Leningrad Region. The primary goal of the Moscow-based Socio-Ecological Union was the promotion of practical solutions to environmental problems.

Democracy was another matter. The Socio-Ecological Union's program clearly spoke out against "red-tape monopolies," and urged taking advantage of perestroika to implement "concrete steps" in environmental protection.[32] Schwartz argued for a second and more radical view, that without a fundamental change in the economic and political structure of Soviet society,[33] organizations like the Union could ultimately be subverted and brought under the control of what was then the still-existing government monopoly.

Schwartz's concerns went to the heart of the split over tactics that cut through the international environmental movement as a whole, and now influences environmental politics in the former lands of the

Soviet Union. Instrumentalists argue that the environment can be preserved by appropriate legal and economic measures and focus on getting laws passed and regulations implemented, that is, on attempts to reform the system as it now exists. Radicals call for a restructuring of modern society away from the domination of what the Greens call the bureaucratic-corporate-intelligentsia (BCI) and toward what Barry Commoner terms "ecodemocracy."[34] Reforms in Eastern Europe and the former Soviet Union thus produced two revolutions: The first, started by Gorbachev, sought to influence government policy to the profit of production, while the second emphasized values: democracy, peace, environmental security, the interdependence between humanity and nature.[35] In my view, these two revolutions were and are mutually exclusive. So long as society's dominant purpose remains economic growth, the human and natural environment can be expected to continue to deteriorate. The formation of Green Parties independent of the nationalist popular fronts in virtually all of the western republics suggests that even those environmentalists who pretend to be apolitical are acutely sensitive to this problem.

Perestroika came to Central Asia somewhat later than it did in the European part of the Soviet Union. Because the area had no dissident movement, the opposition of recent years was the first to have emerged in the past half-century. To Central Asian leaders, perestroika meant freedom from the Russian center. The exploitation by the Central Asian leaderships of what might be called "the Russian card" to secure their own position meant that environmental issues remained under republican control and, even today, have yet to take on the transforming symbolism they acquired in what was the Soviet west or among the native peoples in Siberia.

The primary concern in the region was and is the economy. Central Asia is largely made up of rural inhabitants who retain a patriarchal way of life and thinking. There is a deep gap between the mentality and way of life of villagers and of the intellectuals who head the national movements.[36] Popular reaction to deteriorating economic conditions was rooted in traditional ethnic and religious rivalries. The first riots in the Ferghana valley in 1989–90 were prompted by the center's attempt to resettle Meshketlan Turks under persecution in the Caucasus. Those that followed were between Kirghiz and Uzbeks over housing and deteriorating living conditions. As the central economic structure collapsed, unemployment in the area increased. The public is a long way from understanding that one of the culprits fomenting the violence is not rival ethnic claims over scarce economic goods but decades of environmental mismanagement.

The reasons that serious air, water, and land pollution[37] have yet to generate a substantial environmental movement in these republics is that environmental problems have been considered symptoms, not causes, of the regions' current economic difficulties. The officially stated cause was Moscow's colonial policies, and all over the area there has been a search for ethnic and religious identity, manifested in a resurgence of Islam as well as Tajik, Kazakhi, and Uzbeki nationalisms.[38]

The strong reaction against the Russian center, and the increase in inter-regional ethnic strife, argue poorly for the emergence of either a strong national or regional environmental movement in the near future, with or without support from Moscow or abroad. The sole exception is to be found in the Nevada-Semipalatinsk environmental group, whose demonstrations brought about the halt of nuclear testing at the Balkanur testing grounds in Kazakhstan.[39] As long as environmental tragedies are seen in terms of the consequences of colonial rule, the focus of popular action will be against domination by the center and against resident European Russians, and thus increasingly ethnically oriented. In contrast to the European republics, nationalism is not associated with democracy in Central Asia. Hence, environmental remediation is not necessarily predicated upon a democratic system. The establishment of new national states free of colonial relations with Moscow takes precedence above all else.

Form Follows Function

During the six years of Gorbachev's tenure the function of each of the attractors went through a profound change. This change produced an equally important shift in the interactive pattern between them. In 1985, the CPSU was the attractor of the forces of change, including democracy, and to a lesser extent nationalism. By 1987, the democracy and nationalism attractors were pulling the republican periphery into their orbit. The popular fronts in the western part of the Soviet Union used the environment as a symbol for both decentralizing values. In Central Asia, democracy was purely negative, anti-center and anti-Russian. There, the opposite pole to centralization was nationalism.

From 1989 to 1991, the main thrust of political development was thus the polarization between the center and the periphery. The aborted attempts to forge a union treaty reflected the changed function of the democratic attractor. Whereas the notion of a "Union of Sovereign Republics" had previously served as a positive counterweight to totalitarian government, by 1991, the idea had taken on a negative connotation, and was seen as a means of maintaining the old *nomenklatura* with the illusion of republican control. Decentralization in this context did not promise a program of democratic institution-building within the constituent elements of the union.

The August 1991 coup brought democracy back to center stage. Democratic national institutions were utilized to connect democratic elites with popular demonstrators to create a mass opposition to the conservatives at the center of the Party and the military-industrial complex. If Yeltsin is successful, the turbulence surrounding the democracy and nationalism attractors could stabilize into some kind of spontaneous, as opposed to imposed, organization at all levels of government.[40]

The intensity of the turbulence around the three attractors of centralization, democracy, and nationalism has, for the moment, thrust environmental issues to one side, as sentences in political statements to be forgotten. Despite the persistence of nationalist-based environmentalism in the European republics, the fact is that, since 1989, the environmental attractor has increasingly operated in its environmental, as opposed to symbolic, capacity. But what distinguishes the environmental attractor from the others is its scope and dynamic. The operation of the nationality attractor in the Soviet Union was divisive and fragmenting; it remains a conservative force. The motivation that inspired the signing of the Treaty of Westphalia lay behind the notion of a new union treaty for the USSR, just as it did behind the formation of the Commonwealth of Independent States (CIS): the recognition of territorial entities whose rulers exercise sovereign control over the territory's affairs. Only when nationalism joins with democracy or environmentalism does it become a force for change.

At the present time, democracy may be an attractor of change in the former Soviet Union, but democracies have become status quo states in the international arena to whom rapid change is not all that desirable. When one questions the direction of change, the environment attractor comes once again into play. Gaia not only legitimizes, but demands, global intervention in regional and local affairs. At the same time, local groups are too limited in their means to solve all the environmental problems that face their community and must turn elsewhere for remedy. Only the environmental attractor exercises the kind of force which brings local events into the same political field as global phenomena.

By 1990, the interactive pattern between the attractors began to exhibit a characteristic fragmentation. Democratic and authoritarian differences split the center, the former with virtually no authority and the latter with questionable legitimacy. Nationalism fragmented and in the next two years reverted to a force for the status quo. In the process, nationalism lost much of its attraction as an environmental solution. Unfortunately to this writer it has, nonetheless, maintained its place at the center of the post-Soviet political stage. The environment has lost its mass attraction but its followers are more focused on environmental problems and have reached out for international assistance with them. That outreach has brought home the relevancy of democracy to domestic environmental solutions. It also has begun the process of the full integration of environmental nongovernmental organizations (NGOs) and green parties in the FSU into the global system of nonstate actors.[41]

Summary

The years from 1985 onward have been the most turbulent in the modern history of what was the Soviet Union. At the onset of turbulence, the environment played a critical role both as an element of "surprise," and as a symbol attracting national and democratic forces to the cause of domestic reform. Moreover, because, at least at the outset, the environment was identified as a technical and not a political issue area, it functioned as one means of organizing under conditions of growing political outspokenness. As turbulence increased, the environment lost its superficial common cause with nationalism, and became an issue unto itself, a pole of attraction, drawing democracy inexorably into its "magnetic" field. The process occurred through the formation, dissolution, and reformation of hundreds of informal grassroots groups. Many of the groups in existence today will disappear in the turbulence of tomorrow; others will grow stronger and more prominent.

In August 1991, the conservative forces of the rump center intervened in an attempt to re-impose law and order by force. The thrust of this chapter is that by then the Soviet Union had gone too far down the road through turbulence for change to be reversed. Even now, the chief culprits of environmental degradation in the former Soviet Union remain the economic and industrial ministries at the republican level and the still-state-owned enterprises that have little concern about the environment. Nationalism does not guarantee that these ministries or enterprises will be made responsible nor that their monopolies will be broken. But the onset of chaos has generated a diversity of environmental and democratic groups that have grown in strength through integration into the international community. They have an opportunity to carry through the democratic reform that eluded the conservative center. As new order emerges out of turbulence, these groups can become the guarantors of the institutional diversity and flexibility needed to realize a technical and economic progress that is environmentally sustainable.

NOTES

1. "Very disordered systems spontaneously 'crystallize' into a high degree of order." Stuart A. Kauffman, "Antichaos and Adaptation," *Scientific American* 265 no. 2 (1991), p. 79. The whole article (pp. 79–84) is fascinating reading. For a nonscientific elaboration of chaos theory, see James Gleick, *Chaos: Making a New Science* (New York: Viking Press, Penguin Books, 1987). For my earlier thinking on this topic, see "Chaos as an Explanation of the Role of Environmental Groups in East European Politics," *Green Politics*, no 2 (Edinburgh: Edinburgh University Press, 1992), pp. 156–184.

2. Resilience is defined as the ability of a system to maintain its patterns of behavior in the face of disturbance. Stability refers to the propensity of a system to "attain and retain" an equilibrium condition.

3. This passage has been summarized from a paragraph of the excellent chapter by C. S. Holling, "The Resilience of Terrestrial Ecosystems: Local Surprise and Global Change," in William C. Clark and E. Munn eds. *Sustainable Development of the Biosphere* (Cambridge: Cambridge University Press, 1986), p. 296. The reader is advised to read the whole chapter, pp. 292–317. See also Mary E. Clark, *Ariadne's Thread: The Search for New Modes of Thinking* (New York: St. Martin's Press, 1990), pp. 22–27.

4. James Lovelock, *Gaia: A New Look at Life on Earth* (New York: Oxford University Press, 1979).

5. Holling, "Resilience of Terrestrial Ecosystems," pp. 293–294.

6. Harvey Brooks, "The typology of surprises in technology, institutions and development," in Clark and Munn, *Sustainable Development of the Biosphere*.

7. Among others, James Rosenau makes this point in his contribution to this volume.

8. Barbara Jancar, "Religious Dissent in the Soviet Union," in Rudolf Tokes ed., *Dissent in the USSR* (Baltimore: Johns Hopkins University Press, 1975).

9. For a splendid discussion of Soviet environmentalism in the twenties, see Douglas R. Weiner, "The Historical Origins of Soviet Environmentalism," *Environmental Review* 6 no. 2 (Fall 1982): 42–62.

10. The author made a study of the volunteer and mass organizations in her Ph.d. dissertation, "Czechoslovakia and the All-people's States" (New York: Columbia University, 1965, unpublished). See also Barbara Jancar, *Czechoslovakia and the Absolute Monopoly of Power: A Study of Political Power in a Communist System* (New York: Praeger, 1971), pp. 184–207.

11. Barbara Jancar, *Environmental Management in the Soviet Union and Yugoslavia: Structure and Regulation in Federal Communist States* (Durham, NC: Duke University Press, 1987), pp. 169, 194, 215, 242–3; Gustafson, *Reform in Soviet Politics*, pp. 47–56; and John Lowenhardt, *Decision-making in the Soviet Union* (New York: St. Martin's Press, 1981), pp. 70–76.

12. For a partial listing of Soviet environmental laws and regulations during the 1970s, see Jancar, *Environmental Management*, pp. 337–351.

13. For a more detailed discussion of this point, see Jancar, *Environmental Management*, pp. 213–261.

14. The particular truth of this claim is not at issue; what the claim did was to create a political context for globalizing the lake's importance. On this point, see Ann Hawkins' chapter in this volume.

15. *Literaturnaya gazeta*, January 1, 1988: 5–6. For a discussion of the rural writers and Valentin Rasputin's role in that group and in the resurgence of Great Russian nationalism, see Kathleen Parthe, "Time, Backward! Memory and the Past in Soviet Village Prose," lecture at the Kennan Institute, Wilson Center, Smithsonian Institution, November 18, 1987.

16. Jancar, *Environmental Management*, p. 176.

17. A first Soviet attempt at describing the mushrooming grass-roots organizations was I. Iurii Sundijev, "Unofficial Young People's Associations: Attempting an Exposition," *Sotsiologicheskiie issledovaniia*, 5 (September-October, 1988): 56–62.

18. The *National Geographic* did its customary excellently illustrated description of the Aral Sea disaster in "The Aral Sea: A Soviet Sea Lies Dying," *National Geographic*, February 1990, p. 76 ff. See also "Zona ekologicheskogo bedstviya (Zone of Ecological Poverty)," *Argumenty i fakty*, No. 51, 1989.

19. One highly visible exception is the militancy of the "little peoples" of the Soviet Arctic, who successfully put further oil development in the Yamal Peninsula on hold and who have declared all the land and reserves within the Arctic Circle as belonging to their ancestral territory. (Aleksei Roguinko, "The State of the Environment in the Soviet Arctic," paper delivered at the

Slavic Congress, Harrogate, UK, July 23–26, 1990 and Mike Edwards, "Siberia, in from the cold," *National Geographic* 177 (March 1990): 2–39.)

20. Former dissident and ex-President of the former Czechoslovakia Vaclav Havel dislikes the word dissidence. In his view, dissidence in Communist states represented the emergence of a parallel polis or political community distinct from the dominant state structures. He emphasized that the creation of parallel civic structures was not an escape from society, but an act of "deepening one's responsibility," the re-creation of civil society. Vaclav Havel, *The Power of the Powerless* (Armonk, NY: M. E. Sharpe, 1985), pp. 23–96. For a discussion of religious dissent, see Barbara Jancar, "Religious Dissent in the Soviet Union."

21. Rudolf L. Tokes, "Dissent: The Politics for Change in the USSR," in Henry W. Morton and Rudolf L. Tokes eds., *Soviet Politics and Society in the 1970's* (New York: Free Press, 1974), pp. 11–24.

22. Symbolizing the more open official attitude toward culture and science was the holding of the first U.S. book exhibit in Moscow's Sokolniki Park in the summer of 1959. One of its main attractions was an exhibit of abstract art. When Khrushchev visited the exhibit in the company of then Vice President Nixon, the Soviet leader insisted upon seeing the art display. Afterward, during what came to be known as the "kitchen debate" held in the model kitchen of the exhibit, Khrushchev would have none of abstract art, shouting at the Vice President that abstract art was ____, an unprintable four-letter word.

23. For a discussion of the history of the MGU Young People's Council on Environmental Protection, see Jancar, *Environmental Management*, pp. 275–279. See also E. A. Schwartz, "Student Druzhiny Movement: A Problem of Politization," *All Our Life* (*Vcya nasha zhizn*) (Moscow: "Master" Publisher, with the Socio-Ecological Union, 1991), p. 22. See also E. A. Schwartz, "Social Portrait of the 'Druzhiny' Movement for The Protection of Nature," Scientific-Research Institute on the Problems of Higher Education, *Sistema vospitaniia v vysshei shkole* (System of Education of Higher Education), Number 5, *Iz opyta raboty samodeiatel'nykh ob'edenenii studentov* (From the experience of the work of independent student unions), p. 30.

24. Interview with Evgenii Schwartz, Institute of Geography, January 1991.

25. Svetoslav Labelin, "Socio-Ecological Union, Political Portrait, 1990," *All Our Life* (*Vsya nasha zhizn*), pp. 7–11.

26. For a discussion of nationalism in the union republics prior to Gorbachev, see Helene Carrere d'Encausse, *Decline of an Empire: The Soviet Socialist Republics in Revolt*, trans. Martin Sokolinsky and Henry A. la Farge (New York: Harper Colophon Books, 1981).

27. For a typology of decision-making in Soviet politics during this period, see Darrell Hammer, "Towards a Theoretical Model of Non-Competitive Political Systems: Conflict and Decision-Making in the USSR," paper

prepared for delivery at the 1967 Annual Meeting of the American Political Science Association (Chicago, September 1967).

28. Two important examples of this tendency were the Armenian protest against the pollution of Lake Sevin, and the focus in Kirghizia on saving Lake Issyk-Kul (Jancar, *Environmental Management*, pp. 172–181).

29. The data come from a computer printer and map overlays seen by the author on her visit to Moscow in January 1991. To the best of her knowledge, the study remains unpublished.

30. Schwartz, "Social Portrait of DOP," pp. 25–30.

31. cf. Valentin Rasputin, *Siberia on Fire* (Bloomington, IN: Indiana University Press, 1988).

32. "Socio-Ecological Union," *All Our Life*, pp. 5–6.

33. Schwartz, "Student Druziny Movement," pp. 21–32.

34. Barry Commoner, "Democracy is the Planet's Best Hope," *Utne Reader* 40 (July/August 1990): 61–63. For a discussion of the Green position on democracy, see Andelko Milardovic, *Spontanost i Institucionalnost* (Belgrade: Kairos, 1989), pp. 61–64.

35. Barbara Jancar, "Democracy and the Environment in Eastern Europe and the Soviet Union," *Harvard International Review* 12 no. 4 (Summer 1990), pp. 58–60.

36. See a discussion of democratic movements in Central Asia by Asal Azmova, "Democratic Asia—Terra Incognita," *Moscow News* no. 24 (3479), June 16–23, 1991, p. 6.

37. For a stolid listing of pollution problems in the area, including overuse of pesticides and fertilizers, the drying up of the Aral sea, chemical pollution caused by the expansion of metallurgical production in the mountains, dust, lead, and nickel concentrations in the newly built cities, and the explosion of a metallurgical plant in Lubinsk, see "Only Facts, Central Asia review," *All Our Life*, pp. 73–76.

38. Radio Liberty has carried a good coverage of developments in Central Asia in recent years. The reader is referred in particular to the many articles by Annette Bohr, Bess Brown, Suzanne Crow, and James Critchlow.

39. The group received support both from the Socio-Ecological Union and American groups. Moscow and U.S.-based organizations were also active in setting up the successful demonstrations against Occidental Petroleum's joint venture to set up a petrochemical plant in Kalush. Concern over the disposal of radioactive waste has also sparked a movement in Uzbekistan. (See Dana Khan Nurill, "What Will Be Left After Us?" *Ozbezistan adabivata va san'atl*, December 15, 1989, p. 2 as cited in James Critchlow, "Uzbek Writer on Threat Posed by Radioactive Waste," Radio Liberty, *Report on the USSR* 2,10 (March 9, 1990):19.)

40. 1990 was the second year of serious strikes with 9.4 million person-days lost to strikes reported for the first quarter of the year. The strikes were increasingly politically motivated. The point was driven home by the Kuz-

bass Workers' Council in its published address to the striking Kuzbass miners: "The majority of Kuzbass strikers have given up their economic demands understanding full well that their hopes for a worthy life can only come true in the course of democratic reforms." (As cited in "Kuzbass miners: 'Freedom not Money!'," *Moscow News* no. 11 (3466), March 17–24, 1991:1). The strike movement served as the catalyst for the development of a permanent independent trade union movement. In the Ukraine, coal miners organized a union in Donetsk. in the RSFSR, a Confederation of Labor came into being.

At the grassroots level, the public in the large cities of the Russian republic, and in the Baltics, Moldova, and Ukraine, came out in the thousands in support of democracy. The size and frequency of demonstrations and especially the political activism of workers confirmed both election results and public-opinion studies that democracy is no longer an elitist idea only, but can successfully mobilize grassroots support. As of the fall of 1991, the majority of the Soviet population was still expressing its willingness to continue to bear economic hardships in the expectation of political reform. Madeleine Albright on Public Television, August 19, 1991, the day of the coup, indicated that her opinion polls showed 51 percent of the respondents in favor of democratic reforms. Tatyana Zaslavskaya wrote in the *Moscow News* that her polls showed only 6 percent of the respondents agreeing that the CPSU can lead them out of the present crisis (Tatyana Zaslavskaya, "When the 'Powers that Be' Err," *Moscow News* no. 13 (3468), March 31–April 7, 1991, p. 3).

41. Probably the most successful in establishing international ties was the Socio-Ecological Union, which could claim to represent most of the environmental groups in the country. In its linking up with the official USA/USSR Environmental Agreement, the Union was able to seize the leadership of the Soviet environmental movement. Other groups were quick to secure their participation in international programs. For example, "ECOTEST," a program to monitor acid rain in the Soviet Union, was carried out by the Audubon Society for the American side, and DOP as well as the Union on the Soviet side. But the Union remains the leader with established contacts with UNEP and environmental groups in the European Community. ("Socio-Ecological Union, Political Portrait, 1990," pp. 8–11).

8

Negotiating Ecological Interdependence Through Societal Debate: The Minnesota Drought

•

LUTHER P. GERLACH

In 1988 Minnesotans experienced severe drought. As the drought deepened, government officials acted through established risk assessment and management techniques to handle water shortages. They determined that their main problem was to supply Minneapolis and St. Paul with enough water from the Mississippi River to meet vital urban needs and yet maintain the biological integrity of the river. They defined the problem in biophysical, technological, and formal legal terms, and sought to solve it using rational and standard operating procedures. Before they completed their decisions they consulted with the various groups declaring specific, and often competing, interests in water. They communicated through the media to help the general public understand and respond adaptively to the drought. Through this, they sought to ration water use and to increase supply by drawing water from lakes serving as reservoirs at the headwaters of the Mississippi.

People generally, and these stakeholder groups particularly, resisted, reinterpreted, reworked, and responded so diversely yet so actively to these government actions and to each other's responses that they frustrated the ability of state officials to carry out their plan. Newspaper writers described what was happening as conflict, confusion, turmoil, and as an exercise in selfishness. A public policy expert talked about it as an exercise of emotionalism. Technical specialists worried that it was irrationalism, a confusion of the real facts with the perceived facts, or perhaps just plain dishonesty.

I interpret this differently. I understand it as an example of people engaging in a societal debate to work their way around the dilemmas posed by their competing environmental, economic, and social goals. In the process, they expand the subjects of their debate well beyond the tidy framework established by the officials to facilitate efficient and timely decision-making. Thus they frustrate the officials and themselves. But people also generate changes in how they define and use natural resources, and in the sociocultural system in which this resource use is embedded. As such, they are involved in the kinds of tasks and actions that face all humans as they seek to manage the dilemmas of global ecological change. All can learn from the trials and discoveries of each other.

I surmise that all people in the urban-industrial society of the 1990s face these dilemmas. I argue that they are developing societal debate as a means to negotiate the dilemmas. I think that people are developing the debate as much by trial-and-error exploration, even by accident, as by design. I worry that the biggest threat to debate is that designers of improved decision mechanisms will not simply ignore but actively suppress the trials and accidents in their haste to get on with real, objective decision-making and implementing. But although societal debate is a sloppy and untidy action in a turbulent world, the action like the turbulence operates in patterned ways. I offer a synthesis of this pattern of debate and of the dilemmas that give debate its context. I begin by examining the dilemmas and then explicate a model of the structure, function, and process of societal debate, using the Minnesota drought as an example.[1]

The Horns of Dilemma: Ecological Interdependence and Ethnolocal Independence

A dilemma is not a problem to be solved. It is a problem whose solution creates new problems. It is a set of contradictory goals. Negotiating a dilemma is navigating between such contradictions, the proverbial rock and the whirlpool, the horns of dilemma.

In the dilemma of managing global ecological change, one horn is that of institutionalizing interdependencies, the other that of protecting independencies.[2] The interdependencies are those of ecology and economy and security; I summarize these simply as ecointerdependence. The independencies are those of ethnic or cultural or gender identity, local control, freedom and liberty, individualism, other particularisms, the sentiments expressed in the phrase "Don't tread on me" or "Not in my backyard."[3] I summarize these independencies as ethnolocalism.

Both ecointerdependence and ethnolocal independence are driven by powerful social forces.[4] Ecointerdependence is driven not only by the environmental movement seeking to protect the biosphere, but also by transnational industry seeking to institutionalize a world economy, labor seeking to survive, big government and its technocratic advisers seeking to manage systemically, researchers in academia and think-tankia seeking to understand and influence all of this, and the media reporting about and even crusading for it.[5] Ethnolocal independence is driven by well-known movements for civil and human rights, and more recently by movements for private rights and local control of decision-making, including those with such names as the Sagebrush Rebellion and the Wise Use Movement.[6] Ethnolocalism is also reinforced by the pushes for devolution and decentralization coming from many directions, including political conservatives, environmentalist think tanks, the futurists, and Green movements.[7]

Thus driven, both ecointerdependence and ethnolocal independence become structurally entrenched and culturally legitimate in the modern world. Among the big events in which they interact in tension are those of efforts to change open-access resources and private property into global common property—that is, into property whose uses must be managed on vast scales, ever more comprehensively and systemically rather than fragmentally.[8]

The changes thus proposed are difficult. This is so because the causes and effects of environmental risks are embedded in the core technologies, techniques, and strategies of modern society. They are woven into the economic, social, political, and religious structures and values that interrelate with these technologies and strategies. Technologies, structures, values, and environmental impacts interrelate because they have co-evolved as humans have adapted successfully over the years. Changing a part of these, such as property rights or technology, means changing very much more.

Noted researchers have defined this change in scholarly and positive terms as that which will "manage better the long-term, large-scale interactions among environment and development to achieve sustainable improvements in human welfare."[9] Managing interactions sounds less manipulative than managing people, but ultimately it is people who are managed. Changing whole ways of life and managing people is a task that elevates the tension between ethnolocalisms and the isms of ecointerdependence.

These tensions become elaborate. But they are probably rooted in a deeper tension expressed quite simply as that between individual rights and system duties, or between freedom and order.[10] This root tension grows and branches out to interweave with the system problem. Thus humans must deal with three forces that drive each other in a spiral of mutual causation: those for orderly management of complex ecological and socioeconomic systems, for human rights defined as tangible opportunity to be secured through orderly development of environmental resources, and for human rights defined less tangibly as freedom, identity, and locality.[11] These forces interact so that braking one drives the others and so that changing one changes all. Officials in government, industry, and other established institutions and their expert advisers attempt to dissect the forces into problems to be solved precisely, one by one, according to rationally established tasks and priorities. People mobilize in groups to join in these efforts at problem solving, but as they participate they expand even small problems into elaborate issues. People criticize officials for not acting decisively to solve problems; at the same time, they use decision-making about specific issues as occasions to conduct ever expanding debates about the past and future of society, culture, humanity, and nature. The forces, and the responses to them, operate and interact regularly across many different specific events, frustrating those looking for orderly and timely resolution of problems. It is the regularity of chaos, and of people trying to work their way through the chaos to a better life.

Davis and Lawrence propose that people will seek to have both freedom and order, the benefits of decentralization and centralization.[12] Trying to have both, they build more complex organizations, requiring more complex management. I would add that in trying to have more personal and local freedom, more economic opportunity, and a natural environment that is better protected, people increase the requirements for complexity and management. Resource management is a euphemism for managing how people use resources, which means managing people. Managing how people use resources in ways that promote economic opportunities while protecting or enhancing local control, cultural and ethnic identity, personal liberty, and all the other manifestations of civil and human rights, is complex management indeed.

The Debate Process: Wars, Working Things Out, or What?

One major element in this quest for complex management is a process: the process of wide ranging and drama-like public dispute and debate. The dispute-debate-drama process includes sometimes militant confrontation, as groups advance rival interests, visions, and procedures to manage these disputes within rational frameworks, and as wide-ranging and often dramatic deliberations spin out well beyond these frameworks. It is for this reason that the process seems so disorderly and uncontrolled to officials searching for a rational way to meet the organizational and management challenge.

As the debates expand, they typically delve into questions of technological adaptation to the environment, and of the social and political relationships among those involved or affected. They also reach out to critique contemporary cultural models and to promote ideas about culture change. Furthermore, the debates refer to issues and problems in the personal, social, and cultural history of the participants, and offer opportunities to talk about and to heal wounds rooted in this past. As the debaters draw from this collective history, they are also tied up in present problems of technological and economic adaptation, and are organized through social and political arrangements that developed over time but that have current control on their lives.

A main way that people launch and participate in debates is by organizing into groups. These groups then dispute with each other, in actions often angry enough to be called wars—energy wars, water wars, ecowars, Arctic wars, forest wars. These are usually wars of words and lawsuits, conducted to win not only legal and legislative battles but also public opinion. They take on the form, feeling, and quality of a drama: events are episodic, and while episodes may end in legal decisions and formal agreements, the problem often re-emerges in a new dispute, a new episode. Other disputes fade away, to be replaced by new ones. Whether they fade or reopen, each episode leaves a changed world in its wake. Through them people work things out: they negotiate and renegotiate social relationships, and construct and reconstruct culture. The negotiations are often very informal; even formal negotiated settlements may represent only a small part of all of the working-out that goes on.

Some, perhaps much, of this working-out process is like counseling. Sometimes participants work through a grieving process, grieving for what they have lost through changes in their way of life, their standard of living, or their political power.[13] Sometimes they work through a process of gaining and digesting success. Or they work out their social and cultural revitalization, even as they change how they see and use their environment. The changes range from slight to significant.

In the United States, the main actors often include people mobilized in social movements, the established orders that the movements challenge, ordinary citizens aroused to some temporary interest or simply observing, people organized in conventional interest groups, officials—secular or sacred—who help the participants conduct or manage the dispute, media reporters, and scholarly researchers. The episodes take place on many battlefields or stages, from streets and protest fields to courts, legislative halls, university auditoriums, and other formal meeting places. They also take place in and through the media, which not only record and replay the episodes, but encourage them, give shape to them, indeed conduct them.

I have no one good term for these events, which are at once wars, disputes, debates, and dramas through which people negotiate society, culture, and ecology. In the pages that follow I will call them debates, and describe the actions of their participants as negotiating or working things out.

Market, Command, Collective Management, and Persuasion

A public debate process is an institution that complements the well-known and officially recognized mechanisms of management: market exchange and command and control. It is commonly recognized that, while the market may optimize independence of action and individual pursuit of opportunity, it does not adequately account for the costs these actions impose on others and on the environment. And while command and control arrangements can account for these externalities if those in charge are adequately informed about the systemic impacts, command and control structures may not obtain such information or know how to use it adequately. Also, people resist the imposition of command and control from above. When dictators and their security apparatus are overthrown, people quickly rise to express their search for freedom. Frenetic fission frequently follows forced fusion.

Another type of management institution, and one that is increasingly being considered to manage resources defined as global common property, is collective management.[14] Collective management can be a compressed version of the debate. By definition, management occurs through the combined or collective efforts of all or most community members. They make and implement decisions together, through discussion (sometimes discussion arising from some dispute) and consensus. Ideally, collective management can overcome the impersonal market forces that put natural resources at risk, while also giving society the local control, self-determination, and participation that are not found in top-down command and control.[15]

Collective management works well in culturally homogeneous, small-scale societies, in isolated communities, and even in corporations; people can work things out face-to-face and efficiently arrive at a consensus, and participants have been inculcated in a culture of close cooperation. In such settings, the property arrangement known as common property is not necessarily one of tragedy. Instead of abusing that which they hold and share in common, participants who work things out face-to-face through well-established rules can manage wisely and well.[16]

Collective management built around the consensus of users is problematic, however, when the common property to be managed extends well beyond communities in which people can interact face-to-face. The efforts of the various local communities must be coordinated. One way to coordinate would be through a strong central government, which would direct its many communities in their collective management, perhaps reinforcing this by mass education or tutelage. Clearly this would be unacceptable to most people and impossible in today's polycentric world system. Centralized direction of myriad communities managing through local collective action and thought control is not what people have in mind when they envisage a better world through innovative governance. Yet the idea of community management through the deliberations of most of its members, through their consensus building, or simply through thinking globally but acting locally, does figure in such visions.[17]

Education and persuasion to produce voluntary compliance in

resource use is another management tool. Education and persuasion internalize in individuals and local communities an awareness of the downstream costs of market activities. People educated to respect the environment and the rights of others will regulate their own activities, and less government will be needed. However, as Lindblom argues, education/persuasion can be controlled and used by central government as part of its concerted effort to shape the actions of its people.[18] Through such tutelage, people lose the freedom to know that they are not acting freely.

It is not likely that as the societies of the world shake off dictatorial regimes they will use tutelage, but it is likely that they will use education and persuasion to shape resource management. Indeed, education and persuasion will be tools that help manage resources on the large scales projected in the concept of global ecological interdependence and in the idea that the atmosphere, oceans, great watersheds, and so on are commons that must be managed. In the United States and other market democracies, education and persuasion about managing the environment is decentralized and diffused, with much teaching done through schools and public service advertising. But much also occurs through the environmental movement. Indeed, a major function of social movements (or more precisely that form of them which we can call a moral crusade) is this public education and persuasion.

Combining Management Arrangements

The institutional arrangements for societal management work because they work together. While a society may emphasize market, command, collective management, or even education/persuasion as its dominant means of managing its affairs, most employ all of these in various complementary configurations. For instance, the United States is ideologically committed to market exchange as its dominant institution, but certainly it employs command and control (to control the externalities of market forces, for example). To make command and control work more democratically, various governmental and nongovernmental bodies in the United States educate and persuade people to do their civic duty. Once involved, people may continue to push open government and other established institutions to evermore public scrutiny and participation, actions that add elements of collective decision-making.

Small-scale and territorially localized societies such the Digo people of coastal Kenya in the 1950s, on the other hand, emphasize
collective and consensual decision-making processes, including collective management of resources.[19] Many adults, especially adult
males, sit down together, face-to-face, to talk things over and to
negotiate mutual agreement. The communities are small enough in
size and population to make this feasible. But the members of the
society also use market exchange principles for some of their dealings, and for others organize under the authority of a chief appointed
by and subordinated to a central government. Furthermore, the Digo
prevent their collective management system from becoming too intrusive and oppressive by diffusing it, by enabling its participants to
use and manipulate an array of competing cultural rules and social
roles learned through culture contact and change. In this, the Digo
demonstrate characteristics of the big public debate found in larger
scale societies.

Across many urban industrial societies, social movements and
debate processes play a major role in weaving together market, command, persuasion, and collective management. Movements and debates interact with and complement market and government by challenging them; by driving government to control market excesses, and
to use market incentives to improve effectiveness; by motivating both
government and market enterprises to be more responsive to the
public will; and indeed by helping to define this will. Social movements are often the major force to push a subject into public debate
and then to push the debate from a narrow technical argument to a
broad and penetrating deliberation about many factors that can be
connected to the subject.[20]

Widening and Escalating the Subjects of Debate

It is this process of widening the subject area—of escalating deliberations to include issues and concerns well beyond initial frameworks—that perhaps most frustrates officials in government, industry, or universities seeking to use conventional command-and-control or market-exchange approaches. Those using a market approach
will seek quickly to get down to the financial bottom line; those using
command and control seek to make decisions that can be justified on
established legal or technical grounds and routinely administered.
Under growing pressure from social movements and professional

advisers alike, firms or government offices may open decision-making to a wider public, but seek to manage this participation within their cultural frameworks.

Scholars seek to explain why and how decision-making escapes this tidy framework. Maxwell and Randall cite the general erosion of confidence in the ability of science objectively to determine the facts and reduce uncertainty, the loss of faith in government's ability to move society forward up the ladder of progress, and the growth of pluralism and public demand for participation in making decisions.[21] Dryzek examines such debates as steps in a growing discursive democracy, in which communicative rationality triumphs over instrumental rationality.[22]

Theorizing about the role of science in helping society manage environmental risks, Funtowicz and Ravetz argue that what I call widening and escalating of debate results from the interplay of two factors: decision stakes and systems uncertainties. When the stakes and uncertainty are low, assessment can proceed with the routine use of ordinary science and technology to help government set rules.[23] As the stakes and/or uncertainties rise, ever more stakeholders join the debate, with competing assessments of risks and benefits. Technical consultants help make these assessments, while consultants in procedure management (mediation, for example) help to make agreements. Funtowitz and Ravetz call this level, with these frameworks, that of technical consultancy.

When the stakes and/or uncertainties rise to very high levels, the decision-making process produces enduring debate and dissension rather than agreement and clear decision. Diverse people and groups enter the debates, which include the broadest range of dimensions and components and eschew accepted methods for solving problems. "The problem is total in extent, involving facts, interests, values, even lifestyles."[24] This type of wide open and participatory process characterizes what I here examine as societal debate.

Ravetz hypothesizes that the conflict over decision stakes is more influential than that over uncertainty. If a group sees its vital interests threatened by a decision, then it is likely to fight the decision even if scientific evidence objectively reduces uncertainty. As part of its fight, the group will challenge this evidence; it will push up uncertainty and increase public concern. Environmental movement groups do this as a part of their organizational and ideological dynamics.[25] In order to broaden its base of support a movement group will warn others that their interests are also threatened by the decision. To do this, the movement group spreads the scope of the decision, "globalizing" it by showing how it will set in motion a chain of systemic consequences that will affect ever more people. Through this, the group can recruit from this expanding circle of alarmed people and also build alliances with other groups. The circle can be expanded by defining local actions as part of a general process to save the world.

For example, a leader in a California anti-toxics coalition observes that the coalition is born by recruiting people through their selfish opposition to a local hazard—through the infamous syndrome of NIMBY, or Not In My Back Yard—but then grows by involving people in broad efforts around the principle of NOPE, or Not On Planet Earth.[26] People who believe that they are serving higher principles will then bring these concepts into debates, expanding the discourse. In addition, activists in movements for one type of social and cultural change will seek alliances with groups promoting another type of change. Each party in such an alliance will bring the issue of its allies into a public debate, even if such issues do not easily fit. This action and interaction raises uncertainty and stakes. Debates are also expanded to include ever more factors and actors because of the participants' memory of past events—their local or group cultural history, including grudges against others in the process. The debate offers opportunity to rethink this history, to revenge past wrongs, or to overcome the past and work for reconciliation.

Reconciliation and Negotiating a New Way

Debates may seem to defy reconciliation. Each side seeks to advance and legitimate its position, to win the public relations battle, and to influence media, political leaders, administrators, legislators, other interest groups and voters. But in this there is opportunity for resolution.

Ravetz observes that this opportunity arises because in trying to win over others, competing participants invoke the symbols of universality and rationality.[27] Thus they produce what I call overarching rationales. They also generate parallel rationales—that is, they express their local concerns and show that these are as rational and legitimate as those of their opponents. Further, as these rivals contest, each seeks leverage by discovering and proposing new and alternative solutions. As each weighs the resulting new knowledge, all can negotiate from a new basis, and all can help change society and culture by using these products of their creativity.

Thus it is through the debate that people conduct a social conversation about all the factors that are worked into the discourse. People see connections, and show how their interests are affected. The debate functions on several levels of discourse: to produce the great ideas, sacred values and visionary worldviews that explain, encompass, and legitimate what people do; to develop agreements among interest groups to renegotiate social and political relationships; and, on a basic level of technological and economic adaptation, to define what is a natural resource and why, and to work out how people can and should manipulate nature. Across these levels, the debate takes groups and individuals through a kind of social psychological counseling, so that they adjust to the decisions, even accept them as their own, and grieve their way through that which they have lost because of economic or social change.

Working with social movements and with conventional institutions, from schools to public affairs advertising, the debate educates people to change, and enculturates them to make the new ideas part of their design for living. Interacting with market, command, and movements, the debate generates the complex system people need in managing the tensions between systemic binding and fragmentation, interdependence and independence, freedom and order. The debate enables people to work through these tensions to negotiate a more satisfactory future on all levels, from personal to ideological. Thus, people create new ideas, organization and technology for resource management, and weave these into their changing way of life or sociocultural system.

The Minnesota Drought Debates

Managing biophysical resources is really managing how people use resources, which gets down to managing people. Changing resource use means changing how people live. Thus it is not surprising that debates initially defined as being about managing environment or resources provide one of the main means by which people can debate and work out changes in technology and economy, social and political relationships, and cultural values, ideology, and worldview. Conversely, it is by working out these broader changes that people work out new ways of adapting to their environment and using natural resources.

The two actions come together because resource use is part of sociocultural life. A resource is more than a tangible natural object—it is a relationship between the biophysical environment and culturally valued goals and means of manipulating nature, and a relationship among people and among groups.[28] A resource is nature modified by social action according to cultural interpretations. Debates are an institution that generates these actions and interpretations. The debates (1) define a resource biophysically and socioculturally; (2) define independencies and interdependencies of the resource users, including the impacts of their uses on each other; (3) work out the rights and duties of the resource use and the sanctions to enforce these rights and duties; and (4) build the systems to coordinate resource use on an appropriate scale.

To learn more about how the debate works to work out resource management and related sociocultural change let us look at a case study, managing the 1988 drought in Minnesota.[29] The drought, a biophysical event with major social and cultural consequences, functioned as a societal debate. The debates were launched as people responded to the biophysical effects, to each other's actions, and to the actions of government, which sought to manage these effects and interactions. People responded, as individuals and as participants in groups, based on a variety of material interests and symbolic identities. Through these responses they expanded the framework of drought management well beyond the simple, direct, narrow approaches envisaged by government. As individuals and members of groups, people talked about the impact of the drought and of management efforts on them personally, given their interpretation of their stakes in the matter and their uncertainties about outcomes. They tended to push stakes and uncertainties ever higher.

People—as individuals and especially as members of groups—also discussed these impacts as a problem in social relationships, relationships among neighbors, groups and parts of the state. They related the drought and management efforts to their collective history, reminding themselves of past wrongs that needed righting. And they used drought management issues to critique their way of life, and to begin to work out some changes. As they did this people kept exposing new areas of uncertainty, finding new stakes in the decisions, and raising the value of these stakes.

The debates enlarged the pool of participants in water resource management, and then helped the participants to build informal and interdisciplinary networks of communication and collaboration. The networks cross different levels of government and nongovernment organizations, and cross different functions of water resource management. Further, the debates helped to educate people about water, environment, and much more, and to begin to persuade people to conserve. The debates encouraged government and citizen groups alike to explore new technologies of water management, to look for new water sources, and to consider raising water prices to generate conservation and better account for the many costs of water supply. In so doing, the debates interacted synergistically with institutions of government command and control, market exchange, local collective action and social movements, as well as with applications of technology.

This expansion of the discourse frustrated debate participants. But it had positive effects. It helped people to begin to work out or negotiate new water resource management arrangements more appropriate to changing society and culture, even as it helped to make these changes. Through the debates, resource management arrangements, society, and culture co-evolved.

The Drought as a Biophysical Crisis

The event known in Minnesota as the drought of 1988 began in 1987. The drought effects were not apparent then over most of the state, however, because of unusually wet weather in 1985 and 1986. In 1987 the limited rain that fell came at critical points in the agricultural season so the public was not exposed to stories about crop loss. Most Minnesotans were pleasantly surprised to find that weather continued relatively warm and dry through the winter of 1987–1988. These conditions made life easier: it was easier to drive; people did not have to shovel snow. But the same conditions irritated skiers and snowmobilers and hurt the businesses that help people to enjoy or cope with cold and snow. The conditions helped farmers to get into their fields early, but hurt them and tree growers by depriving soil and crops of snow cover and moisture. Throughout much of 1988, urban newscasters reflected the views of most of their audience by lauding the mild weather, but by March reporters reflected growing public unease by looking for some rain.

But instead of rain, there was only heavy wind. The wind blew clouds of topsoil from dry farmland, fanned local grass and forest fires into infernos, and carried clouds of smoke from fires raging in Canada and Yellowstone. The fires threatened not only the livelihoods of the Minnesotans working in the forest industry but also all of the people who depend upon forest lands, or whose homes lay in the path of fire.

In response to the fire threat, local and state governments banned burning, prohibited open campfires, and asked people not to smoke outdoors. When fires continued to burn the outdoor recreation industry became alarmed. In Northern Minnesota, people remembered how their resort season was curtailed and their economy shaken when state government closed the hunting and fishing season to reduce the risk that people would start fires and be trapped in them. They remembered that government did this without consulting them, and readied themselves to respond to government actions.

By early spring of 1988, drought concerns had spread to agriculture. Seeds did not germinate, crops did not grow, and winds eroded dry soils. Farmers were asked to stop irrigating from rivers as water flows diminished to trickles. The media told the public that the drought threatened farmers, farming, food production, and thus everyone. People had growing cause to be anxious.

By June, many records for persistent high temperatures and lack of rain were set. Old timers told reporters that this was as bad as the dust bowl years. The drought began to affect urban dwellers as well as those living in rural areas; officials worried that there would not be enough water in the Mississippi River to supply the Twin Cities metropolitan area for power production, waste assimilation, and domestic water. St. Paul is about 85 percent dependent on the Mississippi River for its water (with the rest coming from wells and lakes), and Minneapolis is completely dependent. By summer, decisionmakers were focused on managing the river water to serve the Twin Cities' needs. The governor took visible charge of the management efforts, while the division of waters of the Minnesota Department of Natural Resources (DNR) played a major role.

Managing Water Supply for the Twin Cities

The governor and his team led city officials in deciding to reduce urban water use and obtain additional water from lakes at the headwaters of the Mississippi, some 180 miles north of the Twin Cities area. It is the issue of obtaining water from the headwaters lakes that most drove the debate. One reason for conserving water in the cities was to legitimate drawing it from the headwaters lakes. These lakes have long been designated as reservoirs to manage flows in the river and to supplement urban supplies. The officials determined that if water from the reservoir were to reach the cities in time to meet critical urban needs it should be released when the flow over a dam at Coon Rapids, just north of Minneapolis, fell below 1000 cubic feet per second (cfs). They added procedural and formal legal elements to these biophysical and technological factors. They had to consult with the U.S. Army Corps of Engineers, which had the federal mandate to manage the river and its flows. It was necessary for the Corps, through the Colonel commanding the St. Paul district, to give permission for water release. The Minnesota officials also talked to the people living and working on and around these lakes, notably the Euro-American owners and managers of resorts and the Native Americans, Ojibwe, who held much of the land and water in their reservation. Such consultation was important in a state that prized itself on being an early leader in encouraging public participation in decision-making. And consultation was also required legally. The Ojibwe had traditional rights to lake resources, recognized by treaty with the U.S. government. One objective of consultation was to have Ojibwe and resort owners agree with official estimates about how much water could be released from these reservoirs without jeopardizing local uses of the lakes for recreation or growing the wild rice used and sold by the Ojibwe. Also, state officials consulted with major water users, notably officials of area cities and utilities, agricultural irrigators, and barge operators to negotiate possible supply reduction.

During this time the officials also worked with the general public. They held press conferences to inform citizens, encourage more efficient water use, explain how grass, plants, and trees respond to reduced water, etc. The governor, the state meteorologist, and other officials reminded people that the drought had begun in 1985 following an usually wet period, and might continue for some years. This might be the beginning of greenhouse climate warming. Minnesotans should prepare for the worst. The governor and his staff organized task forces, first to handle the drought emergency, then after the emergency to plan future water managing. The postemergency task force recommended that these functions be turned over to an established regional planning and coordinating body, the Metropolitan Council; the state legislature approved. The Council then explored management measures including charging the market cost of water to encourage conservation, and finding sources of water supply for the Twin Cities other than the headwaters lakes.

Officially, the emergency ended because it rained. It rained on August 22, 1988, just as the Army Corps was considering the governor's request to release water from the headwaters lakes. Corps officials could say that the rain ended the emergency. Minnesota authorities could accept this gracefully. River flows were again above 1,000 cfs at the Coon Rapids dam.

Thus described, government operated in textbook fashion: it recognized a threat, showed that the threat jeopardizes the public interest, developed an immediate response and longer term plans, and mobilized public support. Its bureaucracy functioned effectively, and within the framework of modern pluralistic participatory democracy. Minnesotans organized and made claims according to their interests. Government met with them in public gatherings, consulted with their representatives, and put some representatives on management task forces.

But this summary of what government did officially is only part of the story. Most of the rest is one in which state officials were frustrated in their efforts to release water from the reservoir, and in their efforts to make decisions within the framework of instrumental rationality and controlled participation that they established. The rain was timely, biophysically and politically. As one official agreed, it got government "off the hook."

Government on the Hook: Expanding the Debate

The Ojibwe living around the northern headwaters lakes and activist Native Americans in the Twin Cities warned that, if the Corps of Engineers agreed to release water, they were prepared to resist, some through direct action, some through legal action. One protester, representing a group in the American Indian Movement, was pictured in a newspaper standing on the banks of a headwaters dam brandishing a rifle; stories circulated of shots being fired. Euro-American resort owners and others living in the northland demonstrated angrily at a public meeting convened by the governor to explain the plans for water release.

In addition to such grassroots protest, there was turmoil at the top. Corps officials thought that if they agreed to the water release, the Ojibwe would follow recent legal decisions and sue the Corps for not having lived up to trust obligations under the treaty.[30] The Corps would in any event be embroiled in an Ojibwe confrontation with the state. If the Corps did not honor the governor's request for release, this would provoke political confrontation involving Washington. If the governor backed off on the water request he and his staff might lose face and be held responsible for water shortage in the cities. The rain that ultimately fell was real, but it also provided an excuse to escape these problems. It was in this context that Minnesotans conducted their drought debate, expanding the subject well beyond the framework established by government.

It was the governor who launched the debate expansion process. His definition of the problem (water supply to the Twin Cities) and the answer (headwaters reservoirs) was the cornerstone of an instrumentally rational approach. But it was also a symbolic act that reassured the people and helped the leaders assert their authority. As many other Minnesotans entered the debate process they brought to it their own symbols, meanings, and interpretations, and expanded it to include their ideas about problems and solutions.

They expanded the debate at four levels: individual adaptation, social relationships, cultural history, and cultural critique and change. Through such debate they in effect thought through and reworked water as a resource. They defined water in biophysical and sociocultural terms, connecting it to specific material qualities and technologies on the one hand and sweeping ideologies and worldviews on the other. They defined the water users, how the users are related, and how uses affect each other. But even as they defined these mutual interdependencies they also identified their claims to various forms of local, ethnic, and individual independence. Through this, they began to lay the basis for official restatement of legal rights and duties in various types of water resources, that is, for more clearly distinguishing among types of water as open access, common property, or private property. This process of legal restatement is still underway.

The drought debates did this, but not according to this sequence or formal outline. Minnesotans did not participate in a referendum or other formal system to hammer out a new water management system or to design a plan for their social and cultural system in the next century. They debated the issues in a variety of often fortuitous exchanges. If exchanges were planned, as in a public meeting, the plans usually called for limiting debate to technical or legal questions about water or drought management. In addition to government meetings, people carried out the debates in protests, religious assemblies, classrooms, the media, and in their neighborhoods, at the cafe, the mall, or over the proverbial backyard fence.

Individual Adaptation and Social Responsibility

Many people responded according to their personal and material adaptive strategies. Farmers complained that the drought was killing the crops on which they depended to recover from several years of poor markets and huge debt payments. As soon as restricted food supplies and increased prices were forecast, commodity traders bid up prices.[31] Boaters complained that they could not easily use their craft because of receding lake and river levels. Transporters of grain and other goods on the Mississippi were troubled as the river fell, preventing passage into the Twin Cities ports. On the other hand, sellers of windsurfers and boats were happy to see business increase when the lakes were freed of ice and opened early. And a state transportation official declared, "This kind of weather has been real good for building roads."[32]

People sought to defend themselves against the drought or to take advantage of it in ways that troubled others. Some quickly hoarded food, further driving up prices. Some hurried to use "their share" of water before it was too late. On the day before lawn-sprinkling bans took effect in Minneapolis, water use among homeowners surged.[33] When a bank gave fans to seniors and the needy it was reported that affluent and young people joined the distribution lines to get the gift.[34] Hearing of these events, newswriters, government officials, and religious leaders worried that "neighborly spirits wither in a dry time."[35]

People spread the issue further, to express concerns about relationships among people, groups, cities, and sectors of the state and world. They said or implied that good relationships were those of being neighborly, fair, honest. In the cities, debate focused on watering lawns and washing cars. Media reported that people suspected their neighbors of cheating, watering in spite of voluntary and then mandatory bans—indeed, sneaking out to water or wash cars at night.[36]

Some uses of water had a big symbolic impact. One person re-marked "They watered the Capital lawn during a drought! What does that tell you about the state?" A legislator from farm country was upset when he saw city people lining up to have their cars washed. He found it hard to believe that automatic car washes recy-cle much of their water.

More than eighty farmers asked officials why they had been de-nied permission to pump irrigation water from rivers while Twin Cities residents continued to sprinkle lawns.[37] Others asked why some could keep pumping water from wells while neighbors' wells ran dry. A northerner, after telling us how important water and the lakes are to the tourist industry in northern Minnesota, said, "There was bitterness that people (in the Twin Cities) were demanding water for their lawns and golf courses. It is their responsibility to get an alternative supply at their own expense without having a negative effect on a second group in the North."

On the other hand, a member of the Governor's task force on water supply said that a study he conducted on water use from 1932–1976 showed that the North usually fared very well: "Ninety-five percent of the time the Headwaters Lakes are maintained at a level that is very helpful and supportive of that region of the State. Five per cent of the time the Twin Cities area needed water from the Headwaters Lakes. Is that too much to ask?"

A St. Paul resident talked about the competing demands for water and argued that city uses are as important as Northern ones: "My wife doesn't care at all about fishing, but she loves rose bushes. A yard in the city without grass is like a Northern lake without water."

People disagreed and fought, but also cooperated to cope with the drought. The residents of a rural town that has become a bedroom community for people working in the Twin Cities voluntarily banned lawn watering. They did so to conserve now rather than when the wells ran dry, and because it did not seem right to water when neighboring farmers were in trouble. Public service and religious institutions adapted to provide material aid, spiritual comfort, and counseling, particularly in agricultural areas. The National Guard brought water to homeowners whose wells had dried up. Banks and volunteer associations gave fans to the needy. Community leaders formed groups to measure and cope with drought impacts.[38]

Discussions about personal impacts and social responsibility af-fected how Minnesotans interpreted the plan to send Minneapolis and St. Paul water from the headwaters. Do the claimants show that they know water is precious? Are they conserving? Do they recognize that they need not only water but also other help from the north, and do they reciprocate? If St. Paul deserved water from the Mississippi because it dug local wells and built local reservoirs after the 1976 drought, does Minneapolis not deserve water because it did not?

Some debaters asked about plans for change. Will the Cities and the State avert future crises by developing a long-term program to manage water supply not dependent on the headwaters? Will they include conservation in this plan? Others asked: If the headwaters lakes are not a reservoir for when the Twin Cities face a water emergency, then what are they? Is it fair that the headwaters people act as if the lakes are their own private property? Is one group's use of water more right or less right than another's? If the cities will conserve, what about others?

The Cultural History Level

The questions and tensions expressed in this debate derive from a long history of economic and political competition, rivalry, and tension between northern Minnesota and "the cities," between rural and urban Minnesota, between Minneapolis and St. Paul, and between EuroAmericans (whites) and Native Americans (Indians). As part of their debate, participants quickly added other concerns rooted in this history to those of water-supply decisionmaking. They used the water-supply issue dramatically to recount this history and build arguments for change.

For example, a Native American representative interpreted the issue of taking water from Reservation lakes as "a parallel action to taking the kids away to boarding schools." Government in both cases has been "very heavy handed and hit the panic button too soon. It does not respect our traditions, our rights." A member of the chamber of commerce in one of the headwaters communities stated, "we are not pitting the North against the South up here, but the frustration of the North with respect to the Twin Cities is that we have gone through this before and probably will in the future." A cartoonist whose work appears in northern newspapers neatly mimicked the north-south tensions during the drought.[39] In one cartoon the Headwaters Lakes shout "Hands Off." In another, a Paul Bunyan–like woodsman guards the lakes with an axe, proclaiming "make my day, city slicker." The allusion to Twin Cities people as slickers appears in several editorials in northern papers, suggesting that city people are out of harmony with nature, ignorant of it, and untrustworthy or unfair in dealings with the north.

Minnesotans know these tensions well. They surface time and again, particularly during disputes over resources. They have been reinforced as the northern economy has suffered through the decline of its natural-resource-based industries (chiefly iron mining, logging, and pulp and wood production). Water has figured prominently in these industries, for transportation, power generation, and industrial processes including waste disposal. From their beginning in the late-nineteenth century, many of these industries have been controlled directly or financially by metropolitan interests. To this day, a characteristic sentiment of northerners is to decry this history of dependence and to protest evidence of its continuance. Letters to northern newspapers described the drawdown as an attempt to perpetuate these relationships. One writer said that Governor Perpich seemed more a mayor of the Twin Cities than a governor of the whole state.[40]

Vulnerable to fluctuating world markets and resource depletion, the traditional northern industries have declined. Many see water-based tourism and recreation as poor substitutes for mining and logging. Projected expansion of wood-products industries depends in part on environmental protection decisions, which seem to be made in the cities. With these changes the North loses population while the Twin Cities gain. In fact or perception it has also lost political power, control of its resources, and shares of state spending. Northerners think of themselves as protecting the northern environment because, "after all, we live here." They say to city people, "The reason you come up here and have an environment to enjoy is because we have taken care of it." Many are offended when environmentalists from the cities tell them what to do, and when outside government imposes myriad regulations.

But even as northerners criticize the cities and government and outsiders in this way, they are ambivalent. They dislike being made to feel dependent on the cities and government, but they recognize their interdependence. They are tied to the cities through products they sell, vacationers they host, children and friends they have in the cities. Some are migrants from the cities, coming north to retire or open businesses. The drought debates gave northerners a chance to ask city people to show that they need the north, and thus to make a more balanced interdependence.

Perhaps a similar process is reshaping relationships between some Euro-Americans and Native Americans. The Native Americans are the Leech Lake and Cass Lake Bands of Chippewa Indians, but they prefer to be identified as the Ojibwe, or Anishinabe, nation. An Army Corps of Engineers representative suggested that under treaty rights the Ojibwe had a justifiable and deserved opportunity to participate actively in decisions about resources in which they had major interest. Ojibwe expressed similar sentiments in interviews and in a report on the drawdown issue which the Leech Lake Band submitted to the Corps of Engineers. Ojibwe said they did not object to sharing needed water, but they must be invited to participate as equals in deciding such distribution.

They say that whites took everything from them without their approval. This was so when the dams were built on the reservation more than one hundred years ago by powerful milling and logging interests based in the cities. The lakes on the reservation were enlarged when the dams were built, destroying gardens, rice fields, haylands, fisheries and burial grounds. As the Commissioner of Indian Affairs said in 1889, "The injury done them in building the reservoir dams was without doubt very great. Two or three of their burying grounds were so washed by the overflow that the remains of their buried dead were unearthed and scattered along the shore. This desecration but added poignancy to the sorrow caused by the loss of subsistence." [41]

The Ojibwe finally received compensation for this loss of subsistence one hundred years later. In their report to the Corps of Engineers, the Leech Lake Band cites more recent incidents in which the lake levels are controlled to serve resorters and other white interests (such as preventing flooding of white agricultural lands). The Band explains that this control causes severe damage to Ojibwe wild rice crops, which grow best in "naturally fluctuating" lake levels. [42]

Native Americans also note that outsiders control their treaty-protected fishing activities, which have traditional and dietary significance and could be important commercially. The state seeks to attract recreational fishermen to northern lakes, some located in reservations. To maintain a good supply of game fish, the State compensates Native Americans to abstain from harvesting such fish, except to eat. When the governor was at the headwaters lakes to explain the drawdown plans, Native Americans were gathering in the area for a tribal election, and with this to talk about fishing policy and other resource issues. They engaged in vigorous and sometimes angry debate about the policies they should follow to manage their resources and elect leaders. The proposal to divert water to the city provided a powerful focus for this political debate, and political debate reinforced resistance to drawdown.

The Cultural Critique Level

As the Natives Americans developed their arguments they returned time and again to the threat to their rice crops, reminding themselves and others of the importance of rice to their way of life. *The Circle*, a Native American newspaper published in the Twin Cities, explained that destruction of the rice crop would be a financial and nutritional loss and a further assault on traditional Anishinabe religion and other core values.[43] A spiritual leader of the Leech Lake Reservation and members of his family explained to us that these threats to "ricing" are but one of many examples of changes from the outside that are destroying "the people." They told how the care, harvesting, preparation, and use of wild rice was an activity that helped bind their people together. In its native form, prepared traditionally, wild rice is very nutritious. In Minnesota and California, non-natives are now growing it commercially, in vast quantities but of lesser quality, ruining the Ojibwe rice business. Worse, as the native peoples cease to harvest and prepare the crop, they increase their dependence on the outside. They have moved out of harmony with the rhythms of nature and spiritual forces that once assured a long, bountiful rice harvest. All of this has produced a bad diet, alcoholism, drug abuse, and other ruin. This, they say, has its most visible impact on human health in the form of "sugar diabetes." The water drawdown challenged the Ojibwe to think and talk about their way of life or culture, and the deadly threats to its existence.

Similarly, Americans across Minnesota and indeed across the USA found in the drought and water shortage indications that something was fundamentally wrong with Western culture, or with their role in this culture. This was expressed in gatherings of churchgoers, conferences of scientists, presentations of celebrities, deliberations of government officials, and throughout the mass media.[44] Under the caption "Environmental Balance Is Vital or Life as We Know It Is Finished," an Ann Landers advice column addresses one of the many who worried that the drought showed that humans have upset the balance of nature.[45]

Just as Ojibwe expressed concerns through the symbol of wild rice, others focused on the significance of watering lawns and golf courses, diluting sewage, and washing cars in suburban driveways. To the northerners, the cars were "BMWs," and the lawns and driveways were "in Minnetonka," a wealthy lakeside suburb. To be fair, why not pump water from this lake?

People used symbols such as lawns to express general criticisms of the Western way of life, including our misuse and abuse of nature. Letting the lawn go brown in dry weather would be natural, and if the grasses were appropriate for the environment they would grow back. Why not find a natural ground cover? Why do we cover our lawns with chemicals to kill insects and other living things and make grass grow faster, then cut it and dump it in plastic bags in landfills? Lawns were also used to question social values. Growing lawns was decried as "keeping up with the Joneses," and especially bad when neighbors sneaked out and watered their lawns at night during bans. Lawns are symbols of false values—an emulation by the masses of the ostentatious gardens and lawns of the Victorian upper classes. One writer looked forward to a post-drought urban landscape of "natural things" such as front-yard gardens.[46]

People tied such general critique to their equity concerns. A legislator from an agricultural district asks why, with all the pressure to curb chemical use on farms, is there not also action to cut chemical use in urban homes and lawns? A woman who has led fights to curb the farmland conversion to suburbs sees this conversion mirrored in the replacement of food crops with lawngrass. When suburbs draw water from aquifers used by farmers, suburbs should ban lawn sprinkling.

While some people focused on lawns in critiquing Western culture, others saw the drought as a harbinger of the greenhouse effect. This concern went public in late June 1988, after NASA atmospheric scientist James Hansen testified to Congress that "the greenhouse effect has been detected and is changing our climate now."[47] Suddenly, the greenhouse effect was popularized with such media headlines as "warmup of the Earth has Begun," "Greenhouse Effect Coming, Ready or Not," "Heat Trap: Facing a Disaster in the Making," "The Endless Summer?" and "Deadly Drought."[48]

The Hansen story was quickly followed by reports that many scientists did not agree that the warm weather of the 1980s signalled the greenhouse effect. In Minnesota and across the country commentators on the issue acknowledged that, while Hansen's claim was probably premature, it could have the desirable effect of prompting people and governments to conserve energy and cut back on fossil fuels. Scientists and environmentalists used the drought and its alarms as an opportunity to make their concerns part of the public agenda. Americans heard their warnings while suffering from intense heat, and while barraged by panicky reports of drought-related illnesses and deaths and economic doom. Hard on the heels of these stories came those of environmental catastrophe: ozone holes, cities smothering in smog, seas dying, oceans and beaches littered with hospital waste, perhaps from AIDS wards. Some observers worried that environmental concern was becoming "ecophobia," while others called for a crusade to rescue "The Planet of the Year." [49]

Religious leaders joined others in talking about how the drought and the greenhouse effect showed that humans are vulnerable to forces above and beyond themselves. Is the drought a sign from God? asked one writer in a newspaper opinion piece, answering that earth cannot sustain human abuses, whether they be material or moral.[50] For some, the drought called on people to see that they are stewards of the Earth, with an obligation to protect living things now and into the future.[51]

A rabbi cautioned that the drought and the greenhouse effect do more than challenge people to respond through science or even good stewardship. These environmental forces show humans that they cannot take their blessings for granted.[52] Others considered that the drought reflected societal and spiritual as well as environmental ills. In a sermon at the height of the drought, an Episcopal minister in the Twin Cities used a biblical example to support the idea that when people "don't live well together, the earth withers in drought." [53]

Farmers and rural townsfolk in communities across the region held special prayers for rain, and, in at least one case, were joined by Native Americans who asked for rain through traditional ritual. In North Dakota, extension agents collaborated with rural ministers to provide counseling for farmers under stress. The farmers wanted to know if it was their sin that led to the drought, as the bible said. What accounted for the great unevenness in rainfall, for getting rain when others didn't? "Living right," explained one farmer. Farmers watched clouds carry rain elsewhere, and explained that "the [Twin] Cities" are a heat island which pushes rain away. One told us, "It just isn't natural, all that in one place."

Interpretations of the Debate

The official drought managers were frustrated by this multilevel debate and resistance to their decisions, which prevented them from bringing their tasks to a conclusion within the official decision-making framework. The public changed the framework. When officials sought to decide the volume that could and should be released from a headwaters lake, they were met with discussions about everything from the importance of lawns in a city backyard to the future of the planet, from the naturalness of lakes to the unnaturalness of cities. It is small wonder that many officials and their advisers interpreted these debates as irrational, emotional, even dishonest and media-driven deviations from objective efforts to manage the crisis effectively. Officials asked people to use "real" not "perceived" facts.

And yet, by debating on many levels according to their perceptions of the problems, people were able to work out new water resource management arrangements more appropriate to changing society and culture. In doing so, they helped to make social and cultural change. Through the debates, resource management arrangements, society, and culture changed together. Furthermore, as Minnesotans debated they also worked out how they could reconcile their differences and work together. They generated and exchanged overarching and parallel rationales for their cooperation, and learned more about water and its management to apply as they cooperate. These efforts cut across and wove together the various levels of debate.

Overarching and Parallel Rationales

In the drought debate, northerners, Ojibwe, farmers, and city people each advanced particular claims to water under the universal theme of rights and reason. It made sense to share water, to use reservoirs as reservoirs, to conserve water to avoid crisis management, to protect nature, to honor treaties with the Ojibwe. It made sense to recognize that Minneapolis was vulnerable to water shortfall as long as it relied solely on the Mississippi as its source, and if the source could be cut by drought or by upstream pollution. It made sense for northerners to recognize that if the cities needed them for water and other basic resources, the north needed the cities for markets, goods and services, tourists, and recreation home buyers. Minnesotans north and south are economically interdependent. They are also connected through kinship, marriage, and friendship. They have good reason to move from conflict to cooperation.

Minnesotans also responded to each other's claims by proposing parallel rationales, equally valid justifications for using water. To the northern claim that wild rice and recreational boating were more important than green lawns, city people responded that the lawns, plants, and trees made their urban life more liveable. Farmers told city people when you watch your grass dry, think of us watching our livelihood die. To the farmer losing an annual crop, the grower of Christmas trees said that his trees take many years to replace. To the resort manager losing customers, the golf club operator said that unwatered, dead fairways meant financial ruin and loss of a public amenity.

Declaring their particular and local rationales for needing and using water, people explained who they are in the division of labor, and how they came to their interpretations of drought and water. By explaining water needs with common vocabulary, people affirmed social and economic identity within the overall system. Through this they were able to listen to each other. And from this, as one official told us, the debates finally "got all the issues out on the table" so that people could move "to real cooperation."

New Knowledge

The parties in debate were thus able to generate and learn new knowledge about water in its social and cultural context. Through this they could change the terms of the debate. The drought debates moved from being about releasing water from headwaters lakes to become deliberations about water supply options and use management in the Twin Cities. People found new reasons to cooperate to pursue these new approaches, using a variety of institutions.

One result of the debates is that the state legislature mandated planning for existing and future water use, supply, and conservation in ways that would be acceptable statewide. To lead this planning, the statute identified the Metropolitan Council, an agency operating since the 1960s to coordinate government actions and guide development across a seven-county metropolitan area.[54] The Council was given authority to manage water across this area, but was required to consult with the governmental and nongovernmental parties, which played major roles in managing water during the drought. These parties examined a wide range of alternatives: relying more on urban aquifers, holding more water along the Mississippi in restored wetlands, obtaining supply from adjacent watersheds, reducing demand through significant conservation. The parties advised those writing new legislation to manage water, including wetlands, and they considered how the market and education could be integrated with government regulations to institutionalize these approaches. They did not, however, consider ways to incorporate ongoing debate as one of these institutional arrangements.

The Debate as a Water Management Institution and a Force for Change

It may be that people cannot design and plan to employ societal debate as an institution. But debate happens, and people should be better prepared to accept it and work with it when it does. When it happens it is not the antithesis of rational management, but part of this management. It is complex, but complexity is what we can expect from efforts to live with powerful tensions for freedom and order, for ecological protection, economic opportunity, and sociopolitical liberty.

The debates helped construct a new regime of water management. We have seen that they helped people to define water and related resources biophysically and socioculturally, to identify the independencies and interdependencies of the resource users, and to re-work their rights and duties in the resources. The debates worked out these ideas at all levels of discourse: individual impacts and adaptations, social relationships and responsibilities, cultural history and critique.

For instance northerners defined the headwaters lakes as a natural system that had been impounded, while Twin Cities residents defined the lakes as reservoirs. Northerners showed how they needed the lakes, Citians showed how they needed the river. All recognized that the headwaters offered recreation, giving Citians pleasure and headwaters people income. Each reminded the other that water was a precious resource that must be protected. All were reminded that neither natural resources nor social relationships may be taken for granted, but rather must be fostered.

During the debates, people worked out the interdependencies of those using the river and the headwaters lakes, and accounted for the rights and duties of each. Northerners said they would share their water if the Citians demonstrated their appreciation. Citians acknowledged this, but wanted the north to appreciate the cities. Northerners and Citians reminded each other that they lived in the same state, were related and interdependent. And within local communities people reminded each other of their neighborly responsibilities. But even as they argued their interdependence, people also reminded each other of their individuality, their personal and group interests and local independence. The debates prompted state and local government to begin to translate these ideas about rights and duties in water into investigative commissions and legislation.

Further, the debates helped to educate people about water, environment, and culture, and to begin to persuade people to conserve. The debates encouraged government and citizen groups to look for new water sources and new water-management technologies, and to consider price increases to foster conservation and meet the costs of water supply. In so doing, the debates interacted synergistically with institutions of command and control, market exchange, local collective action, and social movements, as well as with applications of technology. And as they generated and exchanged rationales, people and groups built the formal and informal structures necessary to cooperate across their many differences of jurisdiction, culture, administrative level, and function.

The pace of change in water resources management has been slow. With the end of the emergency, the drought debate faded away. Government and its task forces took over the deliberations and returned them to a routine and narrow frame. Yet the drought debate had changed the subjects of these deliberations. Also, the public turned to carry on a new version of the debate episodes around new issues. By 1989, rapidly expanding logging and wood products manufacturing had emerged as one of the new but related issues.[55]

Change through debate is change that is hesitant and uneven, but persistent. People build on their existing culture and organization, challenging this, shifting this, getting people involved, talking it out, working it over, and weaving it into a new arrangement. The organization and conduct of the process is complex; because it is untidy and rambling, the complexity seems that of disorder. Yet it is a complexity derived from the very human effort to find both order and freedom, and to handle the tension between them: to manage environment, economy and society ever more comprehensively, yet to protect individuality, locality, ethnicity, liberty.

Conclusion

As humans seek to institutionalize their global ecological interdependence, under conditions in which claims for ethnolocal independence remain as strong as ever, they will continue to sort out the tensions in debate. The debate is itself an institution of societal management, sometimes frustrating, sometimes complementing government, market exchange, education, and persuasion. It operates somewhat as does collective decision-making in that the public talks things over and works thing out, together. But this public is far flung, diverse and does not move to consensus but rather launches into a new debate without resolving the old. Yet the new debates carry on with the themes of the old, and society and culture are changed even as they are continued. A frequent focus of debate is the biophysical environment and its conversion to natural resources through technology, social action, and cultural interpretation. In turn, these debates expand to reshape the social and cultural context in which the resource definitions, uses, and management are embedded.

There are many such debates across cultures and history, and a comparative examination of a sample of these as case studies would help advance the theory of debate. In the debate examined here, I have argued that Minnesotans expanded efforts to manage the drought as a narrow water-supply problem into the complex arrangement of a debate about adaptive strategies, social relationships, collective history and cultural capabilities and limitations. While this multilevel debate and complex structure frustrated government efforts to apply narrow technological and regulatory solution, Minnesotans used it to revitalize not only their water resources management but also their society and culture. Through debate they continued their efforts to work out better ways of living in their environment, together.

NOTES

1. The research for the study of social responses to the drought in Minnesota was funded by a grant from the Charles K. Blandin Foundation,

Grand Rapids, MN, with additional support from the Hubert H. Humphrey Institute of Public Affairs, University of Minnesota. With the author as principal investigator, research was conducted by a team including Ursula M. Gerlach, Elizabeth Whitaker, Marsha K. Soucheray, Jan P. Stanley, Catherine M. Sleezer, and Leah Foushee. The Charles K. Blandin Foundation also sponsored and held a "Water Management-Drought Report Conference" April 19–20, 1989 in which the research team presented its findings for critique and discussion to an assembly of people representing the various public and private organizations and groups who played major roles in the 1988 drought management. As background for the conference, the research team authored a report "Risk, Resources, and Relationships: The Human Dimension of Drought and Water Management." The author wishes to thank the Blandin Foundation for this support. He also wishes to thank the members of the research team for their many contributions.

2. Luther P. Gerlach and Betty Radcliffe, "Can Independence Survive Interdependence?" *Futurics* 3 (Summer 1979): 181–206.

3. Nicholas Freudenberg, *Not in Our Backyards: Community Action for Health and the Environment* (New York: Monthly Review Press, 1984).

4. See Luther P. Gerlach and Gary Palmer, "Adaptation Through Evolving Interdependence," in Paul C. Nystrom and William Starbuck eds., *Handbook of Organizational Design Volume 1, Adapting Organizations to their Environments* (New York: Oxford University Press, 1981).

5. Harvey Brooks, "The Typology of Surprises in Technology, Institutions and Development," in W. C. Clark and R. E. Munn eds., *Sustainable Development of the Biosphere* (Cambridge: Cambridge University Press, 1986); Thomas Sancton et. al., "Planet of the Year," *Time*, January 2, 1989, pp. 26–30.

6. Luther P. Gerlach and Virginia H. Hine, *People, Power, Change: Movements of Social Transformation* (Indianapolis and New York: Bobbs Merrill, 1970); Jo Freeman ed., *Social Movements of the Sixties and Seventies* (New York: Longmans, 1973).

The Wise Use Movement is explained and endorsed by one of its philosophers in Alan M. Gottlieb ed., *The Wise Use Agenda* (Bellevue, WA: The Free Enterprise Press, 1989). Another of its philosophers explains the need for it and further explains its agenda in Ron Arnold, *Ecology Wars: Environmentalism as if People Mattered* (Bellevue, WA: The Free Enterprise Press, 1987). See also Daniel B. Wood, "Sagebrush Rebellion Revisited, Land-Use Advocates Make Gains," *Christian Science Monitor*, Thursday, October 3, 1991; Margaret N. L. Knox, "The Wise Use Guys," *Buzzworm: The Environmental Journal* 2 (6): 30–36, Alan M. Gottleib ed., *The Wise Use Agenda* (Bellevue, WA: The Free Enterprise Press, 1989); Robert Menneley, "Getting Wise to the 'Wise Guys:' The New Sagebrush Rebels Ride East," *The Amicus Journal* 14 no.3 (Fall 1992): 35-38.

7. Robert W. Gage and Myrna P. Mandel eds., *Strategies for Managing*

Integovernmental Policies and Networks (New York: Praeger, 1990); Alan B. Durning, "Mobilizing at the Grass Roots," in *State of the World 1989* (New York: Norton, 1989); Frank Feather ed., *Through the '80s: Thinking Globally, Acting Locally* (Washington, DC: World Future Society 1980); North Country Greens (Minnesota and Wisconsin), "Principles and Goals," mimeo, n.d.

8. Luther P. Gerlach, "Opportunity, Liberty, Ecology: Challenges of the Post-Cold War Future," in Robert B. Textor ed., *The Peace Dividend as a Cultural Concept: Anticipating the Possible Benefits to American Life from Human Effort Released by the Ending of the Cold War* (A special issue of *Human Peace*, organ of the Peace Commission of the International Union of Anthropological and Ethnological Science, vol. 9 nos. 1–3 [1991]: 13–28).

9. W. C. Clark, "Sustainable Development of the Biosphere: Themes for a Research Project," in Clark and Munn, *Sustainable Development of the Biosphere*.

10. On tension between individual rights and system duties, see J. W. Fernandez, "The Call to the Commons: Decline and Recommitment in Astruias, Spain," in Bonnie J. McCay and James M. Acheson eds., *The Question of the Commons: The Culture and Ecology of Communal Resources* (Tuscon, AZ: University of Arizona Press, 1987). On tension between freedom and order, see S. M. Davis and P. R. Lawrence, *Matrix* (Reading, MA: Addison-Wesley, 1977).

11. Gerlach, "Opportunity, Liberty, Ecology."

12. Davis and Lawrence, *Matrix*.

13. Peter Marris, *Loss and Change* (New York: Pantheon Books, 1974).

14. Gerlach and Rayner, p 9.; McCay and Acheson, *Question of the Commons*.

15. Green movement members have something like this in mind when they call for decentralized government up from the grassroots. See Luther P. Gerlach, "Global Thinking, Local Acting: Movements to Save the Planet," *Evaluation Review* 15 no. 1 (February 1991): 120–148.

16. McCay and Acheson, *Question of the Commons*. While it may do all of these good things, common property arrangements managed through collective action are not simple, routine, or designed to maximize freedom. Participants monitor each other's behavior to assure that the resource is properly used; they do so by watching, talking, interacting, reminding, praising, and punishing. Thus collective management of common property can control individualism at least as much as does central command and control. It can easily be more intrusive and thoroughgoing than most centralized command systems. Common property arrangements can, however, produce "tragic" results when the sum total of individual actions, rational in themselves, combine to produce a conclusion of resource ruin that is collectively irrational and a common bad.

17. One expression of such vision is that of futurists advocating harmonic

globalism or decentered globalism; see Feather, *Through the '80s*; See also Gerlach, "Global Thinking, Local Acting."

18. Charles E. Lindblom, *Politics and Markets: The World's Political-Economic Systems* (New York: Basic Books, 1977).

19. For greater detail see Luther P. Gerlach and Ursula M. Gerlach, "Egalitarianism, Collectivism, and Individualism: The Digo of Kenya, in J. Flanagan and S. Rayner eds., *Rules, Decisions, and Inequality in Egalitarian Societies* (London: Gower Press, 1988).

20. It is through social movements that people mobilize outside established orders to challenge and change established culture, and as part of this, to trigger and drive public debate. I have elsewhere examined the structure and function of social movements in detail, and other contributors to this volume deal with this subject at length. Accordingly, in this essay I will touch upon social movements only in respect to their role in triggering and driving debate. See Luther P.Gerlach, "Protest Movements and the Construction of Risk," in B. B. Johnson and V. T. Covello eds., *The Social Construction of Risk* (Holland: D. Reidel, 1987); Luther P. Gerlach, "Energy Wars and Social Change," in Susan Abbott and K. John van Willigen eds., *Predicting Sociocultural Change* (Southern Anthropological Society Proceedings no. 13, Athens, GA: University of Georgia Press, 1979); and Luther P. Gerlach and Larry R. Meiller, "Social and Political Processes: The Minnesota Hazardous Waste Case," in Donald E. Johnson, et al. eds., *Theory and Methods* (Ames, Iowa: Iowa State University Press, 1987).

21. Judith Maxwell and Alan Randall, "Ecological Economics Modelling in a Pluralistic, Participatory Society," *Ecological Economics* 1 (1989): 233–249.

22. John S. Dryzek, "Discursive Designs: Critical Theory and Political Institutions," *American Journal of Political Science* 31 no. 3 (August 1987): 656–679; and "Complexity and Rationality in Public Life," *Political Studies* 35 (1987): 434–442. Dryzek following Habermas: Jürgen Habermas, *Strukturwandel der Offenlichkeit* (Neuwied: Luchterjand, 1962); "Toward a Theory of Communicative Competence," *Inquiry* 13 (1970): 360–75; and *The Theory of Communicative Action I: Reason and the Rationalization of Society* (Boston: Beacon, 1984).

23. S. O. Funtowicz and J. R. Ravetz, "Three types of Risk Assessment: A Methodological Analysis," in C. Whipple and V. Covello eds., *Risk Analysis in the Private Sector* (New York: Plenum, 1985).

24. J. R. Ravetz, "Usable Knowledge, Usable Ignorance: Incomplete Science with Policy Implications," in Clark and Munn, *Sustainable Development of the Biosphere*, p. 425.

25. Gerlach, "Protest Movements and the Construction of Risk."

26. Glenda Chui, "Environmental Activists Try to Heal a Planet. Fear Sparks Grassroots Efforts, " *San Jose Mercury News*, April 9, 1990, pp. 1a, 11a.

27. Ravetz, "Usable Knowledge."

28. T. O'Riordan, *Perspectives on Resource Management* (London: Dion, 1971).

29. The Minnesota drought case study is based on data and analysis developed in 1988–89 with a grant from the Blandin Foundation, Grand Rapids, Minnesota. Research assistants were Marsha K. Soucheray, Jan P. Stanley, Catherine M. Sleezer, Lea Foushee, Elizabeth Whitaker, and Ursula M. Gerlach.

30. For example, *Winters v. United States,* 207 U.S. 564 (1908), *Arizona v. California,* U.S. 546 (1983), *United States v. Adair,* 723 F.2d 1394 (9th Cir. 1983), cert. denied 104 S. CT 3536 (1984), and *Mississippi River Headwaters Lakes in Minnesota Feasibility Study, Appendices,* U.S. Army Corps of Engineers, St. Paul District (September, 1982).

31. "Drought Conditions Worsen," *Princeton Union Eagle,* July 7, 1988; "Continued Drought Beginning to Affect More Farmers," *St. Paul Pioneer Press,* June 26, 1988.

32. "Drought Has Highway 12 Project Running Ahead of Schedule," *Minneapolis Star Tribune,* (hereafter *MST*) August 11, 1988.

33. "Water Use Rate Jumps Sharply in Twin Cities," *Pioneer Press Dispatch,* August 18, 1988.

34. "What Kind of Person Would Steal Cool Air From the Needy?" *MST,* July 20, 1988.

35. "Neighborly Spirits Wither in a Dry Time," *MST,* July 28, 1988.

36. "Day 1 of Watering Ban Brings Queries, Complaints," *MST,* July 28, 1988.

37. Editorial, "Who Gets Water? Questions Flourish as Drought Deepens," *Pioneer Press Dispatch,* July 21, 1988.

38. Pamela Barnard, "Family Stress Heightened in Crisis Like Drought," *Minnesota Extension Service Responds to People in Drought* (Minneapolis, MN: University of Minnesota, August 1988); "Catholic Bishops Ask State's Parishes to Pray for Rain," *MST,* July 1, 1988; "National Guard Trucks Bring Water to Homeowners Near St. Cloud," *MST,* July 22, 1988.

39. "The Dry Humor of Peter Kohlsaat," *Brainerd Daily Dispatch,* July 1988.

40. "Letter to the Editor," *Bemidji Pioneer,* August 31, 1988.

41. Division of Resource Management, Leech Lake Business Committee, *Emergency Water Withdrawals From the Mississippi Headwaters Lakes and Their Effects Upon the Leech Lake Band of Chippewa Indians* (August 1, 1988).

42. Minnesota Department of Natural Resources, *Drought in 1988* (St. Paul, MN: Division of Water, January 1988), p. 52.

43. This point was also in "Review of Thomas Vennum Jr., Wild Rice and the Ojibway People," *Minnesota Daily,* August 22, 1988.

44. For example of a workshop, see "Water Supply Issues in the Metropolitan Twin Cities Area: Planning for Future Droughts and Population

Growth," sponsored by Water Resources Research Center, University of Minnesota, October 25, 1988.

45. *MST*, September 4, 1988.

46. "A Self-Imposed Sprinkling Ban," *MST*, July 16, 1988; "Sneak Water Down the Rules," *MST*, August 2, 1988; "Sprinkling Bans Will Tip the Odds in Lawn Game," *St. Paul Pioneer Press Dispatch*, July 29, 1988; "A City Without Lawns—Or Maybe Just One," *MST*, August 1, 1988.

47. "Warm-Up of Earth has Begun, Congress Warned," *MST*, June 24, 1988.

48. "The Endless Summer? Scientists Fear that Man-Made Greenhouse Effect Will Warm the Earth, Creating a Hot, Dry Climate That Could Seriously Threaten Our Way of Life," *Newsweek*, July 11, 1988; "Heat Trap: Facing up to a Disaster in the Making," *MST*, July 17, 1988; and "Greenhouse Effect Coming, Ready or Not: Experts Say Even Harsh Measures Will Only Buy Time," *MST*, July 19, 1988 (reprinted from New York Times).

49. "Is the Earth Warming Up? Yes, Say Scientists, But That Might Not Explain This Year's Heat Wave," *Time*, July 4, 1988; "Report Urges Greenhouse Action Now," *Research News in Science*, July 1988; "Has Our Weather Made You Fear the Greenhouse Effect," *Chicago Tribune*, June 23, 1988; "Keeping Cool and Healthy in Hot Weather," *ABC Newspapers*, July 22, 1988; "Inflation Up as Economic Growth Slows," *MST*, July 28, 1988; "A Long Summer of Smog: Air That's Dirty Enough to See Makes Breathing Hazardous to Your Health," *Newsweek*, August 29, 1988;' "North Sea Pollution: The 7000th Seal," *The Economist*, August 27, 1988; "EPA Orders New Steps to Protect Ozone Layer," *St. Paul Pioneer Press*, August 2, 1988; "The Dirty Seas," *Time*, August 1, 1988; "Talking About the Weather: The Lazy Days of Summer Lead to an Attack of Ecophobia," *Time*, August 15, 1988; "Planet of the Year," *Time*, January 2, 1988.

50. "Is Drought a Sign From God?" *St. Paul Pioneer Press*, August 6, 1988.

51. "A Year of Drought Must Not Squelch Quest to Save Land," *MST*, July 21, 1988.

52. "Drought Teaches Humbling Lesson," *MST*, July 8, 1988.

53. Reverend Henne, *Sermon to the Congregation of the Cathedral Church of St. Mark*, Minneapolis, Minnesota, July 10, 1988.

54. Minnesota Statues, Section 473.155; Metropolitan Council, *Metropolitan Council Report to the Legislature*, February 1, 1990 (Mears Park Centre, 230 E. 5th Street, St. Paul MN 55101, document No. 590–90–035).

55. Luther P. Gerlach, Lisa Kaye Brandt and Jessica Morgan, "On Conflicts about Forests: Understanding Turbulent Process as an Evolving Institution for Natural Resource Management." Unpublished manuscript, University of Minnesota, June 1991.

9

Contested Ground: International Environmentalism and Global Climate Change

•

ANN HAWKINS

Environmentalism's close affinity with scientific research and the scientific community makes it the prototypical modern social movement. Contemporary environmentalists formulate their claims and agendas with the imprimatur of scientific evidence and research in mind, and the legitimacy of modern environmentalism obtains from its basis in "science" and not mere "ideology" or "values."[1] The rhetorical tussle over environmental issues thus comes to rest on persuasion: "our" science versus "their" science. Armed with the authority of scientific empiricism, environmental issues and the environmentalist position on these issues has increasingly assumed a unique role (at least from the vantage point of its proponents).

But the struggle over science and its data is only a part of a larger drama. A number of metathemes are also being played out: which issues or topics have been included or left out of international discussions; which actors, voices, and concerns are considered legitimate participants; and who will bear the costs of whatever agreements are finally, if ever, reached and implemented? These conflicts revolve around disputes over context, and over the social construction of global climate change. If how we frame solutions is contingent on how we construct problems, then outcomes are very dependent on these struggles.

In this chapter, I consider three themes related to the "contested ground" of international environmentalism and global climate change. First, I explore the notion of contested ground and how it is expressed in struggles over the construction and definition of the climate-change discourse. Second, I discuss the different ideologies that have emerged among the claimants to this contested ground and the struggles that result. Finally, I explain why these struggles are taking place, and examine their implications for international efforts to address global ecological interdependence. I explore these conflicts not only between North and South, but also at the national, subnational, and local levels of developing countries. Analyzing these conflicts at different levels and among different actors is crucial for assessing the viability of any "global" environmental conventions or agreements. "North" and "South" are also social constructions of the divisions among different nations in the world. The criteria for judging who gets included where, with what implications, have become hard to determine as countries increasingly display multiple characteristics and indicators. It should also be noted here that other designations of the differences between nations (First World/Third World, developed/developing countries, industrialized/nonindustrialized) also face similar problems. None work well. I use the terms as they exist with a great deal of reservation. We all await new ways to speak (and think) of differing countries.

Defining Contested Ground

Since 1987—when the Brundtland Report [2] was released, the first warnings of global warming began to appear in the popular press, and the international environmental community's pressure on the World Bank finally began to take effect [3]—the mainstream international environmental movement has grown in strength and sense of purpose. It now has a more clearly focused agenda: bolstering the Montreal accord on chlorofluorocarbons (CFCs), negotiating a meaningful international agreement on greenhouse gas emissions, saving tropical rainforests, and protecting biological diversity. [4] The environmental movement also has considerable, if diffuse, public support for these goals. Its efforts, moreover, are paralleled by nationally focused environmental movements, such as those in the United States that focus, for example, on water conservation and allocation in California, logging of old-growth forests in the Pacific Northwest, and the disposal of toxic wastes, especially in economically depressed areas. For international and national environmental organizations the ground that must be contested has become ever clearer: it is a political struggle over how the biosphere and its resources will be exploited or preserved, to what extent, and by whom.

Whereas the political struggle is apparent, I would stress that contemporary environmental battles must be seen as contested ground in another, equally fundamental sense: as struggles over environmental science within science, over the representation of scientific data by environmentalists and environmental scientists, and over its interpretation by policymakers. The increasingly scientized veneer of modern environmentalism lends to itself an air of objectivity and neutrality where differing values and norms are concerned. But while this objectification of the environmental movement gains it popular credibility, it does not, at heart, represent a purging of ideology.

Thus, the struggles going on here involve contested terrain in several senses. First, they are metaphoric and symbolic struggles over the perceptions and worldviews that become the foundation of how issues themselves are subsequently defined, presented to the public, and articulated in political conflicts with adversaries. Second, as environmentalism has increasingly become a scientifically ordered ideology, two interrelated dynamics assume growing importance. We see this in the translation of environmental science into environmental ideology (via, for example, the appropriation of the concept of "global change" from environmental science as an umbrella for justifying a range of policy agendas), as well as the focusing of environmental science on issues as defined by environmentalists and/or their opponents. Third, the scientization of environmentalism also means that it has been rapidly transformed into a depoliticized, managerialist discourse, in which neoclassical resource economics and national environmental accounting are being merged into frameworks that serve to sharply limit public input.

But these struggles are not just conceptual or symbolic. They are also material, in the sense that framing of environmental issues will have major implications for the livelihoods and wellbeing of particular social groups, classes, regions, and nations. Consequently, not only does global climate change promise to have physical impacts, but the outcomes of these struggles to define and "construct" the parameters of global climate change—and thus the responses to it—

will also lead to real, material effects. Moreover, environmental issues of global scope provide an opening through which formerly
excluded participants within nation-states can express discontent for
past development decisions, call for new voices to be heard, and
articulate new visions to be encouraged. And, in situations where
neither discontentedness nor new visions can be openly named and
legitimately discussed, scientific and technical debates can also serve
as proxies, providing a shield behind which other ideas may be
advanced or explored. As we shall see, such debates are already well
underway.

Environmentalism: A Platform from Which to Speak

Uncertainties about the scientific, technical, and ecological questions
surrounding global climate change can be seen as perfectly valid in
their own right. As the many studies and meetings of the past few
years show, a tremendous number of questions remain unresolved,
and new ones are continually being uncovered. It is also important,
however, not to overlook the questions of power, structure, and
distribution that are embedded in the sorting out of these uncertainties. These points return us to a key question: Why have "environmental" issues attracted such a diverse array of social and institutional actors, and why have these actors become centers of such
controversy?

Environmental issues have also become an arena in which the
previously unresolved struggles between rich and poor nation-states
can be raised once again (as graphically seen during the Earth Summit). In this light, the tendency of Third World policymakers to link
global climate change to economics, trade, and development issues,
and their apparent reluctance to discuss "only" issues of environment, makes perfect sense. If environmental issues have indeed
become global in scope, there are legitimate questions about their
place and impact within the World Order that go far beyond mere
ecological concerns. How would such issues be handled if left within
the context of an (unchanged) World Order? Are there reasons to
believe that this Order is presently changing, or will it simply continue to re-create the structural inequities of the post–World War II
era? While the answers to these, and other, questions are still unclear, they do provide us with a template for understanding the

wariness of developing nations to enter into a narrowly defined "environmental" global discourse.

The extent to which international agreements on atmosphere/climate, global forests, and biodiversity either restrict or significantly shape economic, and therefore social and political realities, has yet to be directly confronted and openly discussed, especially among nations. Scientists, world environmentalists, and others decry such explicit discussions as political (often implying that these discussions are of a "leftist" or of "Third Worldist" bent).[5] But to dismiss these issues as extraneous is to disregard the real pressures Third World governments face, caught between the need to generate and borrow foreign currency to repay debts, and the need to face and resolve severe domestic problems. Rarely are the two needs complementary or compatible.

Hence, the Third World's reluctance to participate in decidedly one-sided negotiations—a reluctance often described as obstructionist—is, instead, related to issues that have yet to be legitimated as part of these discussions. Such issues include, but are not limited to, the sources of future international assistance; resolution of the debt crisis; the structure of trade agreements, protectionism, sanctions, and world markets; and the roles of international and multilateral bodies in the global economy.[6]

Elsewhere, I have written about the strategies of weaker institutional actors in the face of unequal power relations. Often, the strategy of such actors consists of the appropriation or use of dominant norms and rhetoric to argue the legitimacy of their own concerns, thus applying the very terms that more powerful actors claim to respect and accept.[7] This strategy has often been employed among nation-states, but with the emergence of "environmentalism," subnational actors appear to have found a way to frame topics that allow for relatively open dialogue with those in power. These, I would argue, are attempts by non-state actors to become part of the policy dialogue at national and subnational levels. In some cases, nongovernmental organizations (NGOs) have gained visibility and credibility at a time when state budgets and governing capacities are under severe pressures. Under such circumstances, some of these non-state actors now find themselves taking on traditional state responsibilities.

The extent to which nongovernmental organizations have become key actors, with a major influence on current versions of environmental discourse, is often downplayed or dismissed.[8] I would argue that, in contrast to such dismissal, NGOs are playing a growing role in current environmental discussions, and have been important for some time. The rise of national and local NGOs within developing countries is an extraordinary phenomenon, as are their multiplying transnational linkages to international environmental organizations. This phenomenon can be viewed as, among other things, the NGOs' bid to be included as participants in a "democratic dialogue" on issues of national development and resource use.[9]

Consequently, the language of official resistance to the "globalization" of Southern resources and environments, and their being taken out of the hands (and control of) national and local governments and local communities, has centered around a number of issues. These include questions of scientific credibility (data collection and methodological problems), the application of generalized scientific methods and data to all parts of the world (with no attention paid to variability in social systems using or embedded in these environments), and measurements of ecological flows and absorption capacities (e.g., as in the raging debates over the magnitudes of the carbon sources and sinks that tropical rainforests and global oceans represent). If it is not possible for national governments, especially those in a dependent or weaker relationship to the larger world order, to directly raise their concerns about the future directions of North-South associations, what then becomes the means by which their voices may be heard?

Global Environmentalism for Whom?
Managerialist, Redistributive, and Sustainability Paradigms

Issues of boundaries, legitimacy, history, and ideology operate at all social levels; reality is achieved through social processes. How these "unspoken" concerns influence a particular discourse, such as that of global climatic change, will profoundly affect the nature of future international relations. Berger and Luckmann observe that what we regard as "knowledge" is created, shaped, and sustained within particular social situations.[10] Global environmental issues—and the very real consequences they entail—reflect a process of social construction among actors at various levels, each of whom perceives the international implications of biophysical changes and processes in different ways.

What are possible social constructions, then, that could emerge as the dominant discourse? How are they based on different visions of the relationship between environment and development? While the future will most likely present us with combinations that differ from what I suggest here, there are currently three ideal-type paradigms in contention. I label them the "global managerialist," the "redistributive development," and the "new international sustainability order" paradigms.

The global managerialist paradigm grows out of the belief that there has been a globalization of the commons. Solutions to address problems in this globalized commons will essentially entail a division of labor between governments and international organizations, with NGOs fulfilling a kind of advisory role on the sidelines. This paradigm relies on the structure of nation-states and international organizations as they already exist. Within this paradigm, strong arguments are made for the need for central protection of environments everywhere, based on the notion that "global" interpenetration has occurred everywhere, which in turn necessitates "global" or centralized solutions.

The globalization of the environment lends itself to a managerial approach—that is, to the notion that "expert" bodies or individuals are best suited to determine how, when, and under what circumstances resources should be allocated and used. Globalization, and the entry of experts, frequently displace local perceptions and definitions of problems, with the result that poverty and poor people themselves are blamed for causing environmental degradation.

Such a presumption, while ostensibly about the "environment," is not significantly different from the notions underlying most international development efforts during the post–World War II era. Although different development strategies have come and gone over the last four decades, a basic core theme regarding the relationship between foreign assistance and the determination of development policies has been maintained. Environmental problems become just another in a long list to be analyzed, managed, and solved within the existing or slightly modified paradigm of asymmetrical North-South relations.

Among examples of such thinking are proposals that developed countries "compensate" for the carbon dioxide emissions from new power stations via reforestation projects in developing countries. Debt-for-nature swaps are another illustration of solutions to environmental problems in developing countries being shaped by preexisting unequal relations between rich and poor nations. Such proposals are often offered to developing countries in some combination with "debt forgiveness" or a promise of future lending.[11]

A second social construction of environment and development issues, the redistributive development paradigm, could grow out of greater attention toward equity issues, especially with regard to developing countries. In this sort of construction, such factors as the inequitable economic balance between rich and poor countries would play a larger role. Proposals emanating from such a paradigm might include, for example, a call for developed countries to provide special assistance to developing countries in order to encourage energy-efficient infrastructure. Such proposals often stress the "double burden" of poverty and debt borne by these countries. A number of Third World voices try to contrast the economic indebtedness of Southern countries toward the North with the ecological indebtedness of the technologically advanced but more resource-poor North toward the South; the argument is that some sort of even trade already does exist, and that the South is not somehow "more" indebted than the North.[12] Within the context of the redistributive development paradigm, the resolution of global environmental problems would be linked to outcomes having to do with economic and trade issues. Raising the issue of the economic and environmental effects on developing countries of the General Agreement on Trade and Tariffs (GATT) and other free-trade agreements is a prime example of such linkage.

With specific regard to climate change, a redistributive approach might include separate funding facilities to assist developing countries in meeting their commitments under international atmospheric agreements. Such a fund was, in fact, set up at a November 1990 meeting of twenty-five North and South countries, where one billion dollars was pledged toward a pilot Global Environmental Facility (GEF) or "Green Fund" within the World Bank.[13] The Green Fund does, however, have environmentalist and Third World critics, who argue that it allows the World Bank and other international lenders to avoid the more difficult task of revising lending policies so as to account for environmental concerns in a structurally meaningful way.

Other measures linked to a redistributive development approach might include the next round of discussions about the still-lingering and large international debts of Third World borrowers. By now Western developed countries, the commercial banking sector, and the multilateral development banks are sufficiently eager to see action on this issue so that they are ready to link repayment with the fluctuating fortunes of world commodity prices. While debtholders might not be pleased with such arrangements, there does appear to be growing recognition by lenders of the unfairness—not to mention the low likelihood—of repayment in the face of declining commodity prices and weak export markets.[14]

A third paradigm for global ecological interdependence could be called the new international sustainability order. The phrase is meant to imply not only environmental sustainability, but also economic and social sustainability. The character of such an order falls, today, within the realm of futurist vision, with much of it being dismissed as utopian, unrealistic, and not sufficiently pragmatic.

The managerialist paradigm stresses world conservation and global environmental services, while the redistributive paradigm stresses past global inequities and future Third World development. The sustainability paradigm challenges both to consider whether economic development, as well environmental wellbeing, can be sustained indefinitely given current projections of either of the other two trajectories.

Some take hope for an international sustainability order from the expanded role and strengthening of the UN system, seeing in that body the seeds of future international decision and enforcement mechanisms. Efforts such as the 1992 Earth Summit, the participation of non-governmental organizations at national and international levels during that event, and the preparation of International Conventions on atmospheric and biospheric issues for presentation at the conference, could be seen in this light.

Others see different, less favorable implications of an international sustainability order based on existing institutions. The 1991 Gulf War has led many Third World countries and individuals to think more carefully about the relationships among "national" resource ownership, international dependence, resource "scarcity" (often defined in terms of national security interests), and the potential role of military dominance and force in "globalizing" these resources.[15]

Of these three ideal-type scenarios or paradigms, can we point to one as an emerging dominant construction? Which scenario or set of assumptions appears to be winning the hearts and minds of those engaged in discussing and negotiating at the international level? Within this particular paradigm, what are the principal underlying issues that the emerging social construction of climate change fails either to acknowledge or to address?

At the present time, the global managerialist paradigm, with its concomitant globalization of the environment, appears to be the prevailing construction of the climate-change issue. As I pointed out above, the globalization of environmental problems lends itself strongly to the removal of problems—and problem-definition—from the local and regional levels. Few would argue, of course, that we do not need to look at the global level in order to understand the vastness of the problems we are confronting. But to argue that the responses to these concerns can be determined and legislated primarily at the global level not only overlooks but also oversimplifies causes, relationships, and realities at the regional, national, and subnational levels. As this paradigm becomes increasingly dominant, it is highly unlikely that domestic equity issues will develop as major areas for discussion or redress at international levels.

Participants in international discussions now underway are already attempting to deal with some global equity issues that are, in themselves, immensely complicated, whether tackled from a scientific or policy perspective. Furthermore, the solutions offered do little to address fundamental causes as opposed to more superficial symptoms. In pursuit of the globalist paradigm, moreover, we may fall into the trap of thinking that the hard work of achieving a global consensus will, somehow, translate automatically into the even more difficult task of articulating, recruiting, and affecting the millions of micro-level beliefs, behaviors, and actions that might add up to preventing or alleviating global climate change.

The growing dominance of the paradigm of climate change as a global environmental issue is more than just a triumph of perspective, however. In being accepted as a "true" description of reality, it also becomes a "transforming theory," that is, one that affects the ways in which problems are addressed.[16] We see this in the discourses of development, as well as in the ways both definitions of problems and their solutions are being contested. Indeed, as we shall see, these contestations are, to a large degree, a function of the practical effects of that transforming theory.

Internationalized Environmental Issues and Development Discourse

There are several key elements involved in this process of social construction: first, the new role of transnational environmental groups in shaping the international discourse of development; second, the links between local and transnational environmental groups as modes of controlling the terms and definitions of these problems; and third, as noted above, the globalization and politicization of issues that are primarily local in nature, and for which effective ameliorative or substantive actions will need to be locally generated if international goals are to be achieved.

The ways in which issues of development and environment are now being framed—as global change, global warming, and global rainforests—have pushed into the background some of the key environmental issues in the Third World: soil erosion, land degradation, and deforestation in non-rainforest areas.[17] These environmental changes produce a host of social problems, too: fuelwood shortages, loss of community access to traditional resources, land degradation, and declining agricultural production. A growing number of groups—grassroots organizations, NGOs, governments, and development agencies, each with different ideologies and agendas—have been working to address these problems. As a result, it is here that the "contested ground" is often found, in the form of conflicting assessments of what needs to be done, by whom, and at what level. That primarily local problems are being discussed in "globalized" terms points, as we shall see, to the ideological nature of the local issues themselves. It also raises the question of who is allowed to participate in discussions about those issues.

An important global discourse has been created as a consequence of the international popularization of the environmental movement during the last twenty years. This discourse has permitted "local" groups (often oriented toward social equity) and international groups (often oriented toward the environment) to perceive common ground where "natural resources" are concerned. Most recently, concern for local sustainable development on the one hand and global climate change on the other seem to offer some common concerns between these disparate groups. But this ostensible commonality is more imagined than real, and often stands in contrast to the actuality of remaining differences and struggles among various actors, both locally and between the local and global levels. Constructing such local-global commonalities is often rhetorically useful, to be sure. But different perceptions and interpretations become clearer when difficulties are encountered in the effort to "mobilize" local populations in the implementation of globally agreed-upon solutions. As a result, contestations emerge, even where there seems to be agreement over goals. We can therefore identify three levels of contestation resulting from the globalization paradigm: Northern states versus Southern states; states versus social movements; and the empowered versus the disempowered.

Development Discourse and the Global Environment: The Struggle of North and South

Global environmental issues, including climate change, should be seen as part of the longstanding debate over the structure of relationships between North and South. The construction of international environmentalism, rather than standing apart from previous development discourse, reflects many long-standing struggles over these relations. Where discussions of global climate change are concerned, the primary foci for the North remain the science and the technical feasibility of proposals for control or amelioration. Any broader questions having to do with a restructuring of the present world order remain largely unarticulated, or sub rosa at best. Within the developing countries themselves, similar debates exist about the relationships among state, economy (e.g. domestic business interests, multinational corporations), and society (community or populace of a given country).

Recently, there has been much talk about the emergence of a "New World Order" (which actually predates the military and political events in the Middle East during 1990–1991). It is worth dwelling for a moment on this terminology, now picked up by those on the conservative end of the American political spectrum. When developing countries called for a "New International Economic Order" (NIEO) in the 1970s, the response from developed countries was, by and large, that there existed no deliberate world order structuring economic and political outcomes. In that context, the recent use of the term "New World Order" is perhaps the best acknowledgement we have from Western industrialized nations that there was and is some kind of "Order" articulating dependency and interdependency among the nations of the world.[18]

On what was the Old World Order based? What were the perceptions of relationships between developed and developing countries? Development theorists have constructed a history of the post–World War II era as a series of "development decades," with each marking a new rung on the ladder of progress. Each "decade" has represented the efforts of national elites and international development agencies to fashion combinations of economic and social development strategies for the underdeveloped. These strategies have been based on prevailing Western notions of progress, modernization, and the good life.[19]

Development decades notwithstanding, many critics of international development schemes argue that relations between North and South have been strongly influenced by the nature of the donor/recipient roles played by developed and developing countries. The national policies and development trajectories of the latter have often reflected dependence on the strictures (e.g. "conditionality") of international foreign aid.[20] Seen in this light, the last forty years of "development" have been not a drive toward progress but rather an ongoing struggle between rich and poor countries over the balance of dominance, dependence, and autonomy with which countries, especially the developing ones, would be left.

To be sure, relations between North and South were not solely a consequence of the foreign-aid and development regime of the past forty years, since the "social construction" of this particular set of relationships was the product of a dialectic between the "rich" and "poor" countries involved, and not just an imposition by the stronger upon the weaker. Foreign aid was only one element in this dialectic, which also rested on the after-effects of colonialism and the willingness of Third World national elites to embrace the ideology of modernization and development.

As the issue of global climate change has gained international prominence, it has become a factor in this development struggle, especially in the discourse on environmental agreements between more- and less-industrialized countries. Environmental issues, therefore, have become one more item in the development dialectic between developed and developing countries. This could be seen in the Earth Summit's agenda, which focused ostensibly on three major goals: an international convention on the atmosphere (carbon emissions), a global forest agreement (carbon absorption), and a world biodiversity convention (preservation of germplasm and genetic resources).[21] That the Summit's conferees were able only to sign less-than-comprehensive treaties was, curiously enough, as much the result of U.S. concern about "development" as it was the result of conflict between developed and developing countries.

Future global climate change has been a low priority for most developing countries. Other problems—political, social, economic, and environmental—are generally regarded as more immediate and pressing. Moreover, many developing countries also fall within equatorial or tropical zones, for which current climate-change projections are less definitive or promise less dramatic consequences. Since computer-based climate models are unable to provide precise predictions of effects at the local and regional levels, researchers in developed countries already find it difficult to make a water-tight, scientific case for immediate action. And because the models tend to scrutinize primarily the impact on Northern temperate zones, the level of imprecision is even greater where Southern countries are concerned.[22]

The emerging conflict can be seen, in particular, in the reactions and responses of many developing countries to the climate-change agenda as it has emerged from developed countries. On the one hand, international discussions among many of those involved, including scientists, appear to have reached near-consensus on the plausible implications of, and possible technical responses to, climate change. Based on this, negotiations have been aimed at "working out" potential environmental and technical obstacles to international accords.

On the other hand, Third World states are reacting to this drive toward consensus. Developing countries recognize the serious economic implications of global environmental agreements, and a growing number feel that the Intergovernmental Panel on Climate Change (IPCC) has been dominated by experts from developed countries, whose conclusions are therefore likely to be skewed in favor of those countries' concerns. Thus, in January 1991, the UN General Assembly passed a resolution putting itself in charge of any final climate change agreements, a move some observers interpreted as a Third World attempt to gain some degree of control over the negotiations and their outcomes.[23]

A classic reaction to the domination of industrialized-country perspectives can be seen in the response of several Third World countries (Indonesia, Brazil, and India, among others) to the 1990–91 edition of World Resources, published by the World Resources Institute (WRI) and the UN Environment Programme. The volume includes a "Greenhouse Index," which lists the world's top fifty greenhouse-gas emitters.[24] On this list Brazil, China, India, and Indonesia rank among the top ten (along with the United States, the Soviet Union, Japan, and three European countries). A number of representatives from developing countries believe that these figures are based "less on science than on politically motivated math."[25] A response by India's Centre for Science and Environment severely criticizes WRI's calculations, asking:

Can we really equate the carbon dioxide contributions of gas guzzling automobiles in Europe and North America or, for that matter, anywhere in the Third World with the methane emissions of draught cattle and rice fields of subsistence farmers in West Bengal or Thailand? Do these people not have a right to life? But no effort has been made in WRI's report to separate the "survival emissions" of the poor, from the "luxury emissions" of the rich. Just what kind of politics or morality is this which masquerades in the name of "one worldism" and "high minded internationalism"? [26]

A debate has ensued between WRI and the authors of the Indian report over the nature of the science and calculations involved. Brazil's then-Secretary for Science and Technology, José Goldemberg (later, for a short time, the Environmental Minister), also reacted strongly to: "the illfounded rumors that Brazil is the world's third largest creator of greenhouse gases after the US and the Soviet Union. Such rumors originated in a recent report from the World Resources Institute. Its figures regarding Brazil are plainly wrong." [27]

The Indonesian National Working Group on Global Climate Change has also raised explicit doubts about the scientific validity of certain IPCC claims about climate change, and has expressed skepticism about the databases and analyses of Western institutions used to quantify various aspects of global warming, especially those involving tropical equatorial countries. [28]

In the minds of many from developing countries, these doubts raise a series of questions about the true nature of these "global" environmental issues. Are such issues really just an indirect way for the industrial countries to continue to control and regulate the economies, trade, and development of less industrially advanced countries? Are they just another means of extracting resources and surplus value from developing nations, going well beyond the decapitalizing debt crises of the last decade or so? Attempts to unlink technical regimes for environmental management from these issues, at international conferences or in other forums, assure a continued backlash of contestation.

Development and Environment Inside Nation-states: A Second Level of Struggle

Issues related to global change and global ecological interdependence are, at once, scientific problems and crisis scenarios that combine ideological commitments and policy options at the international level.

It is less recognized, but also true, that such issues also exist at national and subnational levels, and if we look closely we can see manifestations of the essentially contested nature of climate change at these levels as well. Such contestation has both national and international implications, especially for developing countries.

What are possible responses to a global environmental issue within Third World countries? National governments are, it is true, called upon to represent themselves at international meetings such as the Second World Climate Conference, those conducted by the IPCC, or the Earth Summit. But attendance should not be interpreted as a clear national consensus on global climate change, or that dealing with it is actually accepted as a national priority. Within any given developing country there are often a broad range of perceptions, from both official and nonofficial institutions, about what climate change is, the likelihood of its occurrence, and how important it is to that country and its people. Agencies of the national government generally have multiple and conflicting agendas for a country's development, too, as well as urgent bureaucratic and organizational needs. These agendas and needs are potent forces for shaping not only their responses, but also for influencing how an issue such as global climate change is viewed in the first place.

A brief case in point is the recent discourse on tropical deforestation within Indonesia—a nation second only to Brazil in terms of territory covered by tropical rain forests and the abundance and diversity of attendant species.[29] Tropical deforestation was discussed previously using a terminology that ranged from the "effects of slash-and-burn agriculture" to "problems of soil erosion" to "forest and park encroachment by local people." Now, however, tropical rain forests have been linked to global climate change, thereby shifting the emphasis to rain forests as both contributors to, and absorbers of, carbon dioxide in the atmosphere.[30] As a result, the discourse has been globalized, and its focus shifted away from the local and regional effects of deforestation in political, economic, and legal terms.

Within a national context, however, tropical deforestation is likely to be the subject of heated debate among government forestry officials, agricultural officers, resettlement staff, major timber company representatives, national biological and ecological scientists, and nongovernmental organizations. This debate asks several questions: How much deforestation is actually going on? (Is it quantified? Does anyone actually know? Who has the information? Is it possible to get access to existing information?) What are its major causes, and which groups of people are most responsible for deforestation? (Shifting agriculturalists? Resettlement projects and migrant settlers? Timber and mineral concessions? Infrastructure such as access roads?) These debates occur in addition to the standard ones about losses versus benefits: Who loses? Who benefits? In what ways are benefits either public or private?

Over the last five to ten years, nonofficial actors and nongovernmental organizations within many Third World countries have become increasingly involved in debates over issues of national significance such as those described above. The environment has become particularly prominent as an arena in which the participation of nonstate actors is often allowed. With the publication in 1987 of the Brundtland Commission's *Our Common Future*, NGOs have been virtually "institutionalized" by official recognition, especially within the United Nations system. Why has this happened? What does such participation represent? How does it relate to environmental issues? [31]

Many of these voluntary organizations were established during that period of development history when emphasis was put on "basic human needs," with the goal of extending basic services to the poor: basic health care, nutritional services, adult literacy training, water supply and sanitation. Over time, these concerns were broadened to include wider social-justice and equity issues, as NGO participants identified ways in which external policies and actions affected local communities. In recent years, however, environmental issues have risen to the fore. But why?

In countries where little public discourse about social equity is permitted, discussions about the physical environment often provide an opening for more fundamental debate. NGOs and others are often allowed to discuss "technical" problems of soil erosion, water pollution and toxicity, even when it is not possible to question directly the links among political power, national elites, and resource use. Therefore, to categorize the interests of NGOs as strictly environmental would be a mistake, since their concerns may be deeper, often reflecting the development discontent discussed earlier.

Some observers have pointed out, moreover, that the imposition of Western environmentalist categories on Third World NGOs and environmentalists may obscure more than it reveals. [32] Describing Chipko in India, or the rubber tappers' movement led by Chico Mendes in Brazil, as expressions of Third World "green" sentiment are oversimplifications, if not downright misreadings, of local and national phenomena. International and Northern environmental organizations have been able to make common cause with such groups, which requires a closer reading than simply the "spread of environmentalism."

International and national environmental/NGO connections have become fairly complex and sophisticated over the past decade. Prominent in the eyes of many Western observers have been such efforts as the long-term lobbying campaigns targeted at multilateral agencies (including the World Bank, the Inter-American Bank, the Asian Development Bank, etc.)[33] and events such as the large demonstrations in Bonn during the G-7 Economic Summit that took place there in the mid-1980s. But this disregards the growing impact of these transnational linkages throughout the Third World at the national and local levels.

Indeed, more and more, international agencies—whether governmental or nongovernmental—are focusing their attention on the domestic activities and participation of developing-country grassroots and nongovernmental organizations in development, environmental protection, and conservation. This interest is captured in the remarks of Dr. Ronald Roskens, Administrator of the U.S. Agency for International Development (AID): "Enabling non-governmental organizations to play a more important role in the [national] decision-making process within their governments is critical. Therefore grassroots institution building will be one of our highest priorities."[34]

Consequently, whereas much of this interest previously took the form of funding for discrete projects or specific goals, the growing attention being paid by outside organizations is encouraging developing-country governments to include national NGOs within governmental decision-making.

While environmental issues at the international level may be important to NGOs in developing countries, these are often not their main concern. Instead, the connection with outsiders often serves principally to strengthen and protect "environmental dissidents" within their own countries. For example, in the late 1980s, when the Malaysian Prime Minister arrested social agitators, "World Zionists," and environmental activists in the name of state interests, world attention and external pressure played a significant role in securing the relatively speedy release of many people.[35]

The spate of activities linked to the 1992 Earth Summit and the parallel Global Forum, for which a group of umbrella organizations took on the job of coordinating information, highlighted a number of NGO concerns. International preparations for the conference called for "broad based independent sector participation in the process."[36]

The Centre for Our Common Future in Geneva was especially active in publicizing regional and national planning meetings, as well as providing updates on the drafting of national reports from individual countries. There was clearly a kind of oversight of the process taking place, with the Centre and others (e.g., the Global Tomorrow Coalition, the UN-Nongovernmental Liaison Service, PeaceNet/EcoNet) actively organizing and networking among NGOs, and with close attention being paid to the drafting of national "state of development and environment" reports.

This activity by the independent international sector clearly indicates two things. First, national NGOs and environmental groups ("ecodissidents") are being strengthened within their own countries by association with outside groups. Second, the right of "access to information," increasingly raised at both national and international levels, is being highlighted. This latter issue can be understood in at least two ways, the first of which is the right of national governments to have access and input to the structures of power that determine multilateral foreign assistance to their countries. Secondly, the issue of access to information reflects tensions within countries over which groups have the right to participate in domestic policy making—essentially, issues of accountability between a government and its people.

These concerns can be seen, for example, in the positions of the NGO Working Group on the World Bank, which call for project planning and information in developing countries that encourages the:

> active participation of the people of these countries that is not managed and controlled by others and that is promoted not only in the design and implementation of small-scale activities but also in larger-scale projects and in programme, regional and national-policy planning. Grassroots groups must have the right to reject outside initiatives that threaten to do fundamental damage to their communities and livelihoods. The Bank can, and should, work diligently to help remove the internal and external constraints to participation. This can be done in good part by helping to decentralize the development process and by ensuring maximum public access to information about planned development interventions.[37]

The attention paid to the drafting of national reports for the Earth Summit indicates a growing bid by national NGOs, grassroots organizations, and others to participate as equal partners in national decision-making, based on notions of shared and open information. While this is clearly only an ideal in many countries, notions such as free information, equal participation, pluralism, and even democratic process and dialogue are gaining prominence. They are gaining in credibility as catch words or symbols—even if not as actual practices—that legitimate the claims of national NGOs and others to a place within national development decisions. These claims for legitimacy, participation, and dialogue are often strengthened by transnational linkages, whether those linkages are made with international NGOs and outside environmental groups or through pressures from international lending institutions, bilateral assistance agencies, UN bodies, and others.

I do not mean to suggest that these bids by NGOs and other nonstate actors have been simple or smooth processes. As I have tried to point out in preceding pages, these efforts have been both controversial and conflictual, and outcomes are still uncertain. Bids for legitimacy by NGOs with transnational backing may put them on a collision course with the state; there also exists the possibility that NGOs will be co-opted into becoming quasi-bureaucracies, providing "social services" but not political critiques.

Unheard Voices, Other Visions: Local and Indigenous Communities

Even with the calls by NGOs and other for democratic dialogue within decision-making processes, there are still those less-powerful actors whose voices and concerns have yet to be accorded equal treatment in global environmental debates. These include local communities and residents, whose roles in the overall debate have been limited. As these groups begin to make themselves heard, there are likely to be further conflicts, not only with official agencies but with NGOs and environmentalists as well. Such an emerging conflict can be seen in the public statement of an indigenous peoples' federation in the Amazon Basin, addressing their concern over being excluded from the regional development planning process. In 1989, they sent a petition to the "community of concerned environmentalists" and the World Bank warning that:

> We are concerned that you have left us, the Indigenous Peoples, out of your vision of the Amazonian Biosphere. The focus of concern of the environmental community has typically been the preservation of the tropical forest and its plant and animal inhabitants. You have

shown little interest in its human inhabitants who are also part of that biosphere.

We are concerned that you have left us Indigenous Peoples and our organizations out of the political process which is determining the future of our homeland. While we appreciate your efforts on our behalf, we want to make it clear that we never delegated any power of representation to any individual or organization within that community.[38]

In their petition, the federation proceeded to call for recognition of indigenous ownership rights over territories, and promotion of its models for living within the biosphere.

Another example of an indigenous people's voice can be seen in the stand of the Huaorani Indian Nation of the Ecuadorean Amazon against environmental exploitation of oil resources within their territories. In January, 1991 they sent a set of resolutions to the DuPont-Conoco Company, which read in part:

The oil companies enter our territory without taking us into account, they come in and do their work despite the fact that they know we have the property rights over this [sic] lands, disrupting our organizational process; the Conoco company wants to work by itself, using, in an isolated Huaoranis from Cononaco and Yasun! [sic]

That the Conoco company is discussing about the life of the Huaoranis in meetings in which the Huaoranis are not present and that we are treated as if we were guests, when we cannot be guests when the discussion is about our lives, we have to take care of that without anybody disposing of our lives.[39]

Such cases clearly expand the current boundaries of the debate, drawing on issues linked to human rights, citizenship, and other topics having to do with equity and social justice. These cases also show that, although the issues of tropical rainforest protection and indigenous peoples' rights have to a large extent been globalized and institutionalized, the implementation and structures of these efforts are still very much contested.

This use of environmental rhetoric by local communities linked to human rights, local equity, and social justice, can be seen as a mode of protest, resistance, or bidding for autonomous participation. Often these groups first emerged internationally in conjunction with an NGO or an international environmental organization. The irony is that this process of "globalization" of environmental issues has created the very springboard for local groups to publicize their protests, and even their differences with their NGO allies. New actors who speak on their own behalf about these differences and conflicts with their presumed allies represent a phenomenon I call "claiming voice." [40]

Conclusion

In this chapter, I have looked at the contested nature of "global" environmental problems. These contestations are the result, in part, of the globalization of environmental issues, with the appearance of a seeming consensus among a multiplicity of institutional actors. While such a strategy allows disparate actors to share a common rhetoric, practice and implementation often lead to the disintegration of the consensus. Conflict and contestation emerge because the importance of boundaries and the legitimation of certain issues and actors has been overlooked, suppressed, or ignored.

At all levels of the world system, there are boundary issues and social constructions based on different assumptions and perceptions of development and environmental needs. These have to be recognized if the many aspects of global ecological interdependence are to be addressed. To a certain extent, the "official" system has begun to recognize this point, making room for the development discontent of national NGOs and other oppositional groups within Third World nations. The attention—while welcome—has often been half-hearted or placatory at best, and is no indication that the contestations between states and national NGOs have been resolved. Further, it is quite likely that with the emergence of the voices and concerns of a previously ignored level—local communities speaking for themselves—the conflictual nature of global environmental issues will not decline, but rather, will be increasingly contested at all levels.

NOTES

1. "Legitimacy" here is a term to be considered carefully. As the remainder of the chapter discusses, not all actors within the system consider modern environmentalism to be automatically legitimate; see for example, the comments of C. Boyden Gray and David B. Rivkin, Jr., "A 'No Regrets' Environmental Policy," *Foreign Policy* 83 (Summer 1991): 49. Those who see legitimacy per se in modern environmentalism tend to be interacting primarily at international and, sometimes, national levels.

2. World Commission on Environment and Development, *Our Common Future* (New York: Oxford University Press, 1987).

3. Pressure on the World Bank began in the late 1970s when environmental organizations such as the Sierra Club, the Environmental Defense Fund, and others started their campaign against the Bank's funding of the environmentally destructive "Five Fatal [Development] Projects" (including funding of hydroelectric dams in Brazil, dams in China and India, and transmigration projects in Indonesia). In 1987, after several years of this campaign and other pressures, Bank president Barber Conable announced the considerable expansion and reorganization of the Bank's Environment Division. See, e.g., Bruce Rich, "The Emperor's New Clothes: The World Bank and Environmental Reform," *World Policy Journal* 7 (Spring 1990): 305–30.

4. The relative failure of the 1992 "Earth Summit" should only serve to strengthen these goals.

5. See, e.g., Gray and Rivkin, "No Regrets' Environmental Policy,"

6. Chakravarthi Raghavan, *Recolonization: GATT, the Uruguay Round and the Third World* (Penang, Malaysia: Third World Network, 1990), pp. 32–68.

7. I have labeled this strategy "the counterappropriation of progressive symbols," meaning that weaker actors take back powerful language and symbols, often demanding "accountability" by stronger actors to the mutually agreed-upon rhetoric. Ann P. Hawkins, "Swapping Debt for Nature: Emergence of a New Global Order?" Ph.D. dissertation, Cornell University, 1990, pp. 114–118. James C. Scott also discusses issues of "the social production of hegemonic appearance" in his most recent book, *Domination and the Arts of Resistance: Hidden Transcripts* (New Haven: Yale University Press, 1990), pp. 70–107.

8. Richard Elliot Benedick, *Ozone Diplomacy: New Directions in Safeguarding the Planet* (Cambridge: Harvard University Press, 1991).

9. See the chapter by Steve Breyman in this volume. The concept of "democratic dialogue" comes from Bjorn Gustavsen, "Workplace Reform and Democratic Dialogue," in *Economic and Industrial Democracy* (Beverly Hills, CA: Sage, 1985), 6: 461–479.

10. Peter L. Berger and Thomas Luckmann, *The Social Construction of Reality* (Garden City, NY: Doubleday, 1968), 3.

11. Mark C. Trexler, *Minding the Carbon Store: Weighing US Forestry Strategies to Slow Global Warming* (Washington D.C.: World Resources Institute, 1991), pp. 3–17; Hawkins, "Swapping Debt for Nature"; D. Kline and B. Hager, "Developing with Debt," *LatinFinance* 12 (December 1989): 13–16.

12. Latin American and Caribbean Commission on Development and Environment, *Our Common Agenda* (New York: Inter-American Development Bank and UNDP, 1991), pp. viii–ix.

13. *NGO Networker* 12 (Winter 1990): 6.

14. *Our Common Agenda*, pp. 5–16.

15. James O'Connor, "Murder on the Orient Express: The Political Economy of the Gulf War," *Capitalism, Nature, Socialism* 2 (June 1991): 1–17.

16. David Dessler, "The Use and Abuse of Social Science for Policy," *SAIS Review* 9 (Summer-Fall 1989): 222–23.

17. I am indebted to Frederick H. Buttel for making this point in his comments on an earlier version of this chapter.

18. Indeed, the whole concept of "World Order" is, in some sense, a conservative one, in that it implies a high degree of stability and slowly changing, if at all, relations within political and economic hierarchies. We would also do well to remember the "New European Order" that was the objective of Nazi Germany. Perhaps what we desire is not "order" at all.

19. Alan Wolfe, *Whose Keeper? Social Science and Moral Obligation* (Berkeley: University of California Press, 1989), pp. 1–23; and Christopher Lasch, *The True and Only Heaven: Progress and its Critics* (New York: Norton, 1991), pp. 40–78.

20. Economic Commission for Latin America and the Caribbean (ECLAC), *Latin America and the Caribbean: Options to Reduce the Debt Burden*, Santiago, Chile: United Nations, 1990, pp. 9–17, and Robert E. Wood, *From Marshall Plan to Debt Crisis: Foreign Aid and Developmental Choices in the World Economy* (Berkeley: University of California Press, 1986), pp. 1–138.

21. Elissa Wolfson, Interview, "Dr. Noel Brown: Uniting Nations for the Environment," *E: The Environmental Magazine* 2 (July/August 1991): 60.

22. The major exceptions to this seem to involve the small low-lying states of the Maldives, Tuvalu, the Marshall Islands, and the deltaic regions of Bangladesh, Egypt, and Vietnam, where effects from sea level rise or storm increases seem imminent.

23. National Center for Atmospheric Research, *Network Newsletter* 6 (Spring 1991): 3.

24. World Resources Institute, United Nations Environment Programme, United Nations Development Programme, *World Resources Report 1990–1991* (New York: Oxford University Press, 1990), p. 15.

25. Anil Agarwal and Sunita Narain, "A Case of Environmental Colonialism," *Earth Island Journal* 6 no. 2 (Spring 1991): 39.

26. Anil Agarwal and Sunita Narain, *Global Warming in an Unequal World: A Case of Environmental Colonialism* (New Delhi: Centre for Science and Environment, 1991), p. 5.

27. José Goldemberg, "Letter on Ecology: Brazil's Small Share of the Greenhouse," *New York Times*, July 28, 1990.

28. These comments are based on research by the author in Indonesia during December 1990 and January 1991, including meetings and interviews with Indonesian government policy makers, NGOs, and academic researchers working on climate-change issues.

29. Jeffrey McNeely, Kenton Miller, Walter Reid, Russell Mittermeier,

Timothy Werner, *Conserving the World's Biological Diversity* (Washington D.C.: IUCN, 1990), p. 94.

30. Mark C. Trexler, "Carbon Storage Forestry," in Conference Proceedings on Tropical Forestry Response Options to Global Climate Change, Sao Paulo, Brazil, January 1990, pp. 166–179.

31. Compared to organizations such as churches,which have been active over long periods of time, the emergence and growing influence of national or indigenous NGOs—and especially those in developing countries—are fairly recent phenomena, occurring only over the past ten to fifteen years. Without getting entangled in complex typologies and varieties of NGOs— grassroots organizations, community organizations, social movements, self-help groups, charitable organizations, etc.—suffice it to say that in many places, they have grown in number and strength since the mid-to-late 1970s (see David C. Korten, *Getting to the 21st Century: Voluntary Action and the Global Agenda* (West Hartford, CT: Kumarian Press, 1990), pp. 95–133.) Some observers date the influence of NGOs in the international arena to the 1972 Stockholm Conference on the Human Environment.

32. Ann Hawkins and Frederick Buttel, "The Political Economy of 'Sustainable Development,' " paper prepared for ASA meetings, August 1989), 15–16; and Susanna Hecht and Alexander Cockburn, "In Defense of the Forest," *The Nation* 248 (no. 20): 695–702.

33. Steven Schwartzman, *Bankrolling Disasters: International Development Banks and the Global Environment* (Washington, D.C.: Sierra Club, 1986); and Bruce Rich, "Multilateral Development Banks, Environmental Policy and the U.S.," *Ecology Law Quarterly* 12 (1985): 681–703.

34. *NGO Networker* 11 (June 28, 1990): 6.

35. Stan Sesser, "A Reporter at Large: Logging the Rain Forest," *The New Yorker*, May 27, 1991, pp. 53–54.

36. Centre for Our Common Future, "Independent Sector Reports," *Network '92* No. 4, Feb 1991.

37. NGO Working Group on the World Bank, "Position Paper of the NGO Working Group on the World Bank," (Geneva, Switzerland: ICVA, 1989), p. vi.

38. Coordinating Body for the Indigenous Peoples' Organizations of the Amazon Basin, "Two Agendas on Amazon Development," *Cultural Survival Quarterly* 13, no. 4 (1989): 78.

39. Ramn Huanoni Cobi, Moi Enomenga Nantohua, and Eugenio Quemperi C., "Carta de los Huaoranis a Conoco," Lasnet e-mail message, sent April 24, 1991.

40. I explore this topic more fully in Ann P. Hawkins, "The Politics of Claiming Voice: Development and the Rhetoric of Environment," in *Biopolicy International*, Nairobi, Kenya, 1993.

10

Not Seeing the Forest for the Trees: Rights, Rules, and the Renegotiation of Resource Management Regimes

•

RONNIE D. LIPSCHUTZ AND JUDITH MAYER

> What is the good of a house if you don't have a tolerable planet to put it on? —Henry David Thoreau [1]

> We will reclaim the wilderness, secede from the nation, and live as sustainable bioregions. —Ecotopia E(arth) F(irst)! [2]

Consider Redwood Summer, the effort at celebration and protection of old-growth redwood stands in Northern California that took place during the summer of 1990. In mainstream media accounts Redwood Summer was tinted by recollections of the 1960s; it was a "back to the future" kind of event, bringing together old political activists and new environmentalists, all pitted against the capitalist despoilers of nature and dedicated to a civil rights of trees. [3] The circus atmosphere of the proceedings, as well as the way clashes between participants and loggers were portrayed, led many outside observers to expect either thrilling victories or agonizing defeats. Thus, it is not surprising that, after the dust had settled, Redwood Summer was assessed by the media as unsuccessful: No grand movement emerged, there was no mass conversion of the blue-collar inhabitants of the region, and not much happened to indicate that the old-growth trees would, in fact, be protected (although, more recently, there has emerged a recognition that, as an exploitable resource, the old-growth forests of the region are on the verge of disappearing). [4]

Yet, we claim here that Redwood Summer was symptomatic, and symbolic, of an increasingly common transformative process in modern society that is altering the nature of political transactions and activity. This process has both local and global implications. The participants in Redwood Summer were engaged in an effort to change the very basis of the relationship between trees and people, between nature and society. They sought to redefine the constitutive rule structure of the "resource management regime" put in place so many years before by state and federal governments, together with lumber companies. If successful in this effort, Redwood Summer would have led to the creation of a new social choice structure, within which there would apply new types of property right relationships that would alter the nature and locus of control of the forest resource.[5] At the same time, participants in Redwood Summer made a conscious effort to generalize the legitimacy of these new constitutive rules into the global arena—even if only symbolically—in an effort to extend the principles of Redwood Summer into the realm of international politics.

In this chapter, we are interested in exploring how fundamental conceptions of space, ownership, and relationship may be altered as a consequence of a growing awareness of this interdependence. We also examine how this awareness lays the groundwork for political change, generally, and new modes of resource management, specifically. We focus on the concepts of constitutive rules and property rights as fundamental elements of resource management regimes. We ask where these rights and rules come from, how they are changed, and what such changes mean in terms of global ecological interdependence. We address the relationship between constitutive rules, as the repository of a regime's authority, and more conventional notions of power. And, we suggest that actions such as Redwood Summer should be seen as part of a larger process of renegotiation of social choice systems, informed by a developing awareness of global ecological interdependence.

In this chapter's three sections we first delve more deeply into the notion of constitutive as opposed to regulative rules, their relationship to property rights and resource regimes, and the question of who gets to "define" these rules. In the second section we explore how contact between conflicting sets of property rights, at the constitutive level, has been played out under different conditions. We examine three cases, in terms of differing sets of rules and rights in colonial New England; in terms of movements in Northern California and India to replace non-native stands of eucalyptus with native plant species; and Redwood Summer. Finally, we offer some speculations (to be taken up again in later chapters) about the ways these and other manifestations of global ecological interdependence may reflect a process of international political transformation that is taking place simultaneously in many places and at many levels.

Property Rights and Constitutive Rules

Property rights, as we use the term here, delineate the right of actors to behave in particular ways in various arenas, establish liability for actions, and convey rights to ownership and exploitation of physical goods. These rights can also be defined in terms of systems of rules, customs, norms, and laws that specify relationships between actors and their political, economic, and physical environments.[6] Gary Libecap writes:

> Property rights are the social institutions that define or delimit the range of privileges granted to individuals to specific assets. . . . Property rights institutions range from formal arrangements, including constitutional provisions, statutes, and judicial rulings, to informal conventions and customs regarding the allocations and use of property. . . . By allocating decision-making authority, they also determine who are the economic actors in a system. . . . [7]

Although property rights, according to Libecap's definition, designate who the "economic actors" in a system are, they say nothing about how these actors come to occupy their position of economic or more general social and political power, or whether that position might be changed or undermined by forces other than the market or revolution. As we shall suggest, the positions of economic actors can be affected by processes other than these.

Constitutive rules are fundamental organizing principles of social institutions and politics (or social choice mechanisms, in Dryzek's terms). Rather than regulating behavior, constitutive rules establish qualifications for engaging in particular types of behavior. In other words, constitutive rules grant authority to act and, rather than specifying rules of play, prescribe frameworks for play.[8] Constitutive rules delineate eligibility requirements. This includes who constitutes a legitimate actor within a particular social arrangement and what the criteria are for this designation of legitimacy. Regulative rules define norms of behavior within a specified social arrangement in which legitimate actors are already identified or given.[9]

Thus, for example, we might look at particular fishery regimes and note that only certain qualified individuals (or actors) are eligible to participate in the exploitation of the resource, and only under very specific conditions. Such required qualifications are constitutive of the fishing system. Given eligibility, rules may also exist for the taking or dividing of the resource—how much at one time, when during the year, open and closed areas, etc.—but these rules are regulative. An actor must be eligible before being allowed to exploit the resource. The system of participation and exploitation constitutes a resource management regime; indeed, on a larger scale, such systems not only constitute regimes, but also legitimate the very idea that such arrangements can exist.[10]

David Dessler points out how this works at the international level: "When two nations sign an arms control treaty, they not only adopt a set of operative arms control regulations, but they also reproduce the rules associated with the underlying practice of sovereignty (rules that give the nations the very identity required to make treaties possible)."[11]

We see, therefore, that the authority to act under such circumstances derives not only from the relative power or wealth of actors, but also from the legitimacy conferred on them through the constitutive rule system. A powerful actor can, of course, violate the rules, but potentially at the cost of having others decide not to participate any longer in a system.[12]

Rules and Regimes

In order to clarify the difference between constitutive and regulative rules, and their relationship to resources and property, it may be helpful to clarify what we mean by the term regime. Because of the way the term has come to be applied in international political economy[13] we tend to think of regimes as existing only in the international realm; in fact, such management schemes are ubiquitous in human society. A regime is a management or social choice scheme—in effect, a social institution—for providing a collective good or dealing with a public bad. A regime creates a "conjunction of convergent expectations and patterns of behavior or practice" through the rules and roles that make it up. The result of this conjunction is, as Oran Young puts it: "Conventionalized behavior or behavior based on recognizable social conventions . . . [that] are guides to action or behavioral standards which actors treat as operative without making detailed calculations on a case-by-case basis." [14]

According to Young, "Social institutions may and often do receive formal expression (in contracts, statutes, constitutions, or treaties), but this is not necessary for the emergence of or for the effective operation of a social institution"(p. 18). He identifies three types of regimes: spontaneous, negotiated, and imposed. A spontaneous regime is one that "[does] not involve conscious coordination among participants, [does] not require consent on the part of subjects or prospective subjects, and [is] highly resistant to efforts at social engineering"(pp. 95–96). Language, he claims, is such a regime. Negotiated regimes are "characterized by conscious efforts to agree on their major provisions, explicit consent on the part of individual participants, and formal expression of the results," and can be either "constitutional" or "legislative bargains"(pp. 96–97). Finally, "Imposed orders . . . are fostered deliberately by dominant powers or consortia of dominant actors" and can take the form of either "overt hegemony" or "de facto imposition"(pp. 98–99).

Young's identification of regimes with social institutions as culturally and/or politically accepted patterns of interaction among members of a society gets to the core of the argument we present here. Social institutions are underpinned by certain established principles that define roles, rules, and rights. Rights and rules, in other words, lie at the core of every regime. Rights are "anything to which an actor (individual or otherwise) is entitled by virtue of occupying a recognized role"(p. 20). Accordingly: "Property rights are properly construed as bundles of rights, the content of which varies from one society to another as well as over time within the same society"(p. 20). Rules are "well-defined guides to action or standards setting forth actions that members of some specified subject group are expected to perform (or to refrain from performing) under appropriate circumstances"(p. 25)

Renegotiating Resource Regimes

From where do such arrangements come? There is no reason to think that the constitutive and regulative rules and rights embedded in resource management regimes are always the product of negotiated bargains. Although much recent scholarship has been focused on the deliberate construction of international regimes under conditions of anarchy,[15] and the process of negotiation, most resource management regimes are the outcomes of decades, even centuries, of material production, ecological change, and social interaction. They may, for example, be historical and cultural artifacts, arising out of long-held customs, the structure of society, and the nature of the resource being managed. To be sure, regimes are a reflection of power relations as they have developed within a society, but these are not unfettered relations of power. Rather, it is their historical constitution within a society that legitimizes such power relations. Thus, such regimes are changed, if at all, not through a revision of regulative rules, but by changing constitutive ones.

Regimes are often constituted by so-called customary rules. Many long-standing, customary property rights systems—not only in so-called indigenous or traditional cultures but also in Western ones—fall into this category. They may also appear to be spontaneous (perhaps autochthonous is a better word), in the sense described above. In reality, the process of "negotiation" is one that takes place at a cultural level over a long period of time. In many indigenous or traditional cultures, constitutive rules are defined in terms of lineage or group membership; in Anglo-American legal cultures, they are defined through "Common Law," which is the result of a history of past legal precedents.

In general, such regimes tend to change slowly and do so mainly under the influence of exogenous forces.[16] Thus, for example, the regimes governing use of the English common fields, about which so much has been written, seem to have arisen between the tenth and fourteenth centuries, partly in response to population growth and the need to farm more intensively than was possible or necessary under earlier agricultural systems and, partly as a result of changing ruler-society relations during that period. These systems remained in place—largely for customary reasons—until the enclosure movement began several centuries later.[17]

Today, in much of the world, resource management regimes are dominated by rules of private property. Title to a resource—or a private right to exploit a resource—entitles owners to gather as much as they are able. These rules are constitutive of the legal-cultural system we call "capitalism."[18] In the event that such resource exploitation is deemed not to be in the interest of society, regulative rules may be imposed by a user group or by the state. These limit the quantity of a resource that may be taken over a given period of time or how it is used.

Different societies impose different regulations, but all generally require some sort of evidentiary process that demonstrates real harm if exploitation is not controlled. The important point is that the legal mechanism for altering or moderating the resource regime focuses largely on regulation and not constitution. But this is not the only means by which such regimes may be created or changed.

Regimes may also be altered as the result of cultural redefinition—a process that Luther Gerlach has called the "cultural construction of the commons." In this process, the constitutive rules of social choice mechanisms for resource management are changed as a result of contestation within the public domain, but outside of the bounds of the authoritative political process.[19]

John Dryzek points out that:

> The concept of social choice is not coterminous with governmental authority systems: governments constitute just one category—or, in some cases, just one component—of social choice. . . . It should also be noted that social choice mechanisms can have informal as well as formal components. Thus, social choice in most political systems proceeds in the context of constitutional rules; but in addition, all such systems possess informal channels of influence and communication, without which they could hardly operate.[20]

Moreover, it is an error to think that process or change outside of constitutional channels is somehow illegitimate or represents a wholesale challenge to the legitimacy of a political system.[21]

In principle, there is no reason that the constitutive base of a social choice mechanism or, in this case, a resource management regime, must remain fixed, or subject only to change through state-sanctioned institutionalized procedures. As Charles Lipson notes, constitutive rules, such as they are, are never fixed permanently, because one of their central purposes is the "rationalization and maintenance of social relations"[22] in the domestic arena, as well as the international one. Therefore, observes Lipson: "Challenges [to constitutive rules] are important because . . . they do not have fixed meanings of decontextualized significance. Rather, [the rules] . . . are continually reproduced and redefined in the dispute process as the actors use or resist existing standards."[23]

At the domestic level, the development and application of constitutive rules in social choice systems or regimes incorporate not only interests and authority, but also sociocultural rules and values. Concepts of property arise out of the economic and political history of a society, reflected in institutionalized relationships within the society. The principles used to explain these rules reflect and justify social and class structure and the distribution of wealth and power as they exist within that society. In different societies and states, both the explanations for the distribution will vary and basic constitutive rules will differ. But, because the roots of these rules, and their explanations, are to a large degree cultural, in addition to being legislative, change can take place through cultural transformations, and not only via legislative procedures.[24] Thus, Gerlach notes that: "The participants in a global-resource management controversy . . . inhabit and may officially or voluntarily represent nation-states or other territorial units. As such, they possess particular cultures of adaptation that shape the way they view the problem and contribute to its resolution." [25]

What do we draw from the notion that what we here call cultural change can affect the constitution of what look to be institutionalized resource management regimes? At one level, what we might characterize as "environmental battles" are attempts by established interests to protect their claims to various types of resources. At another level, however, such controversies involve efforts to redefine the constitutive basis of an existing regime for resource management.

These struggles do not take place in an informational vacuum. Although the grounds for altering resource regimes may be expressed in cultural-historical terms—witness the frequent evocation of Gaia, Mother Earth, or Native American principles in many environmental conflicts or, conversely, the principle that resource privatization leads to better management—there is usually also a strong knowledge base to the struggle, even among those strongly oriented toward culture and history. That is to say, many of the participants in these ecological dramas are quite knowledgeable about basic ecological principles and interconnections as well as the potential consequences of environmental degradation and destruction. Indeed, many trained experts are actively involved in these movements. Hence, the struggle takes place not only over cultural and political claims, but over knowledge claims and problem definition, as well.[26]

In the remainder of this chapter, we look more closely at "resource management regimes," their constitutive basis, and their relationship to culture and, more broadly, to global ecological politics. Our focus is on colonial New England (as an example of an imposed regime), a comparative study of restoration in California and India (spontaneous) and Redwood Summer (negotiated). As we shall see, the "negotiation" or "renegotiation" of such regimes varies from place to place, and time to time, as do the consequences flowing from their operation.

Colonial New England

In colonial New England, we find a well-documented case of how one resource management regime was forcibly imposed over another. This episode closely parallels events throughout the history of European colonialism, and which are still taking place in many parts of the world today. Indeed, the radical changes that transformed the bases for ecological and social relationships in the region serve as archetypal reference points for identifying challenges to both resource regimes and constitutive rules within an increasingly pervasive and influential world system.[27] Once European trade and colonization began to impose new constitutive rules in New England, a variety of radical ecological changes followed almost inevitably. The most obvious of these was that European dominance of New England replaced Indians with colonists. It also supplanted precolonial Indian village systems of shifting agriculture and seasonal migrations for hunting, fishing, and gathering. In their place appeared colonial agriculture based on English styles of crop and pasture rotation, domesticated livestock, household production within fixed property boundaries, and linkages with often distant commercial markets.[28]

Between about the years 1600 and 1800, three major changes took place in New England: (1) new diseases decimated indigenous populations; (2) Europeans appropriated, cleared, and occupied most of the Indians' land; and (3) to serve growing local and global markets, Indians and colonists exploited dozens of mammal, fish, and bird species to virtual extinction. The patchwork of habitats that the Indians had created, adapted to, and managed in a diversified year-round subsistence pattern—based in large part on mobility and provision for long fallow periods—were overtaken by narrower European-style crop, pasture, and forest systems. These new systems were based on such alien (to the Indians) concepts as fee-simple private property. They also included basic redefinitions of natural resources and the worthiness of human communities and multiple species to coexist on the land. The outcome of conflict on all of these levels was the disruption and replacement of the precolonial resource management regimes by new ones that enabled, justified, and guided European colonization.

The process entailed several steps. On the Indian side, there was a shift from pre-European-contact conditions of relatively large populations in an environment of biological diversity and abundance, effective tribal or clan sovereignty, autonomy, seasonal mobility to follow resource availability, and management of common property resources, to colonial-period population decimation, biological impoverishment, collapse of indigenous social structures, and sharply curtailed abilities to exercise both property and sovereignty rights. On the European side, these steps were paralleled by a transition from vestiges of English feudalism to Yankee frontier liberalism, ultimately underpinned, by the time of U.S. independence, by the eighteenth-century world's least restrictive definitions of both property and sovereignty.[29]

The first step in this process entailed a gradual change in the definitions of natural resources. On the European side, abundant fisheries, wildlife, and forests had attracted attention and considerable European extractive investment long before European permanent settlement was attempted in New England.[30] On the Indian side, the opening wedge was the fur trade between coastal Indians and European fishing and trading expeditions during the sixteenth century. Thus, for example, before any permanent European settlement had occurred, Micmac, Abenaki, and other northeast coast Indians traded pelts, especially beaver and otter, for European metal implements such as knives, axes, fish hooks, cooking pots, and needles, as well as food.[31]

But it was not exchange at this rather simple level that triggered the larger changes in relations of property and production. Those changes had to do, on the one hand, with changing definitions of the roles of humans and aspects of the natural world and, on the other, a shift in modes of production and exploitation focused primarily on use values to modes focused on exchange values. Before the start of the fur trade, Indians valued wildlife for direct use and ritualized exchanges among kin groups, and not as a market commodity. But the growing demand for goods available only through trade led to the commodification of fur-bearing wildlife. As a consequence, for example, the idea of what beavers were, and their role in the Indian world, changed. Beavers no longer simply represented warmth or food or fellow creatures on earth, but a means of accumulation and of gaining power over others. Beavers became "natural resources," to be killed for the market and exploited for gains far beyond subsistence or older concepts of prestige. In self-defense and so as not to be left out or overwhelmed by neighbors acquiring new European technology, even the more hesitant and further-inland peoples were eventually drawn into the fur trade.[32]

The result was the emergence of Indians' treatment of animals, trees, and other forms of life as marketable commodities, rather than as means of subsistence or totems or co-descendants of common tribal ancestors.[33] This signaled a fundamental change in the constitutive rules underlying "management" of the environment, thereby clearing the way for the colonial-era regime of unfettered exploitation. In the wake of the transformation of wildlife into commodified "resources," Indians hunted and trapped beaver to near-extinction in many areas of New England, paradoxically threatening one of their own major bases of subsistence. In similar ways, commodification of other fur-bearing mammals, coastal fisheries, wild fowl, and timber led to exploitation beyond sustainable levels, with major consequences in terms of environmental degradation.[34]

As colonists overwhelmed native peoples in New England, a next step in the transformation of prevailing constitutive rules had to do with concepts and definitions of property rights. These were associated with concepts of appropriate land use, sovereignty, and even concepts of personal worth. The imposition of new concepts of rights to use land, water, other resources, and the productive potential they embody is crucial to understanding the impact of this change. Differences between colonial and Indian concepts of property emerged repeatedly in misunderstandings over colonists' land purchases from Indians, and in the content of land grants made to the colonists by the English Crown. Conflict arose because the package of culturally defined rights under which the colonists believed they had bought or received deeds to land were very different from those under which the Indians believed they were granting or releasing them.

Generally, Indians dealt in rights to carry out specific activities on the land or to take specific products from it (what we today would call "use" rights). With the exception of rights covering cultivated fields, however, these rights were rarely exclusive, and they could not be granted by any single Indian individual except as a representative of a kin or other use-right-holding group. For example, an Indian kin group might sell to one group of colonists the right to build a village or plant corn in a specified area. To other colonists, or Indians, they might give the right to collect walnuts in the same area, without in the process giving up any of their own hunting or gathering rights there. In other words, they were selling only a bundle of specific and limited usufruct rights in the specified area. In such situations, colonists were likely to understand the transaction as an outright sale of the land itself, encompassing rights to resell the land and everything on it as a commodity in the future. But the Indians were unlikely to recognize their own or anyone else's right to sell the land itself.[35]

The transition in constitutive rules became more apparent as such misunderstandings gave rise to colonists' demands for sanctions against property-right or use-right violations. Indians might believe that they had retained the right to gather walnuts from an area in question where they held customary rights. The colonist-purchasers could now assert that the Indians were trespassing on the colonists' lands and pilfering walnuts from their trees, and support their claim under colonial law (in Massachusetts, for example, the law was administered in the name of the English Crown by the Massachusetts Bay Company). Colonial rules generally did not recognize overlapping usufruct rights, or any Indian kin group's sovereign right to transfer any land or usufruct rights in the first place (except over fields under current cultivation).[36]

Yet, it was not quite so simple to deny indigenous peoples' land rights. In line with much seventeenth-century thought on the origins of property, English law recognized that Indians might have "natural rights" to land they occupied, even though neither the English Crown nor any other recognized sovereign had granted them. Later colonial deeds concluded with Indians were therefore careful to extinguish all Indian "natural rights," transferring through civil law all use rights over land to the English purchaser alone, whether as individual or corporate body.[37]

There remained one final impediment to justifying the new regime in land rights under colonial domination. A new set of assumptions was created, and rules set into place, to deny the very worthiness of Indians to occupy their native lands. Early colonists were well aware that many of their new settlements had been located deliberately on the abandoned sites of Indian villages that had succumbed to epidemic diseases only a few years before the colonists arrived. These Indian village sites were often complete with recently cultivated land and surrounding forest undergrowth fire-cleared to improve hunting. Colonists might have doubted their right to appropriate such "improved" land were it not for another fundamental belief justifying the new regime of occupation and land use (at least in the initial settlement of the Massachusetts Bay Colony). Puritan colonists interpreted the epidemics that swept away the natives as a sign of God's Providence, clearing their title to the place. This ideology of appropriation of the depopulated lands defined who was worthy to live there, with legal land tenure protection, and who was not.[38]

The rules defining who was qualified to participate in and be protected by New England property transaction law did not finally crystallize until the mid-seventeenth century. Transitions among several Indian property/use right systems, English civil law, and certain aspects of English common law made for a muddled patchwork of rights in the growing colonies. The imposed ways of defining property, sovereignty, and eligibility to occupy land were alien to the indigenous peoples of the region and, so, those who were left were at a permanent disadvantage. The Indian systems—of common use rights, assigned or transferred through negotiations by sovereign-like groups, and not based on permanent, exclusive boundaries divorced from ecological functions—were usurped in favor of English land commodification, for the most part with clear boundary delineation on the land itself, regardless of the land's prior ecological function.

Thus, a new regime for environmental management and exploitation was created through the replacement of one set of constitutive rules—largely underpinned by the authority of custom—with another—backed by civil and royal authority. This new regime was well-suited to encourage rapid colonial expansion. It permitted colonists to transform New England's landscape from the Indian-managed patchworks—oriented mainly toward subsistence, and sustained by seasonal migrations for cultivation, hunting, fishing, and gathering, and regulated mainly by common property rights—to colonial models—based on fixed settlements, bounded fields, and cultivation and livestock, and increasingly oriented toward expanding commercial production and embodying individual property rights. This regime also marginalized those remaining Indian populations that had survived the epidemics of the 1600s. Finally, it facilitated privatization of land, and rapid exploitation and depletion of New England's forest, game, and fishery resources.

An important point here is that, although the new regime was an imposed one, colonists did not simply impose it through force (as was frequently the case in later settler-Indian encounters). The New England colonists were careful to negotiate the transfer of title, as they understood the meaning of the term, so as to make legal (at least in the eyes of God and the Crown) transactions in land and other resources. This conveyed legitimacy on such transfers on the basis of the new constitutive rules of the colonial regimes, and not simply the greater power of one society over another.

Eucalyptus and Native Species Restoration

Australia's native ecosystems have long been overwhelmed by a plethora of imported species, especially from Europe, Asia, and America. But Australia has been able to strike back. Eucalyptus trees, a native Australian genus that includes more than 500 species, are among the few Australian biological exports now thriving around the world. With so many varieties to choose from, there is likely to be one that will thrive in almost any tropical or temperate climate. Eucalyptus trees were first exported more than a century ago, and exports accelerated when silviculturalists proclaimed them to be an ideal answer to the challenge of growing hardwood trees quickly in poor soil. As a result, over the past 100 years, eucalyptus species have become the backbone of many afforestation and reforestation projects around the world.[39]

In the tropical developing world, in particular, eucalyptus planta- tions have become a mainstay of commercial wood production. In northern industrialized countries, they are mostly the debris of proj- ects launched many decades ago and subsequently abandoned. Worldwide, over the past decade, perspectives on eucalyptus have begun to change. In particular, foresters and policy-oriented environ- mentalists have sharply criticized massive plantings of eucalyptus, especially in dry, economically troubled regions, and in areas where it has replaced native forest species and indigenous agriculture.[40] Critics of eucalyptus plantations assert that although (and possibly because) the commercially planted species grow very quickly, they also draw down water tables and strip the soil of nutrients. Because water is drawn down from the soil surface, eucalyptus groves are also usually devoid of other vegetation, such as forage grasses, and livestock cannot eat eucalyptus leaves. Rural people complain that new eucalyptus plantations deprive them of important free livestock fodder, and that this cuts severely into their subsistence. In poor, land-scarce areas, resentment has been mounting against the conversion of former cropland or native forest (however degraded) into plantations designed to supply raw materials to paper and rayon mills.

Indeed, since the late 1980s, village groups, particularly in India and Thailand, have stormed eucalyptus plantations, uprooting or burning the trees. In one protest in Thailand, 12,000 villagers planted native fruit trees on or near the destroyed eucalyptus plantations.[41] More recently, Kenya's President Daniel Arap Moi responded to problems with eucalyptus reforestation projects by decreeing that 90 percent of seedlings raised in government forest nurseries must be species native to the country, despite the lack of any proven indigenous tree species as fast-growing as the exotic Eucalyptus. The World Bank, which had provided heavy support for massive eucalyptus plantings as part of its "social forestry" programs, has been forced to reconsider its strategy, and it has begun to refocus its programs in several areas toward fast-growing native species.[42]

Parallel to the Third World antieucalyptus movement, groups opposed to the species have sprung up in the United States, although with somewhat different motivations and goals in mind. Strong links have emerged between the antieucalyptus movements in the Third World and native habitat restoration movements in several industrialized countries. Northern California, home of Redwood Summer, is one of the major nodes of native habitat restoration activity, and in much of the region, eucalyptus has become a target of restoration activists.[43]

Eucalyptus eradication first became an issue in Northern California after a hard freeze in 1972, when millions of eucalyptus trees in the green belts of the San Francisco Bay area appeared to have died, and were feared to be a serious fire hazard. Many of these trees had been planted decades earlier as part of a get-rich-quick land development scheme in the East Bay hills. Following the freeze, a broad range of "concerned" citizens and several regional park departments struggled with the decision to deforest rather than run the risk of wildfire from the freeze-damaged trees. Although in 1973 few individuals suggested eradicating undamaged stands of eucalyptus, there were strong grumblings that the exotic water-suckers should never have been planted in the first place. Proposals were made to replace the damaged eucalyptus with native redwoods, which use less water and constitute less of a fire hazard. This was done in a few locations.[44]

In the early 1970s, however, not all "green space" advocates opposed keeping the eucalyptus in place. Many environmentalists defended the trees and warned against assuming that the trees were dead; in their view, keeping any tree in the landscape was better than eradication. By this time, however, a new ecological perspective was beginning to emerge. One East Bay park district ecologist pointed out that native California bay laurels were already invading the eucalyptus groves and would be likely to take over in time.[45] Due largely to arguments in favor of any trees, and lack of funds for costly eradication, the eucalyptus groves remained.

Almost two decades after the 1973 freeze, however, the native habitat restoration movement has gained new momentum. In the late 1980s, public agencies began joining with voluntary citizens' movements and organizations to eradicate opportunistic exotic species, including eucalyptus, and to gradually restore ecologically probable biological relationships. (In Northern California, this movement has been further spurred by the indictment of fire-prone eucalyptus, in a drought-stressed landscape, which played a major role in the fast, uncontrolled wildfire that, in October 1991, destroyed more than 3,500 dwellings in the Oakland-Berkeley hills. The call for native genetic diversity inherent in this movement is identical to that behind virtually all world conservation efforts, but the willingness to go through painstaking efforts to seek and restore an ecological heritage all but destroyed by American-style development is something new.[46]

From the perspective of constitutive rules, the antieucalyptus protests in both the Third World and the United States are significant. First, poor rural people are demanding a voice in and taking a clear stand on a "technical" issue important to both their local environment and their largely subsistence livelihoods. As a result, wealthy landowners and government forestry agencies are less and less able to transform local environments in a social vacuum. In several cases, the managers of eucalyptus plantations have evicted local peasants planting subsistence crops—legal or illegal—or prevented them from gathering free forest products such as fuelwood and fodder. The consequent protests indicate that evictions of poor peasants will no longer be tolerated in the name of afforestation.[47]

Second, although much of the opposition to massive eucalyptus plantings stems from demands for social and economic justice, involving issues of land rights, the protests have often been formulated in terms of local environmental or ecological integrity, stressing rural peoples' intimate relationships, history, and indigenous knowledge systems associated with native species. Third, the antieucalyptus movement, largely centered in poor peripheral regions in the Third

World, asserts local rights against central authority. But the movement has not done so in an isolated, particularistic way, as has often been the case with so-called NIMBY ("Not In My Back Yard") protests. Instead, the antieucalyptus movement's rhetoric has been cast in opposition to a wide range of commercial, exotic monoculture systems that provide few subsistence benefits to local people, but large profits to industrial corporations and landowners. These protests are taking place simultaneously, in widely dispersed locations, but in awareness of each other. The protests do not simply demand ecological integrity for a locale, but assert that all areas should be able to sustain their own native species and demand their own social justice. Thus, Third World poor peoples' movements, following the example of India's Chipko movement, have taken on a bioregionalist political form also highly appealing to a "Northern" environmental ethic.[48]

From the perspective of constitutive rules, there are also clear parallels between the Third World and California movements. Both insist on new definitions and values for productivity, arguing that the production and reproduction of species indigenous to a particular site or region are worth more than those of species imported for commercial concepts of development or for investors' quick profits. Central to both movements are dedication and organization to challenge and resist to prevailing development patterns backed by "big money." Also common to both are righteous anger against state co-optation by profit-oriented land-development interests. The movements also share a determination that positive action by "little people" acting together can transform the consciousness and action of governments and power, the physical reality of the world, and society's sense of propriety with regard to what is worthy of living on the earth (and where), and what is not. Ultimately, in the United States at least, the habitat restoration and antieucalyptus movements can be seen as responses, several centuries later, to the frontier development ethic of Yankee New England. Both movements insist that indigenous (and, perhaps, less "profitable") ecosystems, and the ways that societies can speak up in their mutual interest, do have normative and ethical content and legitimacy.

Reconsidering Redwood Summer

This brings us back to Redwood Summer. What were its goals? How was it played out? What, if any, were its effects? As noted earlier, Redwood Summer began as an effort to halt the logging of the few remaining stands of old-growth redwoods in northwestern California. The event was consciously modeled along the lines of the "Mississippi Summer" of 1964, when civil rights groups called on college students to come to the Deep South to protest and campaign for black civil rights.[49] Via a broad media effort, Redwood Summer organizers hoped to generate a similar response on behalf of the California redwoods, especially among students and environmentalists within the state.

Campaigns to protect the redwoods are nothing new; the first "Save the Redwoods" efforts took place in the early years of the twentieth century, leading to the establishment of the Cowell, Armstrong, Muir, and Big Basin reserves in California and, later on, to Redwood National Park.[50] In a number of cases, however, what was being protected was second-growth trees: those that sprang up after the old-growth had been logged over. What, then, was different about Redwood Summer? First, whereas previous campaigns were based on protection of the aesthetic quality of the redwoods—and their managed exploitation for economic purposes—Redwood Summer focused on the ecological and symbolic features of old-growth stands, arguing that they were linked, even if only philosophically, to the global arena. Second, there was a critical time factor involved in preventing the old-growth stands from being logged. Economic pressures, plus the impetus to increase revenues as the result of leveraged buyouts of the logging firms involved, had placed a premium on more-rapid harvesting. Finally, data were emerging that seemed to indicate the importance of old-growth forests to the survival of several animal species, in particular, the Northern Spotted Owl (and, possibly, its California "cousin"), which was declared a threatened species by the federal government in 1990.[51]

Redwood Summer itself consisted of a series of efforts and protests to block logging in old-growth stands. In a number of well-publicized confrontations, participants managed to slow down harvesting, engage loggers and others in spirited debates about the relative merits of logging versus protection, and generate widespread media coverage. But, in the final analysis, what did Redwood Summer accomplish? In immediately quantifiable terms, perhaps very little. The number of participants was far less than organizers had anticipated, and none of the logging companies that came under attack halted their old growth logging activities.

Yet, the entire effort cannot be considered to have been ineffective. Redwood Summer was, to a large degree, a consciousness-raising exercise. If it could not halt old-growth logging, it was at least intended to raise public awareness of the issue. Redwood Summer, in conjunction with the endangered status of the Northern Spotted Owl, and the so-called Forests Forever initiative that appeared on the California ballot in November 1990 (but which failed to pass) had the effect of mobilizing a great deal of public sentiment against the logging industry. This, in turn, influenced the practices of several major lumber companies.

As Luther Gerlach puts it, "The shadow of Redwood Summer was cast over Washington [State]," where the Weyerhauser Company began to talk in terms of sustainable management of forest resources. In early 1991, the Portland-based Louisiana-Pacific Corporation held a news conference in San Francisco to announce that it was phasing out the practice of clear-cutting on its lands in California (a step not immediately followed by any other company) in response to, among other things, changing public sentiment. In Sacramento, the state and federal forest services have launched an internal program to educate its employees on "sustainable forestry." The Sierra Club, in collaboration with several logging firms, lobbied for the passage of a "Sierra Accord" by the California Legislature that would control clear-cutting on privately owned tracts of land. This has since been followed by an even more complex bioregional initiative that seeks to institutionalize coordinated resource management in designated bioregions. Finally, there was a growing recognition that the days of logging in California, if not the Pacific Northwest, were numbered, because of the depletion of the resource as well as restrictions resulting from the Endangered Species Act. The result of these actions and recognitions will be a changed forestry management regime that will come about less as the result of legislation in Sacramento or Washington, D.C., and more, we would argue, as a consequence of cultural change within California at large.[52]

It could be argued that Redwood Summer was really of no consequence at all, and that the changes observed arise from economic causes and interests (logging out) or institutionalized political processes and political power (the Endangered Species Act). But such changes would not, by themselves, have arisen out of self-interest or institutionalized politics. Indeed, the logging firms had an incentive to continue as before (and as some have done) so as to realize the maximum short-term return on investment. The California public has little idea of the condition of the state's forests: whether they are old or new growth, how much is left, or where logging is taking place. And the local participants in Redwood Summer were, likely as not, to find themselves shunned in the logging regions as the result of participating in the protests.

As far as politics and power are concerned, it is clear that in this contestation, the logging firms possess a great deal of local power. They employ large numbers of workers throughout the Pacific Northwest,[53] and contribute to a not-insignificant portion of the economies of California, Oregon, and Washington. The companies can, if they so choose, log their privately owned land. Yet, in the context of the $700 billion plus economy and the more than 35 million mostly-urban inhabitants of the Pacific Coast, logging must be seen as a declining industry. But, until recently, the potential for political mobilization of public feeling about forest protection was quite limited. Hence, the weight of political and economic power in the ultimate outcome of this drama is not at all clear.

What one is left with, therefore, is an explanation constructed largely on the basis of an effort to disseminate new ideas and change constitutive rules. By tying old-growth forests not to standard wilderness arguments, such as aesthetics and enjoyment, but rather to global environmental questions such as species survival, Redwood Summer posed a challenge to the constitutive basis of the forestry regime. As some analysts have argued, structural political transformation takes place at the level of constitutive rules—where relationships are fundamentally defined—and not at the level of regulative rules.[54] So, if we are to look for the "signposts" of transformation in resource management regimes, we must look for change in the former type of rules, and not the latter, that is, not to how property is assigned, but to how rights to define property, and its uses, are determined.[55]

Actions such as Redwood Summer represent an effort to redefine these constitutive rules governing the relationship between human society and nature. Whereas the relationship as codified in existing law rests on the possession and exploitation of resources by the legal owner of the resources, the participants in Redwood Summer were attempting to define a new set of rules. These involved not only control but also appropriate relationships among participants in and objects of social choice mechanisms and resource management regimes.[56]

What Does This All Mean?

In this chapter, we have presented three main arguments. First, we have proposed that what are often seen as relatively straightforward efforts to assert control over the exploitation of resources are actually much more complex struggles over the constitutive rules that define the shape and structure of resource management systems. Second, following Oran Young's typology, we have suggested that the struggles to create or redefine these systems come in three forms: imposed, spontaneous, and negotiated. Beyond this, however, cultural change can also alter such regimes. Finally, we have asserted that these struggles have global resonance—they are often framed in such terms—and global implications—they are often replicated elsewhere.[57]

Our final point is this: Just as, in 1917, the notion that the Soviet state's ability to nationalize resources within its territory represented a constitutive challenge to internationally accepted rules of property at the level of the state system, so may the types of actions described here represent a similar challenge to the authority of states and the allocation of property rights. This is an ambitious claim, and we do not claim to have documented it conclusively in this chapter. It is also of course possible that, in the end, these particular calls for new constitutive rules will be taken up, modified, and incorporated into the existing legal system as a set of regulative rules governing use rights. Nonetheless, we suggest that actions such as Redwood Summer, which are being replicated in many places around the world, in a variety of different forms, all have the potential to lead to constitutive shifts in both local and global politics.[58]

NOTES

1. According to David Brower, quoted in John McPhee, *Encounters with the Archdruid* (New York: Farrar, Strauss and Giroux, 1971).
2. "Redwood Summer II: Ecotopia Summer," *Earth First!* 11 no. 6 (June 21, 1991): 1.

3. Darryl Cherney: "Earth First! [organizers of Redwood Summer] is the civil rights movement for Mother Earth." Catherine Franke, "An Interview with Redwood Summer Organizer Darryl Cherney," *The Monthly Planet* (Santa Cruz), July 1990, p. 16. There has been discussion about the possibility of granting legal "rights" and "standing" in courts to elements of nature, to be accomplished by some sort of legal ruling or legislation; see, for example, Christopher Stone, *Earth and Other Ethics: The Case for Moral Pluralism* (New York: Harper and Row, 1987).

4. See, e.g., "Tree-lover, spare the woodman," *The Economist*, June 22, 1991, pp. 19–20, 23.

5. John Dryzek uses the term *social choice mechanisms* to denote the more general case: " A social choice mechanism is a means through which a society . . . determines collective outcomes . . . in a given domain." *Rational Ecology—Environment and Political Economy* (Oxford: Basil Blackwell, 1987), p. 7.

6. Tim Ingold, quoting M. Godelier, writes that: "[I]n all societies the holding of property constitutes a relation between persons, so that forms of ownership of territory function as social relations of production." M. Godelier, "Territory and property in primitive society," in: M. von Cranach, K. Foppa, W. Lepenies, and D. Ploog eds., *Human ethology* (Cambridge: Cambridge University Press, 1979), quoted in Tim Ingold, *The appropriation of nature—Essays on human ecology and social relations* (Manchester: Manchester University Press, 1986), p. 136. The notion of property rights is developed in Ronnie D. Lipschutz, *When Nations Clash—Raw Materials, Ideology, and Foreign Policy* (New York: Ballinger/Harper and Row, 1989), ch. 2. Elsewhere, I have used the term "relational rights" to denote what I am describing here; see "Bargaining Among Nations: Culture, Values, and Perceptions in Regime Formation," *Evaluation Review* 51, no. 1 (1991): 46–74. We have returned to the term "property rights" here because they are more appropriate to the discussion of environment and resources.

7. Gary D. Libecap, *Contracting for Property Rights* (Cambridge: Cambridge University Press, 1989), p. 1.

8. Thus, regulative rules describe how one *plays* baseball; constitutive rules establish what *is* baseball. The original example is, apparently, to be found in John Rawls, "Two Concepts of Rules," *Philosophical Review* 64 (1955):25, as cited in John G. Ruggie, "International Structures and International Transformation: Space, Time, and Method," In Ernst-Otto Czempiel and James N. Rosenau eds., *Global Changes and Theoretical Challenges—Approaches to World Politics for the 1990s* (Lexington, Mass.: Lexington Books, 1989), p 33, n. 6.; John G. Ruggie, "Territoriality and Beyond: Problematizing Modernity in International Relations," *International Organization* 47, no. 1 (Winter 1993): 141–76. See also David Dessler, "What's at stake in the agent-structure debate," *International Organization* 43 no. 3 (Summer 1989):454–58; Lipschutz, *When Nations Clash*, ch. 2.

9. Ruggie, "International Structures," p. 23; Dessler, "What's at Stake," pp. 454–58.

10. Note that for "open access" resources," there are, in effect, neither constitutive nor regulative rules: exploitation is open to whomever has the capability for taking. "Common property" and "private" resources are subject to both types of rules. Such systems are described in David L. Miller, "The Evolution of Mexico's Spiny Lobster Fishery," pp. 185–98; James M. Acheson, "Where Have All the Exploiters Gone? Co- management of the Maine Lobster Industry," pp. 199–217, in: Fikret Berkes ed., *Common Property Resources—Ecology and community-based sustainable development* (London: Belhaven Press, 1989). See also Libecap, ch. 3; Bonnie J. McCay and James M. Acheson eds., *The Question of the Commons—The Culture and Ecology of Communal Resources* (Tucson, AZ: University of Arizona Press, 1987); Elinor Ostrom, *Governing the Commons— The Evolution of Institutions for Collective Action* (Cambridge: Cambridge University Press, 1990).

11. Dessler, "What's at Stake," p. 469.

12. Obviously, a powerful actor can also redefine constitutive rules through coercion, but this still requires at least some cooperation from those being coerced.

13. As in, for example, Stephen D. Krasner ed., *International Regimes* (Ithaca, NY: Cornell University Press, 1983).

14. Oran Young, *Resource Regimes—Natural Resources and Social Institutions* (Berkeley: University of California Press, 1982, p. 16). It should be noted that, on the one hand, Young's models of regime formation are not wholly accepted by many regime theorists working more closely with the economic tradition (e.g., Krasner, Keohane, Gilpin). On the other hand, these models are widely accepted, albeit often in a different language, among those working in an institutional or anthropological perspective. See, for example, Dryzek, *Rational Ecology*; Elinor Ostrom, *Governing the Commons*. A somewhat different view of regimes can be found in James F. Keeley, "Toward a Foucauldian Analysis of Regimes," *International Organization* 44 no. 1 (Winter 1990):83–105.

15. An assumption that is not necessarily the case; see Nicholas Greenwood Onuf, *World of Our Making—Rules and Rule in Social Theory and International Relations* (Columbia: University of South Carolina Press, 1989); Albert Bergesen, "Turning World-System Theory on Its Head," pp. 67–82, In: Mike Featherstone ed., *Global Culture—Nationalism, Globalization, and Modernity* (London: Sage, 1990); and Alex Wendt, "Anarchy is what states make of it: the social construction of power politics," *International Organization* 46 no. 2 (Spring 1992):391–426. Ronnie D. Lipschutz, "Reconstructing World Politics: The Emergence of Global Civil Society," *Millenium* 21, no. 3 (1992): 389–420.

16. It is this quality of longevity (or of no discernable origin) that makes such regimes "traditional" or "customary," but there is no reason why they should be regarded as just or equitable.

17. "[A] loose but recognizable form of the common-field system took shape in old-settled areas of southwestern Germany, northern France, and England when localized population growth was associated with transition from an extensive combination of pastoral and arable husbandry to one in which cereals played the dominant subsistence role." Richard C. Hoffman, "Medieval Origins of the Common Fields," in: William N. Parker and Eric L. Jones eds., *European Peasants and Their Markets* (Princeton: Princeton University Press, 1975), p. 45. It should be noted that this period also corresponds to the rise of centralized polities in Europe, which required, as well, greater food production.

The reasons usually given for the enclosure movement are many, but there seems to be general agreement that market forces were critical. Landowners, finding that they could generate greater returns from privately-owned property than from rents from commons, imposed consolidation on a peasantry that lacked legal title to the lands. Moreover, enclosure came about largely *after* the consolidation of the state as the primary political form in Europe and *during* the rise of mercantilism; see Hoffman, "Medieval Origins." It should also be noted that enclosure required centuries.

18. Although one could differentiate between resource management regimes in market and centrally-planned economies, we prefer to distinguish among varieties of capitalism: market, state, corporate, larcenous.

19. Luther P. Gerlach, "Cultural Construction of the Global Commons," In: Robert H. Winthrop ed., *Culture and the Anthropological Tradition* (Washington: University Press of America, 1990), pp. 319–41.

The U.S. Federal Government has also been known to "create" commons outside of the normal legislative process, for example, using the Clean Water Act of 1972 to designate as marshlands what appear, at first glance, to be dry farmlands. See William Robbins, "For Farmers, Wetlands Mean a Legal Quagmire," *New York Times*, April 24, 1990 (nat'l ed.), p. A1.

20. Dryzek, *Rational Ecology*, p. 8.

21. A view often held of social movements; as Richard Darman, Director of the Office of Management and Budget in the Bush Administration once observed, the label "environmentalist" is "a green mask under which different faces of politico-ideology can hide." It would be, he said, a "regrettable irony" if, just as American values have prevailed "in the East-West struggle, they were to be lost in what some environmentalists like to term the struggle for 'global management.' " Quoted in Philip Shabecoff, "U.S. is Assailed at Geneva Talks for Backing out of Ozone Plan," *New York Times*, May 10, 1990 (nat'l ed.), p. 1.

22. Charles Lipson, *Standing Guard—Protecting Foreign Capital in the Nineteenth and Twentieth Centuries* (Berkeley: University of California Press, 1985), p. 32.

23. *Ibid.*

24. It should be noted, nonetheless, that such rules are often legitimated,

crystallized, and offered "protection" through government coercion by legal action and sanctions.

25. Gerlach, "Cultural Construction," p. 327.

26. The literature on the sociology of knowledge as it applies to activist environmental movements is, so far, limited. There is a growing literature on the role of "epistemic communities" as advisors to governments; see, for example, Peter Haas, *Saving the Mediterranean* (New York: Columbia University Press, 1989); Peter M. Haas ed., *Knowledge, Power, and International Policy Coordination*, special issue of *International Organization* 46, no. 1 (Winter 1992), and the chapters by Karen Litfin and Steve Breyman in this volume. What has not been investigated in any great detail is the role of such experts in environmental movements. For a study of this sort in other movements, see Lily M. Hoffman, *The Politics of Knowledge—Activist Movements in Medicine and Planning* (Albany, NY: Suny Press, 1989).

27. A combination of perspectives from ecological anthropology and the *annales* school of history help to illuminate the interrelationships between massive ecological, social, political, and economic changes resulting from two centuries of European colonization and expansion in North America. Much of the material summarized in this section is developed in William Cronon, *Changes in the Land: Indians, Colonists, and the Ecology of New England* (New York: Hill and Wang, 1983); and Carolyn Merchant, *Ecological Revolutions: Nature, Gender, and Science in New England* (Chapel Hill, NC: University of North Carolina Press, 1989).

28. Cronon, *Changes in the Land*, pp. 160–61.

29. For definitions and the historical progression of property and sovereignty, see C.B. MacPherson ed., *Property: Mainstream and Critical Positions* (Toronto: University of Toronto Press, 1978), esp. ch. 1–4.

30. Cronon, *Changes in the Land*, pp. 20–21.

31. Merchant, *Ecological Revolutions*, pp. 54–55.

32. The fur trade grew especially in northern New England, where Indians cultivated little corn. There, furs were traded to Europeans in exchange for corn grown, first, by southern New England Indians and, later on, by colonists. Thus, even for their subsistence, the Indians became increasingly dependent on the fur trade. For a discussion of the beaver's role in the Indian world see Merchant, *Ecological Revolutions*. The pattern described here has been repeated many times in many places; see Nancy Peluso's chapter in this volume.

33. Merchant, *Ecological Revolutions*, pp. 46–48.

34. On the one hand, the emergence of abandoned beaver dams and ponds neatly fit the colonists' needs, as they made good mill sites. If the ponds were drained, on the other hand, they provided "natural," high-quality pasture for livestock. See Merchant, *Ecological Revolutions*, pp. 36–37; Cronon, *Changes in the Land*, pp. 97–99, 105–107.

Later in the colonial period, some northern Indians no longer treated beaver as an "open access" resource, subject to over-exploitation in a "tragedy of the commons." They began instead to use common property management measures to limit taking, for example, by establishing kin group rights to exclude others from hunting and trapping in particular watersheds.

35. Such differentiation between use rights and comprehensive ownership rights over land and everything on it continues in many societies, and can even be seen in the distinction between surface and mineral rights in the United States. See Louise Fortmann and John Bruce eds., *Whose Trees? Proprietary Dimensions of Forestry* (Boulder, CO: Westview Press, 1988). See also Tim Ingold, "Territoriality and tenure: the appropriation of space in hunting and gather societies," In: T. Ingold, *The Appropriation of Nature*, pp. 130–64. See also Cronon, *Changes in the Land*, p. 67.

36. To avoid confusion, and to centralize authority over land, the Massachusetts Bay Company eventually insisted that the company authorize or review any purchase of land from Indians.

37. Cronon, *Changes in the Land*, pp. 68–69.

38. *Ibid.*, p. 90.

39. Alfred W. Crosby, *Ecological Imperialism: The Biological Expansion of Europe, 900– 1900* (Cambridge: Cambridge University Press, 1986). See also "Eucalyptus Plantations Now Deadwood," *Berkeley Gazette*, Feb. 13, 1983.

40. R. K. Kohli, *et. al.*, "Negative Aspects of Eucalyptus Farming," in: R. K. Khosla and D. K. Khurana eds., *Agroforestry for Rural Needs* (Solan, India: Indian Society of Tree Scientists, 1987), pp. 225–33. See also: Third World Network, "Adverse Ecological and Social Impacts of Large-Scale Eucalyptus Planting in the Third World," Penang, Malaysia, 1988.

41. See: Christopher Joyce, "The Tree that Caused a Riot," *New Scientist*, Feb. 18, 1988, pp. 54–59; "Some Second Thoughts on Eucalyptus Planting," *The Nation* (Bangkok), June 15, 1988; "Eucalyptus Planting Sparks Fiery Protest," *The Nation*, June 14, 1988; Michael Richardson, "The Eucalyptus Tree: World's Savior a Menace?" *International Herald Tribune*, May 18, 1988.

42. See "Action Alert" packages from the Asian-Pacific Peoples Environmental Network (APPEN), Penang, and the Rainforest Action Network (RAN), San Francisco, undated, 1987–1991.

43. Interestingly, one of the strongest of these movements is in Australia, where the goal is often restoration of indigenous eucalyptus forests.

A directory of organized restoration groups and the projects with which they have been involved has been produced in the San Francisco Bay area, the urban center of political support for Redwood Summer. See *Ecological Restoration in the San Francisco Bay Area* (Berkeley: Restoring the Earth, 1989); Chris Clarke, "Restoration? A Look at Restoration in Concept and In Practice," *Ecology Center Newsletter* (Berkeley) 20 no. 4 (April 1991):1–7.

44. A repetition of this freeze, during the winter of 1990, seems to have killed a smaller number of trees. But, in conjunction with a six-year (or

longer) drought, the fire hazard is greater than ever, as demonstrated by the October 1991 wildfire in the East Bay hills of Berkeley and Oakland. See also James B. Roof, "A Proposal for the Initial Clearance of Eucalyptus from the East Bay Hills," East Bay Regional Parks Botanic Garden, 1972; "Faking Death," *Berkeley Gazette*, Aug. 24, 1973; *Grassroots*, Nov. 1974; and Gordon Robinson, San Francisco Bay Chapter of the Sierra Club Press Release, undated, circa 1974.

45. Roof, "Proposal," p. 31.

46. See *Bulletin of the California Native Plant Society* 21 no. 2 (April-June 1991).

47. *Asian-Pacific Peoples' Environmental Network Action Alert*, 1990.

48. Vananda Shiva and J. Baudyopadhyay, *An Ecological Audit of Eucalyptus Cultivation* (Dehra Duni: Research Foundation for Science and Ecology, 1987); Thomas Weber, *Hugging the Trees—The Story of the Chipko Movement* (New Delhi: Penguin, 1989); Vananda Shiva, *Chipko: India's Civilizational Response to the Forest Crisis* (New Delhi: Intach, 1988).

49. "Redwood Summer," *The Daily Planet* (Santa Cruz), July 1990, p. 16.

50. Greg King, "The War Against the Redwoods," *Ecology Center Newsletter* (Berkeley) 20 no. 2 (Feb. 1990):5–6.

51. Jane Kay, "Tree Wars," *Image* (San Francisco Examiner), Dec. 17, 1989, pp. 6–14, 16, 34; Timothy Egan, "U.S. Declares Owl to be Threatened by Heavy Logging," *New York Times*, June 23, 1990 (nat'l ed.), p. 1. We should note here that the California branch of the spotted owl family is now being considered for endangered status.

52. Andrew Pollack, "Louisiana-Pacific Will Stop Clear-Cutting in California," *New York Times*, March 7, 1991 (nat'l ed.), p. C1.We received information on the sustainable forestry program from a personal communication, Mark Nechodom. Ultimately, the "Sierra Accord" failed. The governor of California, Pete Wilson, vetoed the original bill, claiming that its 20 acre limit was too restrictive. He proposed, instead, that private landowners be allowed to clear cut parcels of up to 40 acres. This, in turn, was rejected by the Sierra Club and the California Legislature. As noted in the text, bioregionalism is seen as the next step in this process. See Beth Delson, "Bioregional Planning from the Grassroots," *Bay Area Action* 3 no. 1 (Jan/Feb 1992).

53. According to one report, 10,000 loggers would lose their jobs as a result of protection of the spotted owl; another (by the same writer) suggested 28,000 jobs would be lost; see Timothy Egan, "10,000 Are Expected to Lose Jobs to Spotted Owl," *New York Times*, April 25, 1990 (nat'l ed.), p. 6.

54. Ruggie, "International Structures"; Dessler, "What's at Stake." To expand the illustration given above, constitutive rules would describe the *structure* of baseball; regulative rules how one *plays* the game and *scores*.

55. Bruce Andrews, "Social Rules and the State as a Social Actor," *World Politics* 27 no. 4 (July 1975):525.

56. Suffice it here to say that these new rules do not simply propose the

transference of ownership from Georgia Pacific to the U.S. Government or the county or the "people;" rather, they appear to have more to do with the "common heritage of mankind," and relate to the re-emergence of the public trust doctrine in the United States.

57. Even the New England case has such resonance, if only because it is an archetype of the sorts of imposed resource management regimes that are being created in developing countries even today.

58. On the Soviet system see Lipson, *Standing Guard*, pp. 66–70. See also chapter 1. On property rights note, for example, "Each Government possesses in virtue of its sovereignty over its various territories rights which are really rights of property. It has the power to delegate out of these rights concessions and privileges to private people." R.G. Hawtrey, *Economic Aspects of Sovereignty*, London: Longmans, Green, 1930/1952, p. 16. See also see the chapter by Dan Deudney in this volume.

Act III

GLOBAL ECOLOGICAL INTERDEPENDENCE AND THE FUTURE OF WORLD POLITICS

The Earth is one but the world is not.
—World Commission on
Environment and Development[1]

In the first set of chapters in this book, we saw that governments are likely to lack the capacity to manage effectively, either alone or jointly, the emerging reality of global ecological interdependence. In the second set of chapters, we examined the process of broadening the locus of debate over how best to manage those effects, a process manifest in various types of contestation and cooperation among an increasingly heterogeneous group of actors. In this final section, we speculate on the consequences of these trends for the future structure of world politics. Understanding those consequences requires, we would argue, a much greater sensitivity to the question of whether and how interdependence (or its social corollary, globalization) is eroding or changing the ability of national governments to practice "politics as usual."

In chapter 1, we argued that the traditional tools and language of international politics do not lend themselves to the analysis of global ecological interdependence. This is so, we speculated, because the phenomenon calls into question not only the global distribution of power but also the meaning of power, the legitimacy of rules, and the nature of authority in the international system—circumstances that would by definition alter that system, making it into something else.

Most of the global-change literature has stopped short of examining such questions of system transformation. Instead, the tendency has been to project historical assumptions about cooperation and conflict onto new contexts and new issues. As James Rosenau has suggested elsewhere about theories of conflict and cooperation:

> If the dynamics that drive world politics are to be meaningfully incorporated into the theory, it makes a huge difference whether systems are viewed as always on the verge of collapse (so that the theorizing is oriented toward probing what holds them together and enables them to get from one moment in time to the next) or always capable of reproducing themselves (so that the theorizing focuses on how they come apart and break down).[2]

As in the larger literature on international relations that it reflects, most of the contending conceptual approaches to global environmental politics fit neatly on one side or the other of this conceptual divide between collapse and continuity. As such, they either define cooperation derivatively, rooted in the larger conflictual "state of nature" of international life, or define conflict derivatively, as a byproduct of the failure to collectively manage cooperative opportunities. In both cases, process and structure tend to be defined derivatively of outcomes.[3]

In a world of growing ecological interdependence, this sole focus on either conflict or cooperation as the predominant tendency obscures a more complex dynamic at work. This is because the tendencies toward collapse and continuity referred to above are both inherent in the phenomenon itself. The tighter systemic binding that states face is typically seen as a further constraint on their ability to pursue unilateral action or "opt out of the game" in the name of self-interest. But it is also an opportunity to re-create the state system itself, and the privileged position of states-as-actors, in working out new roles and relationships. At the same time, governments are hard-pressed to internalize the skills necessary to coordinate responses to what are basically a new set of demands and pressures, emerging simultaneously from within and without their jurisdictions. This inability to respond can be a threat to state legitimacy, either from above or below; it could also be an opportunity for the state to extend itself into new realms of social life.

What are the implications of these general observations for efforts to speculate on the future of the international system? We see two.

First, because of the contradictory tensions that constitute global ecological interdependence, increasing conflict, intensified competition, and heightened cooperation are plausible at all social levels, and seem likely to coexist in complex fashion. Without abandoning the desire to understand these modes of interaction from a common framework, we must consider them not as discrete, polar alternatives but rather as equally plausible, and potentially coexisting, responses to the prevailing conditions of environmental change and ecological interdependence. Instead of simply asking whether the world will be more or less conflictual, we must ask how existing social institutions—state, market, cultural identity, etc.—will channel patterns of conflict and cooperation, and whether the effect of such channeling will be to re-create the world, or to transform it.

Second, the issue of rule contestation raised in the previous section must be considered at the level of world order as well. This is not to say that the opening shots have been fired in what will be a full frontal assault on the nation-state system. The ideas that non-state actors are gaining power in the international arena, and that states are growing increasingly dependent on institutions beyond their unilateral control, are not new ones.[4] And as suggested above, such changes present states not merely with constraints, but opportunities. As Ken Conca argues in chapter 12, *Our Common Future*, the influential report of the World Commission on Environment and Development—with its clearly articulated division of labor between nation-states and international organizations—can be seen as a response to ecological interdependence that actually strengthens the principle of national sovereignty.

Rather than this, we may be seeing a far more subtle and complex process of systemic change, with the partial undermining or coopting of many of the contemporary functions of the system of sovereign states, its corona of international agencies, and its legitimating authority. Under such circumstances, we may find that the tendency toward systemic binding prevails, and extends far deeper into state and nation. It is entirely possible that feedbacks and interconnections have become so numerous and pervasive that a fundamentally new arrangement of actors and networks is emerging in place of the older states system. In this new "system," interdependence becomes more than just a potentially manipulable (or undesirable) two-way connection; it acquires the characteristics of the physical forces present in a multibody constellation, in which perturbations in one part of the arrangement may give rise to sympathetic responses in another part a great distance away.[5] Or it may be that the tendency toward fragmentation will prevail; the modern state system, which has shown great resilience in shifting between periods of intense conflict and periods of broad stability, may prove far more brittle under circumstances of simultaneously intensifying cooperation and conflict. Either way, catching a glimpse of the future hinges on seeing not only the distributive patterns of conflict and cooperation emerging from global ecological interdependence, but also these deeper, constitutive issues of system structure.

With these thoughts as prologue, the chapters that make up this final section consider a number of directions in which world politics might be moving. In chapter 11, Dan Deudney speculates on the political and social consequences of a successful global effort to "rescue" the environment. Without prejudging its likelihood, Deudney posits two developments if such an effort were in fact forthcoming. The first is the emergence of what he refers to as complementary international regimes—regimes that go beyond merely supplementing or augmenting the capacities of states, to the point that continued state existence depends on the services such regimes would provide. The second is the emergence of an ethos of global-scale "household management," fostered by the rise of a green culture and an associated cosmopolitanism. Functioning as a replacement for older nationalisms, green culture could supplant loyalty to state with loyalty to planet, as the inhabitants of the world become "naturalized" citizens of Earth. Taken together, these developments point toward the emergence of what Deudney describes as "world domestic politics," marked by a diminished political role for both state and nation.

In chapter 12, Ken Conca examines the "implicit" character of institutional responses to ecological interdependence. He begins with a very different premise than does Deudney: that the bulk of global environmental "policy" will remain, as it is today, implicit—in the sense of being embedded in institutions, agreements, and actions not typically interpreted as "environmental" in character. Because such institutions tend to reflect the organizing principles of sovereignty, capitalism, and modernity that define the current world order, so too does the bulk of "implicit" global environmental policy. Conca argues that, under such circumstances, the crucial question is not whether the dynamic of environmental destruction and social response undermines modernity, capitalism, or sovereignty directly, but rather whether that dynamic exacerbates or mitigates the larger tensions that are currently being played out between and among these organizing principles themselves.

NOTES

1. World Commission on Environment and Development, *Our Common Future* (New York: Oxford University Press, 1987).

2. James Rosenau, "Before Cooperation: Hegemons, Regimes, and Habit-driven Actors in World Politics." *International Organization* 40 no. 4 (Autumn 1986): 849–894.

3. Much of the emerging literature on "environmental security," for example, has been based on the traditional geopolitical notion of struggle over scarce or unevenly distributed resources—transferring the idea from the realm of natural-resource goods to the realm of environmental services (e.g., air quality, nutrient cycling, climate stability, the water cycle) that until recently have been regarded as neither finite nor strategic.

4. For a discussion of these ideas with specific regard to the state, see James A. Caporaso ed., *The Elusive State: International and Comparative Perspectives* (Newbury Park, CA: Sage, 1989); and Ronnie D. Lipschutz, "Reconstructing World Politics: The Emergence of Global Civil Society," *Millenium* 21 no. 3 (Winter 1982): 389–420.

5. Without the $1/R^n$ dependence, of course.

11

Global Environmental Rescue and the Emergence of World Domestic Politics

•

DANIEL DEUDNEY

Like all biological organisms, humans are vitally dependent upon their physical environment. Since the emergence of human life on earth, humans have been profoundly shaped by environmental factors. With the spread of the industrial revolution, the human relationship to and impact upon the natural world has been quantitatively and qualitatively transformed. During the last several decades, evidence has accumulated that human activities have begun to cause significant changes in the earth's life support system. A wide array of environmental stresses, including soil erosion, deforestation, water pollution, carbon dioxide build-up, species loss, and stratospheric ozone depletion, threaten human health and well-being. Left unat-

Earlier versions of this paper were presented at the workshop on "Global Environmental Change and International Relations," at the University of California at Berkeley, sponsored by the Pacific Institute, the Energy and Resources Group, and the Institute for Global Conflict and Cooperation Studies, February 1 & 2, 1991; the "Environment and Human Sciences" seminar, Princeton University, February 1991; and the International Studies Association, Vancouver, British Columbia, Canada, March 1991. Thanks to the participants at these meetings and to my colleagues at the Center for Energy and Environmental Studies for helpful comments to earlier drafts.

tended, these accumulating environmental stresses could severely diminish the well-being of future generations.

To cope with these problems, environmentalists have called for changes in political institutions at the local, nation-state, and international level. Thus far political scientists interested in environmental issues have been concerned mainly with analyzing the ways in which existing institutions impede effective response, and in conceiving of institutional innovations and reforms. More such efforts are needed.

The aim of this chapter, however, is different: to analyze in a somewhat speculative manner the likely impact of environmental rescue upon world politics. This chapter is a thought experiment based on an extrapolation from the nascent environmental responses beginning to be visible in world politics. My aim is not to examine the barriers posed by the nation-state system to environmental amelioration. Rather, I seek to examine the consequences for world order of successful response to the environmental crisis. In short, I assume for purposes of the argument that environmental rescue will occur along lines spelled out by environmentalists, and then ask: how will these developments shape world order, and the status of the nation-state system in particular?

The consequences of global environmental rescue will depend heavily upon the form such rescue takes. It is, of course, entirely possible that the responses of human beings to these problems will be insufficient, and that the dire consequences outlined by environmentalists will occur. However, given the importance of the values at stake, it is certainly possible, perhaps even probable, that humans will make the myriad of changes necessary to ameliorate these growing environmental problems and to arrange their affairs in a sustainable fashion. For purposes of this analysis, I assume three features of global environmental rescue (beyond the assumption that rescue will occur). First, I assume that achieving global sustainability will involve economic costs, but that these costs will not be so high as to prevent the continued qualitative growth in the world economic product. Second, I assume that global environmental rescue will entail changes in the behavior of individual human beings throughout the world, rather than a series of technical fixes achievable without the extensive involvement of consumers and citizens. Third, I assume that the steps taken to achieve environmental rescue will be widely distributed geographically, so that the consequences of environmental rescue will not be concentrated in any one or few regions. Although widespread, such action need not be universal or uniform. All of these assumptions may prove to be inaccurate. But none of these assumptions are glaringly implausible, and therefore can serve as a useful basis for preliminary analysis.

My main proposition is that a form of "world domestic politics" will emerge, significantly altering, but not eliminating, the nation-state from the center of world political life. The emergence of a world domestic politics thus implies a diminished role for the state[1] and the national institutions that currently occupy the central position in world politics. To argue that the state and nation will decline in importance is to tread well-travelled ground. As Stanley Hoffmann noted, the writings of international relations scholars tend to resemble entries into the contest for the best essay on the "persistence or demise of the realist paradigm" and the nation-state system.[2] Unfortunately, resolving the status of the state and the system of states in contemporary world politics is no simple matter. The essence and extent, even the existence, of the state is highly contested ground. As James Rosenau recently observed, whether the state is thought to be widening its competence, a withering colossus, or merely weathering change depends upon which of several wavering concepts one employs.[3]

In order to flesh out the concept of a "world domestic politics" much of the conceptual work of liberal internationalism is relevant. Two broad theoretical literatures, on "international government" and cosmopolitanism, envision world orders in which the state and nation have been displaced. The first is concerned with institutional and organizational alternatives to, and alterations in, the interstate system and the second with the cultural and normative alternatives to nationalism.

Domestic Politics

In contemporary political parlance, the expression "domestic politics" is used widely, and without controversy, to describe the politics that occurs within the borders of states among citizens of one community, usually a national political community. There are, however, neglected dimensions and tensions in the relationship between the "domestic" and the "political." The English term "domestic" derives from the Latin "domus" meaning home or house. For the Greek political theorists who first conceptualized the political and the public, the domestic and the political were antithetical. In initially conceptualizing the distinct sphere of "political" activity, Aristotle drew a sharp line between the household and the public space of the polis. In his view, the domestic sphere is constituted by relations that are "prepolitical" in the sense that they are concerned with the maintenance of life (production, consumption, and reproduction). Success in the art of household management (oeconomicos) made politics possible, but was not itself political.[4]

Although not itself political, the disposition of the domestic sphere shaped and limited the political. This way of viewing the domestic-political relationship is alien to moderns, in part because Aristotle conceptualized the public or truly political sphere as the realm of relationships of free consent and deliberation, rather than of domination and subordination. In this classical conception, relationships of power existed in the prepolitical sphere and in the relationships between political communities, or what moderns call "international" life. The political sphere proper was constituted by reciprocity and persuasion rather than domination and coercion.

Since the era of the Greek city-state, the relationship between the domestic and the political has undergone considerable evolution, both in theory and practice. Relationships of consent have increasingly come to penetrate and constitute the domestic sphere, and the tasks regulating human-nature interaction have increasingly spilled over into the realm of politics. Since the industrial revolution, the political life of states has become increasingly "domestic" as matters of economics and welfare have required increasingly complex and large-scale regulation. Modern industrialism (whether organized by capitalism or state socialism) has intensively connected all the previously prepolitical spheres into one giant national "household," and forced its complex concerns upon the political sphere, making politics within states predominately "domestic." The political realm has declined as a realm of free association and become the arena in which various private interests compete for a larger share of the polity's product.[5]

With the further intensification and globalization of industrialism, the domestic sphere has now become planetary in scope. The tasks of human-nature mediation that were performed largely within the family unit in preindustrial economic systems have now become too big even for the domestic managers of nation-states. The global environmental crisis is at its core a "domestic" phenomenon, but one occurring at an unprecedentedly large scale. It is about global-scale household management, about disequilibria in the system of production, consumption, and reproduction. If global communications and transportation has created a "global village" of shared images and consciousness, then the global environmental crisis reveals the existence of a "global household." Attending to the global environmental crisis thus promises to domesticate the relationship between independent political communities, to create "domestic" politics on a global scale. The term "domestic" is appropriate to describe a world political order produced by large-scale earthkeeping activities because these activities will break down the distinction between the "domestic" world of "internal" or intrastate affairs, and the world of "foreign" interstate relations.[6]

International Government

Since early in the twentieth century, analysts of world politics have been debating the feasibility and prerequisites for "international government." For realists, the idea of "international government" is something of a contradiction in terms: government occurs within states, not between them. The main effort to conceptualize institutions and organizations among states that are of more than trivial importance has been made by liberal internationalists, mostly in Britain and the United States.[7] Since World War II the density of interstate organizations and institutionalized transactions has expanded enormously, and theorists have sought to capture these developments with concepts such as "spillover," "integration," "informal penetration," "linkage politics," "incremental functionalism," and "complex interdependence." The essential underlying trend has been the increase in what John Ruggie calls the "dynamic density" of world politics.[8] These categories can help explicate the features of global environmental interdependence.

Welfare Functionalism

One useful set of tools for thinking about the large-scale interstate cooperation on the interstate system is provided by David Mitrany and functionalist theory.[9] In his famous 1943 essay, "A Working Peace System," Mitrany divided international life into two streams, the traditional domain of "high politics" (war and diplomacy) dominated by realpolitik, and a "low politics" centered around economics and welfare. Like many in the late-nineteenth and early-twentieth centuries, Mitrany was struck by the great growth of international interactions in the sphere of low politics and he expected that such interactions would grow with the spread and intensification of industrialism and democratization.

Mitrany hypothesized that as cooperation in mundane matters of welfare grew, the habits of cooperation would "spill over" into the domain of high politics, permitting the gradual resolution of military and diplomatic conflicts and the eventual dismantling of the war system. Mitrany argued that this indirect approach would be more effective than the efforts of many in the peace movement to resolve the conflicts of high politics directly by creating of international arbitration and world peacekeeping systems. Mitrany predicted—and urged—the creation of "a working peace system" beneath or outside the war system that would over time neutralize the conflicts of high politics.

For a number of years Mitrany's argument was extensively developed and tested by political scientists, and in general found to be wanting.[10] Realist critics claim that states which were antagonists in high politics would not allow extensive low politics collaboration. Indeed, the realists argued, the spillover occurred in the opposite direction to that predicted by Mitrany: economic and welfare collaboration would be retarded by high politics conflict between states. Mitrany was "unrealistic" to think that economics and welfare would ever be allowed to operate autonomously of the high political sphere. Thus the low politics collaboration between long-time antagonists France and Germany after World War II presupposed the American-led military unification of Western Europe. And the high political conflict between the United States and the Soviet Union greatly impeded substantial welfare and economic collaboration between the blocs.

There is, however, another possible reason for the apparent refutation of Mitrany's hypothesis: the absence of a real test case of his claims. Mitrany took it for granted that the requirements for welfare cooperation were so compelling that modern industrial societies would be drawn irresistibly toward them. If in fact these imperatives to realize welfare gains were weaker than he thought, then his hypothesis may be more untested than disproven. Also, Mitrany believed that the welfare state was increasingly displacing capitalism, and that the welfare gains that states stood to gain through cooperation would require extensive government-to-government interaction. In retrospect, market exchanges during the last half century have proven to be a much more powerful engine of exchange across international borders than government-to-government transactions. Since so much of the welfare gains available from cooperation across borders can be accomplished with markets, the institutional "spillovers" that Mitrany expected to alter international relations are kept to a minimum. Also, the gains from intraregional cooperation have continued to be much more important than interregional ones.

The global environmental crisis may provide the first test case of Mitrany's proposition on spillover from low to high politics. The environmental problem poses a set of global-scale (rather than simply regional) welfare gains. The combined benefits of environmental protection are, aside from averting nuclear war, perhaps the first genuinely "global welfare function" the human species has yet encountered. Also, the management of global environmental problems cannot simply be left to markets to resolve, but will require extensive governmental involvement. The benefits to be had from global environmental cooperation may be of sufficient magnitude to overpower high political antipathy to common action. Gaining these benefits may require efforts of such magnitude that there will be an institutional and organizational spillover into the domain of high politics sufficient to cause the withering away of the war system itself.

Interstate Regimes

A second set of tools for thinking about the impacts of environmental rescue upon world politics in general and the interstate system is provided by regime theory. Although the term "regime" first came into popularity among political scientists during the early 1970s,[11] many of the basic issues and ideas of regime theory date back to the beginning of the twentieth century.

Throughout this literature of liberal internationalism is a fundamental disagreement: will the result of international institution-building be the replacement of the state system with some type of full-blown world state, or will the creation of interstate institutions provide various services to the world political community that the independent states were unable to achieve acting alone, thus strengthening the state system?

In order to help answer this question, it is useful to employ a typology of regime and interstate institutions. To generalize, the recent study of regimes has been focused explicitly upon institutions designed to augment rather than replace the state system as the political center of gravity in world politics. The earlier tradition of designing various world states and constitutions is in large measure a moribund branch of political science. The emergence of an increasingly dense set of augmenting institutions since World War II has given political scientists an actual set of institutions to study, a much preferable situation for an academic discipline aspiring to put speculation behind it and become a real "science."

It is useful to lay out the different types of interstate institutions (both augmenting and replacing) on a single scale or continuum. The various "regimes" studied by contemporary international relations scholars are all examples of what might be labeled incidental and supplementary regimes—they provide valuable services for the states, but they remain very much the creatures of the states. Such regimes bolster the independence of many states that would not be viable if they were forced to be self-sufficient militarily and economically, but the more powerful states are not dependent on these regimes for their existence. At the other end of the spectrum are replacing institutions, which still remain in the realm of speculation.

There is, however, a logical alternative not adequately examined by either the earlier world statists or the contemporary students of regimes, namely a *complementary* regime. Such an institution may be defined as performing so important a task that the state system itself cannot exist in the longer term without the institution's services. Like a world state, this is still a speculative category,[12] but a useful one for understanding the character of world domestic politics. The collective weight of environmental measures capable of achieving sustainable human interaction with nature should best be thought of as a complementary regime.

The record so far of creating complementary regimes has not been marked with much success. There are three cautionary lessons for the creation of an environmental regime of sufficient magnitude to be labeled complementary. First, the more a prospective complementary regime seems to be preempting responsibilities which the states have come to see as integral to their "sovereignty," the harder it will be to create such a regime. Thus, the prospects of creating a comprehensive control regime for nuclear materials probably depends upon the degree to which states perceive the nuclear question to be distinct from their traditional role of defending territory by making war. Tangling up environmental restoration with the issues of "national security" (as traditionally defined) could make the creation of substantial environmental regimes a difficult—perhaps impossible—undertaking.[13] Conversely, since the state system has traditionally not defined itself according to environmental factors, solutions to these emerging problems perhaps can proceed without overcoming strong statist presumptions and traditions.

The second cautionary lesson is that states will resist the creation of a complementary regime that looks like the nucleus of a world state. States fear that once power of sufficient magnitude has been aggregated by any trans-state or interstate institution, they would not be able to check its evolution into a world state. Thus the Lillienthal-Acheson-Baruch Plan for nuclear control may have been fatally compromised by the widespread assumption that an international atomic authority would make nuclear weapons available to a "world peacekeeping force" at some future time. For environmental regime building, this suggests that great care must be taken to disaggregate the various solutions into separate institutions and avoid the temptation of building one institution or organization responsible for the global environment. A cluster of strong, but unconnected ad hoc arrangements might avoid this critical-mass problem. However, this may pose significant difficulties in environmental problem-solving since so many of them are integrated, requiring coordinated responses.

Third, the creation of a complementary regime may be inversely related to the existence of a hegemonic power. A complementary regime too closely identified with the most powerful state in the system would be seen as a step toward world imperium, and thus resisted by other states. The post—World War II interstate regimes (viewed by many international-relations scholars as a byproduct of American military and economic preponderance) are an inappropriate model for the creation of a complementary regime.[14] A coalition of states roughly commensurate in strength may be much more likely to create a complementary regime than would a hegemon.

Should environmental rescue involve the emergence of a complementary regime, the state system will have been augmented rather than replaced. In this situation, the political structure of the world polity will not resemble the nation-state model extrapolated to a larger scale. Rather, the architecture of world political institutions will be much more complicated and lacking an institutional center of gravity.[15] From the standpoint of the state system, the primary appeal of creating a cluster of environmental regimes is that such institutions would solve problems that states otherwise would be unable to handle. Thus the creation of a cluster of such regimes, like many reforms that stop short of revolution, has a paradoxically conservative effect. Reform saves the system from its own worst tendencies, permitting its continued, if circumscribed, operation.

Green Culture and Cosmopolitanism

Another important dimension of global environmental rescue may be the emergence of citizen mobilization and transnational environmental norms, coupled with and grounded in ecological philosophies.[16] In this scenario, peoples all over the world come to realize that environmental degradation threatens their immediate well-being and change their behavior in order to combat it. Should efforts to protect the environment come to occupy the attention and activity of large numbers of people, patterns of identity and social relations would be shaped and colored in significant ways. Certain scenarios of environmental rescue may, in short, involve the emergence of new sets of norms and perhaps the emergence of something approaching a full-blown culture.

In thinking about the contours of a possible "green culture" and its political consequences, it is useful to extrapolate from the nascent cultural formations in regions of the world where environmental awareness has reached something of a critical mass. Since environmental consciousness and cultural activities are strongest in the Pacific Northwest, particularly Northern California, the behavior and sensibility of the environmental movement in this area offers a good basis for this kind of speculative analysis. Extrapolating and generalizing from such a limited sample runs the danger of confusing regional idiosyncrasies with global prototypes, but is an unavoidable risk at this early stage of environmental politics.

This cultural aspect of environmental rescue might involve relatively little direct interstate institution-building, but its effects on world political order could nevertheless be profound. Widespread citizen and consumer action to ameliorate environmental deterioration would, however, tend to produce a convergence of the internal political life of states around the world. This in turn could be expected to reduce the severity and frequency of interstate conflict. Even more significantly, the emergence of widespread environmental awareness could crystallize into a powerful new planetary culture, in which case the claims of national identities and loyalties could be displaced, thus providing the basis for real world-wide community.

The most interesting political question is how a greening of culture or the emergence of a planetary green culture might alter, and be shaped by, nationalism. Nationalism is a central component of the current nation-state-centered world order, providing autonomous states with legitimation and dividing members of the human species into numerous, often suspicious and xenophobic communities. The reason that domestic politics occurs much more within states than between them is that a common sense of national identity defines a political community. Disagreement continues about the nature and causes of nationalism, but[17] there is widespread agreement among students of world politics that it is one of the most potent forces shaping world political order. However compelling on functional grounds, global institutions remain weak in part because of the continuing power of nationalism. The key point of the post–World War II realist criticism of "idealism" still holds true: efforts to institutionally augment or supplant the nation-state system are blocked by the limited sense of community spanning national borders. As Hans Morgenthau pointed out, the absence of such community means that plans to erect world-scale political institutions are either utopian or blueprints for tyranny.[18] The idea that nationalism has to be diluted before international governmental problem-solving can get very far is also recognized by advocates of world governance. Internationalist efforts to dilute nationalism have been ingenious and wide-ranging, from international languages such as Esperanto to schemes for world religious unity, but so far largely unsuccessful in displacing nationalism.[19]

To understand how the emergence of a "green culture" might dilute, if not significantly displace, national identity, it is necessary to examine the origins and nature of nationalism, and the reasons why other transnationalist and cosmopolitan ideals have failed to dispel the grip of the national sentiment.

Enlightenment, Nationalism, and Cosmopolitanism

Although people have lived in distinct groups since the beginning of human existence, nationalism is a distinctly modern phenomenon. It arose first in Western Europe in the late eighteenth and early nineteenth centuries, and spread to the rest of the world during the first half of the twentieth century. Of course many of the linguistic and cultural features that constitute particular nations predate the modern period, but their employment as the basis for state legitimacy and political community is a distinctly modern development. Prior to the modern period, humans living in institutions larger than tribes or city-states typically lived in polyglot empires in which either religious or dynastic ties formed the most important cultural basis for political community.[20]

The development and spread of nationalism is in some ways paradoxical and puzzling. Its florescence was largely unexpected by the philosophers and propagandists of the Enlightenment who largely defined the modern project. Nationalism continues to be largely unexplainable by either liberals or Marxists, who in differing ways purport to embody the promise of progressive modernity.[21] In the modernist scenario for the future development of humanity, all forms of group particularity and localism were supposed to decline and be replaced by a universal and cosmopolitan community that would eventually come to embrace all of humanity. In this trajectory of universal modernization, religious, ethnic, and linguistic variations were treated as mere residues of the past, what Engels disdainfully called "ethnographic monuments," increasingly archaic and untenable in a world of rational beings. Their hold on human loyalties was expected to fade as reason exposed the groundlessness of myth and as functional interdependencies created new communities of interest transcending the old borders of communal identity.[22]

But this cosmopolitan outcome remains more a vision than a reality. Nationalism, far from withering away, has flowered luxuriantly in the modern age. What went wrong? Although there is far from a consensus on this question, two powerful and related explanations for the growth of nationalism as a force in the modern era have been set forth by Ernest Gellner and Benedict Anderson.

In *Nations and Nationalism*, Gellner argues that nationalism is a side-effect of the process of modernization.[23] Nationalism, far from being a residue of premodern communal forms destined to wither away with the growth of modernity, has spread because it solves an important social problem posed by modernity. In the preindustrial era humans typically lived in small agricultural communities and seldom traveled far from home. In contrast, the industrial era has produced a great mobilization and a great functional differentiation of human society. As mobility increased, the average individual came into increased contact with more people; but as specialization increased, the basis for common understanding declined. Gellner argues that national forms of identity and community came to be increasingly valued and inculcated because they offered a basis for maintaining a minimum sense of common mutual understanding. Thus nationalism provided a centripetal force strong enough to counteract the centrifugal forces of modern social differentiation.

In *Imagined Communities*, Benedict Anderson provides a complementary explanation that emphasizes the role of nationalism in satisfying what might be called "metaphysical yearnings." [24] Noting that the "dawn of the age of nationalism" was the "dusk of religious modes of thought," Anderson argues that it is a mistake to understand nationalism as a consciously held political ideology, like fascism or communism, for it concerns much more fundamental human urges, and has a "strong affinity with religious imaginings." The great civilizations of the premodern era were organized around great cosmological systems that provided answers to the metaphysical questions that trouble human beings, endowing the contingencies of human existence with purpose and meaning. Whatever their plausibility in the face of modern science, these cosmological systems told people who they were, where they came from, where they were going, and why their privations and sufferings were part of a cosmos that was both meaningful and intelligible. They also created strong communal identities across space and time.

The limits of the Enlightenment project are set by the deficiencies in modern cultural possibilities. The great ethical and political ideologies spawned by the Enlightenment have been much less successful in satisfying these metaphysical yearnings than were the religions they supplanted. The modern project has, as its prophets advertised, ameliorated humanity's material estate, but at the cost of creating the "homeless mind" (Berger) adrift in a "disenchanted world" (Weber).

The great void left by what Schiller aptly called the "disgodding" [25] of the world has come to be filled, at least in part, Anderson argues, by nationalism, accounting for its strong and extensive, yet "irrational," appeal. By telling people who they are, where they came from, where they are going, nationalism (however recently invented or historically unfounded) forged a collective identity, justifying sacrifice for the collective and linking the strivings of the present with generations past and future. Thus the psychic pageant of nationalism so disdained and uncomprehended by the rationalist intelligentsia—flags, parades, heroes, "hallowed grounds," sagas of suffering and triumph—generate ready-made and broadly accessible community, and so provide the decisive ideological underpinnings for state sovereignty. Because it satisfies these human aspirations, nationalism remains the hegemonic political culture of the modern era.

In competing with these "imagined communities" of nations, transnational and cosmopolitan norms and identities have repeatedly proven inadequate. One problem with such efforts to construct a cosmopolitan world culture is that the content of such internationalism is thin and lifeless relative to rich and elaborate national cultures. Thus far, cosmopolitanism is defined more by its stance of opposition to particularistic national cultures than by its own substantive content. Cosmopolitanism is consistently antinational, but lacks the richness and emotional draw of traditional national cultures: myths, heroes, narrative accounts of origins, festivals, folkways, flags, symbols, hallowed graves, and taboos. As Nietzsche pointedly noted, cosmopolitanism was hollow, sterile, and authoritative only to the rational intellectual. The "tablets of value" at the center of vital cultures spring not from the head of Zeus, but from extremes of prophetic experience and epic sacrifice.

The shallow hold of modern ideological cosmopolitanism has been parallelled by the more popular, less programmatic global culture that has emerged in the second half of the twentieth century. As the anthropologist Mary Catherine Bateson has recently observed, a global culture now exists that is a "mixture of the Beatles and the International Geophysical Year." [26] This global culture is centered around shared experiences of consumption, production, and leisure (tourism, sports, entertainment) and woven together by telecommunications and jet aircraft, which have produced the "global village." Unfortunately, this culture is, as Anthony Smith has recently argued, "attenuated," "essentially calculated and artificial," and "affectively neutral." It has only marginally diluted, not displaced, the psychic hold of nationalism because it is "essentially memoryless" and is "context-less, a true melange of disparate components drawn from everywhere and nowhere." [27]

Green Culture as Earth Nationalism

Can the cultural impasse of internationalism be broken by environmentalism? Here I explore how "green culture," the emergent worldview, way-of-life, and cosmology of environmentalism could be both universal enough and substantively rich enough to form the basis for a worldwide cultural formation capable of displacing nationalism. Barbara Ward and Rene Dubois pointed the way to the argument with their suggestion that "As we enter the global phase of human evolution it becomes obvious that each man has two countries, his own and the planet earth." [28] There are two clusters of related aspects of "green culture," the first of credible cosmology, sacred space, and ritual, and a second involving heroism, sacrifice, and intergenerational community. Together these features of green culture are intricate and encompassing enough to be the basis for a "nation of the earth." As Bron Taylor has convincingly argued, radical environmental groups such as Earth First! have an elaborate worldview that resembles religions in many key respects. To make this case fully convincing would require a careful look at the cosmologies associated with environmentalism, a task beyond the scope of this paper, and a task well-performed by others. Rather, the aim here is more specific: to provide a preliminary sketch of how aspects of the emergent "green culture" can satisfy some of the psychic and cultural needs formerly filled by religion and now partially filled by nationalism. [29]

First, environmentalism is the first worldview of the modern era that can present a credible cosmology. The fatal flaw of the great theologies that constituted the center of gravity of the great premodern civilizations was that they are not credible in the face of modern natural science. In the West the recession of Christendom and the rise of modernity was marked by a succession of scientific discoveries profoundly subversive of the religious worldview: the Copernican displacement of the earth from the center of the universe, the discovery of deep geological time, the theory of biological evolution, and the emergence of a mechanical conception of nature hostile to supernatural intervention. From the deistic recasting of God into a retired watchmaker it was but a short step to Nietzsche's "death of God"— the end of monotheistic religion as the axis of cultural life.

A striking feature of "deep ecology" as a spiritual and moral system is that it can make at least a prima facie claim to being compatible with an important science—ecology. The simple deduction of norms and prescriptions from bodies of modern scientific knowledge remains a deeply problematic undertaking, but when linked with a simple set of normative assumptions, particularly the desirability of survival, ecology comes much closer to seeming to provide a set of broad and important norms.

Closely related to green cosmology is emphasis in "green culture" upon the reestablishment of sacred space and ritual. A key feature of the great premodern cultures was the possibility of hierarchical space, of special locations that were deemed particularly sacred and hallowed. These spaces serve as gathering points for ritual and for the spiritual encounters with the extra-human force giving shape and meaning to human existence. An interesting approximation of this sense of sacred space is found in the wilderness "sanctuary."[30] The cliché of the environmental movement, that the great wonders of nature constitute the "cathedrals and sanctuaries" of nature, captures an important feature of the emergent green culture. The parallel is further strengthened by the realization that increasing numbers of people are making what amount to pilgrimages to the great seats of nature all over the planet, and that this type of "tourism" has much in common with the religious pilgrimages of medieval Christians or contemporary Muslims. The movement to create these sanctuaries began in the United States and Great Britain, but has become an increasingly global trend in the last two decades with the emergence of the U.N. World Heritage Program.

Like nationalism, but unlike most modern interest groups, "green culture" also contains powerful claims about identity and community. One reason for thinking that "green culture" has the potential to displace modern state nationalism is that the rhetoric of nationalism is highly naturalistic. Although the "imagined" or ideological character of modern state nationalism is readily acknowledged by political analysts, surprisingly little systematic content analysis has been performed.[31] Some of nationalism's most basic and powerful images are biological. The term "nation" itself, derived from the Latin "to be born," makes the obviously fictional claim that membership in a particular nation is somehow a biological act or natural necessity. In speaking of the "fatherland" and the "motherland," nationalist ideology also casts the relationship between co-nationals in biological terms drawn from the familiar family unit. Foreign "aliens" aspiring to become citizens undergo a bureaucratic process labeled "naturalization." The most extreme merging of natural with national rhetoric flourished in Nazi Germany, where "race," "blood," and "soil" were raised as new tribal totems for a war against cosmopolitan "corruption" and "degeneration."[32] In all these examples, nationalist ideology artfully conflates associations arising from biological necessity with those created by historical convention in order to endow the imagined community with substance, continuity, and inevitability.

One of the most philosophically significant aspects of contemporary environmental thinking is the effort to conceptualize human identities and communities based on natural and ecological factors. In the broadest terms environmental thinkers propose grounding human cultural identity and community in the biologic human body and its ecological contexts. At a rhetorical level, environmentalists propose allegiance to "mother earth" as the true "motherland" of all humans and living things.[33] Thus every human's true "nation," in the etymological sense of "genuine birth group," is the human species itself. Given how extensively modern state nationalism employs the rhetoric of naturalism to legitimate itself, rising ecological awareness may provide the foundation for something approximating an "earth nation" encompassing at least the entire human species.

Beyond this general move to found an identity and community upon ecological grounds, important issues of scope and character remain fundamentally contested among environmental philosophers. Does this new identity and community extend only to the human species or does it extend outward and "downward" so that it encompasses other species as well? One powerful tendency is to extend "rights" and the various forms of community implied in their extension into nonhuman nature.[34] The postulate of a human species identity and community—a radical construct when juxtaposed to actual political practice—has been assaulted by environmentalist philosophers as the ultimate source of ecological problems, which suggests that a cleavage analogous to the traditional national-versus-cosmopolitan may be emerging within green ethics and cosmology.

Various "deep ecologists" present an image of human identity as a species identity contextualized in nature.[35] If this identity, this imagined community between humans and the natural world, catches hold widely, humans will have found (or created) an identity for themselves that answers the questions of who we are, where we came from, and where we are going, thus offering to displace the nationalist identities.

Closely related to the question of identity and community is the status of an "out-group" in this hypothesized "earth nationalism." A central feature of modern state nationalism is its nonuniversal character, and the importance of other different, and potentially antagonistic, communities against which the "nation" defines itself. As Anderson points out, everyone has a nationality, but no nationality claims to be coterminous with the entire human community. Is an earth nationalism, encompassing at least the entire human species, something of a contradiction in terms?[36] Or does earth nationalism transcend this limitation of modern state nationalism, achieving something like the universal community without an out-group postulated by several of the higher religions? Or can we expect to see something analogous to an out-group emerge as earth nationalism emerges?

One possible answer to these problems implicit in the "human species" group identity is that the out-group is the rest of life. However, this line of reasoning collides directly with the probably more central ecological insight that the human species is but one small, if particularly precocious, part of life. If, on the other hand, the borders of the green identity and community are drawn so as to include all life on earth, then the identification of a living out-group is by definition impossible. If the borders of "us" are drawn so as to encompass all life, then the differentiated and threatening "them" may come to be understood as the broader nonliving cosmic context that makes life on this planet and in this solar system untenable in the longer run.[37] In this scenario of "life against death" the longer-term project of the human species is to serve as guardian for the precariously situated "ark" of life on earth. In this scenario James Lovelock's "Gaia hypothesis" is turned on its head: instead of humans being largely irrelevant to a planet-spanning life-complex with teleological nesting capabilities, humans become the "crown of creation," the instrument life produces to preserve itself.

Closely related to nationalist identity and community are heroism and sacrifice, usually in war. There is a strong relationship between sacrifice, war, and modern state nationalism. The historian Michael Howard observes that "It is in fact very difficult to create national self-consciousness without a war."[38] One reason that war is such a formative experience, in fact and in myth, for national identities and communities is that it produces heroes and evokes sacrifice. If the tree of liberty must be periodically watered with the blood of tyrants, the tree of nationalism must be periodically watered with the blood of patriots. Intergroup violence and bloodshed evoke extremes of human emotion and group bonding that give nations their continuing cohesion. What experience can green culture provide that can compete with war as a crucible of identity? If, as Nietzsche suggested, war is the core of a vital culture and can sanctify virtually any cause, how can the pacific green worldview ever successfully compete?

One possibility is that radical forms of environmental activism, such as practiced by Earth First! and other direct-action groups, may produce martyrs and heroes for the green culture. Or perhaps animals—particularly larger ones with which humans can readily identify—may be the heroes of green culture. Another possibility is that some great environmental crisis will occur, producing victims and heroic action that could be mythologized for green culture. Ironically, the more widespread and more severe the crisis, and the more pain and struggle it generates, the stronger will be its potential to generate identity and community. Although each of these possibilities has a certain plausibility, it is not evident that any feature of the emergent environmentalist culture will have quite the power of war for state nationalism.

Perhaps the center of gravity of the emergent green culture will be located in the vernacular rather than in extreme situations like war. Hegel's famous quip that reading the morning newspaper is the modern nation's analogue to prayer in the middle ages indicates that an important part of national identity and community derives from routine, serially performed, and universally accessible actions of citizens. In looking for an analogue in green culture for war in nationalism, it is important to remember that the "ultimate test" of battlefield experience does not necessarily have to be routinely or universally experienced by everyone in a culture in order to generate identity and community. To the degree that environmental constraints are recognized and produce modified behavior on the part of large numbers of citizens, and such environmentally responsible behavior is perceived as requiring a sacrifice, then the identity and community claims of green culture could still be strong. Thus, if technical fixes alone are capable of solving environmental problems, then a sense of sacrifice that could help forge a green identity and community are likely to be reduced. Behavioral changes involving perceived personal sacrifice may be harder to achieve than cost-free technical fixes, but their political inheritance could be much greater.

Another dimension of both nationalism and the emergent green culture is their claims to an intergenerational community. One of the reasons that nationalism remains so much stronger than the cosmopolitan ideologies of liberalism and Marxism is that nations are intergenerational communities, bonding the present to the past and future, justifying sacrifice upon the part of the present for the future, and creating a sense of identity that transcends mere self-interest. The classic statement of this intergenerational feature of viable human collectivities was made by Edmund Burke in his attack on the

French Revolutionaries who were attempting to re-create society anew based solely upon atomistic self-interest. Burke's words, beloved by conservatives, resound with imagery that is clearly relevant to the new deep-conservation worldview of green culture:

> Society is indeed a contract. Subordinate contracts for the objects of mere occasional interest may be dissolved at pleasure—but the state ought not to be considered as nothing better than a partnership agreement in a trade of pepper and coffee, calico or tobacco, or some other such low concern, to be taken up for a little temporary interest, and to be dissolved by the fancy of the parties. It is to be looked on with other reverence; because it is not a partnership in things subservient only to the gross animal existence of a temporary and perishable nature. It is a partnership in every virtue, and in all perfection. As the ends of such partnership cannot be obtained in many generations, it becomes a partnership not only between those who are living, but between those who are living, those who are dead, and those who are yet to be born. Each contract of each particular state is but a clause in the great primeval contract of eternal society, linking the lower with the higher natures, connecting the visible and invisible world, according to a fixed compact sanctioned by the inviolable oath which holds all physical and moral natures, each in their appointed place. This law is not subject to the will of those, who by an obligation above them, and infinitely superior, are bound to submit their will to that law. The municipal corporations of that universal kingdom are not morally at liberty at their pleasure, and on their speculations of a contingent improvement, wholly to separate and tear asunder the bands of their subordinate community, and to dissolve it into an unsocial, uncivil, unconnected chaos of elementary principles.[39]

The striking feature of Burke's vision of the fundamental constitution or social contract is how readily it fits the emergent environmental sensibility. A key slogan of the green culture is the American Indian proverb that "We have not inherited the earth from our parents, but borrowed it from our children." The environmentalist justification for controlling global warming and saving endangered species is that the present generation does not have the right to rob future generations of their birthright.[40] This aspect of environmentalism is thus profoundly hostile to the "nowism" of contemporary consumer culture, the systematic discounting of future value inherent in deriving all social choice from the preferences of the contemporary rational individual.

To the extent that global environmental rescue is motivated by these intergenerational ethical considerations, it forges one of the decisive features characteristic of the "nation." (It is also notable that the effort to constrain contemporary appetites on behalf of the otherwise disenfranchised generations of the future is a fundamentally "constitutional" political act, and thus profoundly domestic.

Earth Nationalism and State Nationalism

If in fact a nascent green culture within the environmental movement has many similarities with religion and state nationalism, how will this new cultural formation relate to the existing nationalisms that are largely connected to states? Logically there are three possibilities: (1) green culture will replace state nationalism, providing a substantive cosmopolitan community for the first time; (2) environmental awareness will color state nationalism, making existing nationalist groupings less truculent and more amenable to international cooperation; or (3) environmental awareness will be captured by existing statist nationalism, giving it additional virulence and thus reinforcing the conflictual tendencies of the international system. The first case would involve a nation of the earth, the second a greening of the nation, and the third the nationalization of the greens.

At least a partial test case of these alternatives may be unfolding in Eastern Europe and the former Soviet Union. Here for the first time a major liberation and awakening of traditional national groupings is occurring simultaneously with significant political mobilization around environmental issues. In some widely publicized instances, such as the Chernobyl nuclear disaster in Ukraine and nuclear testing in Kazakhstan, environmental concerns were a major focal point of national grievance against Soviet control. In these cases, environmental concerns reinforced the desire of long suppressed and dormant national groups to assert their interests in acquiring sovereign states of their own.

The important question, however, is whether these newly emergent nation-states will be more likely to engage in interstate cooperation once their aspirations for national liberation have been satisfied. One reason for believing that the emergence of green culture will replace or moderate state and ethnic nationalism rather than make it more truculent is that environmental awareness brings with it an awareness of the interconnected and interdependent character of the earth's diverse inhabitants. Although environmental mobilization al-

most always begins with some specific local environmental grievance, the increased awareness of ecological principles that accompan-
ies such mobilizations leads toward a globalist rather than a statist or
ethnic sensibility. As Luther Gerlach suggests (see chapter 8), people
first come to environmental issues with a NIMBY (Not In My Backyard) mentality, but as they learn more about the actual issues involved, soon develop a NOPE (Not On Planet Earth) mentality.
Intrinsic to the awareness that constitutes the content of environmentalism is a subversion of the artificial human boundaries drawn upon
nature.

Conclusions

This speculative inquiry into the shape of world political order that
might be produced by the establishment of sustainability has borrowed from the conceptual vocabulary of liberal internationalism to
envision a "world domestic politics." In such a world, the nation-
state system has been pushed somewhat from the center of world
political order, first by a set of interstate institutions with more substantive importance than any before created, and second by the
emergence of a green culture. Since nationalism is such a complex
and diverse phenomenon, it would be foolhardy to predict its complete demise. However, if nationalism's strength derives in significant measure from its ability to provide community and answer
"metaphysical yearnings," then it could well decline in significance
if these needs can be met in another way. The green culture attendant to global environmental rescue may well have at least some of
the major ingredients lacking in previous cosmopolitan alternatives
to nationalism. Should these interstate institutions and green cosmopolitanism emerge, the human species could well be, for the first
time ever, part of one domestic polity.

NOTES

1. Definitions of the scope of "the state" vary greatly. At one extreme
are those, such as Alan James, who define a state as "territory, people and a
government." *Sovereign Statehood* (London: Allen & Unwin, 1986), p.13. More
narrowly "the state" can mean the central administrative apparatus, as when
Theda Skocpol defines the state as "a set of administrative, policy and
military organizations headed, and more or less well coordinated, by an

executive authority." *States and Social Revolutions* (Cambridge: Cambridge University Press, 1979), p. 29. For a penetrating review of these conceptual problems see, Fred Halliday, "State and Society in International Relations: A Second Agenda," *Millennium* 16 (1987): 215–229.

2. Stanley Hoffmann, "International Relations: An American Social Science," *Daedalus* 106 no. 3 (Summer 1977): 41–60, p. 53.

3. James Rosenau, "The State in an Era of Cascading Politics: Wavering Concept, Widening Competence, Withering Colossus, or Weathering Change?" in James Caporaso ed., *The Elusive State: International and Comparative Perspectives* (Newbury Park, CA: Sage, 1989).

4. Aristotle, *The Politics*, Book I. From this term come the English "economics" and "ecology." For discussion see Donald Worster, *Nature's Economy: The Roots of Ecology* (San Francisco: Sierra Club Books, 1977).

5. This understanding of the character of ancient and modern politics draws from Hannah Arendt, *The Human Condition* (Chicago: University of Chicago Press, 1958) and Sheldon Wolin, *Politics and Vision* (Boston: Little, Brown and Co., 1960).

6. The centrality of the "inside-outside" distinction is emphasized by both realists and their critics. See R. B. J. Walker, "Realism, Change, and International Political Theory," *International Studies Quarterly* 31 (March 1987): 65–86.

7. The most important formulations being: Leonard Woolf, *International Government: Two Reports Prepared for the Fabian Research Department* (London: George Allen & Unwin, 1916); H.G. Wells, *The Idea of the League of Nations* (Boston: Atlantic Monthly Press, 1919); and Ramsey Muir, *The Interdependent World and Its Problems* (Port Washington, N.Y.: Kennikat Press, 1971; orig. pub. 1933).

8. John Ruggie, "Continuity and Transformation in the World Polity: Toward a Neorealist Synthesis," *World Politics* 35 (January 1983): 261–286.

9. David Mitrany, *A Working Peace System* (Chicago: Quadrangle, 1966) [originally published in 1943] and *The Functionalist Theory of Politics* (London: Martin Robertson and the London School of Economics and Political Science, 1975).

10. For a good summary of the debate over Mitrany's ideas, see Robert I. McLaren, "Mitranian Functionalism: Possible or Impossible?" *Review of International Studies* 11 (1985): 139–152; and Ernst B. Haas, "The Study of Regional Integration: Reflections on the Joy and Anguish of Pretheorizing," in Leon N. Lindberg and Stuart A. Scheingold eds., *Regional Integration: Theory and Research* (Cambridge: Harvard University Press, 1971).

11. For overviews of regime theory see Oran Young, "International Regimes: Problems of Concept Formation," *World Politics* 32 (April 1980): 331–356; and Stephen Krasner ed., *International Regimes* (Ithaca, N.Y.: Cornell University Press, 1983). For the continuity between older and newer international organizational theory, see: Friedrich Kratochwil and John Gerard

Ruggie, "International Organization: A State of the Art and an Art of the State," *International Organization* 40 no. 4 (Autumn 1986): 753–775.

12. Proposed examples of a complementary regime are several of the League of Nations schemes (intended as a war prevention system for Europe), and the post-World War II efforts to conceptualize an interstate institution to prevent nuclear weapons from becoming instruments of interstate politics.

13. For more extended discussion, see Daniel Deudney, "The Case Against Linking Environmental Degradation and National Security," *Millennium* 19 no. 3 (Winter 1990): 461–476.

14. Robert O. Keohane, *After Hegemony* (Princeton: Princeton University Press, 1984).

15. On the importance of increasing the complexity of world political institutions, see George Modelski, *Principles of World Politics* (New York: Free Press, 1972), chapter 13.

16. The list of those who have attempted to conceptualize a "green sensibility" or an "ecological world-view" is long and would include, among others, Edward Abbey, Gregory Bateson, Morris Berman, Wendell Berry, Fritz Capra, Garrett Hardin, Dolores LaChapelle, Aldo Leopold, James Lovelock, George Perkins Marsh, Carolyn Merchant, Eugene Odum, E.F. Schumacker, Gary Snyder, and Lewis Thomas.

17. See Anthony Smith, *Theories of Nationalism* (New York: Harper, 1971). A useful review of more recent work and a useful typology is provided in Ernst Haas, "What Is Nationalism and Why Should We Study It?" *International Organization* 40 (Summer 1986): 709–744.

18. See also Hans Morgenthau, *Politics among Nations* (New York: Knopf, 1948).

19. Among the useful works on cosmopolitan cultural design are: Andrew Large, *The Artificial Language Movement* (Oxford: Blackwell, 1985); Julian Huxley, "UNESCO: Its Purpose and Philosophy," in F.S.C. Northrup ed., *Ideological Differences and World Order* (New Haven: Yale University Press, 1949); and W. Warren Wager, *The City of Man: Prophecies of a World Civilization in Twentieth-Century Thought* (Boston: Houghton Mifflin, 1963).

20. This point is discussed at length in William McNeill, *Polyethnicity and National Unity in World History* (Toronto: University of Toronto Press, 1986).

21. Although all actual liberal and Marxist regimes have had to cope with nationalism and often have sought to harness it for their ends, nationalism remains in tension with the cosmopolitanism and rationalism of both.

22. Thomas J. Schlereth, *The Cosmopolitan Ideal in Enlightenment Thought* (South Bend: Notre Dame Press, 1977).

23. Ernest Gellner, *Nations and Nationalism* (Ithaca: Cornell University Press, 1983). As Haas points out in "What Is Nationalism," the essential outlines of the theory that nationalism fulfilled an important function in the modernization process were spelled out by Karl Deutsch in the 1950s.

24. Benedict Anderson, *Imagined Communities: Reflections on the Origin and Spread of Nationalism* (London: Verso, 1983).

25. Morris Berman, *The Reenchantment of the World* (Ithaca: Cornell University Press, 1981).

26. Mary Catherine Bateson, "Beyond Sovereignty: An Emerging Global Civilization," in R. B. J. Walker and Saul Mendlovitz eds., *Contending Sovereignties: Redefining Political Community* (Boulder, CO: Reinner, 1990), p. 157. Bateson employs an anthropological concept of "culture" as depending on "community, on the process of continuous and dense communication that sustains shared assumptions" (p. 150).

27. For a good composite picture of this thin nascent "global culture," see "Nascent Norms: Legitimacy, Patriotism, and Sovereignty," chapter 13 of James Rosenau's *Turbulence in World Politics: A Theory of Change and Continuity*, (Princeton: Princeton University Press, 1990). See also Anthony Smith, "Toward a Global Culture?" in Mike Featherstone ed., "Global Culture," special issue of *Theory Culture & Society* 7 no. 2–3 (June 1990): 171–193.

28. Barbara Ward and Rene Dubois, *Only One Earth: The Care and Maintenance of a Small Planet*, (New York: Norton, 1972), p. xviii.

29. Bron Taylor, "The Religion and Politics of Earth First!" *The Ecologist* 21 no. 6 (November/December 1991): 258–266. Among the vast literature, a comprehensive and balanced overview is: David Oates, *Earth Rising: Ecological Belief in an Age of Science* (Corvallis: Oregon State University Press, 1984).

30. For an extensive development of this point, see: Linda H. Graber, *Wilderness as Sacred Space* (Washington, D.C.: Association of American Geographers, 1976).

31. An important and revealing exception is Wilbeur Zelinsky, *Nation and State: The Shifting Symbolic Foundations of American Nationalism*, (Chapel Hill, N.C.: University of North Carolina Press, 1988). In filling this gap, anthropology, sociology, and psychology have much to contribute. This would also seem a natural project for the various techniques of text reading known as "deconstruction."

32. As the identification between the national and the natural approached the complete, so did the claim of the group upon the individual. As this perversion of the natural by the total state reached its climax the ideological ground was laid for the complete reconstitution of humanity via genocidal race-culling and eugenics.

33. The exclusive use of "mother" analogies in eco-philosophy contrasts with the mixture of "father" and "mother" in modern state nationalism.

34. For a comprehensive treatment of this tendency see Roderick Frazier Nash, *The Rights of Nature: A History of Environmental Ethics* (Madison: University of Wisconsin Press, 1989).

35. For an overview see Bill Devall and George Sessions, *Deep Ecology: Living as If Nature Mattered* (Salt Lake City: Peregrine Books, 1985).

36. This would seem to be the implication of Haas' definition of a nation

as "a socially mobilized body of individuals, believing themselves to be united by some set of characteristics that differentiate them (in their own minds) from outsiders. . . . These individuals have a collective consciousness because of their sentiment of difference, or even uniqueness, which is fostered by the group's sharing of core symbols. A nation ceases to exist when, among other things, these symbols are recognized as not truly differentiating the group from outsiders." See Haas, "What Is Nationalism," pp. 726–27.

37. For an overview of the cosmic threats to life on earth see Clark Chapman and David Morrison, *Cosmic Catastrophes* (New York: Plenum, 1989).

38. Michael Howard, "War and the Nation-State," *Daedalus* 108 no. 4 (Fall 1979): 101–110; emphasis in original. Howard further observes: "Inevitably, nationalism was characterized almost everywhere by some degree of militarism. Self-consciousness as a Nation implies, by definition, a sense of differentiation from other communities, and the most memorable incidents in the group's memory usually are of conflict with, and triumph over, other communities." For the importance of sacrifice in nationalism, see Jean Bethke Elshtain, "Sovereignty, Identity, and Sacrifice," *Social Research* 58 no. 3 (Fall 1991).

39. Edmund Burke, *Reflections on the Revolution in France* (Pelican, 1968; first published 1790), pp. 194–95.

40. Annette Baier, "For the Sake of Future Generations," in Tom Regan ed., *Earthbound: New Introductory Essays in Environmental Ethics* (Philadelphia: Temple University Press, 1984); Ernest Partridge ed., *Responsibilities to Future Generations* (Buffalo, N.Y.: 1981); and R. J. Sikora and Brian Berry eds., *Obligations to Future Generations* (Philadelphia: Temple University Press, 1978).

12

Environmental Change and the Deep Structure of World Politics

•

KEN CONCA

We are all prisoners of a rigid conception of what is important and what is not. We anxiously follow what we suppose to be important, while what we suppose to be unimportant wages guerrilla warfare behind our backs, transforming the world without our knowledge and eventually mounting a surprise attack on us.

—Milan Kundera, *The Book of Laughter and Forgetting*

In the opening chapter of this volume, we raised four core questions about global ecological interdependence. The fourth and last of these asked how social responses to global ecological interdependence may be shaping or altering world order. In response to this question, I will argue that the world is already seeing a great deal of environmental conflict and cooperation—far more than typically identified by the literature on those topics. But most such conflict and cooperation is of the implicit variety, in the sense that it is embedded in a social discourse that neither most participants nor most observers tend to interpret in environmental terms. If this is so, we may find that vital clues as to whether and how environmental change and response are altering the world system's deep structure are revealed not in cooperative efforts to save the whales or the ozone layer, nor in conflicts triggered by transborder pollutant flows or the migration of environmental refugees. Rather, the clues may lie in processes that shape or reshape the future in ways that are not at first glance "environmental."

I am grateful to Ronnie Lipschutz, Dan Deudney, and two anonymous reviewers for comments on an earlier version of this chapter.

There are many ways of interpreting the concept of world order.[1] A relatively narrow interpretation would stress the political, economic, and social configurations that currently prevail on a worldwide scale.[2] Questions emerging from such an interpretation might include the following: Is the combination of environmental change and social response helping to produce a nation-state system with one or three dominant poles instead of two? Is it helping nationalist and democratic movements redraw the world's political map? Is it steering global economic growth in new directions for the 1990s?

Although these are important questions, my purpose in raising the world-order implications of ecological interdependence is to probe at a deeper, less transient level of world politics. As Robert Cox points out in a recent essay, this inevitably involves projecting some current sense of order onto the future: "Because we cannot know the future, we cannot give a satisfactory name to future structures. We can only depict them in terms of a negation or potential negation of the dominant tendencies we have known."[3]

Cox goes on to describe three current "dominant tendencies." One is globalization of the world economy, marked by the internationalization of production, a new international division of labor, and associated patterns. A second dominant tendency is represented by the sovereign state system itself. The third dominant tendency cited by Cox is "hegemony"—a term used not in reference to a single, dominant state (as it is commonly employed), but rather to describe "a structure of values and understandings about the nature of order that permeates a whole system of states and non-state entities"(p. 140). For Cox:

> In a hegemonic order these values and understandings are relatively stable and unquestioned. They appear to most actors as the natural order. Such a structure of meanings is underpinned by a structure of power, in which most probably one state is dominant but that state's dominance in itself is not sufficient to create hegemony. Hegemony derives from the ways of doing and thinking of the dominant social strata of the dominant state or states insofar as these ways of doing and thinking have acquired the acquiescence of the dominant social strata of other states. These social practices and the ideologies that explain and legitimize them constitute the foundation of hegemonic order. (p. 140)

If we take these dominant tendencies—economic globalization, state sovereignty, and hegemony—as important features of the deep structure of world politics, (and if we accept Cox's caution that we can imagine their negation but not their replacements), a very different set of questions about world order and ecological interdependence comes into focus. Instead of asking whether environmental change and social response are affecting the number of sovereign states that will be dominant actors, one might ask whether the nature of sovereignty and the underpinnings of the state system are themselves changing. Rather than asking how the type, volume, or location of economic activity may change, we can ask whether capitalism in its current form will continue as the predominant global organizing principle for production and exchange. And rather than asking whether nationalist or democratic sentiment will be strengthened or diluted, we might consider whether the modernist worldview that forms the foundation for such sentiments is itself undergoing fundamental alteration as a result of growing ecological interdependence.[4]

Thus, in inquiring about the implications of ecological interdependence for deep-structural change, I take as my starting point a world that is "ordered" around sovereign states, an increasingly globalized capitalist economy, and the hegemony of modernity.[5] This does not mean that all peoples enjoy a full measure of sovereignty, that all relations of production and exchange are organized in capitalist fashion, or that all individuals, groups, and social institutions are equally infused with modernist "interpretive attitudes and practical dispositions"[6]—such a world would be ordered very differently than the current one (even assuming that all three could be reconciled to coexist simultaneously in universal extent). It does mean, however, that these are predominant modes of social organization, that they are deeply institutionalized, and that they are effectively global in reach. Alternative modes of social organization have always existed and continue to do so—but they stand in fairly stark and, more importantly, isolated opposition to these dominant modes.[7]

Systemic views of world politics posit, either explicitly or by omission, some relationship among sovereign states, global capitalism, and modernity.[8] My own view of their interrelation is an evolutionary one: I assume that, tensions and contradictions notwithstanding, the sovereign state as a social institution has helped more than hindered in the globalization of modernity and capitalism, and vice versa. Charles Tilly's observation that the emerging states of Europe were marked by a growing concentration of both capital and coercive power is generally consistent with this evolutionary view, as is Ernest Gellner's argument that nationalism (a prototypically modern phenomenon, although it is often characterized otherwise) played a crucial role in cementing the social cohesion required for large-scale industrial modernization.[9]

Explicit Environmental Politics and World-order Change

The accelerating pace of environmental destruction, and the recognition that both the destruction and its consequences are somehow global in extent, has provided a stimulus for new theoretical inquiry in the study of world politics. The emergence of environmental issues, problems, and agreements has been an opportunity for those so inclined to reexamine assumptions about interdependence, power, cooperation, and other core concepts that underlie various theoretical traditions.[10] At the same time, we are already beginning to see new conceptual constructs that are explicitly informed by the study of ecological phenomena and environmental politics.[11]

Thus far, most of this work represents an attempt to unearth and identify the components of what I would call an "explicit" environmental politics. In this search, the main features of international environmental politics are typically taken to be the orientation of national interests on environmental issues, the construction of cooperative international environmental institutions ("regimes"), the emergence of a transnational environmental movement, and the growing influence of environmental scientists as actors in world affairs.[12] The existence of several hundred international environmental agreements (see chapter 5) has provided a mother lode of data for this effort. The Montreal protocol on protecting the ozone layer has been perhaps the richest single strike to date, but ongoing efforts to construct international regimes on climate change, biological diversity, and forest protection hold out the promise of rich new strikes in the future.[13] In parallel with these analyses of environmental cooperation, we are also seeing the emergence of efforts to identify the "environmental" roots of various forms of international conflict, and violent conflict in particular.[14]

The main model of systemic change associated with this growing literature is incremental. In this scenario, perceived environmental problems (and perhaps even the threat of environmentally induced interstate conflict) stimulate demand for institutionalized international cooperation. The narrow, functional regimes thus constructed may eventually become a sufficiently dense network, it is argued, to yield broad social and political change.[15]

Seen through the lens of explicit environmental politics, the evidence for deep-structural change appears weak at best, even along this incrementalist path. As Karen Litfin points out in chapter 5, the current flurry of cooperative environmental institution-building has emerged very much within the confines of traditional practices of sovereign-state diplomacy. There is also little evidence that international environmental agreements diverge from such basic premises of late-twentieth-century capitalism as deregulation, the globalization of markets, and the mobility of inputs to the production process. Indeed, the growing popularity of notions such as "marketable pollution permits" and pollution taxes suggests the opposite. Finally, emerging patterns of environmental cooperation suggest an extension of modernity rather than a challenge to it: agreements are informed (or imposed) by what are offered as objective analyses of universal cause-and-effect relations, and by a scientific quest to reduce uncertainty.[16]

The literature on environmental conflict makes an even weaker case for deep-structural change.[17] While environmental destruction and social violence clearly go hand in hand, there is little evidence that this violence differs fundamentally from the extensive violence to which the world of today has shown itself, sadly, to be quite adaptable (see chapter 11). While most of the attention has focused on the likelihood of interstate conflict, the most obvious forms of "environmental" conflict in the world today—local struggles over land, water, forests, and other resources—can be seen as an important part of the process of extending and re-creating predominant structures. Such conflicts tend to place the formidable forces of commerce and the state in opposition to what are very often premodern and/or precapitalist social forms (indigenous peoples, subsistence agriculturalists, and local communities in general).

Thus, rather than deep-structural change, the patterns of explicit environmental politics reflect a marked tendency toward *re-structuring* (in the sense of reproducing), rather than restructuring (in the sense of fundamentally altering), the modern, sovereign, capitalist features of the current world order. International regimes legitimize new regulatory capacities and tasks for states, extending state sovereignty in important new directions. Collective responses consistent with the premises of freely flowing goods and capital are, to say the least, advantaged. And the technocratic, modernist elements within the environmental movement are empowered by their preferential access to the bargaining table.

Our Common Future, the enormously influential report of the World Commission on Environment and Development, provides an example of this process of re-structuring.[18] The report articulates an international division of labor between sovereign states and international organizations that legitimizes and extends the primacy of the state system, albeit while seeking to temper the worst excesses of individual states. The report's tendency to define environmental problems in technical-rational terms, and to call for technological adjustments in response, is thoroughly modern in spirit and substance. The opening paragraph of the report is telling in this regard:

> In the middle of the twentieth century, we saw our planet from space for the first time. Historians may eventually find that this vision had a greater impact on thought than did the Copernican revolution of the 16th century, which upset the human self-image by revealing that the Earth is not the centre of the universe. From space, we see a small and fragile ball dominated not by human activity but by a pattern of clouds, oceans, greenery, and soils. Humanity's inability to fit its doings into that pattern is changing planetary systems, fundamentally. Many such changes are accompanied by life-threatening hazards. This new reality, from which there is no escape, must be recognized—and managed. (p. 1)

And the commission's embrace of "sustainable development" as the key to "a new era of economic growth" represents an attempt to steer the course of capitalist expansion rather than overturn it—particularly when contrasted with earlier "limits-to-growth" formulations of the environmental problematique.[19] *Our Common Future* is a text on sustainable development—but sovereignty, modernity, and capitalism form its subtext, from the report's opening call for a "Copernican" revolution in perspective to its concluding recommendations for institutional adaptation.

There may indeed be current or imminent crises of capitalism, sovereignty, and modernity. Seen through the lens of explicit patterns of environmental cooperation and conflict, however, such crises do not appear to be explicitly "environmental" in character.

Implicit Environmental Politics and World-Order Change

Of course, not all of the processes of environmental change and social response associated with global ecological interdependence fit neatly into the category of "explicit" environmental politics as delineated above. Certainly this is a central message of previous chapters in this volume; we have seen repeatedly in these chapters that individuals and groups use the environmental debate as an arena in which to raise fundamental questions about political and economic structures and processes.

Moreover, this phenomenon of environment-as-arena works in two directions at once: just as "environmental" debates can be a forum for pursuing "nonenvironmental" aims, so too do debates and decisions that are not explicitly "environmental" in character have enormous environmental consequences. The result is a double irony. While on the one hand debates nominally about the environment are often, for most of the participants, really debates about something else, on the other hand debates, conflicts, and struggles not explicitly framed in terms of an environmental discourse may be profoundly "environmental," in the sense of their impact on the planet's life-sustaining capacity. The crucial point is not simply that all policies having environmental consequences (though this is certainly true on some level). Rather, the claim I am making is a stronger one—that those policies and practices that most strongly shape environmental futures lie outside of those arenas that the dominant discourse or customary usage label as "environmental."

Consider the international trade regime defined by the General Agreement on Tariffs and Trade (GATT). By lowering tariffs and stimulating international trade in the postwar era, the GATT has had a profound impact in shaping environmental futures—in ways that dwarf incipient international environmental law and agreements. To take a specific example, the export-promoting trade and economic policies pursued by the Brazilian or Indonesian government have had a vastly greater impact on rates of tropical deforestation in those countries than have explicitly "environmental" trade provisions such as restrictions on exports of round hardwood logs. More broadly, the general inclusion of goods and general exclusion of services from the GATT have helped foster a global economy based on the mobility of raw materials and manufactures rather than of people and services. One result has been to stimulate, as a byproduct, an international flow of hazardous materials and toxic wastes that, again, dwarfs explicit efforts to control or regulate such trade.

The recently proposed North American free-trade zone provides a similar example. The political struggle in the United States over how such an agreement was to be negotiated—culminating in Congressional approval of "fast-track" negotiations that inhibit opponents from intervening as the deal is being struck—did not take on a strongly environmental character.[20] Yet it is clearly environmental policy that is being made when polluting U.S. industries will be able to relocate more easily to Mexico, and when a larger share of goods consumed in the United States will be manufactured in compliance with Mexican (as opposed to U.S.) environmental standards. In terms of cumulative environmental effects, such policy choices far outweigh all but the most salient environmental legislation.[21]

Seen in this light, the environmental-conflict and environmental-cooperation literatures cited above are trapped in a fairly narrow conceptualization of the global environment as an "issue-area," in which definition of issues and issue boundaries are not taken as problematic. International regime theory, which forms the basis for much of the literature on environmental cooperation, betrays a strong tendency to focus only on explicit, formal manifestations of cooperation, and to treat regimes as "benevolent, voluntary, cooperative, and thus legitimate associations."[22] And theories of environmental conflict, although frequently laden with ecological language and metaphors, are heavily tinged by simple, mechanistic models in which cause and effect follow simple and direct, almost Newtonian, patterns. When such lenses are applied, only those social processes broadly and explicitly acknowledged by the dominant discourse as "environmental" will register.

There are at least two reasons for the implicit, embedded character of much of environmental politics, reflecting very different but equally telling forms of power. In many instances, the distribution of decision-making power and institutional control is such that explicit struggles for structural change simply fail. This has been the fate, for example, of recent efforts to "green" the World Bank.[23] The campaign succeeded in forcing the Bank to divert a small percentage of its lending into environmental-protection projects, and to rein in some of its most environmentally destructive lending activities. But the campaign failed in its larger effort to challenge the concept of project-based development lending and the ends toward which such lending is directed. Ann Hawkins's chapter in this volume suggests that a similar struggle may be shaping up in the climate-change arena (and that the results may be similar as well).

A second reason is more closely linked to the idea of a dominant, disciplining discourse (in the Foucauldian sense).[24] By this I refer to the strong tendency for all parties that shape the dominant discourse to argue the terms of the environmental debate within the compartmentalized confines of larger intellectual structures. That this should be the case for the interests of capital and the state is not surprising—but the same has also been true of large segments of the environmental movement, which have come to adopt a discourse stressing planetary imagery over more immediate, local symbols.[25] Ironically, by raising the focus of concern to a global scale, such tactics and tendencies reinforce the idea of the environment as a separate, separable sphere of human activity at the same time that they seek to build a sense of planetary citizenry and global stewardship. There are, of course, alternative discourses—including some that explicitly challenge such intellectual structuring of environmental problems—but they have been marginalized, for the most part, from the emerging processes of international environmental regime construction.[26]

Global Ecological Interdependence as a Catalyst of Systemic Change

To summarize: recognizing what I have termed the "implicit" character of much of international environmental politics broadens greatly the number of avenues by which global ecological interdependence could in principle lead to world-order change. At the same time, however, the question of deep-structural change seems almost tautological in a world where sovereignty, modernity, and capitalism define the social space within which environmental politics is embedded. Anything short of cataclysmic disruption yields, by definition, a strong tendency toward reproduction of prevailing structures as opposed to fundamental change.

To untangle this seeming tautology, two observations are necessary. First, it is important to keep in mind that continuity in world politics comes not from a static structural rigidity, but through a far more complex process in which the actions of individuals and groups reproduce structural configurations. Only the most brittle and static notions of structure overlook this, and do so at their peril.[27] Second, and with this in mind, we need to return to the idea, sketched above, that the current world system is the product of the dynamic interaction of sovereign, modern, and capitalist structures. The notion that these structures form the "pillars" of world order is thus a misleading metaphor, because it suggests that they stand apart and exert an essentially separable influence. If that were the case, it would make sense to ask whether global ecological interdependence were undermining the social structures tied to any one of these ordering principles (be it the state, the market, or modernist discourse). But in historical practice the social structures of state sovereignty, global capitalism, and modernity have been intimately intertwined. The world system thus has a character that we might label interdetermined, in the sense that its main ordering principles have coevolved institutionally; despite considerable tensions among them, they also exhibit strong historical tendencies to reinforce, reproduce, and extend one another.

Consider, for example, the relationship between the state and the market. As forms of social organization both sovereignty and capitalism are dynamic, of course; the modern welfare state differs profoundly from earlier city-states or colonial administrative systems, just as contemporary transnational business differs radically from early forms of merchant capitalism. The key point (and what is missed by so many theorists of both the state and the firm[28]) is that, within this dynamic context, each has evolved under the substantial influence of the other. States have promoted national integration, created and extended markets, and helped spread capitalist relations of production to previously inaccessible areas (both within and beyond national borders)—and states have grown stronger in the process. At the same time, the expansion of capitalism helped generate a surplus that enabled the state to fund its activities and reproduce and strengthen its major institutions—with the further extension of capitalism resulting. The modern corporation is as much a product of this market-creating and stabilizing power of the state as the modern state is the product of an economic surplus.

An analogous pattern of convergence and symbiosis could be sketched between capitalism and modernity, or between modernity and sovereignty. Richard Ashley, for example, argues that the nation-state system is rooted in a "paradigm of sovereignty"—that is, a "specific, historically fabricated, widely circulated, and practically effective interpretation of man as sovereign being"—that is itself grounded in modernist discourse.[29] Ashley further argues that, in acting to frame domestic society in opposition to the dangerous, "primordial zone" of international politics, the practices of statecraft serve to reinforce this modern discourse of sovereignty.[30]

A world system characterized by multiple, dynamic structures suggests an alternate mechanism by which global ecological interdependence may be a force for deep-structural change—even when both explicit and implicit environmental politics tend to reproduce global capitalism, modernity, and state sovereignty as argued above. To see how this can be, consider an analogy suggested by the Latin American debt crisis of the 1980s. As does environmental destruction, foreign debt emerges from and operates within a complex and far-reaching network of social relations. In both cases, this complexity is masked by a high-profile, explicit discourse—a discourse that can distract attention from underlying processes at work and polarize interpretations of continuity and change.

Widespread recognition of the Latin American debt "crisis" was tied to a dramatic, explicit event, Mexico's 1982 suspension of payments, which is often pointed to as the "beginning" of the crisis. In the ensuing decade, there has been a tremendous flurry of explicit activity: debtor-creditor negotiations on rescheduling; IMF pressures for change in national economic policies; attempts among both debtors and creditors to coordinate negotiating strategies; high-profile debt-relief plans announced by U.S. Treasury Secretaries Baker and Brady. Although this flurry of explicit activity has had important consequences for short-term economic performance in Latin America (and for the health of individual banks holding bad loans), it has done little to alter the larger political and economic structures that generated and perpetuate the debt itself.

Nevertheless, political and economic structures in Latin America are changing. The region has seen a wave of transitions from military to civilian rule, a major push for privatization of state-owned industries, a renewed effort to promote regional economic integration, and a growing shift among economic elites toward strategies that stress international competitiveness and technological modernization.[31] As a result, the context of debt in Latin America, and indeed of politics in general, has been transformed. The debt did play a role in these changes—but it did so mainly by accelerating several longer-term social dynamics already at work: exhaustion of the import-substituting-industrialization model of economic development; crisis and fragmentation in the domestic-political coalitions supporting authoritarian rule; changing patterns of foreign investment and world trade.

The debt was important primarily in its effect as a catalyst relative to these underlying social forces and processes. Debt exacerbated some existing tensions, cemented other nascent alliances, and thus helped restructure the world of Latin American politics. Or, more accurately, helped both to restructure and *re-structure* that world, in the sense of altering some structures while reproducing others.

Seen in this light, the central question is not whether explicit patterns of environmental conflict and cooperation will build up to the point of transforming the current structures and institutions of sovereignty, capitalism, or modernity into something else. Nor is it whether implicit environmental politics will somehow produce environmental consequences that lead to more *re-structuring* than restructuring. The question is whether, given the dynamic tensions among capitalism, sovereignty, and modernity as organizing principles for social life, environmental destruction and the social responses it engenders will serve as a catalyst for change. In other words, as the world continues to be both *re-structured* and restructured, is the emergence of global ecological interdependence cementing new alliances or exacerbating emergent tensions among the predominant social structures of world politics?

Capitalism, Sovereignty, and Change

For many students of international environmental politics, seeking answers to this question—indeed, conceiving of the question itself—means moving from the familiar ground of atmospheric treaties and endangered species into unfamiliar new territory. It means, among other things, scrutinizing the bonds between late-twentieth-century global capitalism and the organs of the modern welfare state; probing the links among sovereignty, nationalism, and modern identity; and examining potential tensions between capitalist expansion and modernist notions of the nation and the polity. These are complex, multifaceted, and often ambiguous relationships. In the remainder of this chapter I consider briefly one example of the sort of inquiry which I assume to be called for, focusing on the role of ecological interdependence in shaping the interplay of capitalism and sovereignty as global-scale principles of social organization.

As suggested earlier, while the coexistence of capitalism and sovereignty has not been without its tensions, the relationship has been on balance a mutually productive one. Each has played a crucial—

and on balance, supportive—role in shaping the increasingly global character of the other. This historical symbiosis notwithstanding, there are today at least initial signs of newly emergent tensions. As Susan Strange and others have argued, capitalism in the second half of the twentieth century has outgrown national markets (as it outgrew national resource bases at a much earlier stage). Driven by changes in the global structure of production and finance, both firms and markets are becoming increasingly transnational in extent.[32] As Robert Cox suggests, "In the last half of the twentieth century, the relationship of states to the world political economy has altered. Formerly, the state's role was conceived as bulwark or buffer protecting the domestic economy from harmful exogenous influences. Latterly, the state's role has been understood more as helping to adjust the domestic economy to the perceived exigencies of the world economy."[33]

Such changes may foreshadow the emergence of more-or-less traditional forms of state sovereignty, but at a more aggregate level. European integration is the obvious example, although the possible emergence of parallel trading blocs in East Asia and North America could also be harbingers in this regard.[34] Or it may be that resurgent sovereignty will somehow rein in freewheeling global capitalism and the destabilizing potential it carries. Come what may, reconciling the globalization of production, finance, and markets with the tasks of stabilization and redistribution from which the modern welfare state derives its legitimacy will be, at the very least, a source of significant tensions. The question is whether global ecological interdependence—which as we have defined it embodies a strikingly similar tension between the global and the local—tends to exacerbate or mitigate such tensions.

It seems likely that capitalist expansion will continue to require of the sovereign state system two conditions: (1) at least minimally "open" international access to crucial components of the process of production and exchange (markets, raw materials, capital); and (2) a measure of stability and predictability in international life. In return, sovereign states require from the capitalist system both an adequate surplus and enough social satisfaction to forestall revolutionary social upheavals. Does global ecological interdependence make this partnership easier or more difficult to sustain? Considering (very briefly) each part of the bargain in turn:

Open access. One reason for thinking tensions may be exacerbated more than mitigated is a theme stressed repeatedly in this book: the managerial weakness of the state on environmental matters. Perhaps more so than any other pending challenge, ecological interdependence points up the limits of state capacity. In the short run this may lead to efforts to strengthen state capacity, particularly in those countries where it is currently weakest. The dilemma, however, is not simply that state management may be ineffective, but also that the (relatively few) tools available to the state may run counter to the expansionist logic of capitalism. It may well be that the sort of centralized policy instruments available for economic coordination (tariffs, exchange-rate manipulation, monetary policy, etc.) cannot be fashioned for environmental policy, leaving only the most blunt instruments of the command-and-control variety.

There may thus be a crucial difference between the ability of the sovereign-state system to manage the world economy in ways that support the global extension of capitalism, and its ability to manage the global environment toward similar ends. If so, the alternatives— ceding real decision-making power to local groups, erecting blunt barriers to certain forms of activity—point in directions that are diametrically opposed to current developmental trends in the global economy.

Predictability and stability. Ironically, there may be new strength for the weak emerging to parallel this weakness of the strong. As Karen Litfin discusses in chapter 5, the strongest states in the system may be incapable of enlisting support for, imposing, or coercing a hegemonic program for ecological stability. The South may wield a substantial veto power over actions intended to stabilize the current order.

The contrast with the "New International Economic Order" debate of the 1970s is instructive in this regard. The NIEO was premised on the notion that the South could exert an effective veto over business as usual. This veto power, an important component of which was thought to be control and cartelization of natural resources, proved to be ephemeral. The NIEO failed because its success would have required willful acts by the industrialized countries to change existing tendencies—and simply by not acting, the North was able to thwart the South. In the case of environmental destruction, however, the burden of coordination and compliance has been reversed. Given the scope and accelerating pace of such destruction, the South appears to hold an effective veto over reform-minded, stabilizing programs for international environmental protection—merely by staying on its current course of growth and development.[35]

Adequate surplus and social satisfaction. Collective efforts by states to manage ecological interdependence may create new sources of state revenue, in the broad form of pollution taxes. Such efforts may also create new channels for redistributing income from North to South (presumably an important system-stabilizing mechanism, particularly as the gap between rich and poor grows wider). On the other hand, social stability may be threatened by the downward spiral of environmental destruction, declining resource-based productivity, and falling living standards predicted by some proponents of environmental-conflict theories.

A less obvious but equally critical question is whether the benefits of environmental protection can substitute for the benefits of environmental destruction in building key state-society alliances. Throughout (but not limited to) the industrialized world, environmental destruction has historically been an important component in the process of cementing the bonds between state and national bourgeoisie—whether it be via the granting of property rights in "public" spaces, the guarantee of resource monopolies, the stabilization and subsidization of commodity prices, or even state ownership of extractive industries. Such tools and processes effectively *are* the state in primarily resource-extractive national economies, and they remain important even where they have been partially supplanted by defense spending and other means in more complex, industrialized economies. Whether state-sponsored initiatives to promote environmental protection can play the same role remains to be seen.

One could follow a similar logic in examining the implications of global ecological interdependence for tensions between capitalism and modernity, or between modernity and sovereignty.[36] Obviously, this brief sketch does not even begin to resolve whether any of the potential tensions cited above are sufficient to derail the evolving compact between globalizing capitalism and state sovereignty. But these are the sort of questions that must be asked if we are to gauge the full impact of ecological interdependence on the deep structure of world politics.

Conclusion

It is possible that global environmental change and the social responses it engenders are a force powerful enough to undermine the capitalist, modern, sovereign structure of the current world system. Assuming that this is inevitably the case, however, overlooks a powerful tendency of social structures to reproduce themselves. In a modern, sovereign, capitalist world, the ways we perceive and respond to ecological interdependence are likely to be structured along modern, sovereign, capitalist lines. For this reason, both explicit and implicit responses to global ecological interdependence tend to recreate modernity, sovereignty, and capitalism. This does not mean that global-ecological interdependence has no meaningful world-order implications; I suspect that quite the opposite is true. It does mean, however, that those implications are not likely to be manifest in the form of directly "environmental" challenges to the predominant ordering principles and social structures of the current world system. Rather, change seems more likely to emerge through a process of exacerbation of emerging tensions or the cementing of potential complementarities among those principles.

The globalization of capitalism, sovereignty, and modernity has not been premised on ecological sustainability. Had it been, the struggles of modern social history—driven in part by tensions among these three principles—would no doubt have looked quite different. So too would the sweeping changes that have come about when these three forces have converged (as they did, for example, to facilitate the subjugation of most of the non-European world to European rule). But because none of these ordering principles have until now required ecological balance for their institutional recreation, questions of sustainability tend to be subsumed in the struggle to maximize something else, be it wealth, order, legitimacy, or control. This may not be true indefinitely, depending on the gravity of environmental problems and the speed with which they manifest themselves; but it is not implausible to imagine that it will remain true for some time to come. If so, we need to look for the most important social responses to global ecological interdependence outside the explicitly "environmental" arena, recognizing the latter for the narrowly constructed discourse that it is.

NOTES

1. I do not use the term "world order" to describe, as some do, a program of global reform seeking a worldwide system based on more humanistic values (See for example Richard Falk, *The Promise of World Order: Essays in Normative International Relations* [Philadelphia: Temple University Press, 1987]). Nor do I refer, as others have, to explicit programs such as the balance of power or collective security that seek to impose a measure of stability or predictability in world politics; see Hayward R. Alker, Jr., Thomas J. Bier-

steker, and Takashi Inoguchi, "From Imperial Power Balancing to People's Wars: Searching for Order in the Twentieth Century," in James Der Derian and Michael J. Shapiro eds., *International/Intertextual Relations: Postmodern Readings of World Politics* (Lexington, MA: Lexington Books, 1987). Rather, I take the world system as, by definition, ordered; the question is the scale on which we can identify such patterns of order, and the principles of ordering that we can identify underlying such patterns.

2. This is the sense in which George Bush used the term when speaking of the "New World Order" over which he hoped to preside. It is also the sense in which more idealistic programs have used the term. As Richard Falk characterizes his concerns with world-order studies in the 1960s:

"It does not posit any overall organisational alternative to the state system. In this regard, a central aim is to demilitarise international relations within the existing framework of states and empires, as well as to promote reformist policies of a functional (management of interdependence) and humanistic (human rights, development assistance) character."

As Falk goes on to point out, his work has subsequently grown increasingly sensitive to deeper questions of system structure. See p. 17 of his volume.

3. Robert W. Cox, "Towards a Post-hegemonic Conceptualization of World Order: Reflections on the Relevance of Ibn Khaldun," in James N. Rosenau and Ernst-Otto Czempiel, *Governance Without Government: Order and Change in World Politics* (Cambridge: Cambridge University Press, 1992), p. 139.

4. As Ernst Haas has suggested, "Nationalism is 'modern' because it stresses the individual's search for identity with strangers in an impersonal world, a world no longer animated by corporate identities. . . . The kind of identity we seek to understand is only an issue since the onset of the industrial revolution." See Ernst B. Haas, "What is nationalism and why should we study it?" *International Organization* 40 (Summer 1986): 709–744.

5. I refer to modernity as a specific example of the general phenomenon Cox describes in using the term "hegemony." Modernity invokes the universalist posture of the values and understandings which Cox describes as hegemonic; as Anthony Giddens points out, the global spread of modern orientations and institutions is a logical product of the paradigm of modernity itself. See Giddens, *The Consequences of Modernity* (Stanford, CA: Stanford University Press, 1990), ch. 1. I use the term "modernity" because it stresses not only universalization but also the character of the values and understandings thus universalized.

6. Richard K. Ashley, "Living on Border Lines: Man, Poststructuralism, and War," in Der Derian and Shapiro, *International/Intertextual Relations*; Ashley suggests that "modernity is simply not an overarching, homogeneous order susceptible to analysis in terms of some totalizing narrative: some attempt to uncover some deep and total structure that, as a source, generates the surface experience of 'the modern' in all the far reaches of its influence.

. . . Poststructuralist social theory . . . regards modernity as a historical attitude or set of attitudes—a regime—that since its emergence has struggled against attitudes of countermodernity, most often successfully, but very often not."

7. It thus makes little sense to refer to alternative modes as (for example) precapitalist or postmodern; given the effectively global extent and aggressively expansionist tendencies of capitalism, sovereignty, and modernity, I find it more useful to speak of such alternative forms as anticapitalist or antimodern, as well.

8. Often the systemic view is a hierarchical one; thus realists stress sovereignty, world-systems theorists stress capitalism, and poststructuralists stress modernity. Because they tend to see one of these organizing principles as structuring and sharply delimiting the possible configuration of the others, the opportunities for such theoretical perspectives to engage in sustained debate are limited.

9. See Charles Tilly, "Cities and States in Europe, 1000–1800," *Theory and Society* 18 (September 1989): 563–584; Ernest Gellner, *Nations and Nationalism* (Ithaca: Cornell University Press, 1983). On Gellner, see also the contribution of Daniel Deudney to this volume.

10. This reexamination is for the most part a liberal research program; as discussed in chapter 1 of this volume, both conservative ("realist") and radical ("Marxist") perspectives tend to see environmental politics and institutions as a reflection of more fundamental interests and structures in world politics.

11. One example of new conceptual constructs is provided by the work of Peter Haas and others on epistemic communities; see Peter M. Haas, "Do Regimes Matter? Epistemic Communities and Mediterranean Pollution Control" *International Organization* 43 no. 3 (Summer 1989): 395–97; Peter M. Haas, *Saving the Mediterranean: The Politics of International Environmental Cooperation* (New York: Columbia University Press, 1990). A second example is provided by James Rosenau's notion of turbulence, one of the driving forces of which is a list of "interdependence" issues that prominently includes transborder environmental problems. Theories of environmental conflict are also beginning to emerge, although for the most part based on traditional ideas about conflict; see Thomas Homer-Dixon, "On the Threshold: Environmental Changes as Causes of Acute Conflict," *International Security* 16 no. 2 (Fall 1991): 76–116.

12. See for example John E. Carroll ed., *International Environmental Diplomacy: The Management and Resolution of Transfrontier Environmental Problems* (Cambridge: Cambridge University Press, 1988); Marvin Soroos, *Beyond Sovereignty: The Challenge of Global Policy* (University of South Carolina Press, 1986); Richard E. Benedick, *Ozone Diplomacy: New Directions in Safeguarding the Planet* (Cambridge: Harvard University Press, 1991); Haas, *Saving the Mediterranean.*

13. Such new discoveries do not depend on the successful construction of new regimes; regime-building efforts provide the stuff of case studies whether they succeed or fail. Thus the largely failed efforts of the Earth Summit provide as much new data in this regard as did the relatively successful effort to build a regime on ozone depletion.

14. See, for example, Homer-Dixon, "On the Threshold"; Reidulf K. Molvær, "Environmentally Induced Conflicts? A Discussion Based on Studies from the Horn of Africa," *Bulletin of Peace Proposals* 22 (1991): 175–188; Jessica Tuchman Mathews, "Redefining Security," *Foreign Affairs* 68 (1989): 162–177; Michael Renner, *National Security: The Economic and Environmental Dimensions*, Worldwatch Paper 89, Worldwatch Institute, Washington, D.C., May 1989; Arthur Westing ed., *Global Resources and Environmental Conflict: Environmental Factors in Strategic Policy and Action* (Oxford: Oxford University Press, 1986); Norman Myers, *Not Far Afield: U.S. Interests and the Global Environment* (Washington, D.C.: World Resources Institute, 1987). See also the proceedings of the Conference on Environmental Stress and Security, Royal Swedish Academy of Sciences, Stockholm, December, 1988. For a critique of this literature, see Daniel Deudney, "The Case Against Linking Environmental Degradation and National Security," *Millennium: Journal of International Studies* 19 (Winter 1990): 461–476.

15. See chapter 11 of this volume, by Daniel Deudney. As Deudney points out, this is essentially an extension of the so-called "functionalist" arguments of the early post-World-War II era, which held that interstate cooperation in relatively mundane areas could expand to cover ever-more conflictual and controversial issues in international politics.

16. Ironically, this is true even though the challenges raised by environmentalists are often framed in terms that reject modern notions of progress and of the human-nature relationship.

17. One reason for this is the difficulty in isolating "environmental" factors from the stream of social phenomena that "cause" conflict. As Reidulf Molvær suggests, "Social facts, such as conflict, cannot be explained by natural facts, such as the environment, but only by other social facts" (Molvær, "Environmentally Induced Conflicts?" p. 175). The growing literature on environmental conflict suggests a number of hypothetical causal pathways— from simple mechanistic models of states fighting for their share of declining resource goods and environmental services, to models in which environmental stresses trigger already potentially explosive situations, to models invoking a more gradual "spiral of decay" among environmental degradation, declines in resource-based productivity, and falling living standards.

18. World Commission on Environment and Development, *Our Common Future* (New York: Oxford University Press, 1987).. See in particular the chapter on institutional and legal change; ibid., pp. 308–347.

19. See Frederick H. Buttel, Ann P. Hawkins, and Alison G. Power,

"From Limits to Growth to Global Change," *Global Environmental Change* 1 (1990): 57–66.

20. The so-called "fast-track" approach, approved by the Congress in 1991, gave the executive branch broad authority to negotiate the provisions of a free-trade agreement without substantial public notice, hearings, and comment. Environmentalists, labor activists, and others raised fears that, with limits on the opportunities of opponents to intervene, the result would be a final "take-it-or-leave-it" agreement, with little or no possibility of amendment or revision.

21. Environmentalists have recognized this, of course, joining with labor unions and other groups in a coalition that sought (unsuccessfully) to derail the Bush Administration's fast-track approach. That they failed in their attempt to define the discourse surrounding the agreement in environmental terms illustrates that the distinction between implicit and explicit environmental politics is largely defined by such discourse struggles.

22. The quote is from James Keeley, "Toward a Foucauldian Analysis of International Regimes," *International Organization* 44 (Winter 1990): 83–105, p. 84. See also Susan Strange, "Cave! hic dragones: a critique of regime analysis," in Stephen D. Krasner ed., *International Regimes* (Ithaca, NY: Cornell University Press, 1983). On regime theory and international environmental cooperation, see the contribution of Karen Litfin to this volume.

23. On environmental policies of the World Bank, see P. Aufderheide and B. Rich, "Environmental Reform and the Multilateral Banks," *World Policy Journal* 5 (1988): 301–321; Bruce Rich, "The Emperor's New Clothes: The World Bank and Environmental Reform," *World Policy Journal* 7 (Spring 1990): 305–329.

24. See Keeley, "Toward a Foucauldian Analysis."

25. On changing global imagery over time within the environmental movement, see Buttel, et al. "From Limits to Growth."

26. For a discussion and illustrative citations of the range of such perspectives, see the contribution of Steve Breyman to this volume.

27. Unfortunately, many of these particularly brittle conceptions of structure have been brought to bear explicitly on questions of world order and deep structure in the international system. For a critique of such notions of structure in international relations theory, see Alexander Wendt, "The Agent-Structure Problem in International Relations Theory," *International Organization* 41 (1987): 335–370; John Gerard Ruggie, "International Structure and International Transformation: Space, Time, and Method," in Ernst-Otto Czempiel and James N. Rosenau, *Global Changes and Theoretical Challenges: Approaches to World Politics for the 1990s* (Lexington, MA: Lexington Books, 1989).

28. This point is made with regard to theories of firm behavior in Susan Strange, "Big Business and the State," *Millennium Journal of International Studies* 20 (1991): 245–50.

KEN CONCA

29. Ashley, "Living on Border Lines," p. 269.

30. Ibid., pp. 303–4.

31. See for example Jorge G. Castañeda, "Salinas's International Relations Gamble," *Journal of International Affairs* 43 (1989–90): 407–422; Ben Ross Schneider, "Brazil Under Collor: Anatomy of a Crisis," *World Policy Journal* 8 (Spring 1991): 321–347.

32. Strange, "Big Business." Strange sees accelerating technological innovation as the principal change in the productive structure of capitalism, and the global integration of capital markets as the principal change in the financial structure.

33. Cox, "Towards a Post-hegemonic Conceptualization of World Order," p. 143.

34. Both in Europe and in East Asia, intra-regional trade has grown more rapidly than trade with the rest of the world in recent years; a similar process may be unleashed by bringing Mexico into the proposed North American free-trade zone. See John Zysman et. al., *The Highest Stakes* (New York: Oxford University Press, 1992).

35. Energy-consumption trends illustrate this point in stark fashion. John Holdren presents an "optimistic" scenario for world energy use, based on "relatively low population growth, progress in energy efficiency, and closing the gap between rich and poor" ("Energy in transition," in *Energy for Planet Earth*, special issue of *Scientific American*, September 1990, p. 162). In this scenario, total energy consumption in the industrialized countries declines from 9.0 terawatts in 1990 to 5.3 terawatts in 2025, while energy use in less-developed countries increases more than threefold, from 4.5 terawatts in 1990 to 15.0 terawatts in 2025.

36. The argument of Daniel Deudney in the previous chapter, for example, suggests at least the possibility that environmental protection could form the "moral glue" for a new phase of state institution-building.

13

The Implications of Global Ecological Interdependence

•

RONNIE D. LIPSCHUTZ
AND KEN CONCA

If Change Is the Answer, What Was the Question?

Global ecological interdependence is more than just a physical or social phenomenon; it is an intellectual one as well. It has changed—and continues to change—how we look at the world, and it is also changing how we interact with one another. Indeed, the very act of naming a phenomenon can lead to an explosion of popular and academic curiosity about it that was not previously in evidence. It can also lead to conflict, as others dispute not only the name itself, but also the process: the evidence offered in support of a particular name, the right of different individuals and groups to define or impose a name, and the real consequences of that naming.

This is not to suggest that global ecological interdependence is imagined, but it is to say that the ways it is understood and acted on are constructed. And, because it is being constructed before our very eyes—rather than coming down to us as tradition or hagiography—global ecological interdependence is the subject of active contestation. Because the resulting construction gives form to people's lives, we cannot separate the very real causes and consequences of environmental change from this process of naming and contestation. To understand the particular patterns of conflict and cooperation that may emerge from such change, we must understand global ecological interdependence not simply in political terms, but also in its cultural and social dimensions.

Nowhere is this link clearer than in the mainstream discourse on global environmental politics and the state. Suppositions about responses to global environmental problems are usually framed in terms of the nation-state system; that system is seen as both the locus of causes and consequences and as the level at which appropriate policy responses must take place. Given the anarchy assumed to prevail in the system as a whole, interstate cooperation around shared interests is said to be essential if these "inherently transnational" problems are to be addressed effectively. But framing the phenomenon in this way may limit the universe of possible policy responses (if, for example, global-scale solutions are presented as the only effective response). And it also serves to delegitimize what could well be effective alternatives, claiming them not to have sufficient "reach" or to lack authority. Our purpose in this concluding chapter is not to offer a specific agenda of alternative responses, but simply to point out some of the ways we find this statist logic wanting.

In chapter 1 we posed four central questions. How we express these questions has changed since this project began in 1989, reflecting a process of convergence among the authors participating in the workshops and represented in this volume. As indicated in chapter 1, we found that our thinking converged around the multiple social levels of environmental cooperation and conflict, and the multiple social meanings of the global environment itself. This common ground proved to be the basis for two broadly stated conclusions. We found ourselves in general agreement that the social and political complexity inherent in these multiple levels and meanings was not reflected in the rational-technical paradigm that is coming to predominate in the discourse on global environmental politics—rendering that discourse at best ineffective and at worst an exercise in social control. We also concluded that the dominant discourse overlooked some emerging patterns of social interaction that may contain hopeful alternatives for "managing" our environmental futures, albeit in forms very different from those which the dominant discourse offers. With the benefit of the insights contained in preceding chapters, we now develop and extend these conclusions by returning to the questions raised in chapter 1.

From Global Environmental Change to Global
Ecological Interdependence

Our first question asked how global environmental change contributes to global ecological interdependence. On one level, this means asking whether the former contributes to the tighter systemic binding and the decay of traditional authority structures that we take to define the latter. We see little in the preceding chapters to suggest that this is not the case, and much to suggest that it is. And yet our collective sense of what is driving this binding and fragmentation differs somewhat from the usual description of these processes. While the tighter binding is usually taken as an inevitable consequence of the "inherently transnational" character of environmental degradation, we would point to a far more complex and active social process: while we see existing social institutions magnifying and globalizing what are often local causes and effects, we also see groups at all levels of social aggregation involved in active processes of constructing some new sense of the global.

The other side of the equation—the decay of authority structures— is generally expressed in terms of a functionalist logic. Traditional institutions, including the state, are said to lose authority when they fail to craft effective solutions to the problems inherent in tighter interdependence. An implicit corollary is that successful responses reinforce traditional authority. We have indeed seen in this volume examples of success reinforcing, and failure undermining, traditional institutions. But again, we would stress a far more complex social mechanism by which either the decay or the reinforcement of traditional authority structures may occur. We have also seen that failure, and resulting pressures on the state from within and without to "do something," can be an opening for the state to pursue its traditional agenda along new avenues. And as described by Karen Litfin, success is sometimes subversive; the "ordinary international practices" that have prevailed thus far in the construction of international environmental regimes have also meant an encroachment on national sovereignty and the empowerment of new, non-state actors. Perhaps most important of all, the erosion of authority may come not simply from a failure of traditional institutions to "provide the goods," but also from a more active process in which individuals and groups use growing awareness of ecological interdependence to redefine how they relate to those institutions.

Thus, probing the link between environmental change and ecological interdependence also means understanding how a prevailing sense of the former is giving rise to the latter. As largely untapped territory, the concept of "global environmental change" is itself something of a commons for disciplinary analysis. Until very recently, there was no crowding or scarcity evident in terms of investigations of the subject. Now there is, as the practitioners of politics, economics, law, anthropology, public policy, sociology, and international relations, among others, all struggle for a piece of the action, trying to define the issues in terms of their proprietary language and tools. And yet, the complexity of the phenomenon repeatedly defies this tendency toward analytical fragmentation, as the poor fit between disciplinary borders and environmental change as a subject of inquiry becomes clearer.

This resistance to intellectual fragmentation holds both great promise and great danger. The promise lies in the possibility of building conceptual and language bridges among the isolated frames of reference that constitute academic disciplines (much as we have sought to do with this book). The danger is that in doing so a single dominant discourse on the global environment will emerge to such an extent that it crowds out other ways of knowing and expressing. Something akin to the latter can be seen in the way that, as scientists, politicians, and the public became aware of how human activities increasingly affect nature on a global scale, the idea of "global environmental change" (or, more commonly, "global change") has come to assume pride of place in the environmental policy lexicon over the past several years. Within this dominant paradigm, the study of economic, political, and cultural causes and consequences is given such unwieldy names as "human dimensions of global environmental change"—a rubric that hints at, without fully crediting, the causal role of social institutions in environmental degradation.[1]

Thus defined, the two most visible manifestations of global environmental change are the destruction of the ozone layer (particularly the seasonal erosion in the Antarctic region and, more recently, in the planet's northern reaches), and the possibility of global warming as human activities deposit "greenhouse gases" into the atmosphere. There are also, however, a host of geographically local phenomena that are being conceptualized as "global" because they are linked, both in terms of causes and consequences, to social systems of global extent. In this category we find such issues as deforestation and the loss of species diversity—"local" phenomena that are being replicated in many locations around the planet, and that are also being conceptualized in global terms, as part of "global change."

This generalized naming of phenomena has a twofold effect: it blurs potential conceptual distinctions that could be sharpened if other criteria were applied, while at the same time erecting other conceptual barriers (as does any system of classification). As we suggested in chapter 1, phenomena such as climate change that are depicted as "global"—and thus emphasized—are, in fact, the sum of geographically variable environmental effects that result from geographically dispersed activities. By the same token, phenomena such as soil erosion and land degradation that are depicted as "local"— and thus relegated to a lesser sense of urgency—are in fact linked by economic, political, and social institutions of much broader, and often global, extent.

Thus we find the distinction between "global environmental change" and "global ecological interdependence" to be a crucial one. The latter represents the totality of interconnections between the social and the physical which, taken together, constitute a global "ecosystem." [2] Thinking in terms of global ecological interdependence thus helps us, on the one hand, to disaggregate generalized phenomena into their local manifestations and, on the other hand, to see how they fit into the larger scheme of things. The important point, however, is that this is not simply an analytical tool; it is also a reflection of the various ways that individuals and social groups are defining relationships between local ecosystems and the idea of a generalized, global one.

Global environmental change is thus a "cause" of global ecological interdependence, in the sense that it produces the countervailing tendencies of binding and fragmentation. But it is also a "cause" in the sense that global ecological interdependence is an increasingly important symbol through which individuals and social groups are coming to make sense of processes of environmental change. This is a key point, for we will argue below that it is here, at the localized level of individuals and groups, that one must look to understand the full extent of the countervailing tendencies toward centralization and fragmentation that make up the core of global ecological interdependence.

Managing Global Ecological Interdependence

What global ecological interdependence underscores is not so much the "global nature" or "transnational character" of environmental problems—which is mostly a matter of border definition—but rather, as Luther Gerlach observes, the very messiness of human social systems and their politics. Given this messiness, what are the prospects for collectively managing environmental change and ecological interdependence (our second question)? Not only are the techniques for such management untested and controversial; so too is the locus of management. The overwhelming presumption of academics and policymakers has been to think in terms of models of "collective management" articulated through some sort of regime-based system.[3] Such a model does not necessarily posit a centralized management authority (the latter being decidedly out of fashion). It does presume, however, that the locus of policy-making lies at the nation-state level, with individual governments acceding to international agreements that bind them to collective action in pursuit of specified goals.

Here we simply reiterate the skepticism expressed throughout this volume. As many observers have pointed out, one problem with this approach lies in what are often referred to as "barriers to collective action." Absent a central coordinating authority, a single predominant actor (or "hegemon"), or effective small-group (or "k-group") coordination, the barriers of mistrust, defection, free-riding, and lack of information make explicit cooperative agreements difficult to attain and sustain in world politics.[4] As Karen Litfin points out, the possibility of such hegemonic direction or the emergence of a central coordinating authority seem remote with respect to environmental matters. And the likelihood of effective multilateral coordination seems small as well, because of major uncertainties about the costs and benefits of environmental protection and management.

To these generalized barriers and conditions we would add a number of factors that stem from the nature of the state itself: the fundamental incapacity of governments to control the destructive processes involved, the scarcity of effective policy levers, and the importance of certain forms of resource extraction (and hence environmental destruction) for key state-society alliances. As the chapters in section 1 indicated, weak states lack capability and authority; stronger states are often forced to use coercive and other powers that ultimately reflect an underlying weakness; and at all levels of state capacity, the task of managing ecosystems sustainably often runs counter to traditional state interests and alliances. And, as Jesse Ribot and Nancy Peluso make clear in their chapters, under such circumstances policies intended to promote environmental protection and regulation may be captured to serve more fundamental purposes of powerful social groups or the state itself. Often, such policies exacerbate the problem they were meant to address; Ribot's discussion of forest regulations in Senegal clearly illustrates this, and Peluso's case study suggests that coerced conservation might well lead to none at all.

But what of the relatively strong (in the sense of capable) states of the industrialized world? Do they possess the competence, capabilities, and inclination to manage the effects of global environmental change and global ecological interdependence? Can the traditional techniques and practices of statecraft be brought to bear effectively, within the traditional social spaces where these states have operated? Perhaps they can. The dominant states in the current system have one advantage: most of the networks of social processes causing widespread environmental change either originate in, or make multiple passes through, the economic and political systems of the industrialized countries. And while the challenge of learning to be an effective environmental manager is an enormous one, it is perhaps not unprecedented. Throughout the evolution of the modern state system we have seen states learn to make war, colonize remote territories, manage increasingly complex national economies, and even manage (after a fashion) their economic interdependence.[5]

Thus governments in the developed countries may be able to learn how to limit greenhouse gas emissions, and how to deploy a wide range of fiscal, regulatory, and other instruments to reduce the environmental impact of a whole host of human activities. But the marginal costs of doing so are likely to become quite large, and the distribution of the social burden will vary greatly depending on the specific policies applied.[6] For this reason, states face not simply their own incapacity and barriers to collective action, but also the various forms of contestation, at all social levels, highlighted throughout this book. As Luther Gerlach indicates in chapter 8: "Resource management is a euphemism for managing how people use resources, which means managing people. Managing how people use resources in ways that promote economic opportunities while protecting or enhancing local control, cultural and ethnic identity, personal liberty, and all the other manifestations of civil and human rights, is complex management indeed."

Whether the traditional barriers to collective action, the inability and unwillingness of individual states to be effective environmental managers, or the intensely contested nature of global solutions will prove to be the largest obstacle to effective management of global ecological interdependence remains unclear. But combining these factors, we conclude that the collective-management paradigm in its technical-rational form is likely to be exceedingly difficult to implement. It is true that, as Karen Litfin indicates, the state system has thus far shown a certain adaptability in the construction of some fairly narrow and limited environmental regimes. In particular, the regime designed to manage ozone depletion seems well on its way to functioning effectively, and is often cited as a model for other agreements. But an agreement to phase out a single family of chemicals, for which substitutes are increasingly available, is a weak test at best. Most of the phenomena that make up the global-change litany are far more complex in terms of sources, effects, and linkages to social systems of global extent.

Solutions that seek (as most do) to impose the cost of adjustment on the weak and the poor face the barriers of state incapacity in the Third World directly. They also face the prospect, described by Ann Hawkins, of widespread North-South contestation—in an arena where the opposition of the weak may hold a veto over the plans of the strong. Responses imposing the brunt of adjustment costs on the industrialized world have the advantage of facing a less formidable level of state incapacity. And while they too are likely to be intensely contested, they may have available more effective channels for the sort of "working out" process described by Luther Gerlach. But the turn to such solutions, and their effective implementation, would almost certainly mean that the dominant states in the international system participate in world politics in new ways. With each of the major "learning episodes" in the history of the modern state system, the character of the state and the ways in which it participated in world politics changed. There is no reason to think that ecological interdependence does not present a similar challenge. This leads to our third question, that of changing processes in world politics, which we take up below.

A prior question remains, however: can we conceive of the local management of global ecological interdependence? The very content of the term suggests that this is not possible; yet what we see in a number of the chapters in this volume is an emerging paradigm or construction of the phenomenon that originates at the local level. Ann Hawkins's discussion of contesting paradigms only begins to unwrap the growing complexity of political and social relations surrounding global ecological interdependence. Hawkins illustrates how the framing of a question—in her case, global climate change—can influence management strategies and techniques and, in the process, generate contestation and conflict. The "global management paradigm," as she calls it, makes assumptions not only about the specific nature of the global warming problem, but also about who possesses the requisite knowledge needed to deal with it. This, however, is very dependent on the framing of the question as a global one, rather than as the aggregation of a myriad of localized human activities. Addressing an issue such as global warming at the international level does reduce, at least in theory, the traditional barriers to cooperation. But, as we noted above, in doing so it places the burden of responsibility on nation-states and their governments, who may or may not possess the requisite competence or inclination to manage the system sustainably.

Both Jim Rosenau and Steve Breyman address the competence question, taking a perspective that highlights the possibilities of local management. Rosenau suggests that:

> with their analytic skills enlarged and their orientations toward authority more self-conscious, today's persons-in-the-street are no longer as uninvolved, ignorant, and manipulable with respect to world affairs as were their forebears. Most important for present purposes, the refined skills of citizens have diminished their habitual patterns of compliance and heightened their sensitivities to the diverse aggregative processes whereby micro actions get converted into macro outcomes.

Breyman focuses on the role of knowledge as motivation for environmentally oriented social movements and organizations. His argument, which follows from Rosenau's point, is that this knowledge has both symbolic power and practical uses. More to the point, locally oriented movements and organizations may have access to geographically specific knowledge and techniques that, although not denied to governments, require such detailed management and co-ordination as to defy the best efforts of bureaucrats.

Ronnie Lipschutz and Judith Mayer suggest a second function for groups oriented toward local management of resources: the reconstruction or revision of what they call "resource management regimes." By calling attention to, on the one hand, the local and regional importance of the conservation of various resources and, on the other hand, the linkages among dispersed resources, mediated via global systems, these movements and organizations create the basis for changes in the constitutive rules underlying those regimes. More than that, through their public and highly visible activities, these groups make nonparticipants collectively aware of where they are located within the global social ecosystem and create possibilities for political and economic change that are more protective of dwindling resources, imperiled ecosystems, or threatened species.

What is not yet evident in all of this is what could be called the "coordination function." There are many groups operating in many different venues at many different scales. No one, to our knowledge, has even made an effort to try to map out what is an increasingly dense network of knowledge and skill flows related to the environment.[7] This network serves to transmit not only data, in a traditional sense, but also modes of social organization—ways of doing things—that can be replicated in many places. In this process, cultural values are not homogenized—to do so would be to deny the relevance of locale—but successful modes of social organization do begin to appear and recur in culturally diverse places.

Global Environmental Change and the Processes of World Politics

Our skepticism regarding the technical-rational management paradigm leads us to our third question, whence we asked whether and how the processes of world politics are being altered by global ecological interdependence. We speculated that important new actors might be emerging, traditional actors altering how they participate in world politics, and patterns of conflict and cooperation changing as a result. Neither the idea that new actors (notably social movements) are emerging, nor the idea that traditional actors (notably states) face a new set of challenges, originates with us.[8] Typically, the two ideas are taken to be directly linked: the failure of traditional institutions to solve emerging problems or distribute resources satisfactorily is seen as the stimulus for new forms of social organization.

Certainly the emergence of environmental movements, and the global-scale interconnections being built among such movements, are intimately connected to the state system's inability to respond. What we would stress, however, is that the nature of the challenge posed is not simply distributive, but also constitutive. To see why this is so, we need to examine the idea raised earlier, that centralization and fragmentation are not simply global-systemic phenomena but also local, even personal, ones. Although individuals often think of themselves as members of social collectivities on a broad scale—the nation-state, for example—their experience of and participation in collectivities takes place largely at the micro-level—family, neighborhood, community, tribe or ethnic group, social movement or organization—on a scale where identity can be seen most clearly.[9]

Even as these micro-level identities (both individual and collective) stand in some relationship to the larger structures of social life, they remain differentiated from those larger structures and in constant tension with them. The reason for this is that groups tend to organize on the basis of defined or constructed differences from other groups. In other words, the constitutive rules for membership differ across groups. In many instances, this does not matter: stamp-collecting clubs differ from bird-watching clubs, but there are no points of overlap or contestation between them, and most individuals can easily meet the constitutive requirements of each. The same is not true, however, for groups constituted around ethnic characteristics, the occupation of particular bits of land, or differing conceptions of how resources should be used or managed. In such cases, the constitutive basis of competing groups is fundamentally different, intergroup "conflicts of interest" are endemic, and common bases for cooperation may be difficult to find.

It is at this level, then, that we can begin to see how the tensions between micro- and macro-level structures emerge, and why tendencies toward centralization and fragmentation appear simultaneously. Smaller collectivities, although nested within larger ones, come to see themselves as the guardians of particular truths and the holders of specialized knowledge denied to others. Larger collectivities see themselves as the guardians of more generalized truths and the holders of more generalized knowledge that, in the interest of the larger collectivity, must override or subsume the interests of the smaller ones.

For example, the state and federal governments are the presumptive guardians of certain property rights and economic arrangements within the State of California. Within this region there exist particular collectivities ("loggers" and "lumber companies") that avail themselves of what is a well-established pattern of property rights and relations of production. But these collectivities now find themselves in conflict with movements and organizations ("environmentalists") that claim to possess specialized knowledge regarding the consequences of deforestation and truths describing the global effects of existing practices. As Lipschutz and Mayer discuss in chapter 10, this conflict takes place over basic constitutive rules, rather than simply over the division of the resource itself.

Fragmentation is evident here because the specialized knowledge that is claimed has only local applicability. Environmentalists try to make their claims to knowledge and truth universal, but ecosystems—natural and social—differ from one place to the next. Centralization is also evident; government, on behalf of loggers and companies, seeks to reassert its more generalized truths and knowledge as a means of protecting and maintaining existing relations of production. But this, too, is problematic, because there is no way that such generalized knowledge can be uniformly applied to local problems and issues.[10]

Do such constitutive challenges, grounded as they are in the tension between centralization and fragmentation, mean the way in which the state participates in world politics is inevitably changing? Not necessarily. It is true that, as Steve Breyman points out, movements may "engage" the state by seeking to bypass it or to challenge it directly. But they may also (or instead) act in ways that support the state and prop up its authority—pressuring the state for incremental reforms, or even carrying out local management functions that suit the interests of the state. Much will depend on whether and how new and traditional actors come to be joined, on a broader scale, in the sort of "working out" process that Luther Gerlach describes in the case of the Minnesota drought debates. Perhaps the emerging contestation described by Ann Hawkins in the climate-change debate represents the first halting steps in such a process.

Global Ecological Interdependence and World Order

Whether such processes of "working out" are occurring, will occur, or even can occur on a global scale remains unclear, of course. On the one hand, we have seen repeatedly in this book that the global environment serves as an arena into which actors can and do bring fundamental, preexisting struggles; thus the principal effect of global ecological interdependence could be to re-create and reinforce the current divisions and structures that obtain in world politics. On the other hand, to the extent that raising such issues presents a constitutive (and not merely distributive) challenge, the effect on the current state system could ultimately be profoundly subversive. Thus we see yet another way that the global environment represents contested ground; in this case, what is contested are the fundamental organizing principles that constitute the "deep structure" of world politics. This was the focus of our fourth question, in which we asked how social responses to global ecological interdependence are shaping or altering world order.

As we have seen, even the rational-technical paradigm for managing ecological interdependence hinges on at least a limited reconfiguration of the international system as it exists today, in the form of states ceding a measure of sovereignty to new international regimes for environmental protection. That reconfiguration is generally assumed to be the work of the important states that give the system its character; hence the focus on powerful states as the engineers of collective management. Even in these limited terms, we can see global ecological interdependence having effects that may undermine traditional presumptions of a world in which international anarchy and national sovereignty combine in the form of clearly differentiated nation-states. As suggested above, pursuit of common interests (including the common interest of protecting the residue of sovereignty) binds states together more strongly; this in turn means that as sovereignty is progressively subsumed to collective management, the differentiation among states that underpins both sovereignty and anarchy becomes less strongly pronounced. Yet, as we have suggested, this discovery of shared interests does not do away with the politics of identity; indeed, it intensifies it. Thus the tensions between centralization and decentralization noted by several authors in this volume can be seen at work even in the limited context of a business-as-usual approach to international environmental politics. If anarchy and sovereignty are not eliminated, neither are they simply reproduced.

Given our skepticism that this model for international responses to environmental challenges can function effectively (even assuming it can be imposed), we take ecological interdependence seriously as an agent for even more profound deep-structural change. But we see no simple correlation in the chapters of this book between the success or failure of "management" initiatives and the prospects for such change. As we suggested earlier, successful adjustment may both stabilize the system and plant the institutional seeds of change;

failure to respond effectively may provoke both forces for deep structural change and new channels along which traditional forms of
power may be exercised, in ways that reproduce current structures.

Dan Deudney and Ken Conca present two very different approaches to this question, each pursuing the world-order consequences of a plausible (though by no means determined) scenario.
Deudney sees two plausible consequences of a broadly successful
international response to environmental destruction. The first is the
sort of functionalist institutional binding described earlier, a result of
ever-more-comprehensive international environmental regimes; the
second is the possible emergence of an overarching ethic or set of
norms (which he labels "green culture"). Deudney sees in these
trends the possibility of "world domestic politics"—the emergence
on a global scale of the sort of shared ethos and political community
that currently define domestic politics by their presence and international politics by their absence. The process he describes reflects an
environmentally stimulated social reconstruction of global politics
away from anarchy.

Ken Conca follows a very different initial premise: that the bulk of
substantial international environmental "policy" will remain embedded, as it is today, in institutions not typically thought of as "environmental." Such institutions tend to reflect the organizing principles of sovereignty, capitalism, and modernity that define the current
world order; for this reason, so, too, do the most consequential
international-scale environmental policy initiatives (whether they are
recognized as "environmental" in content or not). Conca argues that,
under such circumstances, the crucial question is not whether the
dynamic of environmental destruction and social response undermines modernity, capitalism, or sovereignty directly but, rather,
whether that dynamic exacerbates or mitigates the larger tensions
that are currently being played out between and among these organizing principles themselves.

Because Deudney's scenario is one of transformation and Conca's
one of reproduction, they may appear to stand as mutually exclusive
possibilities for the future (though by no means the only two such
possibilities). And yet the very "embeddedness" Conca describes
could be a powerful spur, ultimately, to the same sort of overarching
ethos Deudney examines, providing ground for the sort of oppositional character and "sense of other" on which identity and mobilization may hinge. And Deudney's image of the extension of international regimes—from state-supporting "supplementary" regimes to

state-enabling "complementary" ones—could be a specific pathway to Conca's image of structural reproduction of sovereign, capitalist modernity in world politics. As Deudney suggests, the creation of a cluster of complementary regimes, "like many reforms that stop short of revolution, has a paradoxically conservative effect. Reform saves the system from its own worst tendencies, permitting its continued, if circumscribed, existence."

Finally, while the two differ somewhat in their notion of the social structures that comprise world order (Deudney stressing sovereignty and nationalism, Conca modernity and capitalism), they reflect similar processes in which structures are not merely given, but actively reproduced or transformed.

Conclusion

A final question lies implicit in all the others: is ecological interdependence part of something bigger, some larger process of social transformation in the world system? As Ken Conca points out in chapter 12, we are hindered when looking for the implications of the patterns and processes we describe by the fact that the international system is itself a moving target. With the end of the Cold War, the precise configuration of the world system—and whether it is in transition from one "metastable" state to another—has become the subject of intense and active debate. On the surface, much of the debate is preoccupied with understanding the relative importance of military and economic power, the shift from bipolarity to multipolarity, and the consequences of technological change. Below these issues, however, lurk a number of questions the consideration of which can no longer be held back by the various ready answers and arguments of the Cold War—questions about the character of anarchy, the nature of sovereignty, the meaning of territoriality, and the sources of change.

We do not argue that global ecological interdependence is in itself producing a broad, systemic transition. Instead, we suspect that it represents one strand in a thread of developments having to do with politics, culture, identity, growth, and mobility that, taken together, are changing world order and world politics. Our attention is drawn to global ecological interdependence rather than to other manifestations of these developments because of its prominence, its powerful global imagery, its proven ability to cause (and in turn be deepened by) extensive social mobilization, and its linkage to some of the traditional concerns of states: property rights, territory, sovereignty, and legitimacy.

In one sense, at least, global ecological interdependence is a part of a larger process of systemic transformation. We have defined the global environment as a physical system, an issue-area in world politics, an arena for contesting other concerns, and a social construction. To this list we can add the idea of the global environment as a crucible for the debates, dialogues, and disputes by which people either re-create or transform the social institutions that give form to the future. Given the centrality of issues of power, wealth, legitimacy, and authority to questions of environmental change, we are hopeful that it is becoming increasingly difficult to ignore the former when discussing the latter. The drama of global ecological interdependence is indeed being played out on stages ranging from local to global, foreshadowing the concepts, conflicts, and constructs of a new world politics.

NOTES

1. See for example National Academy of Sciences, *One Earth One Future: Our Changing Global Environment* (Washington, D.C.: National Academy Press, 1990), which characterizes "humanity" as "an agent of global environmental change."

2. We thus see human "ecosystems" as encompassing both social systems and natural environments, and the "global" ecosystem as encompassing human civilization in its entirety.

3. This model is described by Richard E. Benedick, *Ozone Diplomacy—New Directions in Safeguarding the Planet* (Cambridge: Harvard University Press, 1991).

4. See Mancur Olsen, *The Logic of Collective Action* (Cambridge: Harvard University Press, 1971); Russell Hardin, *Collective Action* (Baltimore: Johns Hopkins University Press, 1982); and Joanne Gowa, "Rational Hegemons, Excludable Goods, and Small Groups: An Epitaph for Hegemonic Stability Theory?" *World Politics* 41 (1989):307–24. These barriers notwithstanding, a growing body of work suggests that self-organizing, self-governing forms of collective action are possible under certain circumstances; see Robert Axelrod, *The Evolution of Cooperation* (New York: Basic Books, 1984); Elinor Ostrom, *Governing the Commons: The Evolution of Institutions for Collective Action* (New York: Cambridge University Press, 1990). For an extended exploration of these themes at the micro level, see Robert Wade, *Village Republics: Economic Conditions for Collective Action in South India* (New York: Cambridge University Press, 1988).

5. For a view of the state that stresses learning capacity and adaptation, see James N. Rosenau, "The State in an Era of Cascading Politics: Wavering Concept, Widening Competence, Withering Colossus, or Weathering Change?" in James A. Caporaso ed., *The Elusive State: International and Comparative Perspectives* (Newbury Park, CA: Sage, 1989). For a perspective stressing institutional barriers to state adaptation, see the contribution of Stephen D. Krasner to the same volume ("Sovereignty: An Institutional Perspective").

6. Efforts to improve air quality in the Los Angeles Basin illustrate the range of activities, such as outdoor barbecues, that will have to be managed at the margins. We can expect to see resistance to "cultural" microregulation of this type.

7. Initial efforts to sketch the contours of such a map are projects being undertaken by some of the contributors to this volume. We might note here that such networks are not limited to environmental issues; they are characteristics of movements directed toward issues as diverse as peace, human rights, rural development, gay and lesbian issues, and many others.

8. Claims to this effect are also not new and unique to the recent upsurge of interest in the global environment. Both the idea of emerging non-state actors and the idea of new tasks for states are common themes in the interdependence literature of the past two decades.

9. Even individuals engaged in international negotiations experience that activity in terms of a defined microcommunity of designated negotiators. They may be aware of the global implications of their decisions and activities, but they cannot experience these implications at the global scale.

10. The idea that social units do not map onto natural ecosystems is one that has been championed by those environmentalists who propose the reconstitution of society on the basis of "biomes" or "bioregions," arguing that human social units must subsist on what is available within these areas (this point is made in general terms by Herman E. Daly and John B. Cobb, Jr., *For the Common Good—Redirecting the Economy Toward Community, the Environment, and a Sustainable Future* (Boston: Beacon Press, 1989)). Ironically, in some respects, such an approach is, conceptually, as centralized as any proposals for global "management," since the new constitutive rules of human societies would, in both cases, have to be widely agreed upon by participating parties.

Index

Text: Palatino
Compositor: Maple-Vail
Printer: Maple-Vail
Binder: Maple-Vail